The Old Rectory

The Story of the English Parsonage

— ANTHONY JENNINGS —

Sacristy
Press

Sacristy Press
PO Box 612, Durham, DH1 9HT

www.sacristy.co.uk

First published in 2009 by Continuum International Publishing Group.
Second (revised) edition published 2018 by Sacristy Press, Durham.

Sacristy Limited, registered in England & Wales, number 7565667

British Library Cataloguing-in-Publication Data
A catalogue record for the book is available from the British Library

ISBN 978-1-910519-51-6

Printed by Copytech (UK) Limited, Peterborough, UK

Contents

List of Figures

List of Plates

Parsonages through the ages in chronological order

Plate 1: The vicar's pele—Lanercost, Cumbria
Plate 2: The early priest's house—St Alphege, Canterbury
Plate 3: The early priest's house—Mulcheney, Somerset
Plate 4: The priest's house—Itchingfield, Sussex
Plate 5: The priest's house—St Mary, Stamford, Lincolnshire
Plate 6: Later medieval—Congresbury, Somerset
Plate 7: Later medieval—Cossington, Leicestershire
Plate 8: Later medieval—Methwold, Norfolk
Plate 9: Jacobean—Chilmark, Wiltshire
Plate 10: Jacobean—Thorpe Achurch, Northamptonshire
Plate 11: Queen Anne—Redmarley D'Abitot, Gloucestershire
Plate 12: Queen Anne—West Ashby, Lincolnshire
Plate 13: Early Victorian—Pugin Hall, Rampisham, Dorset
Plate 14: Early Victorian—Wantage, Berkshire
Plate 15: Victorian—Barnack, Cambridgeshire
Plate 16: Edwardian—St Michael, Aldershot, Hampshire
Plate 17: Modern—St Stephen, Canonbury, London

More parsonages through the ages

Plate 18: The vicar's pele—Corbridge, Northumberland
Plate 19: Tudor—Great Snoring, Norfolk
Plate 20: Early with Restoration additions—Bishop's Cleeve, Gloucestershire
Plate 21: Tudor—Headcorn, Kent

More parsonages through the ages

Changes and rebuildings, the parsonage in its setting, porches and gatehouses, London parsonages, some smaller parsonages, curiosities

Foreword

"Old" is not a word that the twenty-first century much cares for. People shrink from it, going to painful lengths to preserve the appearance of youth and acting as though they had never grown up. But bracket "Old" with "Rectory" and the response is entirely different. Together, the words conjure up a vision of the most desirable of house types for affluent living. The Old Rectory has status, but not, in this democratic age, to an off-putting extent.

As this book shows, it may be in any architectural style (though not, since the great age of rectory building had finished by the Second World War, the hideous ones): estate agents will hope for Queen Anne, though Regency and Victorian are more numerous. Whatever the period, the house will have good-sized rooms, high ceilings and architectural presence. The large garden can be developed into a horticultural paradise, while leaving room for tennis courts and swimming pool. Offices and games rooms can be made out of the stables. Old rectories are companionably part of their villages, but remote from the modern estates that have been built on the edge. Their appeal to modern buyers is enhanced by their proximity to the church; newcomers buy into the tradition and history, even if they do not regularly sit in the pews. Perhaps the association with past clergymen, imagined writing their sermons or cataloguing their natural history collections, exerts a subliminal attraction. The spirits of the past are benign. And so, one hopes, are the well-heeled professional families who occupy them today. Buying one of these fine properties provides entry to an exclusive and agreeable club, that of the Old Rectory owner; barristers, newspaper editors, company directors, doctors, software developers, interior designers, and architects belong.

There will be some who still, lingeringly, agonise over the word "Old". Of the estimated 13,000 parsonages that the Church of England owned at the beginning of the twentieth century, only around 900 have been retained. They had come to seem too big. Some vicars loved them: one whom I met in Northamptonshire when he opened his garden for charity denied that heating was a problem—he could always do a brisk half-hour's gardening to warm up before lunch. But many others did not feel it was their role to act as custodians of architecture, when religion in the community was at a low ebb. Clergy, like the rest of the population, had stopped having families on the Victorian scale, nor did they employ servants. With hindsight, the disposal of so many prime properties for, as Anthony Jennings says, "a pittance" was not an inspired business decision, though in line with post-war practice in other spheres (whole villages were being sold by landed estates). Might it not have been possible to divide parsonages into flats, after the fashion of the architect Kit Martin's highly desirable country house conversions? An apartment might have been kept for the vicar, who would then have been able to use the grounds for the church fête.

The retreat of the Church from villages has coincided with the closure of other services. The charity Pub is the Hub has pioneered the idea that sub-post offices, shops, and IT centres can be saved if they share premises with other threatened institutions; the focus is the pub, which can even host church services. What a pity that the initiative is not Parsonage is the Hub. The modern vicar is now housed in the manner of his medieval forebear, in much the same manner as his flock; he does not have room to hold parish events or host other activities in his parsonage house, even if he wanted to – and expectations of privacy are now such that he probably doesn't. As rural vicars attempt to spread themselves between their many parishes, the most appropriate form of dwelling could be a caravan.

But take heart. Save Our Parsonages stands up for those parsonages which still serve their original function (just as the Rectory Society helps the owners of Old Rectories to join hands). Meanwhile, we should be grateful that Old Rectories are for the most part beautifully cared for, and not threatened with collapse or dereliction. It is an irony that the church beside them may quite possibly be in a better state of preservation than at any time in history – albeit that the vicar, as a permanent presence, has often left.

Clive Aslet
Editor-at-Large of Country Life

Preface

What do we think of when we hear the word "rectory"? Lovers of buildings think of architectural features. House buyers think of their dream home. Theologians think of religion. To lawyers or historians a rectory or vicarage is not a building, but an estate, a bundle of rights and duties. To diocesan surveyors it is a headache. Retired vicars either have memories of a wonderful house, or of cold baths and leaky ceilings. Working vicars either dream wistfully of the elegant house they could have had, or delight in the chipboard of their new suburban bungalow. Most of us probably think of an old and gracious house in a large garden near the church at the heart of a country village. Each of these perceptions is just part of the story.

The collective name for rectories and vicarages is parsonages. That is what this book is about: the phenomenon of the English parsonage. However we approach the subject, the history of the English parsonage is also the history of the Church. Church of England parsonages were built or bought to serve its mission—somewhere for the clergy to live and work—mostly by the patrons and clergy themselves. So were their equivalents, the Catholic presbyteries and the Nonconformist manses. Most were purpose-built for that task: one they have fulfilled for over a thousand years.

What is special about them? We only have to visit a few to realise one thing: they come in an astonishing variety of shapes and sizes. Many of us think of Georgian rectories, or Victorian ones, but anybody researching them quickly finds there is no such thing as a typical parsonage. Some are grand, others just homely. Some are sophisticated, others rustic. Some are ornate, others minimalist. Some are architectural gems, some are not. They are medieval, whether stone or half timbered, Tudor, Renaissance, Palladian, Neo-classical, Neo-Gothic, Neo-Georgian, and modern. They constitute perhaps the most admirable, desirable, and aesthetic body of domestic buildings ever built. Some, including the Church of England itself, see traditional parsonages as gloomy, anachronistic, undesirable, and irrelevant. Those who take that view are vastly outnumbered by their admirers, who understand their homeliness, humanity, and charm, or just their quality.

I will start with their history—the historical background, their origins and development, their periods of prosperity and decline, from early times, through the Reformation, to the present day. Then comes the architecture. The medieval rectory looks very different from the Georgian, and again from the Victorian. Why? And what are the similarities? What, if anything, constitutes the essence of the English parsonage? The importance of parsonage architecture seems strangely, perhaps spectacularly, to have been overlooked, and alone justifies this book.

There are wider issues. The twentieth century brought about a major change in the status of the traditional parsonage. For much of its recent history the Church of England has been selling them off. The demise of the old working parsonage must say something not just about the parsonage but the Church itself and the direction in which it is heading, a matter that affects the whole community, so the "great sell-off" is relevant to our entire post-war history. Once The Rectory has become The Old Rectory, how does it fare? Is it equally happy in that more secular role? Or has something fundamental been lost?

Then there is the place of parsonages in the community, and that of those who have lived in them, the clergy, their wives and families, the associations with the famous and influential, the private owners. What has been the contribution of parsonages to society, as symbols of religion, learning, and stability, as architecture? Finally, where does the future lie for these marvellous houses and the communities they were built to serve?

My definition of the term "traditional parsonages" is those built before 1939, an arbitrary date, I agree, but, as a generalisation, the shortage of money after the Second World War led to a decline in standards of construction and materials, as well as a different concept of the parsonage in the eyes of the Church. But I have not ignored the modern parsonage, which is a subject in its own right and a helpful comparison of the past with the present.

Parsonages are as much part of the landscape of England as its churches. Or, for that matter, its timbered cottages, red telephone boxes, and village cricket pavilions. It is only to be expected that they feature prominently in the great tradition of English storytelling. We think of Anthony Trollope and George Eliot, but also of thrillers and mystery novels—in this context, at least, Jane Austen and Agatha Christie can be mentioned in the same breath. Yet there are very few books about the history, architecture, and social importance of parsonages. Books about castles, cathedrals, and churches would fill a library. At the other end of the architectural scale there are books about suburbia, cottages, even such esoteric subjects as dovecotes, lighthouses, tin tabernacles, weavers' tenements, pill boxes, and Dartmoor blowing houses. What about rectories and vicarages, the most popular buildings in the country with house buyers?

It is difficult even to find references to "parsonage", "rectory", and "vicarage" in books on architecture. The index of Sir Banister Fletcher's *A History of Architecture* has none. Most books on English architecture, even English Georgian architecture, make no reference to the parsonage. In the City of London volume of *The Buildings of England* I found no reference to any parsonage in the section on its history and architecture, and only from page 413, in the street perambulations, do some begin to be mentioned. It is mainly from photographs in the property advertisements in glossy magazines, particularly those in *Country Life*, that we have been able to see the great architectural variety of these houses.

This is not an academic study. The story of the English parsonage is not a niche subject. Traditional rectories and vicarages appeal to us for their importance to our religion, culture, and heritage, their aesthetics, the people who have lived in them, for their gardens, their historical and religious associations, their Englishness. We like them as bricks and mortar and we like them for what they connote. Thousands of us are proud owners of old rectories and vicarages, and thousands more covet them. Few, except perhaps the most doctrinaire modernist architects, can resist their charms. Le Corbusier would probably have seen no merit in them. His successors, today's High Tech architects, would happily gut their interiors and rework them in steel and glass, destroying all character instantly, if we were to let them.

I have mentioned more than four hundred individual houses in Chapter 7 and many more in various other chapters. However, I cannot claim that this book is in any way comprehensive, given the many thousands of excellent houses that survive and flourish. There are many more I would like to have included, and I am quite sure there are many I am not even aware of. There is far too much material for one book.

Acknowledgements

Many people have helped with this book in different ways. A project of this kind was first contemplated some years ago by Tony Hodgson, in collaboration with Peter Burman, so the book has had a long gestation period. Their groundwork and enthusiasm were my inspiration. They and many others have helped me by providing research material, commenting on my synopsis, acquainting me with their parish history, giving me the benefit of their wisdom and experience, or simply providing moral support for a complex project. These include Michael Higgins, Noël Riley, Mervyn Wilson, Angela Cook, Anne Toms, Elizabeth Simon, Jeremy Hummerstone, Julian Litten, the former Bishop of London (Richard Chartres), and Anthony Howard.

I have greatly benefited from earlier research, in particular by Anthea Jones and Noël Riley, on parishes and parsonages, Richard Wellby's dissertation on the function and change of use of parsonages, David Shacklock's notes on parsonages featured in *The King's England* (Arthur Mee's county gazetteers), and Julian Litten's archive of all *Country Life* advertisements of parsonages on the market since 1983, later taken on by Anthony Bartleet, now back to Julian, being archived by Angela Cook.

Parsonages illustrated by estate agents are by definition either now, or soon to be, no longer in Church ownership and use, so they bring gloom as well as delight to us traditionalists. I am therefore particularly lucky to have been welcomed into some of the dwindling number of traditional parsonages that are still doing the job for which they were intended, as well as others, and I must in particular thank Jeremy Hummerstone, Gerard Moate, Henry Pearson, Harry Edwards, Andrew Jones, Michael Hewitt, Julian Litten, Noël Riley, Jonathan Farnsworth, Lois Fletcher, Susan Moore, Rod and Maggie Harris, William Garfit, Laura Tomlinson, and Mary Archer for their hospitality.

I have tried to get as much input as possible from owners of parsonages and other enthusiasts, and must acknowledge with thanks the help of the Georgian Group, the Victorian Society, the Twentieth Century Society, the English Clergy

Association, Save Our Parsonages, and the Rectory Society in publicising my quest for information. Those who have helped me include Mark Powell, Rod Searle, Alex Letts, Graham Booth, Raymond Moody, Chris and Penney Thompson, Rod Harris, Julia Abel Smith, Christopher Purvis, Christopher Gibbs, Peter and Viv Riches, Guy Spragg, Hugh Martin, John Patrick, Douglas Hoare, Glenda Parsley, Peter Condon, Martin Thompson, Geoffrey and Rosemary Pengelly, Dr C. Jolliffe, Michael Thompson, Michael Hewitt, Jane Willis-Bund, R. A. Lonsdale, Marie Winckler, Diane Walker, Alec Hamilton, Hugh Bedford, Ian Pringle, Ken Chambers, Michael Pearce, Peter Neumann, Jeffrey Wilkinson, Catherine Croft, Joanna Brown, Ken Gay, Congresbury PCC, Christopher Tull, Alastair Ferguson, Edgar Jeffery, Mary Hallett, Raili Fraser, Karen Northeast, Kevin Morris, Tina Purcell, Dawn Goodman, Oliver Ross, Lisa Chapple, and Simon Cook of the Rifles Wardrobe and Museum Trust. I am also grateful to others who provided information I was unable to use in this book but have carefully retained, for example for my current project "The Parsonage's Tale".

I have also learnt a lot from many parishioners up and down the country, too numerous to mention by name, who cherish their parsonage, or have fought to save it for the Church. Several long-suffering souls have travelled with me in search of parsonages in wind and rain, and I am very grateful to them, in particular my son Jasper, my wife Jennifer, David and Lois Sykes, and Peter Neumann.

My documentary sources are set out in the bibliography, and I have kept footnotes to a minimum. I owe a particular debt to *The Buildings of England*, the series often simply known as "Pevsner", where my research on individual parsonages started, and also to the two pioneering books, both published in 1964, *The English Parsonage* by B. Anthony Bax and *The Parsonage in England* by Alan Savidge. The Westminster Reference Library, Lambeth Palace Library, and the Cathedrals and Church Buildings Library have all been very helpful.

No acknowledgement would be complete without mention of the illustrations. I am very lucky to have had access to the excellent colour and black and white photographs taken by Anthea and Glyn Jones, most of them previously unpublished. The other illustrations are from various sources including The Landmark Trust, Images of England, parsonage owners, Jasper and Felix Jennings, and some are my own. Acknowledgements are on page 318.

I apologise to anyone I have forgotten. I must also apologise in advance for any inaccuracies, particularly any errors in my descriptions of individual houses, which I fear are inevitable.

The National Trust has asked me to mention that its houses discussed here are occupied by private tenants and not open to visit. I must stress that this is true of all houses mentioned in this book. I would ask readers to ensure that the privacy of all owners and occupiers is strictly respected.

Anthony Jennings
Bloomsbury, 2009

I would add the following comments for this second edition. One reviewer of the first edition expressed surprise that the gazetteer of parsonages in Chapter 7 is in chronological rather than alphabetical order. I suppose it would be easier for parsonage owners to identify their house that way, but there is an index, and I have no wish to encourage people to visit private properties. In any case, the idea of chronological order is to illustrate how the English parsonage gradually developed over the centuries in terms of architectural form and style. I therefore remain unrepentant.

This second edition is fully revised and one or two errors have been corrected. I have also taken the opportunity to supplement it with additional material. I am very grateful for the help and encouragement of Sacristy Press in getting it published.

Anthony Jennings
Bloomsbury, 2018

Terminology

When writing about the Church, some technical terminology is necessary, even important, if only to avoid confusion, and the reader should refer to the definitions in Appendix A. Terms can be misleading. The words "rectory" and "vicarage" do not, in their strict sense, refer to physical property at all, but to an estate conferring rights and responsibilities. *Vicarages in the Middle Ages*[1] does not discuss the buildings or their architecture at all, except incidentally when referring to dilapidations.

The historical distinction between rectories and vicarages arises from the differing status of the rector and the vicar. In the early years of the Church, the rectory or vicarage was known as the priest's house. Clergy houses are for communities of ministers. A presbytery is the Catholic equivalent to a rectory or vicarage, and a manse is the Nonconformist version. I therefore use the term "parsonage" as the most accurate term when talking generically about these houses.

Inevitably, the term "the Church" appears quite frequently in this book. I use it in a conveniently imprecise way, but I am normally referring to one or other or all of the institutions that constitute the Church of England, make its decisions, and carry out its policies, and not in the wider sense of the body of its members.

Notes

[1]   R. A. R. Hartridge, *Vicarages in the Middle Ages* (Cambridge University Press, 1930).

Part One: Prologue

"A serious house on serious earth it is"

Philip Larkin

CHAPTER 1

The Appeal of the Old Rectory

"It is no coincidence," said *Country Life*,[1] "that the best addresses in any English village are likely to be The Manor House or The Hall, followed by The Old Rectory or The Old Vicarage. Such is the enduring appeal of these gracious relics of a less secular age that ownership of a former rectory or vicarage is still considered one of the ultimate symbols of status in the community." It quoted an estate agent: "There's something quintessentially English about an old rectory, which conjures up images of elegance, space and cucumber sandwiches on the lawn."[2] "The vicarage and the rectory are two of the cornerstones of English village life . . . the holy grail for any 21st century property developer is to track down one of these properties and sell it on, after an overhaul."[3] In his survey of historic parsonages in Devon, the Revd Jeremy Hummerstone noted: "The very name 'Rectory' adds to the value of these fine houses."[4] "It is what more people want than any other house", said an estate agent of the Grade II old rectory at Coberley, selling in 2005 for £2.85 million.

In breezier style: "Ever dreamt of owning an old rectory? Perhaps the question is—have you ever not dreamt of living in said old rectory?"[5] Or: "Buyers are backed up along the M1 waiting to pull into an old rectory, ignoring its more lowly neighbours . . . a hot spot is the rich slice of middle England between Newbury and Marlborough. If you are thinking of selling your lovely Old Rectory in these parts, don't bother waiting for the spring flowers."[6] Or: "Your sixteenth-century rectory . . . sounds like an idle fantasy . . . they stumbled upon the Old Rectory on the internet and could not believe that it 'ticked every box' on their wish-list, from the practical (it has five bedrooms so guests could stay) to the silly . . . an Aga, a crunchy gravel drive."[7] "Not too large and not too small; not too grand, nor too humble . . . but just right. It has history, style and an ideal position. It attracts buyers like bees to its purple wisteria . . . No wonder estate agents lick their lips when an owner decides to sell."[8] "Take, for example, the gorgeous 17th century

Old Rectory at Haccombe. It's straight out of central casting."[9] "They are the most popular houses by far . . . ask any new buyer . . . what his dream home might be and nine out of ten will say the old rectory."[10] "The wisteria-draped rectory is the ultimate rural idyll . . . Georgian is rectory nirvana; Victorian is popular too."[11] In a more mercenary vein: "Developer X made £1 million in two years after he and his family moved to a rundown former rectory near Reigate . . . Now . . . the early eighteenth-century home . . . could be worth as much as £2.2 million, putting the family well into the millionaire bracket."[12]

We are constantly reminded of the huge popularity of The Old Rectory. But what is it that makes these houses so popular? After all, they have associations with religion in general and Christianity in particular, deeply unfashionable these days, not to say responsible for all the world's ills, if the proudly atheist chattering classes are to be believed. But once a rectory has become a former rectory those associations are often unspokenly but determinedly marginalised. They are now of the past. The term "rectory" nowadays just seems to signify a grand old house in the country.

But don't they also connote outdatedness? That can spell unfashionability, anathema in an age when we are bombarded with the message that we are nothing unless we are trendsetters, "progressive", "cutting edge"! Most of us would describe old rectories as charming, tranquil, traditional, rural, dignified, imposing, and the dreaded "rambling", old-fashioned qualities. Surely England is now modern and multicultural? But old rectories are still status symbols, it seems. They must appeal to something deep-seated in us. Even the trendies of the cultural elite, our architects and design gurus, even the atheists, seem not to begrudge the innocent pleasures of their adherents. In fact, they are by no means averse to owning the odd old rectory themselves. With old rectories, trendiness doesn't seem to matter. They are so untrendy that they are trendy.

We talked about Englishness. The Church of England is very English. What about Scotland and Wales? The Scottish character, and its Presbyterianism, are less aptly characterised by sweeping drives and grand façades. Wales is the land of the chapel and its heritage lies more in the hill farm than the Georgian pediment, but it has some good parsonages.

We mentioned tranquillity. In an age of noise pollution, that is important. Most parsonages are in the country. Many have large gardens. They also seem to have a spiritual tranquillity in the oak and pine panels, and the boards which once creaked to the tread of rectors, their families and dogs, their ferrets and archdeacons. That was their *raison d'être*. Religion may be unfashionable in times of apathy, agnosticism, atheism, and media sages like Richard Dawkins with their corrosive views, but a more politically correct term like "spirituality" or "meditation" has tapped into something more fashionable since the psychedelic 1960s. Most of us still have some time for the metaphysical, even if we no longer eagerly stride up the church path. We may be slaves to fashion, dreading above almost all else to be thought practising Christians, ideas like restraint and self-sacrifice anathema, but a dash of spirituality in the cocktail, just a little drop, why, there can be no harm in that. The chimneypiece, the mullions, and the wainscoting can create the right mood as the pre-dinner chatter begins and the gin and tonics are broached as dusk falls on the backdrop of the lawns beyond the leaded lights. Tranquillity torn from spirituality becomes tranquillity at the altar of secularism.

We also talked of more worldly desires. Rectories symbolise not great wealth, but a comfortable affluence, again a thoroughly English aspiration. Most of us have dreamed of living in a grand house, with fine architectural features, however vague our knowledge of architraves and quoins, however liberal our political views, whatever our professed revulsion for snobbery or privilege. We may not aspire to Longleat, but the Old Rectory will fill the bill. As we greet our weekend guests with their gasps of admiration, we can glance up at the south elevation with a throwaway "yes, not a bad little place". The Old Rectory is a step up the ladder from the Victorian semi of our younger days, on the path to bourgeois respectability. It is where we think we quite rightly should be, as the greying hairs get harder to conceal.

We often resort to that old cliché "rambling" in our attempts to summarise what is desirable about old rectories. We can't resist it; it avoids the need for a more precise architectural vocabulary. It is by no means always accurate. Many early parsonages are too small to have endless corridors at unexpected angles, and there are some surprisingly compact Georgian ones. But there is more to the word than that. It hints at desirability. It suggests spaciousness combined with character, a house which takes time to reveal its secrets, a house which is the very opposite of a modern box. It can mean a house that is grand while still being vernacular and unselfconscious. More broadly, it creates an image of a rosier, less stressful, more reassuring past. Interestingly, we will see in the next chapter that it can be used in a pejorative sense as well.

Is there no downside to the dream? What about the cost of maintaining these houses? The Church has certainly failed to keep them in good repair. To any Church bureaucrat, the mere mention of an old parsonage conjures up a vision of apparently insuperable problems. Yet this is not a great issue for private buyers. They are going to have to spend money, but they are prepared to do so. They understand that the Church is selling the house too cheaply because it has not maintained it properly.

"It seems that whatever state old rectories and vicarages are in and whatever indignities they have suffered, buyers flock to them like vultures to the carcass . . . Buyers climb over each other to bid for the bleak shells disposed of by the Church . . . Put bay trees by the front door, and the rich move in . . . It's a sobering thought that when the village grandees come in for an after-service sherry, their wives are probably mentally measuring up the curtains . . . buyers simply refuse to be put off, whatever the condition of the house."[13]

Unlike the Church, private buyers understand that routine maintenance is not just prudent, but essential. If there is any threat to the old rectory it is that of "over-restoration", not lack of maintenance.

It was not always like this. When rectories first began to be sold in substantial numbers, after the First World War, they were unpopular if not unmarketable, and this remained true until long after the Second World War. When they were sold, it was generally for a pittance, but the families who bought them then now have a substantial asset. That unpopularity seems odd now, but in the context, it is understandable. We had survived the two greatest upheavals in our history, which had brought radical change in our economic circumstances and our attitude to the past. We were now poor; old houses reminded us of old times. Bombing had not only damaged our heritage but our attitude to what remained. There was a desire to move on, to look to the future. Austerity had forced us to crave a new simplicity. At first, the architects of the New Elizabethan era were seen as the solution. They were designing houses for the modern world, compact, practical, economical, technologically advanced, and with the very latest materials and labour-saving devices. The public took its cue from the success of the Festival of Britain, and was eager for the new ideas.

By the 1970s, the backlash had begun. The harsh modernist style was becoming less acceptable. The new buildings could be seen to be no better, even inferior in design and construction. We had tumbled to modernism. Ironically, it was modernism that turned our thoughts to tradition again. The disadvantages of fine old buildings were looking more like advantages. It was the birth of the "heritage" culture. The rigid dogma that form must be unadorned, and of concrete, steel, and glass, was seen to produce houses of little character and less charm. Because concepts such as craftsmanship, even beauty, were alien to the new buildings, they alienated the public. Inferior materials and construction gave rise to hefty repair or maintenance bills, the avoidance of which had first been seen as the main advantage of new houses. A rectory of the proper, friendly kind was not such a bad bargain after all. And there were plenty on the market at ridiculous prices.

In one unforeseen way, then, the Church has been lucky in finding such a ready market for its houses. But, like deconsecrated churches, their true purpose has gone. They are lost to the Church. What has the Church gained in return? Is its mission strengthened? Have congregations increased? Has the exercise at least been a financial success?

"There is real social kudos in owning an old vicarage. Now that the dioceses aren't as heavily underwritten by the Church Commissioners as they were a decade ago, it makes sense for them to cash in on some of their larger assets."[14] But what sort of sense? Practical sense? Financial sense? Pastoral sense? Sense for the parish? Has the "great sell-off" worked?

Notes

[1]   Penny Churchill, *Country Life*, 11 January 2001.

[2]   Edward Waterson, Carter Jonas.

[3]   *Daily Telegraph*, Telegraph Property, "Living on a Prayer", 1 October 2011.

[4]   J. Hummerstone, *Historic Parsonages in Devon*, Save Our Parsonages, 1995.

[5]   Anna Tyzack, *Daily Telegraph*, "Live The Dream", 14 March 2009.

[6]   Anne Spackman, *The Times*, Bricks and Mortar, 17 September 2004.

[7]   *The Times*, Bricks and Mortar, September 2004.

[8]   *The Sunday Telegraph*, "Simply Divine", 10 July 2005.

[9]   *London Evening Standard*, Homes & Property, 23 November 2011.

[10] *Sunday Telegraph*, Life, "Praise Be to Rectories", 29 August 2010.

[11] *The Times*, Bricks and Mortar, 10 May 2013.

[12] *London Evening Standard*, Homes & Property, 2005.

[13] Dixie Nichols, *Daily Telegraph*, 3 December 1994.

[14] Richard Jackson, Cluttons, quoted in newspaper article, 2005.

CHAPTER 2

The Great Twentieth-Century Sell-Off

Strolling around an unfamiliar village, seeing "The Old Rectory", or "The Old Vicarage", or perhaps "The Old Deanery" or "The Old Chantry", we remain largely uninquisitive. We can see that these buildings no longer fulfil their true function. We probably assume there are good reasons for this and the Church must know what it is doing. The Church is probably not unhappy with our relaxed approach to what is the most remarkable continuous and wholesale divestiture of valuable assets ever undertaken by any national institution. Its origins can be traced back to the 1838 Parsonage Act, which allowed the freeholder to sell his parsonage, subject to consents, for the first time.

The Church also likes the word "rambling". But it uses it when seeking to justify selling a parsonage. Here it implies an impractical house, a house with a lot of wasted space, difficult to maintain and heat, a house quite unsuitable for this day and age, not the sort of house the "modern" clergy could possibly be expected to put up with. Also, a garden which needs mowing every so often, and no busy clergy these days can be expected to mow a lawn. In these times of political correctness, it also means an immodest house, far too large for a mere vicar, a house that gives out quite the wrong signals about the priesthood. It is an extraordinary paradox that while the Church calls traditional parsonages unsuitable, they are the very houses most people want to live in. We may say that while that is certainly remarkable, it is not particularly important. After all, most of us are not remotely interested in the Church. Even if we are, it is not as though the house is being destroyed; indeed, it is likely to be highly valued by its new owners. If the Church still needs a house, a new one has been found, for which the vicar is deemed to be duly grateful. All is well. But there are wider issues. The first obvious message is that the Church holds its heritage very low in its scale of priorities. The next is that traditional parsonages have always had a much more important function, particularly in the rural community, than merely that of the vicar's house. At the centre of the village, close to the church, they not only gave the Church a high profile, which cost it nothing, but they were a valuable tool for its mission, and that of any vicar with an "open door" policy. There was even more to the parsonage than that. Like the post office and the pub, it was a symbol of the community as a whole, whether the parishioners were churchgoers or not.

Physically, these houses remain at the heart of the village. But they are now as firmly private as any Englishman's castle. The cries of newly baptised children once rang out above the chink of the sherry glass; engaged couples once glanced at each other on the sofa in nervous silence, resigned to the vicar's homilies; the teacups of hatpinned spinsters once clattered on their porcelain saucers. Today they are silent until the off-road vehicle swirls up the gravelled drive, decants loud children and recalcitrant nanny, and speeds off again to Waitrose for the weekend's supplies.

Nobody seems to know precisely how many have gone, and that includes the Church Commissioners. The rector of Coberley, Gloucestershire, observed:

> Sadly, over the last thirty-six years, nearly all the parsonage houses in the Cirencester Deanery have been sold and only very few have been replaced. In all the changes, Coberley Rectory has stood aloof and alone. Now it appears that, at last, a similar blow is poised to fall here too.

He recalled the fate of others in the area: "Cowley, sold as a farmhouse, Colesbourne, Rendcomb, North Cerney, Bagendon, Daglingworth and others.[1]

For that matter, nobody seems to know how many there have been in the first place. In 1994, there were 16,364 churches. There were only 8,770 benefices (most parishes are now in combined benefices) but 13,083 parishes,[2] about the same as in medieval times, though of course the population was then a tiny fraction of what it is today. If each parish originally had its own parsonage, we have a conservative figure of about 13,000 houses. But that is just the start. The village of Bampton, Oxon, is small, yet had two prebends for much of its history, which provided for no fewer than five parsonage houses and a deanery. That is untypical, but in most country towns and many villages we can find at least two, and often three or four, former vicarages. Over the centuries, parsonages have been successively discarded and replaced. Many towns have several churches, each with its own history of parsonages. If we conservatively quadruple my first figure, we already have over 50,000 houses that have been parsonages at one time or another. That is without even counting the deaneries and the archdeaconries, and the other houses built by the clergy and their families.

Between 1900 and 1914, 251 were sold, or seventeen per year. Then, after the cataclysm of the First World War, between 1919 and 1930, 58 were sold per year. It was a period of economic depression and large houses were difficult to sell, but even so about 1,300 went between 1925 and 1939. The rectory at Asheldon, in Essex, was sold, together with about 40 acres of glebe, for £800. It then sold on for £25,000.

Interestingly, there was some concern about this even at this stage, and the idea of keeping parsonages, with the clergy as shareholders, and letting them to lay tenants was suggested in the late 1930s by the Revd C. E. Douglas. Like the diocesan secretaries of today, the officials were unimpressed. In the 1920s their suggestion that 2,252 parsonages were oversize had led to the 1930 Parsonages Measure, the fount of subsequent legislation. Parsonages were even advertised in the Indian press in case they appealed to returning Civil Service bureaucrats![3]

A joint committee of the Queen Anne's Bounty and the Church Commissioners reported in 1934 on "Over-large Parsonage Houses". The 1938 Parsonages Measure followed. Average sales after 1930 went up from 58 to 90 per year in the decade before the war. After the war, 631 houses were sold in the years 1945–50, or 105 per year. Between 1948 and 1963, 2,627 were sold, or 175 per year.[4]

The concept of "unsuitability" is a rolling one. Vicarages formerly thought suitable magically became unsuitable once the bigger ones had gone. In 1925, 2,252 vicarages out of about 12,000 had been considered unsuitable. In 1959, the figure was 3,769, in a survey that found the total number of parsonages was 10,796.[5] This was the year in which Archbishop Fisher talked of easing the burden of "those freezing passages and those awful cellars".

Adding up these figures, we see that well over 5,000 parsonages had been sold off between the turn of the century and 1963 alone. That meant that many had to be replaced. Savidge, writing in 1964, said there were about 10,800 working houses at that time, not counting some owned by the diocese or patron, so it seems half of those were pretty new. In 1978, Michael Hanson, writing in Country Life, reported that over the 10 years since the 1968 Pastoral Measure, which also provided for the sale of "redundant" parsonages, well over 2,000 had been sold. This makes a total of more than 5,500 since the war. Most had been replaced, leaving about 4,500 older ones still in use. He noted that the definition of "unsuitability" kept changing. Older houses were currently selling for sums in the range between £36,000 and £60,000 and new ones averaged £31,000. One house built in 1968 was already sold for £18,000. In the year ended March 1977, a record number of 348 were sold.

The mission of the Church may not be about money, but it would be nice to think that at least these sales have brought financial benefits. More detailed statistics were obtained by *Country Life*. Michael Hanson reported that in the year ended March 31 1978, 316 "unsuitable" or redundant parsonages were sold at an average price of £25,764 each, for a total of £8.1 million. In the same year, the purchase of 102 replacement houses was approved, at an average cost of £28,832 each, including the cost of repairs or alterations, totalling £2.9 million. The construction of 83 new houses was also approved, at an average cost of £35,337 each, excluding the value of the land. This totalled another £2.9 million. In other words, about £6 million was spent on 185 houses to replace 316 sold for not much more. Indeed, the Church authorities acknowledged the apparent lack of value for money. The high cost of building new parsonages "is increasingly a matter of concern" said the Church Commissioners.

In the following year, 302 parsonages were sold at an average price of £34,450, but the average cost of new ones was £40,490 excluding the site value, and of replacement ones £33,430. In 1980, 211 were sold at an average of £53,930, new ones excluding site value averaging £61,300, and "regarded with some concern" by the Commissioners. In 1983, Michael Hanson reported that more than 2,000 parsonages had been sold over the past decade. The previous year's average price was £61,345, for replacements £59,155, and for the new £73,459. There were 9,200 working parsonages and the average repair cost was £899 each.

In 1983, 308 were sold at an average price of £63,930. But 76 new parsonages were built in their place, at an average cost of £76,199, and 105 houses were bought at an average cost of £60,306. In other words, the unit cost of replacement houses, vastly smaller and inferior, was higher than the sale proceeds of those fine older houses. In 1984, 260 parsonages were sold at an average price of £65,620. But again this was not enough to meet their replacement cost. The building of 85 new houses was approved at an average cost of £82,674. The Church Commissioners said in their report: "Understandably, therefore, progress with the replacement of unsuitable houses was considerably slower than in recent years." Michael Hanson added: "Though one sympathises with the present incumbents of properties that are expensive to run and repair, one wonders whether the Church Commissioners have studied the possible financial advantages of repairing and modernising old parsonage houses before they sell them, as they often do with office buildings. They might then be able to command prices such as that currently sought . . . for the Old Rectory at Bletchingley, Surrey . . . for which offers over £600,000 are invited."[6]

In 1983, a parsonage in mid-Essex, in the diocese of Chelmsford, was sold by the diocese for £60,000, to appear towards the end of the same year in the pages of *Country Life*, advertised as a family house for sale at the price of £300,000. When one member of a Diocesan Synod[7] asked how this was allowed to happen, he was told that since each Diocesan Board of Finance is a registered charity it is unable to enter into development agreements or invest funds in restoration works even though that might give rise to greater returns. Well, but what about maintenance?

In 1961, there had been 10,796 vicarages, but by 1986 there were only 8,887.[8] In 1987, 213 parsonages were sold in England for a total of £23.9 million, still only an average of £112,000 each, in a year when price inflation was rampant. "Surplus" portions of parsonage gardens which were deemed too large were also enthusiastically being sold.

In the same year, the Old Rectory at Bletchingley, Surrey, came back onto the market again, at £1 million this time. £750,000 was being asked for the Rectory House next to St Michael's Church at Warfield, Berkshire. The Old Rectory in Thornby, Northants, lost to the Church for some years, changed hands in 1983 for £122,500. It was sold in 1988 for about £600,000. The Old Rectory at Kislingbury, Northants, considered by Sir Nikolaus Pevsner to be one of the finest in the county, an early eighteenth-century house attributed to Francis Smith of Warwick, after offers over £425,000 were asked for, sold privately in 1988 for £450,000. The Old Vicarage at Castle Hedingham, Essex, cited by *The Buildings of England* as the best classical brick house in town, was for sale privately in 1988 at more than £400,000.[9]

In 1989, Huon Mallalieu in *Country Life* was reporting the asking price for the former rectory at Edith Weston, Rutland, as £700,000, and for the former rectory at Houghton as £1.25 million, showing how much money was being made by private sellers rather than the Church. As to the new houses, he added: "Substitute vicarages are all too often shoddy eyesores and unlikely to prove financial assets in the long term."

In 1983, Julian Litten started his comprehensive collection of advertisements for the sale of parsonages in *Country Life*. By December 1990 alone, he had 828 advertisements.[10] The average asking price of a parsonage from 1984 to 1989 was £155,000 and from 1990 to 1994 was £215,000. The best of those which had been sold off earlier by the Church and were now selling privately were going for considerably more. One in Devon was on offer at £475,000, in Gloucestershire at £495,000, and J. P. Seddon's former vicarage at Princes Risborough was on at £550,000. If the dioceses had kept all those fine houses (worth over £154 million in simple money terms even at the prices then achieved) for the long term and let them out, the Church would now be sitting on substantial capital gains and would still have a good income from them.

The above figures show that, during the 1980s, the annual rate of sales was comfortably exceeding even the huge numbers of the earlier post-war years. The Commissioners said that between 1978 and 1984, 1,982 houses, about one-sixth of the total, were sold.[11] Recent estimates, which the authorities were reluctant to confirm, suggest that between 1945 and 2000,[12] or 1948 and 1994,[13] the Church sold at least 8,000 rectories and vicarages; a huge number when we consider the total number in clergy use over that period must have ranged between 9,000 and 12,000.

Sales of the few remaining pre-1939 parsonages continue, but have slowed down a little. In 1996, for example, there were said to be 102 sales. But that was largely because most of the good houses had already gone. A 1995 survey of Devon parsonages[14] showed the remaining traditional parsonages to be mainly medium-sized houses of about four or five bedrooms. These are now being targeted. All but three of the clergy surveyed said they used these houses for parish purposes, and obviously that is much more difficult with a new small house. Mr Hummerstone concluded by observing that the diocese was now taking the more relaxed view that there was no longer any desperate need to sell off parsonages. But then there could not have been more than 1,000 older parsonages left in the whole country.[15] As one researcher remarked, even if they were thenceforth to continue to be sold at the historically low rate of say 70 or 80 per year, the Church was well on its way to shedding the lot. Since then, sales have continued to slow, and there are signs that in one or two dioceses the merits of older houses are now better appreciated, but it is too late to save the vast majority.

In the 1990s, various experts calculated that somewhere between five per cent and ten per cent of pre-1939 parsonages remained in Church ownership, and some say there are now only somewhere between two and five per cent left. It would be difficult to get a more accurate figure. In response to enquiries about their archives, the Church Commissioners tend to be vague. Worse, the parsonages have for some time been the responsibility of the dioceses, and anyone doing statistical research has therefore needed to approach 43 (now 41) separate offices. The diocesan administrators vary widely in their degree of helpfulness, but they are hardly ever willing to provide a comprehensive response to specific questions; indeed, in most cases they do not respond at all. In 2008, Save Our Parsonages wrote to 41 diocesan secretaries. Only 20 (48 per cent) bothered to reply and only five of these (15 per cent) provided any information. The most common reply was that the information was not readily available, or was confidential, or too sensitive.

It is difficult to see how that can be so, and when asked to clarify this, the great majority simply failed to respond.

In 2005, one diocesan surveyor advised that, at that time, the diocese had 19 houses in category B "suitable but with drawbacks" and 55 in category C "unsuitable". If these figures were to be taken as an average for all 43 dioceses, B would equate to 817 and C to 2,365 in total. With about 8,000 benefices overall, these are high numbers even given the doctrine of "rolling unsuitability", considering the vast numbers that have already been disposed of. It suggests that some of these must be houses recently built or purchased that are now proving too small, or too badly built, and we know that repair and maintenance costs for 1960s and 1970s parsonages have often been high.

Taking a modest hypothetical figure of 5,000 parsonages sold since the 1960s, applying broad average sale prices (1960s £15,000, 1970s £30,000 and so on, average somewhere around £250,000) we get a gross sales revenue of up to £1.5 billion on a crude unadjusted basis. At rental yields of between two per cent and five per cent (depending on market and condition), lost income from £1.5 billion at two per cent is £30 million per annum, or at five per cent, £75 million per annum. At present prices of course, the figure would be much higher; taking the average value of a parsonage at the conservative figure of £500,000, £2.5 billion would yield rental income of £100 million per annum at less than five per cent per annum. That is a lot of money. Moreover, taking the figure of 8,000 parsonages sold since 1945 to date (and it is well over that), at a more realistic present value of £1 million per house (and a lot go for much more), these would now be worth £8 billion. If they had been kept and rented out, the income would be enough to fund the entire annual stipends of the clergy, with money to spare.

Of course, specific financial assumptions can always be challenged, but the principle remains: capital needs to be preserved. When I told someone involved in Church funding work that it had been suggested to me that not all the capital brought in from the sale of all those parsonages had been reinvested, he looked surprised at my naivety. "Oh, no, in the old days, it all just went", he said. He hastened to add that there is nowadays a more businesslike and practical approach to investment in most dioceses.

By 2008, the Old Rectory was more popular than ever. An estate agent was then quoted as saying that former parsonages were one of the few areas of the market likely to be recession-proof, even though the cheapest was now "at least £1 million" and the most desirable "more than £10 million".[16] By 2016, former parsonages in the home counties were regularly selling for at least £1.5 million.

But mercifully, the story of the parsonage is not just about the great sell-off. It goes back for a thousand years, and is also the story of our history, architecture, and heritage. We must now go back to the beginning and consider the history of the parsonage. How did it come into existence in the first place?

Notes

[1]   "Where have all the rectories gone?", *Letter From Home*, Christmas 1995.

[2]   *The Church of England Yearbook* (Church House Publishing).

[3]   Michael Higgins, *The Vicar's House* (Churchman Publishing, 1988).

[4]   Alan Savidge, *The Parsonage in England* (SPCK, 1964).

[5]   Savidge, *The Parsonage in England*.

[6]   Michael Hanson, *Country Life*, 5 July 1984.

[7]   Julian Litten.

[8]   Michael Higgins, former Dean of Ely.

[9]   Michael Hanson, *Country Life*, 14 July 1988.

[10] Julian Litten, *Save Our Parsonages Newsletter*, 1995 (date previously stated as 1994 and number as 836 but recently recalculated).

[11] Michael Higgins.

[12] Anthea Jones, "The Great Selling-Off", *Parson & Parish* No. 158, Trinity 2002.

[13] Tony Hodgson, Anthea Jones, conference notes, "A House for All Seasons", 22-24 November 1999, Cheltenham.

[14] J. Hummerstone, *Historic Parsonages in Devon* (Save Our Parsonages, 1995).

[15] Tony Hodgson.

[16] *Daily Telegraph*, 17 April 2008, "A Safe Place for your Money: The Old Parsonage".

Part Two: The History

"There, where a few torn shrubs the place disclose,
the village preacher's modest mansion rose"

Thomas Gray

CHAPTER 3

The Parsonage in the Parish—the Historical Background

We can only understand the history of the English parsonage in the context of the English Church, people, and parish system. The parsonage exists only because of the parish.

Saxons and Normans

Constantine first permitted Christianity in the Roman Empire in AD 312. The end of Roman rule in Britain came in about 410, when Honorius said it should expect no more support. From the fifth century, periods of paganism alternated with periods of Christianity, as the incoming pagan Saxons took time to be assimilated into the existing Celtic Christian ways. Then Augustine arrived with his missionaries from Rome in 597. Kent became Christian in the early seventh century, Mercia had a Christian king by 654. The Synod of Whitby in 664 was crucial, settling the battle for supremacy between the Celtic Church and the Church in Rome in favour of the latter, paving the way for nine hundred years of Roman Catholic supremacy.

The Roman system was different from the Celtic. Celtic Christianity had been overwhelmingly monastic. The Roman was better suited to the needs of the converted, and thus for the parochial system. In Augustine's day there was already an attempt to create parishes, but they were not yet well developed in the seventh and eighth centuries. Pope Gregory's scheme divided the country into two provinces (archbishoprics) each with its bishops, but it could not be fully realised until later.

The monasteries were owned by wealthy private individuals before they were destroyed by the Viking invasions. The minsters were regional mini-cathedrals from which the clergy ventured forth. Strictly, minsters could be said to be monastic, cathedrals to be families of clergy, but the distinction should not be exaggerated; both sent out priests to the towns and villages in their region.

The Saxons began the process of organisation of the landholding system. The noblemen held the land and smallholders were allowed to cultivate it. The Vikings caused continual disruptions in the eighth and ninth centuries, but eventually settled in better. The pagan Saxon landowner or thegn had often built the temple and the priest had been paid by tithes from his peasants. This system was assimilated by Christianity and when the parochial system became established the thegn instituted the priest, gave him a glebe to live off, and the tithe continued. The parish was the village in its new guise.

Then came the Norman invasion and a more feudal pattern of land tenure developed. The barons held large estates which were tended by the lower classes. It was not a dramatic change and seems to have sprung from a combination of the Roman, Saxon, and Norman way of doing things; as a generalisation the Roman was a collectivist, the Saxon an individualist, the Norman a bit of both. The Normans adopted Saxon administration and tax and a lot of its law. The shires and hundreds remained. But Latin replaced Anglo-Saxon.

Feudalism grew from pressures that forced a loss of independence; the smaller man had no chance without protection; it suited everyone. It was a diluted feudalism, a communal cultivation system. The bishops owed service of knights to the king in return for land given to them. Money came from the land, hence the manor.

The Lord of the Manor was not just a commander but had broad responsibilities towards his estate. There was still no great structure of Church bureaucracy, and when he converted to Christianity, he required a priest to minister to his domain, just as the thegn had done. He dedicated part of his land, and built and owned the church and other Church buildings on it. He needed a parson so he needed somewhere for the parson to live. He built the priest's house and it was under his control. Ownership of the land gave him the right to appoint the priest to the house. This was the beginning of what is called patronage. It was the duty of the priest to live in the house and use it as his tool for the provision of the spiritual welfare of the lord and all those working on his estate. The quality of the house largely depended on the wealth of the lord. As settlements grew, more churches were needed and the big parishes were subdivided into smaller ones. More priests' houses were then needed. All this had developed from the Saxon system.

The priest was like anyone else except in one way: as from the eleventh century, he was expected to be celibate. Celibacy meant being unmarried, and had nothing to do with chastity. Any woman at the priest's house was a "housekeeper". The bishop was represented by the archdeacon in visitations, interrogating the local clergy and their "synods-men" or sidesmen, questioning morality, and celibacy formalised it. The bishops tried to enforce it from time to time, but it was often a losing battle. Unchastity was often less offensive than formal marriage. Pope Paschal II himself said it was better to suffer an unchaste priest than to die without rites. But peccant priests could find themselves paying blackmail to the archdeacon. Many cases which should have resulted in deprivation were settled by private penance and payment of a fine.

The archdeaconries and the rural deaneries, to which the bishops delegated administrative and local powers, are creations that go back long before Norman times and were well established by then, and their roles remain largely unchanged to the present day.

The medieval period

Christianity continued its steady growth from Saxon and Norman times. The rector held the freehold, so was "ruler" of the parish. But abuses by lay rectors encouraged the practice of giving the living to the monasteries. In theory this was better for parish priesthood, but there were major problems. The monks, forbidden by the Pope to do parish work themselves, became just as rapacious as their predecessors. In theory mere trustees, they became "appropriators", converting the church "*ad proprios usus*". The monastery became the rector, and the vicar or "vicarius" was given the work to do, at first with no security of tenure at all. The grant of security of tenure, in what became the freehold, with the requirement for a proper income for the vicar, was the important achievement of Innocent III and his Fourth Lateran Council of 1215. Even so, the social distinction remained. The rector had sufficient property to give him an independent income, while the vicar had to rely on his stipend.

Christianity had not meant destroying paganism; it had merely assimilated it. The temples had been re-used, worship simply transferred from the gods to

God, and the church houses where church ales were brewed still retained many of the pagan customs. The old pagan gods still existed, the Church just called them devils. When a thirteenth-century defendant pleaded that he had killed an old woman with a pitchfork because she had cast a spell, the jury decided it was self-defence against the devil.[1]

The growth of the population of England over the centuries has been an important factor in the requirement for and design of new Church buildings, including priests' houses, and in the need for parish reorganisation. In 1066, the population was still only about 1.3 million. By 1348, the population had grown to about 4 million, but up to 2 million were lost to the Black Death in 1349, so it was down to about 2.5 million in 1450, and would still only be 3 million by 1561.

By the end of the thirteenth century, the Catholic Church had 17 dioceses and 40 archdeaconries. By the time of Edward III, the parish system was fully developed. There were now about 9,500 parishes, and between 300 and 450 souls per parish (fewer than 100 adult males). Estimates of ordained and beneficed clergy vary from 20,000, to 24,000, to 40,000 before the Black Death, and there were about 15,000 monks and 7,000 nuns. Below the priests were the lower clerics, so it seems there was probably at least one cleric for every 100 people.

By 1938, there were still about 20,000 priests serving ten times the population,[2] and nowadays fewer than 8,000 stipendiary Church of England clergy serve almost twenty times the population. The numbers of clergy who had done a university course were low, and even those had rarely studied classics or science; even fewer had a theology degree. Few could understand Latin. There were arguments about whether baptism could be effectual if done by an ignorant priest, but it was held that if there was no theological error it was valid. Most clergy seemed to attain office through apprenticeship. After school and serving the priest, the youth might aspire to become parish clerk, in those days an important job. He could deputise for the priest and keep the school. A clerk had a sort of "benefice", a place in the chancel, and had normally to be unmarried like the vicar. In large towns clerks sometimes formed guilds, as at Clerkenwell.

Lack of education was a problem and perceived as such: before the Reformation there was a general feeling that the Church would not improve until the quality of clergy did. The ignorance of clerics had been debated for centuries, from Bede in 730, St Boniface in 750, St Bonaventura in 1260, and the Bishop of Mende in 1311, to Dean Colet in 1509. Chaucer, Gower, and Langland all paint a poor picture of the clergy. Chaucer censures clergy and monastic morals. Gower savagely criticises the Pope, the cardinals, the bishops, the archdeacons, and the absenteeism, ignorance, and immorality of the clergy.

Pluralism, the right to a number of benefices, which has always gone hand in hand with the problem of non-residence, was, and would remain, a recurring problem. The fattest benefices were often distributed for unspiritual reasons. The more endowments a man could amass, the more dispensations he could buy from Rome, so rights to hold pluralities were bought. A lot of the rich English endowments went to Italian protégés of the Pope, who had not even set foot in the country, with no requirement to do so. The late thirteenth century seems to have been particularly bad. Bogo de Clare, the younger son of an earl, had so many canonries, prebends, and churches that there were only four dioceses that did not have him somewhere among their clergy. He probably never even became a priest. John Mansel, a minister, was said to have 300 benefices.[3] Universities were staffed by absentee rectors. Even bishops were powerless to take action against presentees who refused to take holy orders, though sanctions were (in theory) in place. There was a profession of brokers who dealt in benefices.

Despite disasters like the Black Death and scandals of pluralism and licentiousness on the part of the clergy, the Catholic Church remained powerful. The brainwashed peasant was terrified into fear of hell or purgatory on his deathbed, and deathbed legacies to clergy became so common that their absence was sometimes taken as proof of heresy, enough for burial in unconsecrated ground.

Sabbatarianism was sometimes strictly enforced. One woman who said she had to work on Sunday on peril of starvation was not absolved from God's vengeance. "A beast like a sucking-pig of coal black hue fixed upon the woman's left breast and could not be torn away . . . drawing her blood, it had soon consumed almost her whole body."[4] It was a good way to get conversions.

Despite the power of the clergy, the church itself was not the sacred space of our image. The nave was used for storage of corn, barrels, etc. Talk at services was normal. There are records of "chattering, laughing, jangling and jesting aloud", the priest "smiting his hand on the book" to try to silence them. The friar who wrote "Dives and Pauper" said "they have liever go to the tavern than to Holy Church. Liever to hear a song of Robin Hood or of some ribaldry than for to hear . . . any word of God." Berthold of Regensburg said "it irks some to stand decently for a short hour in church", to be told "we understand not the Mass . . . we know not what is being sung or read, we cannot comprehend it".[5]

No state or secular public authority existed to relieve distress. It was all left to the Church. Even so, there was no systematic charitable giving, for example through the parish priest, just almsgiving. There was no "overview" or co-ordination, so charity was more abundant, because of comparative wealth, in places that needed it least. Shameless seekers of alms who went from place to place thus did better than honest hard workers who stayed at home.

The everyday life of the parish priest was little different from that of his parishioners. He visited the sick, and if he could read or write this at least gave him a sort of authority. The parsonage of the time could have been built for the parson or could have been a farmhouse or a village house. The monasteries were supposed to provide one, but could be slow to build. It was just a hall, timbered, unceiled, unglazed, with a central hearth, with perhaps a dais and a screen at the far end. The priest was obliged to receive travellers. He was often fed by the monastery. But there were many parishes where there was no parsonage, many where the parsonage was in a very poor state, and priests found themselves lodging in the monastery or a monastic house or even the local inn.

The modern Church sees parsonage maintenance as a headache, but dilapidations are by no means just a modern story. The Archbishop of Canterbury in 1236, Edmund Rich, had required the rector to pay for repairs if he "should leave the houses of the church ruinous or decayed".[6] In the visitation of Totnes archdeaconry in 1342, most vicarages were in poor condition, one "vile insufficient and ruinous". The vicar at Birling, Kent, said his house was decayed due to the negligence of Bermondsey Abbey. Not all clergy were responsible for their own maintenance. It depended on what had been agreed.

Diocesan records show that many incumbents presented to benefices were not even ordained clergy, though that improved after the Black Death. The 6,000 or so rectories were given to middle-class men; the 3,000 vicars, and others of the lower orders, were from the peasant classes. But the battles of Henry III and the Edwards with the barons had given rise to a new yeoman class above the peasantry. Sheep farming began—the poor could now get richer.

By the later Middle Ages parish priests were in surplus and many found employment as chantry priests. The merchant classes were better educated and the Church was long established and was no longer quite as dominant as it had been. Whereas once education was entirely in the hands of the monasteries, there were now secular foundations, though the teachers were still clergy.

The Tudors

Huge changes had come about by the end of the medieval period. A Saxon or Norman would have been bewildered by Tudor England. The inventories of church plate in 1500 under Henry VII are double those of 1300 under Edward I. Tudor archdeacons saw their churches as small and dark; they wanted them replaced by something modern in the perpendicular style. The peasant or artisan was for the first time able to think to some extent independently. The printing press had been invented, religious and philosophical works were becoming available, and English was even being used instead of Latin. The population grew slowly to about 5 million under Henry VIII. The basic modern structure was there: there was an archdeacon for each county and a rural deanery roughly corresponding to each hundred. But the town was still scarcely more than an overgrown village, and there were few towns with populations of more than village rank today.

Problems like simony, pluralism, and illiteracy continued. Ordinary people still knew nothing of the Bible other than, perhaps, a few stories like Adam and Eve; Sir Thomas More says a woman of his time was shocked to discover that Mary was a Jewess. Bible knowledge had never been encouraged by the Church; there had been no English version until the sixteenth century. There was nothing like a Sunday school system. Some priests did not know the Lord's Prayer. Little preaching was done. The ordinary priest was incompetent to hear confession. Then as now it seems women were in the majority at church and all sat together while the men "in chirches and in ministres eke, that gon the women for to seke".[7] Church was used to ogle the ladies. The medieval parishioner usually confessed only once a year, before his or her Easter Communion. The Spanish envoy to Henry VIII reported "nearly all the people here hate the priests". There was a medieval superstition that it was ill-omened to meet a priest. There are reports that in the country it was thought necessary to cast the priest into the plague pit in order to stop the mortality. The monks remained powerful: by the Reformation, a third of all rectories had been reduced to vicarages, and two-thirds of their revenues had been diverted to the monks. The monasteries were tolerated because they were devoted to prayer and contemplation, and the Church in the world was glad that others were doing that for them. "Mortify yourselves, and pray for us", was the pact. But the monks got too complacent. Fieldwork was dropped as incompatible with monastic dignity. Finally, even statutory masses were neglected, effectively defrauding benefactors and their souls. Even the celibacy rule was not unbroken. Records of allowances at Canterbury and Westminster show each monk's portion of fish as six and a minimum of a gallon of ale per day.

The Reformation

By the later Middle Ages, huge monastic wealth was giving rise to widespread anticlericalism. The personal difficulties of Henry VIII exacerbated it. His first marriage to Catherine of Aragon was unable to produce a male heir and the Pope refused to grant an annulment, giving rise to a series of Acts of Parliament placing Henry at the head of the Church and enabling him to dissolve the monasteries between 1536 and 1550 and to confiscate their wealth and property, on the basis that they had become too powerful, their teachings had strayed too far from the Bible, and besides he wanted a divorce and needed money. Dissolution could also be justified on the premise that the monasteries did not fit into the parochial system. Henry did not gain the title of Defender of the Faith for the Dissolution; ironically it was conferred by the Pope for his attack on Luther.

The consequences of the Dissolution were huge. It was the end of 900 years of Roman Catholic supremacy and the birth of a new Church of England. Cranmer was the first Archbishop of Canterbury to embrace the Reformation. The abbots were thrown out of the monasteries, though they often became the parson. The buildings were destroyed, converted into "secular" churches, or sold to Henry's courtiers, who became lay rectors, or "impropriators" as they were called, and they in their turn now got all the fruits of the benefice, including glebe and tithe. The 1549 Act of Uniformity requiring use of the new 1547 Cranmer prayer book was resented and there were riots in Devon and the South-West, and rebellions in the Midlands and the North.[8]

The reign of Edward VI, Henry's son, which, unlike his, was truly protestant, pressed reformation with even greater zeal, but this was cut short by his death. Then Henry's daughter Mary, married to Philip II of Spain and a devout Catholic, tried to restore the authority of the Pope, persecuting prominent Protestants, but failed to produce an heir. This time of upheaval saw the end of the great period of English church-building that had lasted for centuries. The great period of secular house-building was beginning. Priests' houses remained largely poor, but some of the many manor houses now being built would later be converted to parsonages.

Elizabethan

Under Mary's half-sister Elizabeth, Reformed theology was back and there was a feeling that it might last. The Act of Supremacy of 1559 established the Church of England under Elizabeth as Supreme Governor (rather than Supreme Head), and the Act of Uniformity of 1563 enforced the Book of Common Prayer and the Thirty-Nine Articles. The clergy had to be approved; others were just licensed readers. The parson's role developed; for example, he had to help the constable supervise movements across parish boundaries—people who crossed them were considered lawless and called vagabonds. The Elizabethan Settlement embodied the *via media* of the Church of England as a Church which was Reformed in doctrine whilst emphasising Catholic continuities. This compromise, however, caused both Catholic and Protestant dissent. After the Papal Bull excommunicating Elizabeth and releasing her subjects from allegiance to her, English Catholics who retained an allegiance to Rome fell under great suspicion. The more radical Protestants were also disaffected. Their fundamental belief was that the Church should not be governed by any Episcopal hierarchy, and they saw mainstream Protestantism as a compromise and insufficiently radical. These Puritans, as they became known, attacked any self-indulgence they could, including the endemic pluralism, and were punished for non-conformity from time to time.

The population was only 3 million in 1561, but it was now rising again. By 1601 it would be 4 million. This was the age when many church houses were built, and they were used for village events, such as holidays and fêtes, particularly after the 1571 Act curtailed the use of the church for these activities. Clergy incomes continued to vary widely, but some new parsonages were much better than the old.

Jacobean and Carolingian

When the Stuarts took over after Elizabeth's failure to marry, some had hopes for a Catholic revival under James I, but he espoused the Protestant cause, though he also antagonised the Puritans. Protestantism had become irreconcilable with Catholicism after Elizabeth's settlement and the Pope's demand for her deposition in favour of Mary Queen of Scots. As a result, Catholic priests were executed and there were a number of "Popish" plots, the last being the Gunpowder Plot. Differences of religious doctrine between Scotland and England also caused frequent problems. The Scots revolted when Charles I tried to align the Presbyterians with the Church of England. Charles was married to the Catholic Henrietta Maria of France and was suspected of having Catholic sympathies.

The new gentry class were with Parliament, against the Stuarts and Archbishop Laud. Puritans attended the Anglican church and the parson had to turn a blind eye. In 1640, Parliament reassembled and impeached Laud. Churchwardens were ordered to remove church ornament and the Book of Common Prayer was outlawed. The King broke with Parliament. In 1645 came civil war, resulting in the abolition of the monarchy in 1649. Justices of the Peace took over church courts. Out of 8,600 incumbent clergy, 2,425 were evicted, and Presbyterians and Baptists took over. One parson was accused of "eating custard scandalously".[9]

Richard Reynolds, rector of Stoke Fleming, fled his parsonage disguised as a farmer. When Cromwell's soldiers asked him the way to Stoke Fleming, he gave directions, adding that he hoped they'd catch that old malignant Reynolds. Peter Grigg, curate of Churston Ferrers, recited the Lord's Prayer with a pistol at his head. William Lane, rector of Ringmore, hid in his church tower for three months, as the intruding cleric preached below. Puritan committees allowed for compensation to those evicted to the extent of one-fifth of the living, but many of those who took over the parsonage did not pay. Milton (1608–1674) thought the lay presbyters just as good as the old hierarchy. Samuel Butler (1612–1680) on the other hand ridiculed them in *Hudibras*: "Such as do build their faith upon/ the holy text of pike and gun".[10]

Civil war was devastating not only to the clergy but to their parsonage houses. Some were deliberately attacked, and they suffered neglect and dilapidations. Few were being built. Their size and status continued to depend on the wealth of the living. Most parsonages were poor, a minority were grand, and there was little in between.

The Restoration and William and Mary

Charles II was invited to resume the crown that was already his by right in 1660. The Act of Uniformity in 1662 required the Book of Common Prayer again. But the problems for the new Church were not over. Charles sought to resolve revenue difficulties by seeking help from France on promising to reinstate Catholicism. Worse, James II was an avowed Catholic. When a male heir was born, it sealed his fate in the Glorious Revolution of 1688 and William of Orange, married to his Protestant daughter Mary, was invited to take the throne.

The Restoration was a new age of building, but a surprising number of serving parsonages were still of medieval origin and restored clergy were often too poor to do proper repairs. Though houses continued to be built, the religious upheavals of these heterodox times caused disruption, and the Great Plague, drought, and in London the Great Fire, did not help, so parsonages of this period are comparatively rare.

In 1688, the population was 5.5 million but not growing. Dissenters continued to thrive, even though persecuted, but after the Act of Toleration in 1689 non-conformists could go to their own meeting houses, and the clergy had no control. Their status remained low and they often still had to be content with a run-down hovel, though big improvements in housing meant good new parsonages for those lucky enough to afford them.

Queen Anne

Inequality of means between the rich and the poor clergy had never been properly addressed. Efforts made during the Commonwealth were slowed by the Restoration. By the end of the seventeenth century clergy incomes were generally still low. But Queen Anne was devoted to Anglicanism and Queen Anne's Bounty, to which can be traced the beginning of the bureaucratisation of the Church of England, was set up in 1704. From the time of Henry VIII the Crown had received taxes from clergy that had previously gone to Rome. The Queen Anne government set up a scheme to subsidise the poorer clergy by giving this money to trustees, to augment incomes. These augmentations were to continue into the early nineteenth century, by which time there had been a great improvement in most clergy incomes. The Bounty's money would also be used to make loans to the clergy, but this would come later.

Greater political and religious stability also now meant that new parsonages were suddenly needed, so while many clergy still had very poor accommodation, some very elegant new houses were now being built by the more prosperous. Richer vicars who were in residence and willing to do so were also able to repair. Some were even able to renovate, and here there are parallels with today's mania for modernisation. The incumbent at Plumland was putting the parsonage "into a more modish frame, in his apartments, windows, stair cases etc".

Georgian

When it had seemed clear the Queen would not provide an heir, the Act of Settlement, settling the succession on the Electress Sophia of Hanover, had been passed in 1701 to prevent the return of the Catholic Jacobites. The Georgian period would become one of much greater political stability, and the Hanoverian line was to continue uninterrupted through to 1837, despite various Jacobite risings and continuing wars overseas.

The eighteenth century is nevertheless known as an age of parsonage dilapidation.[11] The Church had suffered successive blows to its authority in this new age of enlightenment. Many parsonages were still old, and had got more and more dilapidated and run down. There continued to be a gulf between the rich and the poor clergy. Pluralism remained a problem, and that meant empty houses. Fundamentally frowned upon, it was nevertheless permitted by law in some circumstances, for example if the vicar lived within a reasonable geographical distance of his parish, or was simply highly educated; university education was increasing, and the universities were dominated by clergy. Even so, pluralists were supposed to live in their parish for some of the time, and appoint curates, but the temptation was to avoid doing so or to pay as little as possible to get maximum benefit from all their livings.

When Bishop William Nicolson made his triennial visitations in his Carlisle diocese he saw too many "slovenly", "ruinous", and "woeful" houses. Some wealthy rectors lived in their own private house, often in town for convenience rather than in the country, which they generally found disagreeable, ignoring their parsonage, where there might be a curate who had no means, or just a tenant, or the house might even be empty. The parsonage house at Melmerby was "wholly neglected" by an incumbent, who "(being as well Lord as parson), always resided at the Hall". The sons of the landed gentry also often became the parson, tending to leave the parish in the care of under-paid curates when they inherited the estate.

The rich and poor were equally to blame. The parson who had many parishes was absent due to pluralism; he sometimes even lived abroad, a curate in charge if he appointed one. The parsonage got run down. So it did when there was a poor parson, in residence but unable to afford the upkeep. Parsons were also tending to have larger families. The vicar of Irthington was the "wretched and beggarly father of ten poor children" and had been unable to prevent his vicarage from falling into "scandalous ruins".

The plight of the poorer clergyman tended to worsen, encouraging dilapidations. It was not just that parsonages were in a state of decay—many parishes did not have a parsonage at all. Fewer parishes than ever had resident incumbents. In the deanery of Ludlow in 1793 only a third of the parishes had "suitable" houses, and this was having an effect on church attendance. Though there were four clergy, there were no more than seventy communicants, two-thirds of them women.

Livings were bought and sold like commodities. One vicar was incumbent at Stanton Lacy, near Ludlow, as well as Wycombe in Hampshire, and also in the Peak District. Non-residence had become a scandal, even local vicars preferring to live in their nearest market town, not their village. As parsonages deteriorated, more habitable ones had to be provided before new clergy could be found for the parishes, making the problem slow to resolve, and it went on into the nineteenth century.

Agricultural revolution brought a rise in the social status of clergy, leading to rivalry between squire and parson, described by Joseph Addison in *The Spectator*. But neither rich nor poor were conscientious and, as the clergy grew idle, the new Methodists prospered. Wesley's first open-air reading was at Bristol in 1739. The Methodist conference in 1744 did not recognise parishes, resented by Anglicans. Eventually they would be tolerated like the earlier non-conformists, but at the time of the French Revolution there was rioting; dissenters were dangerous to stability.

New taxes were levied for the Napoleonic wars, and food prices went up. There was still great disparity and the wealthy benefices became relatively wealthier. Woodforde was well off. At Long Melford the advowson was bought for £2,600 in 1783 and sold for £15,000 in 1819. But poorer incumbents found parsonage upkeep difficult. The Clergy Residences Repair Act of 1776, the first of the so-called Gilbert Acts of Thomas Gilbert, was a breakthrough, and allowed Queen Anne's Bounty to lend money for improvements. It was still not until 1809 that Sydney Smith was an early beneficiary. Then, in 1811, the Bounty started lending for new building too.

In 1803, bishops were required to provide details of clergy non-residency, about half being non-resident. Where pluralism was not allowed, bishops were still empowered to issue licences. Lack or unfitness of the house was a substantial reason for non-residence. Despite that, many fine new parsonages were built during this period by the wealthy, and many more were to come after the turn of the century. By 1731 the population was still only around 5.2 million, the same as a hundred years earlier, but would now rise rapidly. By 1750 it was 6.4 million, by 1780 it was 7.1 million, by 1801 8.9 million, and 30 per cent had now migrated to the towns, a process that was to continue.

Regency

Due to the incapacity of George III, his son became Prince Regent in 1811. In 1829 Sir Robert Peel, backed by the Duke of Wellington but opposed by the King, passed the Catholic Emancipation Act, and the position of the Dissenters and the Catholics was improved. This was the time of the Industrial Revolution. There was much political reform and the Reform Act of 1832 was to lead to universal franchise; the Church was still very conservative—in 1831, 21 bishops had voted against the Act, and opinion was hardening against them as a result.

Absenteeism continued: Cobbett says 332 incumbents had 1,496 parishes, and 500 others had 1,524. Of 10,800 livings, more than 6,300 had no residence.[12] Non-resident clergy were now under greater pressure. Sydney Smith lived in London but his parish was in the wilds of Yorkshire, and he now had to move there. The percentage of vacant parsonages varied from area to area, but by 1817 Parliament was told there were still over 2,000 "unfit" houses and 2,600 parishes had none at all, not far from half of all parishes. Not only that, but new parishes were rapidly being created, and the provision of new houses lagged behind the increase. In 1835, of 10,533 parishes, 1,728 vicarages were unfit for habitation and 2,878 had none at all, the building having ceased to exist. The vicar at Creaton, Northamptonshire, lived in the local pub for 40 years.[13]

This and the huge population explosion meant new emphasis on church and parsonage-building. In the 1811 census, the population was over 10 million and it was increasing rapidly. The Church Building Act of 1818 gave rise to the "Commissioners' churches". As the cities swelled, new parishes were needed. Because of this and the mortgages provided by the Bounty, the commonest purpose-built parsonage today is that of the early nineteenth century, coinciding with a period of progress in domestic architecture that has provided us with a great number of parsonages in different styles.

The political and social upheavals and population increases prompted the creation of the Ecclesiastical Commission in 1836. It found that there were huge differences in livings, and inequalities were as great as ever. Collegiate churches, deans, and prebends were often even wealthier than bishops. This led to more legislation seeking redistribution. Tithe was commuted. Queen Anne's Bounty was still busy making loans, but institutional patrons tended to do better than private ones, and quite a number of loans were for making existing houses grander rather than building new ones. The Ecclesiastical Commissioners, who eventually became the central authority for clergy stipends, were stricter, and even in the 1830s and 1840s would only give grants for five-bedroom houses, whereas the Bounty would provide for a new wing, or a billiard room.

There was a huge growth in the number of parsonages. New plots were found, sometimes a little further from the church, and the old house, or what remained of it, was abandoned, or alternatively the old house was rebuilt, or if still sound, substantially altered. Great effort was invested by architects and writers into researching earlier architecture in order to determine the ideal parsonage house design. Architects now had to file applications for mortgages with detailed plans, and the Commissioners were now calling the tune on all aspects of parsonage design and standards of construction.

Victorian

At first, the Victorian period seemed a secure one for the Church of England, after the Ecclesiologists had fought its unpopularity. Georgian and Regency advances in clergy status continued, a dash of conscience was added, and the clergy were making the running, setting up schools and organising parish events. Religion was now alive and popular and there was much theological debate, with the coming of the Oxford Movement and the Ecclesiologists, as well as the Christian Socialists and evangelicalism, the Church's answer to Methodism. The Victorian parson, with his philanthropy and parish excursions, his relationships split in a complex way between the squire and common people, more than competed with the Dissenters. Even so, to Ralph Waldo Emerson the Anglicans had nothing left but possession and the bishop was "a surpliced merchant".[14]

In 1838, the Pluralities Act, which reduced the distance at which the incumbent was permitted to live to ten miles from 30 (the 1885 Act would get it down to four miles), had a real impact on the scourge of pluralism. Absenteeism and clergy non-residence sharply declined. This, in combination with parsonage dilapidations and the great population increase, galvanised parsonage-building anew. There remained sharp discrepancies between what wealthy and poor vicars could afford.

Conservatism and prosperity led to the admiration of all things medieval, reflected in the growing influence of Gothic architecture. By now, the size and grandeur of the house usually reflected the wealth of the incumbent, rather than whether he was technically rector or vicar. The status of the clergy was at its height. The second half of Victoria's reign, however, was one of increasing uncertainty as the burgeoning populations in the towns and cities proved intractable. This was reflected in the status of the clergy, which gradually started on its subsequent decline.

By 1851, the population was 18 million, and by 1870, 20 million, more than 50 per cent in towns, the rate of increase still intensifying. The mid-nineteenth century saw an unprecedented surge in church restoration, resulting in the destruction of medieval fabric that led to the formation of the Society for the Protection of Ancient Buildings (SPAB). But before we condemn the architects we must remember that restoration was badly needed; so little attention had been paid to maintenance and repair for so many years. Still more parsonages were renovated or built in tandem with the church restorations, new ones often built in a planned group with new church and school, almost all now in the Gothic style. Between 1872 and 1901, 40 per cent more would leave the land. To cater for population growth and migrations, the Ecclesiastical Commissioners allocated nearly £2 million between 1866 and 1882 for parish and parsonage. Some grants were to supplement gifts by patrons.

Lack of parsonage maintenance continued to give rise to litigation between vicars, and in the housing stock the standard of basic services could still be poor. In 1862, the vicarage of the Revd J. Holdich of Bulwick, Northants, had "not a single drain or spout about it, and no pumps".[15] By the 1870s, the age of clerical affluence was declining with the collapse of corn prices caused by imports. At the same time the Ecclesiastical Dilapidations Act of 1871 was the beginning of the central administrative control of parsonage maintenance. It required archdeacons to inspect all buildings in every vacancy, a practice which had largely disappeared. The Rector of Saintbury, in Gloucestershire, was sceptical, observing that the Act was as good as a small bishopric to the bishop's surveyors, judging from their fees. Incumbents now had responsibility to their successors for dilapidations. But it was up to the vicar to instruct the diocesan surveyor, to get his certificate, protecting him from claims. If he had no certificate and left, the diocesan surveyor had to do the work and chase him as best he could. The next vicar started with a clear five years.

In 1879, Queen Anne's Bounty estimated that there were 13,426 parishes and 11,500 parsonages.

Bishop Goodwin of Carlisle, who helped build or improve many parsonages towards the end of the nineteenth century, said:

> I confess that if I have any anxious feeling concerning parsonages, it is rather with respect to their excellence and their beauty", and: "I would wish that in not a few instances the purse of the incumbent rather than the glory of the architect had been manifestly the first consideration.

Clergy and their families had been at their most affluent in the High Victorian age of grand houses. By the end of the century, worsening economic conditions meant clergy fortunes had suffered. Things were not to recover. With the declining congregations of the early twentieth century, the boom in parsonage construction would be over, and the "great sell-off" would be getting under way.

From the First World War to 1939

The story of the late nineteenth century had been one of increasing diocesan control, and this would only intensify. The Archbishops' Committee on Church Finance in 1911 said there was too much parochialism and recommended that the diocese should be the main unit of the Church, and diocesan boards should be set up for finance and church buildings. Next, the First World War brought fundamental changes to the British way of life. One factor was purely economic—the value of money. Inflation in Victorian times had often been static or non-existent. Prices actually fell for considerable periods. Endowments had been stable. But the war brought high inflation, badly eroding fixed incomes. Landowners were in recession during the two post-war decades. Parishioners were in reduced circumstances. Worse, the war had irrevocably altered attitudes to faith. There was a loss of community feeling, and the start of a long period of decline in respect for the Church as mainstay of the community.

All this affected attitudes to Church buildings. The large traditional parsonage was beginning to be seen as a problem. Only shortly after the new, still large Edwardian parsonages had been built, the "great sell-off" of the twentieth century was beginning.

The Church Assembly was set up, and started to meet in 1920. In 1923, the Diocesan Dilapidations Boards were set up and the quinquennial parsonage inspections became compulsory, and money deducted from the incumbent's income was put in a fund for benefice repairs. The Bounty and the Commissioners continued to provide substantial funds in an attempt to remedy the backlog of dilapidations. They developed firmer guidelines about the cost of parsonages, size of rooms, ceiling heights, and so on. The Church Assembly held lengthy discussions about "unsuitable houses". The argument for the transfer of ownership of the parsonage to the diocese can be traced back to this legislation, and it came up again in the 1930s, but the clergy freehold prevailed.

In 1925, a substantial minority of houses were considered too large, and by 1930 nearly 600 had already been sold, even though there was a depression and large houses were difficult to sell; another 700 went before 1939. By 1938, the population was about 40 million, a massive fourfold increase since 1811. Though the Church was not growing in the same way, more houses were needed as there were now about 20,000 clergy, and about 600 replacements were built and 500 or more purchased. These pre-war houses were a lot smaller than many older ones, but were still of about 2,500 sq. ft (nowadays redefined as "overlarge"). Objectively, the size of these houses could surely be justified by the facilities for the community they could provide, but on the Church's own criteria it seems they were another mistake, giving rise to more future cost in disposal and replacement.

Modern

The nation had still not recovered from the First World War when along came a second one, dealing a further body blow. There was no money. The war had damaged Church buildings: 1,000 or more houses badly, some beyond repair. Others had been requisitioned and thus obviously suffered from the depredations of wartime use. Parsonages were run down. The process of selling them accelerated.

The new houses were considerably smaller even than those of the interwar years, built of inferior materials, and constructed with less care. The status of their occupants, the clergy, deteriorated with them. Responsibility for parsonages passed in 1948 to the new Church Commissioners, formed from the merger between the Commissioners and the Bounty, whose functions had progressively overlapped. The first "Green Guide", a set of guidelines for specifications of parsonages, was produced in 1953. Sales of parsonages continued and some of the early twentieth-century replacements were now among them.

The power of the aristocracy had declined. Tradition was weakened. There was an erosion of traditional values of thrift, conservatism, respect for the establishment and conventional morality, and a decline in the status of the rector and the vicar in the community. War had eroded confidence in cultural values, and this had its impact on the Church.

The view that the Church is in decline now seems widely held, both among the laity and increasingly among the clergy. The last Archbishop of York, for example, opined that we no longer live in a predominantly Christian country. Disagreement seems confined only to whether this decline is slow, rapid, or terminal. In simple terms, it is often measured by church attendance. Congregations are in long-term decline, though evangelicals have increased rapidly and now form a significant proportion of churchgoers. In 1850, the population of England was 18 million. In 1991, it was 48 million. Congregations went from about 3 million to about 1 million, so there was a big decline relative to population numbers. Since 1938, Church of England stipendiary clergy numbers have dwindled from over 20,000 to fewer than 8,000, serving a population at least 33 per cent greater and still growing rapidly.

We have been through periods of belief, followed by periods of so-called enlightenment, or questioning of perceived truths, before, as in the eighteenth century with the rise of scientific methods of study. There was a reaction to this, but the questioning culture is back today. Two world wars, unrest, and debate about the environment have contributed to the climate of scepticism. The disillusioned have become atheists, agnostics, or humanists. Some have defected to other religions or cults, or the vaguer "New Age" mythology of a new Aquarian enlightenment, or paganism, in the hope of spiritual nourishment. Most no longer look to the established Church, some no doubt because of the very fact of its establishment and alignment with monarchy and state. Lack of leisure time results in value placed on weekend privacy. Among remaining congregations, there is division between town and country, the latter more conservative. The number of Christian denominations, to some merely confusing, is to others an obstacle—explicable historically, but to an outsider unattractive, like divisions in a political party. Then, the divisions within the Church of England itself: the latitudinarians, the Anglo-Catholics, the evangelicals; schisms over women and homosexual priests; fundamentalists who believe nothing changes, and progressives, for whom the gospel must be reinterpreted for successive generations. Each creates tensions and disunity, and the leadership is often perceived as weak in dealing with them. The divisions are reflected in differing approaches to liturgy; some potential churchgoers find traditional forms of service off-putting, while others are alienated by "trendification". Many modern vicars see it as their duty to tinker with, if not reject, tradition. The management consultancy culture tends to prevail: the Church is told it must constantly change.

There are also questions about the calibre of the clergy, and of those who rise to the top, and a perception that Church leaders suffer from a failure of conviction and inspiration. The episcopal hierarchy, and their bureaucracies, have become increasingly unattractive, and are much less influential than in the past. If the morale of the clergy is low, that lack of confidence is transmitted to the rest of us on whom the structure of the Church depends for its existence. The Church may not be attracting the right people because the right people are avoiding it.

The chattering classes delight in mocking the Church from their Hampstead villas. God is beneath the intellectual dignity of these atheist or humanist sages. They are apparently privileged to understand what the rest of us cannot. The attack has also come from the scientists. Mankind possesses the key to life, God does not. But they are misguided, and largely unrepresentative. Religion is part of human nature. Few except them see any contradiction between Darwinism and God. The decline of the Church seems to have come about despite fairly wide empathy on the part of the public.

By 1998, the "Green Guide" in its sixth edition was dealing not just with the specifications of the parsonage itself, but with such detailed matters as storage space, security measures, and low-maintenance gardens. The recommended parsonage size was up slightly, to around 2,000 sq. ft.[16]

Notes

1   Surtees Society, 1890, 343, quoted in G. G. Coulton, *Medieval Panorama*, Vol. 1 (Cambridge University Press, 1938, Collins Fontana Library edition, 1961), p. 138.

2   Coulton, *Medieval Panorama*, Vol. 1.

3   Prof. A. Hamilton Thompson, *Pluralism in the Medieval Church* (Ass. Archit. Soc. Reports, Vol. XXXIII).

4   A chronicler of the missionary Eustache, Abbot of St Germer-de-Fly.

5   Coulton, *Medieval Panorama*, Vol. 1, pp. 219, 220.

6   Constitution of Edmund Rich, Savidge, *The Parsonage in England*.

7   Coulton, *Medieval Panorama*, Vol. 1, p. 224.

8   Notably, the Lincolnshire Rebellion of 1536.

9   Lionel Players, rector of Uggeshall, Suffolk, 1644.

10   Samuel Butler, *Hudibras*, Canto 1 Part 1, lines 195–6.

11   The Revd John Conybeare, writing in 1853.

12   William Cobbett, *Rural Rides*, 1821–26.

13   Savidge, *The Parsonage in England*.

14   Simon Goodenough, *The Country Parson* (David & Charles, 1983), p. 38.

15   Michael Higgins, former Dean of Ely.

16   *Parsonages: A Design Guide*, Church Commissioners (<https://www.churchof england.org/more/parish-reorganisation-and-closed-church-buildings/parsonages-and-glebe-guidance-and-forms>).

CHAPTER 4

The Parsonage and the Church Institutions

The monasteries

From Saxon and Norman times, all through the Middle Ages, the Church was central to the life of the people. The monasteries were the embodiment of the Romano-British, then Saxon, then Norman idea of the Church. They were the centres of learning and grew to be, and remained, the great power base of the Church right up to the sixteenth century. Monasticism began with the Benedictines, in England from 598. The term "monasterium" meant the place within which the ecclesiastical *familia* lived, and the word "minster" is of the same derivation. In practice the distinction between the monks in the monastery and the clerks in the minster was not great. Both were bases for missionary work. Like the monasteries, the minsters suffered badly in the late Saxon period from the Viking raids of the ninth century, and their power gradually diminished as the parish system grew, but the monasteries recovered in the eleventh century, particularly when William gave the Church a quarter of all land, and were at their peak around 1300.

Long after the Benedictines came the Cluniacs (sub-Benedictines) in 1078, then the Carthusians, the Cistercians, the Augustinians, and the Premonstratensians, all in the eleventh and early twelfth centuries. Finally there was the only English order, the Gilbertines, founded at Sempringham, Lincolnshire, around 1130. The Knights Hospitallers and the Knights Templar, also of the late eleventh and early twelfth centuries, were other religious institutions. Then came the Friars, mendicants dedicated to good works. The Franciscans (Grey Friars), the Dominicans (Black Friars), the Carmelites (White Friars), and the Austin Friars, all of the early to mid-thirteenth century, were followed by the Crutched Friars in 1298. These more socially minded foundations also had buildings and provided accommodation for priests.

In around 1300, the number of monasteries was between 800 and 1,200. Their relationship with the growing parish system in the early post-Norman days is complicated. The Celtic tradition remained strong in the north of England, and there was also a Celtic influence in Cornwall from Brittany and Wales, and even a "Gallic" pattern of parishes in East Anglia. The wealthy landowners who had created their own church in their parish, outside the monastic system, tended, in the course of time, to bequeath the benefice to a monastery. It was their religious duty, with the added advantage of securing their place in heaven. With this power of persuasion, the dominion of the monasteries increased rapidly.

When they acquired the parish living, they also acquired its wealth from glebe and tithe, in which capacity they were called "appropriators". They took two-thirds of the income from one-third of the parishes without giving much back. They remained the main almsgivers to the poor, but the account rolls show charity of scarcely one-tenth of abbey income. They even appropriated money given to them as charity trustees. They claimed tax deductions for more than they distributed. It was giving them a bad reputation. When this great power and influence came to a dramatic end with the Reformation, many of their buildings were not in fact destroyed, but instead became manors for the wealthy, or deaneries and parsonages for the "secular" clergy.

The diocesan system and the parishes

The term "parish" comes from the Greek *paroikia*, meaning a dwelling apart, or in a strange land. It came to mean the bishop's domain, where he had his *familia* of priests to assist in pastoral work. The parishes are part of a diocese, a Roman term, the administrative equivalent to the bishop's *parochia*, in which sense it is still used today.

When Theodore came to England in 669 to become Archbishop of Canterbury, there were only three bishops. By the time of his death in 690, there were 13 or 14. By 1066, there were 13 bishoprics in the south but only two in the north: 15 in all. The Normans only created two new bishoprics, Ely and Carlisle. After this the diocesan structure was the same for the four hundred years to the Reformation. Yet in Victorian times there were 22 dioceses, and in 1921 there were 31. Nowadays, with a Church in decline, there are 44 dioceses. Their bureaucrats exercise much tighter controls over the clergy.

There were very few local country churches in the seventh and eighth centuries, but by the early ninth century the non-monastic church was already an institution, and by the end of that century the private church, founded by the lord or thegn, was probably normal. The tenth century was the great age of establishment of the parish church. By the eleventh century, before the Conquest, local churches were firmly in local hands. The parish system developed in parallel with the monasteries, but at the expense of the minsters. Being locally owned, it was also independent of the bishops in their diocesan headquarters, but they struggled to get power over it.

Parishes needed to have defined boundaries, and in the medieval period they were sub-divided and new ones created, though the "north-south divide", much talked about these days, certainly applied to the parishes. There were far fewer north of the line between the Humber and the Severn than south, as recorded in the *Valor Ecclesiasticus*, Henry VIII's census and valuation of the Church (1535) motivated by the King's need for money. A total of 8,071 rectories and vicarages were recorded in the *Valor* and only about one-eighth were north of that line. The *Valor* also demonstrated the difference in size of parishes. Average parish sizes varied between three square miles in East Anglia and 70 square miles in Northumbria.

The differences were partly compensated for by the greater number of chapelries, subordinate to the parish church, in the north. In between came Devon and Cornwall, with about eight square miles. Surprisingly, the same was still broadly true at the time of the 1821 census: there was still a population disparity, the northern parishes still contained a lot more open land, moor, and mountain, and several administrative areas were embodied in one parish. Town boundaries therefore differed from parish boundaries in the north, whereas in the south they were mostly the same. The chapelries remained a feature of the north.

There were attempts to survey parish numbers, churches, and incomes in the thirteenth, sixteenth, seventeenth, and early nineteenth centuries. In 1288, Edward I was given powers to collect taxes normally due to the Pope. His survey revealed at least 8,000 parish churches. The *Valor Ecclesiasticus* showed 8,838.[1] It was thought there were about 10,000 by the seventeenth century. In the early nineteenth century, returns to the royal commission enquiring into ecclesiastical revenues came from 10,540 benefices. These surveys were not precise, but the returns made over the centuries were consistent in suggesting a range of 8,000 to 10,000 parishes, despite inevitable inaccuracy in defining a parish and a benefice, considering the time span of nearly six hundred years and the huge population growth over that period.

The nineteenth-century population explosion made it necessary to create more parishes. Brand new parishes with no history took their place alongside ancient ones. Legal complications required successive Acts of Parliament. The end of the Napoleonic wars brought greater stability, releasing funds for church building in areas of population density. In 1843, the Ecclesiastical Commissioners gained the power to create new parishes before the church was built, under the bishop's licence, and the latter half of the century was the catalyst for still more parishes and new chapelries, often financed by grants to match donations.

There was something unsatisfactory in trying to adjust the old parochial system to the new conurbations. It was very difficult to draw a boundary through dense streets, and this was inevitably sometimes arbitrary and unrelated to any sense of community. All these little parishes based on country precedent could hardly be self-sufficient. Still, they emphasised the continuing importance of the parish system, and the urban parish is still very much with us. Despite its differences from the rural parish, it has undergone periods of prosperity and poverty in a similar way.

By the beginning of the First World War, there were 14,000 benefices (parishes or parish groups), but then the population was over 30 million, four times higher than at the turn of the nineteenth century. In 1924, there were just over 13,000, in 1961 just over 11,000.[2] If population is our guide, the decline of the Church can be viewed as having already begun in the later Middle Ages and having been an overall trend since then. By 1994, the number of benefices had dropped to 8,770, as the 13,083 parishes continued to combine into much bigger benefices. There were almost twice as many churches as benefices.[3] More recently, there were 12,600 parishes and the number of benefices had fallen again.

For many centuries, their parish has been central to people's lives. Their births, marriages, and deaths have been recorded in it, their year has been regulated by its festivals, they have been educated in it, they have maintained its clergy, and their community has been represented by the boundaries that were shaped by Saxon nobles and Norman barons. Nowadays the parish system is under threat. Within the Church there is debate about it. The modernisers see it as an anachronism. The traditionalists see it as the core of the Church.

The rectory

A rectory was a benefice, an "estate", not a physical object, such as a house, but a package of duties, land, endowments, income, and rights, that had a value. The rector was the embodiment for the time being of the rectory. He owned the house. He had what we call the freehold. The freehold gave him the flexibility to administer the parish in the way that he wished. He did not personally have to carry out his parish duties or even live in the parish; but if he did not do so, he had to appoint a substitute. This was a vicar, a "*vicarius*", someone appointed to carry out the duties of another. His parsonage was called the vicarage, so there could be both a rectory and a vicarage in the same parish. In the Middle Ages, the monasteries had acquired a lot of the rectories and after the Dissolution they were mostly merely sold off to "lay rectors", whose descendants still find themselves with the traditional legal obligations for repair of the chancel.

In terms of bricks and mortar, there is probably greater kudos in the term "Old Rectory" than "Old Vicarage", though there is no firm principle that a rectory should be grander than a vicarage. It depends on factors such as the age of the house, the historic wealth of the living, and the needs of the parish. Private wealth, historically more often available to the rector than the vicar, has generally given more latitude to the ambition of the incumbent and his architect. But there were significant differences between the wealth of one rector and another, depending on the value of the endowment, and for that reason some vicars, with a good regular stipend, could be wealthier than some rectors.

The vicarage

Historically, there was always a sharp divide between the privileged class of bishops, archdeacons, and senior cathedral clergy on the one hand, and the rector or vicar on the other. But within these broad classes there were also big divisions. Many rectors, whether they were an institution like a monastery or an individual, were also very wealthy and appointed vicars because they often had many livings, and wanted to indulge in other interests. The vicar was funded by a mere stipend from the rector. After the vicar acquired his own freehold, giving security of tenure, he could appoint his own curate to run the parish. But the

Valor Ecclesiasticus continues to show huge discrepancies between the wealthy clergy, usually rectors, and the poor, usually vicars, not to mention mere curates.

By the eighteenth and nineteenth centuries, the vicar's status had improved to the extent that the rector was not always even wealthier. The tithes the rector received varied widely, depending on the prosperity of the village and the glebe lands, and the value of corn. Nowadays the distinction between rector and vicar is a matter of history, and rectors and vicars both receive stipends in the same way.

The curate

A parson had to get a parish. For most clergy, much of the time, that meant flattery and simony, cultivating the influential and paying them cash. By late medieval times, the rector or even sometimes the vicar was educated and prosperous enough to put a curate in his parish and cream off most of the parish income without ever being there. The curate only accepted in order to get a foot on the ladder.

After the Reformation the new lay rectors demanded even more money for a parish, too much even for the educated to pay, so they studied for degrees other than theology and the priesthood declined. Poor ordinands simply could not afford university without the monastic support they had had earlier. Patrons appointed service providers who were not even clergy, so not even ministers. Curates became farmers or teachers. By the eighteenth century, the universities were turning out plenty of ordinands, but curates were little better off, still seen as an inferior breed at the beck and call of the squire. They often lodged with the family but were allowed to stay for only part of the family meal. They became tutors to the heir of the family estate, like George Crabbe (1754–1832) for the Duke of Rutland. Sydney Smith (1771–1845) said "there is something which excites compassion in the very name of curate".[4] Kilvert (1840–1879) was a rare curate in a prosperous period who by this time could enjoy himself.

The curate has always been a mainstay of the Church. He has done all the vital tasks, run the benefice in the rector or vicar's absence, but been paid a pittance for his pains, with no security. Rectors or vicars tended to resent even the small sums they had to pay to keep a curate. Wealthy parishes sometimes had curates' houses, but if not and he could not live at the parsonage, he had to find lodgings.

Parsonages through the ages in chronological order

1: The vicar's pele—
Lanercost, Cumbria

2: The early priest's house—
St Alphege, Canterbury

3: The early priest's house—Mulcheney, Somerset

4: The priest's house—Itchingfield, Sussex

5: The priest's house—St Mary, Stamford, Lincolnshire

6: Later medieval—Congresbury, Somerset

7: Later medieval—Cossington, Leicestershire

8: Later medieval—Methwold, Norfolk

9: Jacobean—Chilmark, Wiltshire

10: Jacobean—Thorpe Achurch, Northamptonshire

11: Queen Anne—Redmarley D'Abitot, Gloucestershire

12: Queen Anne—West Ashby, Lincolnshire

13: Early Victorian—Pugin Hall, Rampisham, Dorset

14: Early Victorian—Wantage, Berkshire

15: Victorian—Barnack, Cambridgeshire

16: Edwardian—St Michael, Aldershot, Hampshire

17: Modern—St Stephen, Canonbury, London

Glebe and tithe

When the lord of the manor instituted the rector, he had to give him a living, so he endowed him with land, known as glebe. The rector was maintained by its income. Many interesting glebe houses, farmhouses, and cottages still survive, often close to the parsonage. Gifts from wealthy benefactors also helped. The rector could install a vicar or curate, pay him what he thought fit or could get away with, and keep the rest. Greedy priests became pluralists. If the monasteries took over, the living became part of their permanent endowment. After the Reformation, lay landowners who had acquired rectories from the monasteries benefited.

Further regular income came in the form of tithes, a concept dependent on the parish system. Glebe was supplied by the lord, tithe by the parish. One-tenth of the produce of parishioners had to be handed over and physically placed in a tithe barn built for the purpose; for farmers a tenth of the harvest, but for traders a tenth of their profit only. The "great tithe" on crops and cattle went to the rector. The "lesser tithes" on other produce, such as cheese, milk, chickens, geese, bees, wool, etc, went to the vicar in the parish itself.

The original idea was to redistribute profits for the poor, but the rector and vicar saw the tithe as their own. A benefice financed in those simple ways could, depending on the state of the economy, be a wealthy estate. The fourteenth-century reformers objected to tithe. Those such as Langland, John Ball, and Wycliffe said it should not be paid by the poor and the parish should only pay what it thought right. But non-payers were allowed to be cursed from the pulpit.

The priest's income was a constant bone of contention in the parish. It was rarely cheerfully paid. Labourers earning a very low wage were sometimes exempted, but this only caused friction from those earning slightly more. The tithe was the cause of more litigation than anything else. Puritans objected to the tithe, but then sought to enforce it when they took over the parish in the Civil War. Friends of the ousted Anglican raided the barn.

William Cowper described the annual tithe party in his poem "The Yearly Distress" in 1779. The farmers who resented having to pay these dues made a good job once a year of trying to drink them all back.

By the latter part of the eighteenth and early nineteenth centuries, the tithe system had had its day. There had been a decline in agriculture after the Napoleonic wars, and the remaining tithes were finally commuted into cash rent charges in 1836. For this purpose land had to be enclosed, a process carried out under the Enclosure Acts. The enclosures of open fields endowed the clergy with additional lands, substituting land revenues for taxes and ownership for collectivisation. The wealth that came to the rectors in this way stimulated parsonage modernisation and new building, but tended to accentuate the gap between the rich and the poor parishes. Church corporations and lay rectors or big landowners gained. It was not until 1936 that the cash rent charges were finally abolished. Glebe lands were appropriated by the dioceses in 1976 and from then on the parishes were deprived of any direct income from them.

Patrons

I have the original sale particulars for the Rectory of Folke, near Sherborne, Dorset, which was to be sold on Tuesday, 8 August 1837. The sale is stated to be of "the next and every alternate right of presentation to the rectory". We are told the parsonage house "with all necessary Buildings, Pleasure and Kitchen gardens" is "distant only 300 yards from the parish church". The Dean and Chapter of Salisbury had the alternate right of presentation. It was to be sold by auction at the Auction Mart opposite the Bank of England. It doesn't sound very attractive at first sight—after all you're not getting the freehold of the parsonage—until you read that the glebe is 18 acres and 14 perches and "the Great Tithes extending over 1700 acres—Worth about £400 per annum". In other words, this is a substantial investment. The glebe is quite a bit of land and the tithe covers a large area. All the buyer has to do is appoint an alternate vicar and cream off the profits.

Patronage is the right to appoint the priest to a benefice, and therefore to confer a living. It grew from the practices of the Saxon thegns and Norman barons. In legal terms it is a sort of property which can be transferred or bequeathed. As the monasteries appropriated rectories, they also acquired a lot of these "advowsons". As a result, after the Crown dissolved the monasteries in the sixteenth century, the patronage of nearly half of all livings changed hands. It sold most of them to laymen, and the King and the bishops or other clerical bodies kept some. If bishops presented livings to relations it was called nepotism. For this reason, lay patrons continued to have a large proportion of advowsons from the early seventeenth century right through the eighteenth. By the early nineteenth century, a number of rectors or members of their family were also patrons of the living, and these were called family livings. The whole system had got rather out of hand and was under attack for encouraging pluralism. One rector could hold several livings and might not appoint a vicar or curate to some.

Owning the living and having the right to present the incumbent to the living both conferred wealth, so had a value. Advowsons were thus bought and sold like any other commodity. This practice was finally ended in 1923. During the nineteenth century, the bishops steadily increased their own patronage—they disliked patronage that they could not control. In the twentieth century, this process continued and the powers of lay patrons have diminished under legal measures. Bishops and trust corporations have acquired their rights on a vacancy, and unification of benefices has sharply reduced their influence. Bishops also nowadays like to "suspend the living", sometimes for long periods of time after an incumbent has retired, to prevent patrons from exercising their rights. It helps them to get their hands on the parsonage.

Patronage was a factor in determining the quality of a parsonage house. Wealthy patrons endowed their parish with a parsonage. The wealthier the patron, the more he could afford to spend, both on the house itself and on subsequent repairs and maintenance, when this was not the responsibility of the incumbent.

The freehold and the parsonage

Parsonages are part of our built environment just like any house. But their differences are more interesting than the similarities. Their location beside or near the parish church has always been a special one. Secondly, without the parish system they would not exist. Thirdly, they pass from one vicar to the next, not to his or her family. The rector or vicar (the incumbent) is not in legal terms a person but a corporation and has the "freehold" in the parsonage house. But the term "freehold" does not have its normal legal meaning. There is no heritable interest, and even life ownership under the freehold is nowadays qualified in many ways—by age or ill health, under disciplinary measures, or pastoral reorganisation. In yet another body blow, the freehold of office has now itself been superseded by "common tenure", though the fragile freehold of property survives. But since 1972 the incumbent has no longer had much responsibility for repair and maintenance and has little freedom to make alterations. Team vicars, increasingly common, only hold office for a term of years, and priests-in-charge do not even have the security of the freehold, so they are now favoured by the bishops.

Notes

[1]   Anthea Jones, *A Thousand Years of the English Parish* (Windrush Press, 2000).
[2]   Savidge, *The Parsonage in England.*
[3]   Jones, *A Thousand Years of the English Parish.*
[4]   Goodenough, *The Country Parson*, p. 53.

Part Three: The Architecture

"God has no real style—he just goes on trying other things"

Picasso

CHAPTER 5

What Counts as a Parsonage?

The great majority of the houses in this and the following chapters are no longer parsonages at all. Most have been sold to private buyers. If we were to exclude them on those grounds, we would be imposing an intolerable limitation for the purposes of this book. But we still have to decide what houses lie within the scope of our architectural survey. You might think that is obvious. We have defined parsonages (see Appendix A) as rectories and vicarages, together with priests' houses and clergy houses. Is that not all?

Churches are obviously outside our scope, but if we start by considering all other church buildings, we will come across at least the following names or titles (in alphabetical order): Abbey Cottage, Abbey Farmhouse, Abbey Lodge, Abbot's House, Anchorite's Cell, Archdeacon's House, Archdeaconry, Bishop's House, Bishop's Palace, Canonry, Canon's House, Chancery, Chantry, Chantry House, Chaplaincy, Chapter Farm, Chapter House, Chorister's House, Church Cottage, Church Farmhouse, Church Hall, Church House, Church Place, Church Rooms, Church School, Church Schoolhouse, Churchwarden's House, Clergy House, Clerk's Cottage, Clerk's House, Curate's House, Deanery, Dovecote, Dower House (ex-vicarage), Friar's Farmhouse, Friary Court, Glebe Cottage, Glebe Court, Glebe Farm, Glebe House, Hermitage, Hostry, Lay Vicar's House, Manse, Minster Bedern, Minster Cottage, Mission House, Moot House, Old Canonry, Old Deanery, Old Priory, Parish Rooms, Parsonage Farm, Prebendal House, Prebendal Manor House, Preceptory, Priest's College, Priest Hall, Priest's House, Prior's House, Prior's Manse, Priory Farmhouse, Priory House, Rectorial Manor House, Rectory Cottage, Rectory Farm, Rectory House, Rectory Tower, Refectory, Seminary, Subdeanery, The Monastery, The Priory, The Treasury, Tithe Barn, Verger's House, Vestry House, Vestry Meeting Room, Vicar's Pele.

We must try to sort these out, and we must first distinguish the types of building from the names. Names can be very misleading. Houses called The Abbey or The

Priory are sometimes, but only rarely, part of the fabric of a dissolved monastery; they are usually private houses which may once have been associated with one, but they are often houses on or near the site of one, or of wealthy rectors or vicars, or survivals that became the local manor house. At Wiggenhall, Norfolk, The Priory is so called because it is on the site of a priory; Nostell Priory, Yorkshire, is a Palladian house on the site of another. Priory Farmhouse at Litcham, Norfolk, is a former chapel or hermitage, not the farmhouse of a former priory. Abbey House at Thorney, Cambridgeshire (1565), is believed to inhabit the site of the original Thorney Abbey, built as a manor house reusing demolished fabric after the Dissolution, extended again in the seventeenth century. At St John Lee, Northumberland, The Hermitage is a house on the site of the seventh century hermitage of St John of Beverley. In Salisbury, Church House is a wool merchant's house. But these names can also all be clues to a former parsonage. Glebe House may well be a renamed old vicarage, as may Church House.

If we now take the types of building, as distinct from the names, they can be categorised in various ways. Some are non-residential. If living accommodation is our criterion, we might say the church schoolhouse is within our scope but not the church school; the chantry house but not the chantry itself. But we must not be too pedantic: a school building may form part of a noted group that includes the parsonage, all designed by the same architect, common in Victorian times.

If we stick to our strict definition of parsonages, then try to categorise the other buildings, we may do so like this:

1. Houses of Church of England clergy or officials other than rectors and vicars, such as Bishop's Palace, Archdeaconry, Deanery, Canonry, Prebendal House, Lay Vicar's House, Verger's House, Chantry House.
2. Houses of other denominations such as presbyteries and manses.
3. Private houses built by or for wealthy clergy.
4. Other residential Church buildings such as Church House, Church Farm or Glebe House.
5. Monastic clergy dwellings: Abbot's House, Priory House and so on.
6. Ancillary buildings: tithe barn, stables, dovecote and so on.
7. Monastic associated houses: Abbey Farmhouse, Abbey Cottage, Friar's Farmhouse.
8. Non-residential religious buildings: Chapter House, Chantry, Refectory, Vestry House.
9. Buildings with missionary or educational functions: Mission House, Seminary, Parish Rooms, school and schoolhouse.

10. Miscellaneous buildings with religious associations: hermitage, Rectory
Tower and so on.

The monastic and non-residential buildings in 7–9 above are in my view the
subject of another book, but I have considered the rest fair game where space has
permitted. Church houses were not necessarily residential, but many are of great
interest; certainly, a whole book could easily be written about them and church
farmhouses. I have included category 10 simply because these odd buildings
are fun, and we must remember that gardens are often of interest or contain
interesting relics.

How the parsonage evolved

To understand the architecture of the parsonage, and how it evolved over the
centuries, we must talk about periods. These are by nature arbitrary; sudden
changes in architectural styles rarely occurred, and certainly not in conjunction
with changes of monarchy, and even developments leading to great changes could
be gradual. In any case, the term "Georgian" covers up to 150 years of changing
fashions and "Victorian" over 60 more. The Regency box and the Neo-Tudor house
are both of the same period, and the High Gothic is quite different from the Arts
and Crafts, though both are Victorian. Faced with those difficulties I have tried
to define the periods in the way I think to be the best compromise between the
historical and the architectural, which is: Saxon and Norman 697–1154; Medieval
1154–1485; Tudor and Elizabethan 1485–1603; Jacobean 1603–1660; Restoration
1660–1688; William and Mary 1689–1702; Queen Anne 1702–1714; Georgian
1714–1811; Regency 1811–1837; Victorian 1837–1901; Edwardian 1901–1918;
Interwar 1918–1939; Modern 1939 onwards.

Saxon

How did the parsonage originate? Where did the earliest priests live? In the Celtic tradition, hermits, the early monks, often set up their cells at the sites of holy wells, so these might be called the first parsonages. The first more conventional parsonage may just have been the church itself. Saxon church towers may have been used, for example those at Sulgrave and Earls Barton in Northamptonshire, Saintbury, Longborough, and Withington in the Cotswolds, Barton-upon-Humber in North Lincolnshire, or Deerhurst in Gloucestershire. But you do not have to go back a thousand years to find clergy living in the church. A friend of mine, commenting on Bax, wrote:

> The entry on Rye greatly interested me as it referred to St Mary's Church where the rector lived in one room in the church wall. The Revd Oscar Brooks, ex-vicar of our church in Brighton, went to Rye after being repatriated from Japan during the war. He was a good friend and Margaret and I visited him during our honeymoon in 1945 when he showed us the room [in the church] where he lived before taking us for lunch. He was tickled pink with the room which was accessed by one or two steps against an outside wall; being a bachelor it suited him but there was no bath so he had an arrangement to go to someone's house.[1]

The Saxons arrived in the fifth century and had converted to Christianity by the seventh. There had been at least four centuries of Christian priests before the Normans even arrived in England, a period as long as the time from the Jacobeans to us. Yet very few Saxon buildings, let alone parsonages, survive. We have virtually no knowledge of so many buildings. Saxon architecture broadly falls into two periods. The early buildings of about 600–800 were of wood or reclaimed Roman brick. Then came the Viking raids. Then the Late Saxon of about 900–1066, a period of which we have a number of surviving stone buildings, though only fragments apart from some fine churches. The wooden halls of the thegns tended to look like barns, the aisle posts coming down inside the hall. The stone buildings were stylistically Romanesque, adapted for local conditions. There are no stone priests' houses of this period, but we can get some idea from the churches of what they might have been like—very modest rectangular boxes. However, the Saxon priest not housed in the monastery or church would have been lucky to have timber, wattle and daub, and turf thatch.

Norman

The Norman parson was a little better provided for. He often lodged at the local inn or stayed at the appropriating monastery. The wealthier ones built quite good houses. But the basic priest's house was just that. One room, timber, wattle and daub, unceiled, unglazed, central hearth, no sanitation. Unglazed windows and opposing doors created a draught. In a bigger house there might be a dais at one end and a screen at the other, with a separate kitchen for fire security. Parsonages did not need to be large; in the eleventh century Pope Hildebrand enforced celibacy.

The Normans used more stone than the Saxons, but continued to use timber and the aisled hall. The Manor House at Boothby Pagnell, Lincolnshire, and the Jew's House in Lincoln, with their delicately moulded round-arched windows and doorways, give a clue to the look of the better priest's house of the period, but a separate parsonage house was not yet accepted practice. Mid-twelfth century stories show clergy continuing to lodge in church. John of Ford's *Life of Wulfric*, an anchorite of Heslebury, Somerset, says the priest usually slept in church. Gilbert of Sempringham and his chaplain lived in the village inn, moving—only to avoid temptation from the landlord's daughter—to a room at the church, then to a house they built at the edge of the churchyard. This was probably not untypical. Still later, Gilbert converted the parsonage into an almshouse and lived in the rooms of the Bishop of Lincoln. The priest in Blackburn lived in Samlesbury Chapel; Scots raiders came down all this way and carried off blankets and vessels. Bishop Nicholson of Carlisle said the choir of Salkeld church had been built as a "secure hold or habitation for the Rector himself". The church at Burgh by Sands had a tower at the east end which "seems to have been intended for a mansion house for the vicar, such fastnesses being necessary". The more socially minded institutions like the friaries also provided accommodation for priests.

Early medieval

Through the Angevin into the early medieval period, the clergy still did not always have a house provided for them and continued to lodge at the abbey or priory. The early medieval priest's house is now a rare phenomenon. What are the oldest survivals? Savidge says there is nothing before the thirteenth century. The earliest stone houses of any kind now existing seem to be of the second half of the twelfth century, like the Jew's House in Lincoln. The houses of the lower classes were built mainly of wood and have not survived. More houses from the fourteenth century onwards exist, though again mostly of the larger kind.

"Full sooty was her hall and eke her bower", said Chaucer of the priest's widow's two-roomed cottage. But the parsonage was by now often a hall house. Sometimes the monasteries provided a plot and the vicar built the house himself; for example, in 1253 the vicar of Conisbrough, Yorkshire, was given land for a manse. In 1287 in Hadlow, Tonbridge, an acre was allocated. But at Halifax, in 1273, Lewes Priory said, "a vicarage house shall be built, in which the vicar for the time being shall reside". A typical plan for a timber-framed house was described in an ordinance for Histon, Cambridgeshire, in 1268. Eynsham Abbey built a house of oak with hall of 26ft by 20ft, chamber and pantry, and a separate kitchen. At Muchelney, the abbey supplied the cooking. A house consisting of hall, two solars, and cellars was given to the vicar of West Harptree, Somerset, in 1344.

The larger houses, of stone or timber, fall into two basic types, the first floor hall and the aisled hall. The hall was the main living and entertaining area. In the case of the first floor hall, the rooms on the ground floor were probably used for storage. Above were the hall, where guests were entertained, and the solar, the private withdrawing room for the owner. The hall was heated, the solar usually not. The more usual aisled halls were double height, with aisle posts, open to the rafters with central fire, and a cross passage at the side, screened from the hall, separating it from the service areas, the pantry and buttery. At the other side there was often a parlour on the ground floor and a private solar above. The kitchen was often quite separate to avoid fire. First floor halls were less common after the fourteenth century, though some say they were just a cross wing to a former aisled hall. As time went by, the hall house developed by the addition of cross-wings at each side, forming an H-shape. The Wealden house, found particularly in Kent and Sussex, was a small hall house with more vestigial cross-wings. The Wealden house is recognisable from its unusual shape, jettied out at the sides, even when the timber frame is nowadays concealed by later materials, such as rendering, tiling, or even stone or brick cladding. We know some of these were parsonages. Again, the hall was open to the rafters with an open fire in a central stone hearth, unceiled, and the windows were unglazed. Later, when fires became more sophisticated and could be placed against the wall, the upper part of the hall was roofed over, creating more space, the upper floor disguising the original configuration.

The medieval parson's solar could be up an external spiral stair. He slept on a straw pallet with a log bolster. Carpets were not introduced until Edward I's reign.

He often had to accommodate assistant priests, and offer hospitality, both to the visiting bishop or archdeacon and to the traveller. This might consist of no more than a "shakedown" of straw in his hall. The parson also usually needed to be a competent farmer.

In the north of England, on the borders and even some way from them (the Scots raided Blackburn), architecture was different. A house had to be defensible. These pele houses or towers (the word "pele" may come from the Celtic "pill" or stone fort) of three or more floors are unique and readily identifiable by their shape. A historian wrote in 1891 that "their number is so great that no list of them has ever been attempted".[2] They were not all parsonages, but he identifies Embleton and Whalton as such, and says those at Belsay, Halton, Chipchase, Elsdon, and Whitton housed "the gentleman or the rector". They are in various stages of decay. The history of the border country from Norman times right down to the union of crowns of 1603 is one of continual strife. After the twelfth century, houses in the rest of England were often unfortified, but here they needed to be. By Edward II's reign there was a proliferation of pele towers, though the surviving ones cannot confidently be dated earlier than the thirteenth century. There was continual war during the reigns of the three Edwards and many were built in the fourteenth century.

Often within a walled enclosure called a barmkyn, there was a rectangular tower of three or four floors, the ground floor, a storage space, and sometimes also a vaulted first floor. The ground floor could house the cattle when under attack. The entrance, usually arched, might be on the first floor for security, or if on the ground, there was a spiral or a wall stair. The ground floor was usually in total darkness, but the first floor was lit, often by moulded or trefoiled lights with an arch on the inside, in the thickness of the wall, with inbuilt stone seats. There was a good stone fireplace, with a tapering hood resting on corbels or columns. The second floor was often similar but more modest, while the parapet was battlemented and there might be angle turrets, projecting on corbels. The parapets were also corbelled out, allowing machicolations for attacking the enemy below. There was little ornament, particularly on the exterior.

There had rarely been a church porch in Norman and early medieval times, but by the fourteenth century a lot more had been built on. The porch, normally on the south side but perhaps on the north if the manor house was there, was now needed for many purposes. Women were "churched" there after childbirth, penitents were given absolution, legacies were paid, coroners sometimes held court there, notices were displayed, and they gave protection to the church door in bad weather. They were usually of stone, but sometimes oak-framed on a stone base. Some of these porches had a room over them, used perhaps for the library, or for church accounts and records, or for wills, or more pertinently, by chantry priests to stay overnight in order to perform their duties to the parish, and sometimes to teach Latin, under the terms of the chantry bequest, so they were the first church schools. And sometimes they were the parsonage.

Late medieval

Quite a few medieval parsonages, called priests' houses, from the fourteenth to the sixteenth century still survive. They are usually smaller and much simpler versions of the manor house. Even so, some are delightful to look at, with their mullioned and cusped or even traceried windows, reflecting the recent modernisation of the church in the new Perpendicular style. They were either timbered or of stone. They tended to be rectangular, without projecting wings, with groups of two or three light mullioned windows, sometimes with ornate mouldings, and an arched doorway with plank and ledge door, their only excrescence often being external newel staircase towers. They could look a little like a small chapel, or like the much earlier first-floor halls such as that at Boothby Pagnell. They were not unlike other small village houses, though often rather better, with two floors and sometimes a cellar and an attic. They were very close to the church and convenient for the priest to get to the service. Priests' houses were adaptable, and when superseded by a new house for an ambitious rector were later used for many purposes such as almshouses, church houses for communal activities, parish halls, clerks' houses, alehouses, lodgings for income, chantry houses, even chantries.

Most medieval parsons lived little more grandly than anyone else, though they were mostly now on a par with the yeoman or the modern parson in his late twentieth century box. As a general rule small houses went through a continual process of enlargement as the years went by and prosperity increased. These successive modernisations have made it difficult to determine precisely what individual parsonages of this date were like when new. The pele towers of the north acquired more conventional wings. The timber-framed houses of the south sprouted cross-wings and outbuildings and more were now built of stone. They had wood or stone mullioned windows or lights with shutters, there still being no glass. The wool trade made many communities prosperous over the fourteenth and fifteenth centuries, particularly in Yorkshire, the Cotswolds, and the south-east, and some parsonages grew substantially in size.

Chimneys and wall fireplaces made it possible for houses to be built with an upper floor over the hall, and this created extra space. In the later fifteenth century this was being done as a matter of course, particularly with priests' houses and other Church buildings, some of the large manor houses continuing to have open halls, mainly for prestige purposes. In wooden houses, more sophisticated roofing and stronger materials had now solved the problem of outward pressure on the walls requiring open aisle posts.

Churches were often greatly enlarged in the fifteenth century and now had much bigger porches with rooms above them. Even now not all clergy had parsonages and the rooms (or parvise chapel) over the church porch could provide spacious and private accommodation. There is a good example at St Sepulchre in Smithfield, London, occupied even until quite recently.

Tudor

Architectural ideas were increasingly coming from the continent, and Italy in particular, and this was creating a greater interest in style. In grander houses, this manifested itself in vestigial Renaissance mouldings and classical features like pilasters which sometimes mixed awkwardly with the English tradition. The parsonage, however, was still often too small to be much affected by this. Marriage continued to be forbidden during Henry VIII's reign (though Cranmer had an illicit wife, as did others), so in theory a big house was still unnecessary, and though wives resurfaced under Edward, they disappeared again under Mary.

Alongside stone, timber was still used in the Tudor parsonage, now of a higher standard than before. Houses were getting larger, with bigger cross-wings. The hall was flag-stoned, the screens passage continuing to separate it from the service wing of kitchen and buttery.

Elizabethan

The Renaissance influence from Europe was now taking greater hold, but classical ornamentation was still poorly understood. It gave rise to sometimes elaborate dressings, or moulded brickwork, still being grafted on to buildings of traditional configuration and style with Tudor mullions and gables. The break with Rome had contributed to a disjunction from Italian and French trends and left English architecture looking rather dated, though ironically it gave rise to a distinctively English style.

By the end of the sixteenth century, the great increase in trade and the rise of the merchant classes meant that housing had dramatically improved. Some now even talked of an excess of luxury, looking back to earlier days with nostalgia. This had its impact on clergy houses. Reconstruction and modernisation meant that more flues were built in the walls, with sophisticated fire surrounds, giving rise to a proliferation of chimneys. These had previously been rare or non-existent. Upper floors over the hall were now normal. There were more and better fittings, furniture, and draperies. When a new priest's house was built, the old one was used for a subsidiary purpose such as a village hall or an almshouse. The parson's wife was now tolerated, and by the middle of Elizabeth's reign half the clergy were married. Some said it was for this reason they were now better fed and the house better furnished. The average Elizabethan parson left a bigger estate than the Tudor.

The new parsonages were gabled and had mullioned windows with casements, but glazing in windows was still uncommon even by the end of the sixteenth century, except for the very wealthy. Windows generally remained quite small, with dripmoulds to deflect rain from the roof.

Jacobean

Improvements in comfort continued unabated. There were more rebuildings of existing houses and houses continued to grow in size. New houses were more urbane. Stone and the fashionable brick were now much more frequently used. New stone or brick façades were added to timber houses, though they still had mullioned and transomed windows with hood moulds for drainage. Elevations generally became more "polite" and sophisticated, less vernacular, with dressed stonework and greater architectural pretension. The Renaissance influence from the continent, which had started in Tudor times, developed apace, bringing greater symmetry of façade. In polite houses, rooms now had to fit the overall design rather than the other way around as before, so much so that in court circles, the Jacobean became a period of a battle of styles. By the 1620s, Inigo Jones was designing buildings in a style new to England, bearing no relation to the Tudor tradition, even though dating back to Palladio in Italy, but Jones had little influence beyond the court, let alone on the parsonage. The next style, this time of Dutch influence, known as Artisan Mannerism, with patterned brickwork and Dutch gables, often with medallions or oculus windows, had more. Such devices were employed on quite vernacular houses if they had some pretension, like the better parsonages of the period.

Restoration

There was still more radical change in mid-seventeenth-century architecture, another sort of revolution after the Civil War. The Jacobean manner was superseded by the new compact double-pile house, of largely Flemish origin, so influential that it is still much of the basis of the house of today. Architecture had metamorphosed from the medieval to that of the Enlightenment by the mid-seventeenth century, Roger Pratt's sadly demolished Coleshill of around 1650 being a fine example. These more compact houses, with their new elegant entrance and staircase hall, were radical, functional, and beautiful, practical as well as grand. Key features were the hipped roofline, complete symmetry, tall sculptural chimneys, and the new double-hung sash windows, possibly an English invention of the 1670s. The new style was rather avant-garde for most parsonages, but it paved the way not only for the Queen Anne parsonage but the Georgian and later. Dare we whisper some regret for the passing of the sprawling gables of medieval tradition?

Despite civil war, clergy prosperity was increasing, though there were huge differentials, as Hearth Tax records show. The tax of a shilling for each hearth or chimney was introduced in 1662, and went on for twenty-seven years. Some clergy now had large numbers of hearths, ranging from seven to eleven up to twenty-seven, while most people had only one or two. Window Tax, which lasted from 1696 right through to 1851, was more architecturally disfiguring, causing many fine windows to be blocked.

William and Mary

What we call the Queen Anne style can be traced back to the later years of the seventeenth century and William and Mary, with the transition from the Restoration house to the Baroque, introduced to England by Wren and Vanbrugh, late as usual, from Italy. But there were political implications and, though influential, the Baroque, hinting at Counter-Reformation, was more muted as a mainstream English style. Though used to dramatic effect in the great houses, it was also less suited to the more intimate scale of the smaller house such as the parsonage. Nevertheless, its influence was felt in stylistic devices found in many parsonages, such as nicely scalloped and pedimented doorcases, elegant quoins and architraves, and, inside, twisted balusters.

Queen Anne

The Queen Anne period saw the culmination of the English Baroque just before its mutation into the early Georgian. Greater use of mellow brick and a simplification of the façade, with its projecting and sometimes pedimented central bays, sash windows, decorative central doorcase, and corner quoins, made the Queen Anne house the model for the "doll's house" look. Though the effect was simple, the use of materials, with contrasting brickwork, lighter rubbed brick dressings round windows and door, and prominent quoin stones, made these houses both charming and quite sophisticated. Chimney stacks were bold and dramatic. The style was highly versatile and suited the parsonage very well.

Georgian

Many call the Georgian period the golden age of the parsonage. The phrase "Georgian rectory" is music to the ears of any estate agent. Georgian architects were perhaps the earliest true ones in the modern sense of being informed in theory. Houses were classical, balanced, civilised. In this so-called age of enlightenment, parsonages were seen more as gentlemen's residences, not necessarily located alongside the church, as once deemed essential, but increasingly in good secular streets of low density.

People often say they dream of retiring to the country to live in a Georgian rectory, but one wonders if they know what they mean. The Georgian period lasted for at least 120 years, and architecture changed throughout that period. In the early years, the Georgian parsonage was a development of the Queen Anne house. A little more sophisticated, it was elegant, symmetrical, typically of five bays, with double-hung sash windows, a central doorcase with classical mouldings and hipped roof, and sometimes a parapet. By the second quarter of the eighteenth century, the Grand Tour of Italy had led to what were perceived as the purer designs of Palladio by architects like Colin Campbell and William Kent, a hundred years after Inigo Jones had originally tried, and failed, to make this style dominant. Palladianism unexpectedly returned to England, perhaps because it seemed to suit English restraint. Its new features included the columned portico and the Diocletian window. Palladianism was more diluted in smaller houses like parsonages, but manifested itself in pedimented façades and doorcases, and sometimes side wings and Venetian windows. The huge square chimneys gave way to smaller or disguised ones. These attempts to recreate the Italian house, if built today, are perversely called pastiche and roundly condemned. Palladianism was, and remains, very popular in England; it was different from contemporary continental architecture and was not Catholic or French. It was also a political tool, favoured by the Whigs, and became the most potent symbol of British architecture.

The broader classicism of Adam, then Wyatt and others, came as a reaction to this excessive purism. Adam took detailed note of the new discoveries about Greek and Roman architecture, enabling him to go beyond Palladianism. He is accused of idiosyncrasy, but he was not seeking to copy in the same slavish way. Palladio himself could be accused of inaccuracy if his aim had been to copy the Romans. By the last years of the century, this sophistication and the more rounded classicism of William Chambers (he spoke of Adam's "macaroni attitude"), then the eclecticism of Wyatt, had become prevalent. Finally came the late Georgian Greek and Italianate Revival.

All these styles could be scaled down for the parsonage, and were well suited to it, which is why the Georgian parsonage is such a successful creation. We must also not forget that Gothicism, though sometimes dormant, was never dead throughout the Georgian period; Gothic Survival ended and Gothic Revival had begun. Parsonages reflecting true medieval Gothic principles were, however, not yet to be found in the high Georgian period and even Gothick parsonages are not very common.

Many parsonages were still not grand houses and the major stylistic developments passed these by; many were built by the jobbing builder with a tired old formula—if in doubt, put up a rudimentary pediment, and a projecting porch with columns if the customer could afford it. But a lot of good work was done by amateurs with only the guide books of Batty Langley, Isaac Ware, and others for guidance. And the parsonage was not at all beneath the dignity of proper architects like John Wood of Bath, Smith of Warwick, and John Carr of York. Georgian rectories vary widely. They can be elegant in the extreme, or frankly dull. Some are full of character, some almost too perfect, some botched jobs. Their great popularity since the early twentieth century is perhaps attributable to the fashionable rejection of Victorian architecture, even though Modernism is contemptuous of symmetry. The classical style of architecture required symmetry, and this meant designing the interior to fit the exterior. Rooms, except for the service rooms discreetly hidden away at the back, tended to be of equal size round a central corridor hall.

The story of the Georgian parsonage is not just about new houses. The Georgians were keen modernisers and no respecters of "original features". Modernisation of the older parsonages by way of perceived improvements to keep up with fashion were a major feature of the period. Jacobean or even medieval houses were refronted or had wings added in the new style quite inappropriate to them. To be fair, this was not always just for show, and some work was urgently needed. John Waugh, Chancellor of Carlisle, observed that "in the best circles" tiles were replacing thatch, showing just how dated some houses still were. (In Onybury, a farmer occupied the parsonage. It was "cheerfully situated" but "parlours without fires and bedchambers full of grain take off from the comfort and dryness of a house very much".) As always, in impoverished areas the old houses remained more untouched and so more unspoilt.

The beginnings of more serious study of the architecture of the smaller house can be traced to this period. Isaac Ware talks in his *Complete Body of Architecture* of "common houses" in the country, and cites a "parsonage house in Yorkshire" as a house of small expense in which "a small family may find perfect convenience".[3]

Regency

I use the term "Regency" for the period from 1811, when George IV became Regent, right through to 1837, because the Late Georgian parsonage very much has its own character. It is ironic that the Grand Tour, the fashion of visiting Italy to study the classical buildings that were now seen as the basis of our culture, should also lead to a return to Gothicism, seen as their polar opposite. 1811 is an arbitrary date, but as good as any to mark this shift from an era of unchallenged classicism which had seemed as if it would last for ever.

Architectural theory had existed since Vitruvius. Less important in the long medieval period, it had gained strength with the Renaissance, and was now acquiring the respectability of academic study due to the popularity of antiquarianism. The Jacobeans and Georgians had become obsessed with style, but the past had been forgotten, and even in the eighteenth century amazingly little was known about the form and structure of historic architecture. Thomas Rickman (1776–1841) studied the Gothic style, and his classifications of Norman (Romanesque might have been preferable), Early English, Decorated, and Perpendicular at once made it better understood. This new academicism gave rise to much study and theorising about domestic architecture in general and parsonages in particular, which had a great influence on the form of the contemporary parsonage. Architectural theory was firmly rooted in tradition and respect for the past while also giving impetus to creativity.

The Regency is also known as the age of Greek Revival. The new classicism was essentially plain and simple, but had certain modish tendencies, such as the use of cast iron in porches and balconies, and a love of curves, characterised by blind arches around fenestration, sweeping staircases, and apsed corridors. But the Gothic Revival meant that Neo-Tudor houses were increasingly being built at the same time as those stucco boxes. This Gothicism would grow in strength, and the parsonage played an important part in its development. The struggle for freedom from the straitjacket of the Georgian classicism which had so long been dominant was under way.

Architects had no idea how to achieve their new aim—at first they simply tacked classical, Renaissance, Italianate, Gothick, or Tudor Gothic features onto the same square box as required. When a Gothic look was required, a gable with a pointed window might be put one side of the doorway to create the required gable-and-bay asymmetricality. One half of these so-called "Frankenstein" houses might be classical, the other Gothic. Some were a mixture. You could call these houses Clathic, or perhaps Gossical. Oddly, these strange hybrids often had charm.

But the architects learned rapidly, and soon became quite skilled in a wide range of styles. Eclecticism was in. They really were architects now, as the Royal Institution of British Architects was first formed in 1834. They were starting to think more radically and would finally shake off classicism when they started designing the whole house from the inside.

There was much theorising about the proper style for the parsonage. J. B. Papworth recommended that its design should be "selected from the church itself".[4] We know quite a bit about the architects of the new parsonages, partly thanks to the detailed plans that they had submitted to Queen Anne's Bounty on behalf of their clients after the Gilbert Acts of the 1770s.

Victorian

For admirers of the Gothic style, the High Victorian rectory is the very embodiment of the concept of the rectory; the massive pile dedicated to the institutionalised mission of the moralising Church. Together with the Georgian parsonage, it is one of the two most fundamental but quite different archetypes of the parsonage. The essence of the Victorian period of Empire and conspicuous prosperity among the middle classes is summarised nowhere better than in the rectory, with its tall gables, steep rooflines, stone dressings, mullioned windows and decorative brickwork, and inside, the gloom of its oak panelling, the daylight filtered through dark stained glass. It is a tradition that continued right into the Edwardian period.

At first, the Victorian parsonage differed not at all from its Regency counterpart. Houses were still being built in classical style. These were often highly practical, and the design of the parsonage at Harlton, Cambridgeshire, as late as 1843 shows the Georgian model augmented by a simplicity of internal plan separating the public rooms at the front from the private family areas behind. But this was deceptive; the reaction to classicism had already become an ideological one, nowhere better exemplified than in the writings of Pugin, who railed about the devastating effect of the Reformation on churches and ecclesiastical buildings. He blamed both modern Catholicism and Protestantism for the way medieval houses had been treated by later occupants: the new clergy "found the old buildings but ill-suited to their altered style of living; what had served for the studious, retired priest, or the hospitable and munificent prelate of ancient days, was very unfit for a married, visiting, gay clergyman, or a modern bishop, whose lady must conform to the usages and movements of fashionable life . . . mullioned windows cut out, and common sashes fixed in their stead . . . "[5]

He saw classicism as the architecture of paganism, and comprehensively rejected it. He saw the old Gothic as the only true architecture, and was determined to revive it.

There had already been a decisive shift towards Gothic, but it had been a Tudor Gothic. Pugin wanted his vision of the real thing. He studied early buildings in real detail, as only a few had done before, noting how they had been constructed, and the practical rationale for their detailing and mouldings: he concluded that hoodmoulds, string courses, and other mouldings should be solely to deflect the rain, not for decoration. His Catholic presbytery at Brewood, Staffordshire, and his parsonage at Rampisham, Dorset, were gabled, with mullions, but simple and unostentatious, in what he saw as the true early manner. In these ways he was to influence Butterfield, Street, then Webb and the vernacular revival. He designed his presbyteries and parsonages from the inside, the outward appearance being subordinate to the internal function. It was a radical approach. Yet it was only what the medieval builders had done. It was a rejection of conscious style. His "functionalism revival" was influential, born of architectural theory of the kind still admired by the modernists. Ironically, in the twentieth century, Victorian churches, rectories, and vicarages were largely derided. But if we look at the Victorian rectories designed by the major architects with fresh eyes, we see good solid materials with finely crafted, but often quite sparse, detailing. Designing from the inside meant creating the main rooms, which by now were the drawing room, dining room, and study or library, to the most practical size and configuration, so that the exterior followed their shape, leading to greater external complexity and asymmetry.

As to Pugin's theory of the primacy of the Gothic, if we reflect that the Gothic period had succeeded the Romanesque in the twelfth century and lasted only until the birth of secularism in the sixteenth century, we might argue that it was really quite a short phase of architectural history—but that is another story. The Victorian Gothic parsonage is unlike any house of any earlier period, and that is its great strength.

Then, just when the High Gothic was accepted as the established style, there came another significant "paradigm shift" in architecture. The Arts and Crafts, or more descriptively "vernacular revival", style emerged. This quiet revolution was ultimately even more influential, perhaps as much as the Restoration house had been. There were really two types of Victorian parsonage, the formality of the High Gothic and the domesticity of the vernacular revival. But despite the Queen

Anne Revival with which it is associated, the latter was not a return to classicism, having much more in common via High Gothic with English medieval buildings. The two styles were different, yet both shouted: we are English, and proud of it.

Edwardian

The Edwardian period, though brief, was one of great prosperity and optimism, and produced some very fine buildings. Some see it as regressive, a blind celebration of glories already of the past, some as too confused, with the great eclecticism of its gleanings from all earlier styles. Some see it as progressive, as its exploration and development of the vernacular revival took it towards modernism. The very fact of those opposing forces makes it a most interesting period. Houses were at their most sophisticated, often making even Victorian standards of construction and detailing seem crude by comparison. But the great days of parsonage building were over.

Interwar

Savidge, author of *The Parsonage in England* and a bureaucrat with the Church Commissioners who broadly favoured selling the old houses for the pittance then obtainable, nevertheless felt that, though the new houses after the First World War were suitable in size and planning, those of the interwar period followed the styles of contemporary housing "in perfect safety"[6] and the post-war ones "had nothing impressive, certainly, about them".[7] Yet a house of this period could of course claim to be "Georgian"; and indeed, the period of George V is one of Neo-Georgian architecture. But it was also yet another period of eclecticism. There were some pleasing late examples of the Arts and Crafts style, hipped roofs and dormers combining with more modern features such as decorative tiling. The period also saw the birth of the eccentric Art Deco style and, more ominously, that of the modernist movement, in the austere "international" style, imported from the continent after 1925 and gaining ground in the early 1930s. The modernist architects derided the stockbroker Tudor and Neoclassical offerings of the more conventional housebuilders, so the houses of the later 1930s can often be sharply distinguished from those of the 1920s. The parsonages of the period tended to be less adventurous, but the interwar period of architecture is an underrated one, and should be growing in reputation.

This period between two world wars was also a time of contraction, both of the Church in general and of the physical scale of its houses in particular, though big ones were still being built. Worth in Sussex, by Paxton Watson (1932–34), had six bedrooms, two attics, three bathrooms, a servants' room and back stairs, and a chauffeur's cottage, in what Savidge called "Wrenish" style, and was H-plan. By contrast, Whaplode Drove, Lincolnshire, by Wilfrid and Laurence Bond (1936), was less than half that size, with four bedrooms and a very small study. The floor area of parsonages between the wars thus varied widely, but averaged out at about 2,600 sq. ft. Some architects continued the tradition of the maid's room, but by 1938 the designer of the parsonage at Wilburton in Cambridgeshire (E. J. Tench) was saying that this was a thing of the past.

There was very little of the avant garde and most of the new parsonages were an uneasy compromise between Stockbroker Tudor and concrete Modernism. Savidge notes that the "central authorities" (an apt term for the way the Church had developed) were neutral on design, being concerned only with construction and accommodation. This is still Church policy today, though many believe that the issue of style in parsonage design should be given more attention, as had the perceptive Victorians.

Modern

The story of the Revd Oscar Brooks at the beginning of this chapter and his refuge in the walls of the church was undoubtedly unusual—the aim was now that the modern parson should have a modern parsonage. After the Second World War, the priorities of contemporary architects and developers changed, and architecture was now seen by the theorists as an instrument for social reform. The whole past history of architecture was widely seen as unsatisfactory. Traditional aesthetics were largely abandoned as undesirable. Victorian architecture was derided. The "modern box" came in. Gas fires, then central heating, were replacing big old chimneys and messy open fires. Much smaller rooms, insulated from the weather, were cosier. Big rooms with uncarpeted floors were seen as antediluvian, cold and draughty. Contemporary designs and colours did not suit venerable mullions and cornices. Parsonages followed the trend, but most were still quite conventional. Generally, they were now much smaller, and less distinctive.

The view that the parsonage should be smaller gathered strength. The first parsonages after the Second World War were limited to 1,500 sq. ft, down from the interwar period by as much as 1,000 sq. ft. The restrictions were lifted in 1952, but houses remained small. In this post-war period, the Church authorities continued to remain neutral on the design of new houses.

By the 1960s, parsonages, while slightly larger, were still much smaller than early houses, rarely more than 2,000 sq. ft, yet cost a great deal more. Contractors on large local developments were sometimes simply asked to add a parsonage, modified to the slightly higher standards specified by the Church, with the diocesan parsonage board perhaps asking for a repeatable plan. There was generally at least a nod towards traditionalism. A typical Wates house had deep eaves and picture windows, a sort of vernacular and modern mix. Where existing local architecture was Georgian, or even Tudor, the new designs often took note of the setting, but not if the former house was Gothic.

Savidge argues that some parsonages stood out as good examples of new domestic design, because they were sometimes designed individually, and after the war few other houses were. The mass production of the 1960s reduced this advantage. There were now only four bedrooms but occasionally two bathrooms; no longer a scullery but a "utility room" sometimes tucked in behind the garage; flush doors and many fitted cupboards. The new "open plan" was quite popular. There is a perceptible parallel between the cultural changes that the Church was trying to impose on its clergy and the architecture of the parsonage in this period.

To the housebuyers and their estate agents, the traditional parsonages are the ones with charisma, and they cannot wax very lyrical about these new houses. They were plain, unadorned, insubstantial, often of poor quality brick, with lower pitched roofs, straight lines, unvaried glass, a general absence of detailing, and, inside, low ceilings. They used fewer natural materials and were often less robust and built with less care. The dominance of the modernist school was used to justify their perceived functionalism and lack of emphasis on aesthetics. While they do not slavishly follow Le Corbusier's statement that a house is a machine, they are perhaps closer to Mies van der Rohe's "less is more". There was little if any attempt to symbolise religious values.

But there is some variation even in this unpromising material. They can be categorised either as in modernist manner or essentially traditional, scaled-down versions of earlier Georgian or Victorian styles. The 1985 house in Amersham,

Bucks, designed by Sir Basil Spence's partnership in a "vernacular modernist" manner, is neither one nor the other, but at least attempts some individuality.

Where older parsonages have been retained in this period, there have often been attempts to reduce them in size to make them what is perceived as more practical for our time. A good example is the Regency vicarage at Humshaugh, Northumberland, modified in the 1970s. The illustrations (Figures 1A–D, pages 74–75) show how the reduction was achieved. It is inevitable that some of the character of a house is lost in this process.

More recent vicarages have tended to be less adventurous, and more traditional, echoing the "executive home" concept, even less overtly modernistic, with archaising features like fake stone quoins.

It is not that there has been no consciousness of the importance of good design. In 1987, *Country Life* had a leading article about the design of new parsonages, couched in critical terms. It said there had been "no attempt to compete with the architectural standards of the nineteenth century", adding that they "seemed to display the worst aspects of modern speculative building".[8] It suggested that a design competition might be a good idea. In 1988, a parsonage design award, with a judging panel of Church Commissioners and ecclesiastical architects and surveyors, gave rise to over 100 entries and thirty-four dioceses were represented. Conversions as well as new buildings were eligible. The panel wrote that the relationship to the environment was the factor particularly sought. Houses that were part of some speculative estate, indistinguishable from other "executive homes", were not selected. Presumably that meant that schemes that were more individual, used sympathetic materials, and were in "context" found favour, in broad terms a rejection of modernist theory. That seems reasonable. On the other hand, buildings which try too hard to be discreet may fall between two stools. Perhaps as a result, the chosen schemes, though mostly reasonable, cannot be said to have been in any way outstanding. But no doubt there was little of merit to choose from.

The judges added that they found the Commissioners' "Green Guide" a very sound document . . . "giving the architect every opportunity to exercise ingenuity in working with it. It should not instruct further on design, nor attempt to standardise plans".[9] Not everyone shares that view of its merits or agrees with the specific point on design. It might be argued that the Guide could usefully contain more to encourage excellence. It is true that recommendations based on aesthetics are difficult, and any attempt to standardise parsonage design, however good, if done on a countrywide basis could be a recipe for disaster. Having said that, the Victorians had no compunction in pushing for the Gothic style as a standard

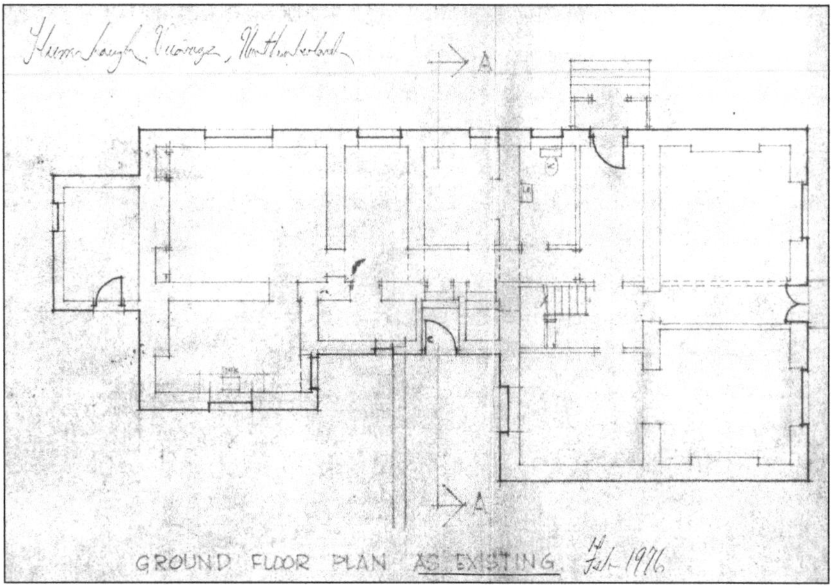

Figure 1A: Ground floor plan of Humshaugh, Northumberland

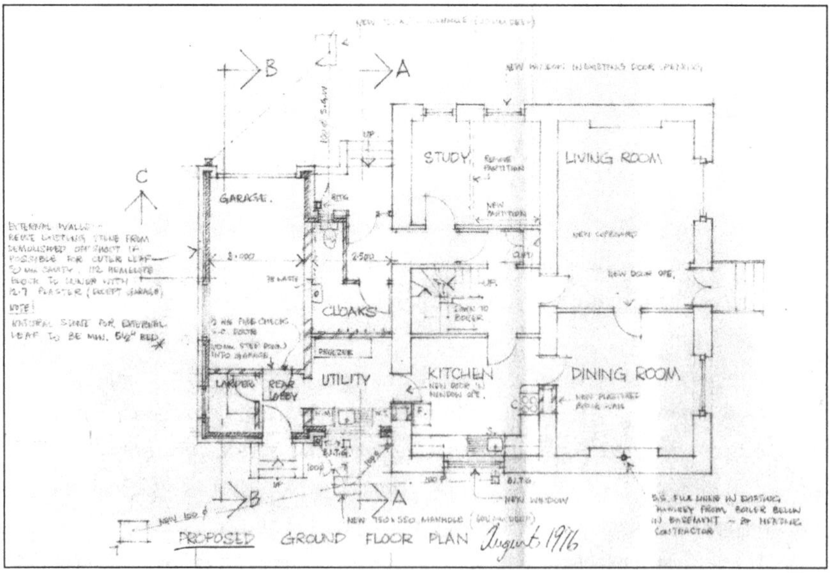

Figure 1B: Reduced ground floor plan of Humshaugh, Northumberland

Figure 1C: East elevation of Humshaugh, Northumberland

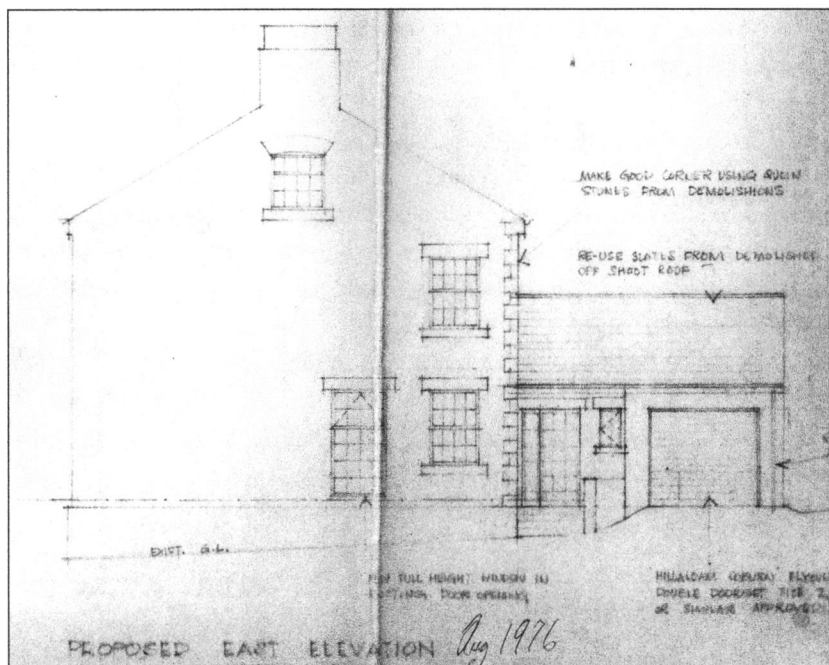

Figure 1D: Reduced east elevation of Humshaugh, Northumberland

for the English parsonage, wherever it was situated, and that sense of direction resulted in many remarkable houses which were of a far higher standard of design and detailing than is prevalent today. An equally individual style for the modern parsonage, if it could be found, would be a most interesting development as a basis for individual designs. But that has to be accompanied by a sense of conviction, and I suspect that the will is no longer there.[10]

The Church House

It is not always understood that the local people, not the state, had, and still have, direct financial responsibility for their parish church. The churchwardens have done their job diligently over the years, through all the turbulence of the Reformation and since. Money had to be raised, and here, particularly after the church was deemed no longer appropriate for the selling of ales in the second half of the sixteenth century, the church house came into its own. Many were built from the mid-fifteenth century onwards. They are often architecturally charming. Many can still be seen beside the church today. Part village hall and part local inn, they were used for festivals and parties. They usually had a ground and upper floor, with a spiral staircase, and could be let for accommodation to raise more income. Drunken parties were nevertheless increasingly frowned on and new uses for charitable or educational purposes had to be found. Some are still used as parish meeting rooms, but they had generally fallen out of favour by the mid-seventeenth century.

Oddly, by far the majority that remain are in the West Country, particularly Devon. It has been suggested that this was because this was a land of scattered farms and hamlets, unlike the nucleated villages of the Midlands. The former priest's house sometimes became the church house when a bigger rectory was needed. Church houses later became pubs, private houses, or schools.

The Clerk's House

The parish also often provided a clerk's house for the parish clerk. The secular (non-monastic) clergy were of two orders, major or minor, the major being the deacons and priests, the minor being the parish clerks. These held quite responsible positions in parish administration. They were permitted to marry, but had certain clerical rights such as clerical privileges in the legal system. The clerk's house was very similar to the parsonage in a modest parish.

The Chantry

A chantry was a financial endowment for the chanting of masses after death. Depending on the wealth of the deceased, the endowment, and the beneficiary, the money might provide for just one or a few masses, or at the other extreme, masses in perpetuity. The landowner could finance a priest, or a college of priests, or even pay for almshouses, with the condition attached that the soul of the deceased or a favoured class of people was to be prayed for. Chantry endowments were able to fund more church services, particularly for the poor, by funding priests and chapels. In the Middle Ages, they employed a lot of priests, who were often expected to find their own lodgings, not live at the parsonage, but some had their own chantry house. Chantries came into disrepute and were suppressed in the Reformation. They were not in such radical need of reform as the monasteries, but the idea that salvation could be paid for rather than earned by devotion was contrary to the new tenets of Protestantism. A number of chantry houses survived, converted to other functions, and still do. Since chantry houses had the same function as the priest's house, they often looked very similar. That at Trent, Dorset, is a fine example, a vernacular stone house with some polite features, innovative when built, with two floors replacing a hall.

Summary

The parsonage started as the humble priest's house, but became the second best house in the village. It was a symbol of the power and importance of the Church, in the days when the Church was not embarrassed by its position in the community. But it has rarely rivalled the manor house. It is usually more vernacular and its design has provided less opportunity for grand expressions of style.

The changes in the architecture of the parsonage over the years followed the major stylistic changes that affected any residential property, but architecture in rural areas could also often lag considerably behind London and the important provincial towns and cities. Even so, the parsonage is often a lot easier to date than the vernacular village house.

In the Saxon, Norman, and Medieval periods, the wealthy were never averse to making statements of their importance, but grandeur was more important than style, and there were few grand parsonages. Apart from the great abbeys, castles, and bishops' palaces, all buildings, including parsonages, were vernacular. Getting their construction right, so that they did not fall down, was important, style was not. It is therefore ironic that the timber-framed medieval house, its construction nakedly visible to all, and particularly the "magpie" black and white house of the late medieval and Tudor period, could be said to be the most essentially English house of all, genuinely indigenous with no foreign influence. That is something that would be remarkably rare later on. No architect was needed. Craft skills with wood, mud, and plaster, and occasionally stone, were all that mattered. That was the early English parsonage.

Conscious style had arrived by the Tudor period and, by Jacobean and Queen Anne times, it had become very important, if only to the wealthy—but they included some of the clergy. In Georgian times, the trend continued. By the Victorian period, style, and the theory of style, had become an obsession, now with a moral aspect, and the parsonage had assumed great importance in that debate. The battle of the styles that followed would finally give birth to the reaction of the modernist movement. Paradoxically, that was a style as much as any other, though it brought decline for the parsonage after a continuous history of improvement.

Parsonage construction was not a constant process. It was at its height when the Church was prosperous or unchallenged, or when population growth or migration created demand, at its lowest in time of religious strife or uncertainty, such as the Reformation and the Civil War. The boom periods for the clergy house were the Medieval, Queen Anne, Regency, and High Victorian.

Though we are more prosperous as a society after a long period of comparative peace, and live in "executive homes", the more spacious parsonages of past centuries are ironically deemed "unsuitable". To be "suitable" they must be modern, simple, and no more than 2,050 sq. ft.

The story of parsonage architecture through the ages is one of astonishing variety. My own highlights are these: the medieval priest's house for its combination of simplicity and tracery; the Elizabethan for its Englishness; the Restoration for the new style and its influence on what was to come; the Regency for the importance of the parsonage in the history of smaller house design; the High Gothic for its magnificence; and the Arts and Crafts for its more informal Englishness, combining progress and tradition. Finally, I suggest the parsonage of the interwar years is under-appreciated.

Now for the more detailed anatomy of the parsonage.

Notes

[1] Ken Chambers, letter to the author.

[2] Charles Clement Hodges, writing in *Archaeological Journal and Review*, Vol. 5 (Bemrose and Sons, 1891).

[3] Isaac Ware, *A Complete Body of Architecture* (London, 1756), Book III, p. 348.

[4] J. B. Papworth, *Rural Residences* (R. Ackermann, 1818), commentary on Plate XI, "A Vicarage-House".

[5] A. W. N. Pugin, *Contrasts* (Charles Dolman, 1841).

[6] Savidge, *The Parsonage in England*, p. 170

[7] Savidge, *The Parsonage in England*, p. 198

[8] *Country Life*, 18 June 1987.

[9] *Parsonage Design Award 1988*, a Church Commissioners' booklet.

[10] Inevitably, *Church Times* featured the first "green vicarage" (in Bradford Diocese), in issue 7628, 29 May 2009.

CHAPTER 6

More About Parsonages

Dating a parsonage

Dating a parsonage is by no means simple. We must first be familiar with general changes in architectural styles; understanding the stylistic differences between the early, mid and late Georgian periods is by no means easy. Even then we can be misled. In the remoter parts of the country, architecture was sometimes decades behind the latest developments in the major cities, and London in particular. Houses with the steep gables and mullioned windows that were being phased out in the mid to late seventeenth century in polite circles were still being built in the country in the mid-eighteenth century. The manor house at Stanbury, West Yorkshire, still had mullioned casements in 1753, seventy years after the sliding sash window had become the fashion. Dates on houses, particularly on fittings like rainwater heads, are not much help either. They should never be trusted. They usually commemorate an alteration or addition, or even deliberately mislead.

That is still only the start of the dating process. Most buildings of any age have been altered, many greatly so; only in recent years, under the eagle eye of the amenity societies and the more conservation-minded owners, may this process have slowed. The church is the classic example: the vast majority have undergone such great alteration that it is rarely possible to talk of a medieval church in terms of any specific period. We like to believe that our churches are ancient. The fact is that a lot are now mainly Victorian. Parsonages have not suffered quite so badly, but they have still undergone more changes than many other houses. An amazing number have much earlier origins than at first seems possible. What is superficially a late Georgian rectory is very often the shell of a much earlier building with a new face; after all, where there is a church, there has always been a parsonage. The natural process of repair and alteration has been accelerated by the changing status of the clergy and type of accommodation needed. The Tudors, Jacobeans, and Georgians were also swayed by the whims of fashion just like the twenty-first-century house owner, and more than happy to add a totally new façade to an older house in a quite incongruous style, to cover timber framing with stone cladding, or to tear out old-fashioned stone mullions in favour of sash windows, without the slightest regret.

Bax observes that in many parishes the parsonage escaped the major changes to churches, the main causes of those changes being Tudor enlargements, the seventeenth-century iconoclasm, the eighteenth-century neglect, and the huge reconstructions of the Victorian age.[1] Perhaps so, in the sense that they were not so often deliberately damaged or quite so arrogantly reconstructed, though they suffered in the Civil War and have been subjected to continual alteration, extension, and reduction. As a generalisation, the Jacobeans refaced timber in stone or brick and added a wing, the Georgians refaced again and stuck on another, the Victorians added yet another or rebuilt, and the new Elizabethans of the twentieth century reduced or demolished. The average old rectory is a mongrel. The old rectory at Sutton, Bedfordshire, next to the church, began as a fourteenth-century wattle and daub priest's house, grew in the sixteenth century, again in the early eighteenth century and then again in the nineteenth century. The Old House, Milford-on-Sea, Hampshire, is a medieval hall with seventeenth-, eighteenth-, and nineteenth-century additions.

So, by what criteria do we speak of a Georgian rectory? If it is an earlier house, at what point does it become Georgian? When its fabric is more than 50 per cent Georgian? A parsonage may be fundamentally Jacobean in its materials yet largely now Georgian in character. Or it may consist of two or more wings of quite distinct styles and periods, one medieval and one Georgian, or one Georgian and one Victorian, with no attempt to reconcile the two. Even parsonages which have not been extended have often been substantially altered. In Bedfordshire, for example, there seem to be quite a few modest parsonages of seventeenth-century origin whose appearance has been greatly altered in the nineteenth century. In these cases the house may still retain a dominant character which belies its superficial style and important architectural detailing. The massing, configuration, and method of construction of such a parsonage will still reveal the period in which the core of the house was built. That requires some architectural knowledge, and it may not be an infallible guide to the spirit of the house. The best feature of a medieval house may be a Queen Anne façade. What do we call the house? Some houses with substantial additions simply have a split personality. Others, despite the changes they have undergone, still have a dominant character.

Victorian rectories are likely to have suffered less radical alteration, but even here a surprising number are earlier houses remodelled. Many also retain later accretions, an ill-shaped annexe, or a utilitarian parish office, though these are usually easier to identify. Even more have been disfigured by partial demolition.

Elevations

The same house can look startlingly different from different angles. From medieval times to the seventeenth century, houses were irregular. Even the simplest of eighteenth-century symmetrical boxes still often had an untidy series of service outbuildings at the side or back. Victorian houses were again deliberately asymmetrical. Subsequent alterations and additions create more complications. As a result, the same house more often than not looks completely different in photographs from different elevations (as the illustrations of Bampton and Northiam demonstrate). A parsonage does not have to be particularly large or grand to have these characteristics. Bulmer Tye House, Bulmer, Sudbury, is the home of Noël Riley, founder of Save Our Parsonages. To all appearances, from the front and side this is a Regency house, simply classical, of formal "Suffolk White" brick. But at the back it starts to reveal its secrets. Here the more complex and irregular pattern of gables has a quite different and earlier character. It started life in about 1600 as a simple timber-framed farmhouse with central chimney and two bays. The curate Robert Andrews in around 1820 (Bulmer never having had a rectory) considerably enlarged it. The prominent bay at the side was added in the 1880s. The house now has a large sitting room and drawing room either side of a wide central hall.

Parsonage spotting

Before we can date the parsonage, we have to find it. In Peterborough, there was once an old vicarage for St John's Church. Where should we look for it? Priestgate, an ancient enclave now besieged by the concrete horrors of a city that resembles one big set for *Get Carter*, sounds a good place to start. And so it proves. There is nothing to indicate any former parsonage. But 51 Priestgate, newly vacated offices at the time of my visit, looks likely. It has a handsome Georgian stone frontage to the road, with a parapet and typical dressings such as quoins, string courses, and architraves round the wide sash windows. Number 49 next door also has a Georgian front, a plainer version. From the car park at the back of these twin properties the story looks different. The elevations are more varied; starting from the east, there is a new range, then an early gable, which must be seventeenth-century, then more seventeenth-century stonework, a tall staircase window, next to a stolid Victorian bay of generous proportions, and finally the back of a smaller outbuilding, again early stonework, which no doubt originally extended to the street front.

Inside, down in the cellars, usually the least altered part of a house, there is a seventeenth-century door still in place, its double thickness of wood and thick mouldings making three layers, and a strap hinge. You can see the old coal chute under the pavement. There are wine racks. There is another small cellar, vaulted in brick, with old flagstones. You can see that this site had probably been occupied for many hundreds of years before the Georgian façade was proudly added. The attic rooms are an extensive warren, until recently still used by solicitors for archiving, and dilapidated. There is evidence of timber framing and again some of the fabric of an early building. There seems to be a seventeenth-century fireplace upstairs in a front room, with a later Georgian surround. The wide main entrance hall, and much of the ground floor, feels late Georgian. There are some Georgian panelled doors, elaborate architraves and dado rails and cornices. But this is deceptive: the landing ones were created after one of the upstairs rooms was reduced to accommodate quite a modern passage, because the mouldings fit the passage. But there is something about the proportions of the main front room; you can still imagine the vicar sitting there, and you can see him going down to the cellars to get another bottle of claret. You can try to imagine the priests of many centuries earlier who must surely have inhabited this site.

The setting

The setting, or what in the jargon is called the "context", of a traditional parsonage is most important and helps to date it, even if the present one is not the first house on the site. The parsonage was traditionally close by the church. The illustration of the house at Stanton, Gloucestershire (the daughter of the rector of Stanton was a friend of Charles and John Wesley), shows it in that setting, as does that of Combe, Oxfordshire, in this case not strictly the parsonage but built by the Archbishop of York and let out to clergy.

The most historic and most attractive street in an English market town or country village is likely to be called Church Street or Church Lane, or if not, Rectory Street or Rectory Lane, Vicarage Street or Vicarage Lane. So often, the guidebook will say: "Church Street is the best street in the town." It will lead to the church, and is likely also to lead to the parsonage or other clergy buildings. Usually relatively unspoiled, it is fertile ground for parsonage spotters, but you still have to identify the house. Many former parsonages bear no name to identify them. Some are in municipal or commercial use, and it has also sometimes been Church policy to require private buyers to rename the parsonage in such a way that it bears no trace of its former status, a dubious practice that obliterates history and is not approved by conservationists. We often have to do detective work. Names like Glebe House can be a clue. One method is to go back in time. Church Lane can be comparatively well preserved, but even so development and "infill" may have obscured the original configuration and former grounds of the older houses, and thus their significance. The more modern development there is, the more difficult it becomes to get a picture of the nucleus of the town or village as it was. But the identity of the parsonage is more likely to emerge if we can visualise its setting at a given date, or at the date the parsonage was built if we have that information.

In the eighteenth century, as in any period, the buildings in a town or village were mainly of an earlier era, and the typical parsonage was not Georgian but more likely a sixteenth- or seventeenth-century house, with other houses of that period, as well as earlier ones, around it. If the parsonage was new it could be further from the church. The Georgian parson sometimes liked to build in a new and more fashionable road. The streetscape in a small town in, say, 1780 was unlikely to have been that of our image of uniformly planned Georgian houses, like much of Bath or Bloomsbury. If the parsonage was newly built, it would be an ultra-modern stucco Palladian house which would have stood out among its mullioned neighbours.

The setting of the parsonage is often also about its relationship with the village as a whole and with other early buildings. At Warmington, Warwickshire, the foot of the green is dominated by the rectory with its early eighteenth-century front. At Upper Arley, Worcestershire, the vicarage is part of the mixture of attractive buildings in the main street climbing from the River Severn.

This relationship with church, village, and village green can be marred by insensitive later development. *The Buildings of England* describes the Old Rectory at Kexby, Yorkshire, of 1853 by F. C. Penrose, as "a fine brick and slate building in the Tudor style" but "its attractive setting with the church has been spoilt by the intrusion of the unsympathetic 1980s house to the south". The old rectory at Whitton, Ipswich, a Regency cube, was advertised for sale at a low price because it is surrounded by a modern estate of "low value terraced houses". In the towns and even the bigger villages, urban expansion has blighted the setting of the Georgian or earlier parsonage, once outside but now almost in the town centre, uncomfortable, marooned in the urban wasteland of offices, shops, pubs, and takeaways. Milton, Cambridgeshire, is a classic example of a once rural village which has had its character completely destroyed by the creeping suburbia of Cambridge. The setting of church and early houses round it is now barely comprehensible.

Adjacent buildings

The church and parsonage are often supplemented by other buildings. There may be successive parsonages. At Winteringham, Lincolnshire, the seventeenth-century parsonage of the Revd Lorenzo Grainger is in the curtilage of the Victorian parsonage, which in turn was replaced by a modern "more utilitarian"[2] building. The three stand in a line. The church house, the clerk's or verger's house, and perhaps also the chantry would typically be close by. The manor house and the glebe farmhouse would not be far away. Some of these buildings will have served different purposes at different times. If the town or village had two churches, these buildings could be duplicated. Aldwincle, Northamptonshire, is only a village but has two parishes, with the churches of All Saints and St Peter, each with its old rectory. The 1866 house is large with spacious rooms and high ceilings in solid Victorian manner, and would be still larger but for having suffered the indignity of semi-demolition in the 1950s by the Church Commissioners. They did take the trouble to save and replace the impressive hall and landing window with its stained glass lights in the retained half, where it lights the new landing with its Gothic staircase. The owner told me of an earlier parsonage nearby, as shown on a 1773 map, and has a print showing a large Elizabethan or Jacobean house described as "Birth Place of Dryden". The new rectory with the inevitable garish plastic windows is next door. A few hundred yards along the road lies the other parsonage, the one where Dryden really was born, nothing like the one in the print. It is described as thatched in *The Buildings of England*, but has for some time had Collyweston tiles. A new Georgian wing was tacked on at the side. The older part has recently been rendered, and inside there are still clear traces of the original medieval house with beams and an inglenook.

Figure 2: Aldwincle Rectory, Northamptonshire, before it was reduced

There are other reasons for clergy houses being found in groups. At Bampton, in Oxfordshire, there was a history of prebendal houses: collegiate endowments, in this case for Exeter Cathedral. There were historically two prebends. One of the prebends served two vicarages, so there were three vicarages, and three houses were required to serve their prebendaries, together with a fourth, a deanery, to oversee them. These have now all been sold off together with another newer vicarage, so, with the current vicarage, there are now no fewer than six existing buildings that are or were parsonages, all in the space of a few hundred yards round the churchyard, in a small equivalent of a cathedral close.

In many, perhaps most, parishes there is more than one surviving parsonage. For example, Stow on the Wold, Gloucestershire, has two, mostly eighteenth-century, and also J. L. Pearson's parson's house Quar Wood, a fine High Gothic house in his French style, sadly mutilated in the 1950s. In North Elmham, Norfolk, *The Buildings of England* mentions two early nineteenth-century houses, one superseding the other as the vicarage and another newer one. No doubt there are, or were, earlier ones too.

Different villages have different configurations of Church buildings. At Fressingfield, Suffolk, the medieval archbishop's house, Ufford Hall, was built outside the village. Next to the church, the Fox and Goose pub is an excellent close-timbered building with dark red brick nogging, facing the churchyard. It used to be the guildhall and is said at one time to have been a church house. The former parsonage, down the hill from the church, is a rendered Georgian cube of 1725, with hipped roof and black pantiles, unexceptional but elegant. No doubt there was, or is, an earlier one.

The new parsonage is often an infill in a traditional spot. Eling, Hampshire, was once a tiny hamlet, but is now in the jungle of the Southampton suburbs, though still an oasis on the river estuary reached by a little toll road. Here, if we enter the churchyard, the picturesque church nestling behind its wall, and take the path down towards the meadow and river below, where container vessels hum and oystercatchers cry, we see first the low yellow brick new parsonage with its plastic windows, and beyond it, the elegant three-storey Regency bows of the old.

Part of a group

The parsonage is sometimes part of a planned development, a purpose-built group of buildings including the church and the school, schoolhouse, and parish rooms. This became common in Victorian times, when, with huge population increase, there was great demand for new churches, along with greater social consciousness and emphasis on education. These groups can be notable in their own right because of the stylistic harmony and subtle relationship between the buildings. Examples in London are those at St Barnabas, Pimlico, by Thomas Cundy, and St Jude and St Paul, North Islington, by A. D. Gough. At All Saints, Nottingham, the church, school, church institute, and parsonage are all by Hine and Evans in High Victorian style, and there are many by Butterfield, such as at Alvechurch, Baldersby, and Hensall, and others by Street, for example All Saints, Denstone, Staffordshire, and Boyn Hill, Maidenhead, Berkshire.

The parsonage as parish history

Figure 3: Tewkesbury Vicarage of 1827

At Tewkesbury, Gloucestershire, before the Reformation, the abbey was the rector, appointing perpetual curates as parish ministers. The curate lived in one of the abbey's houses, with no vicarage, funded by benefactors through the centuries, and by the early eighteenth century the borough council administered the perpetual curate's stipend. In 1827, when more new parsonages were urgently needed, Charles White, the new vicar, raised more funds with the aid of Queen Anne's Bounty and others, and designed and built a new house in the fashionable Neo-Tudor style. In 1846, he borrowed more and called in S. W. Daukes to add a porch and make alterations; downstairs there was a drawing room, dining room, study, hall, kitchen, and butler's pantry.

In 1883, the estate in Tewkesbury of John Martin of Ledbury, deceased, was to be sold, including Abbey House, the much older former abbot's house. This, with its grey lias stone front to the churchyard, and now an eighteenth-century brick façade, and at the east end and inside, a visible timber frame, had, like many, been sold rather than demolished at the Dissolution. Its garden had as one of its boundaries the south wall of the church, and it included what remained of the cloisters, with the south door into the church. The estate included the abbot's gateway and other houses. A Tewkesbury builder, Thomas Collins, who had worked on restoration of the abbey with Sir George Gilbert Scott, bought Abbey House with the then vicar, Hemming Robeson, enabling them to open up the south door to the church. Robeson sold unwanted parts of the estate, bought Abbey Cottage for his retirement, and conveyed Abbey House to trustees for the vicar.

A vicar in 1919 thought that Abbey House was too grand for the vicar of a relatively poor town, and proposed to move back into Charles White's house, but subsequent vicars understood that Abbey House was good and convenient for meetings and activities, and an important part of history.[3] These days such matters are outside the vicar's control.

Polite or vernacular?

Is the parsonage a polite or a vernacular building? R. W. Brunskill[4] distinguishes the two. The polite house makes an architectural statement unrelated to its location, while the vernacular makes use of local materials and styles. Both types of house are intended to be permanent, unlike his third type, the temporary and primitive. Brunskill then speaks of four traditional categories of domestic building, the Great House, the Large House, the Small House, and the Cottage, of which the Great House was normally polite as distinct from vernacular. Brunskill acknowledges that in the case of parsonages there are degrees rather than absolutes, but places rectories generally in the "vernacular large house" category. The Large House included the manor house, the house of the successful yeoman, the small country house of the squire, the house of the successful farmer or businessman, and that of "the highly favoured parson". These all still had vernacular qualities until "the approach of the nineteenth century".

The later the period, the more Brunskill's "vernacular zone" of smaller houses contracts. By the 1840s, the railways meant that materials could be transported longer distances economically. Regional distinctions were not eliminated entirely, but they lessened. The larger Victorian parsonages can no longer be described as vernacular houses. Many architects still sought vernacular credibility, and the Arts and Crafts movement in particular saw a return to favour of vernacular materials, which carried over to a lesser extent into the early twentieth century, but this was self-conscious and contrived, albeit often effective. The International Modernist movement of the 1930s was vehemently opposed to the whole concept of tradition, especially the use of local materials. Convention was anathema. This approach, purporting to be "honest", has turned out to be corrosive. Nowadays, we are appreciating vernacular building more, and that it can be as aesthetically rewarding as the grand house.

In short, as from the early nineteenth century, the region where the parsonage is situated is markedly less likely to be identifiable from its style and materials. But that does not mean that every earlier parsonage is vernacular. If the late seventeenth-century parsonage at Burford is a vernacular house, it is certainly "grand vernacular" by comparison with its "simple vernacular" neighbours. It is eminently dateable to its period by its stylistic features. Brunskill's photograph of a truly vernacular house at Longworth, Berkshire, dated 1783,[5] is much harder to date, differing little from any two up, two down small house of 200 years earlier. The simple Georgian cottage or even farmhouse with no polite features is very different from many contemporary rectories with their attempts at Palladian or Adam features.

Local materials

England has many different landscapes in a small geographical area, because of the variety of the geology that gives them their appearance. For many centuries, houses blended with their local environment because they were built of local materials. Most of us are familiar with the mellow limestones of the Cotswolds, the granites of Cornwall, the gritstones of the Pennines, and the flints of Sussex and Norfolk.

In England, the younger (and poorer) rocks are in the east and they get older as we go west, from the sand, shales, chalk, and clays of East Anglia, the South, and South-East, to the central limestones, the sandstones of the West Midlands, and the older sandstones, slates, and granites of the West. Because the different rocks come in vertical bands running from south-west to north-east, rather than horizontally across the country, there are huge differences in building stones as you go from east to west, but there can be similarities going north to south, as far apart as Dorset and Yorkshire.

A stone house is most likely by far to be of limestone or sandstone. The best-loved stone is probably the Jurassic limestone that runs up the country through Dorset, Somerset, Gloucestershire, Buckinghamshire, Leicestershire, Northamptonshire, and Lincolnshire, then into Yorkshire. This produces the best "freestones", easily worked into ashlar (regular smooth blocks). It is sedimentary rock of compressed fossils, called oolitic because it is granular. Parallel to this is the band of what is called lias, also limestone but with a harder texture and wider range of colours, which does not acquire the same patina of age, giving a harsher look. Older carboniferous limestones occur in parts of Somerset and Derbyshire as well as the North. These are still harder, have often travelled less, and are even more localised as a result. Houses of this hard stone are often finished with dressings of softer sandstones which can be more easily moulded.

The sandstones are more scattered. Gritstone is an older version, mainly north of the Trent, occurring in Derbyshire, Staffordshire, Lancashire, and Yorkshire, unmistakable and grimly impressive. The bright, younger red sandstones of South Devon are in complete contrast, and the older ones of North Devon and Cornwall differ again, as do the greensands of the eastern counties.

The granites, the hardest rocks, are of Cornwall, Devon, and the Lake District, with a tiny bit in Leicestershire. They are hard to work and were only used when there was no alternative; on Dartmoor the clitter was simply gathered and put together as unworked rubble boulders. Granite is heavy, massive, and grey, impervious to light and water. It is frequently rendered with whitewash. Its accompanying slatestones are easier to use but also need much mortar because of their irregular shapes. Chalk is difficult to work for the opposite reason. It is the softest rock, and with its associated flint, forms a wide belt, looping round from the South-East, round London from Kent and Sussex up to Cambridgeshire and into the north and east Norfolk coasts, extending as far west as Dorset and Wiltshire through Berkshire. The hardest chalks are good enough for building stone but require very sound roof protection. Flints look attractive but require much mortar and galleting, and brick or stone quoins, "lacing" courses, and dressings for solidity, giving an equally distinctive look to the houses of these areas.

This paucity of good stone in the south and east, and much of the West Midlands, meant much greater reliance on timber where it was available, or cob, and later brick, in vernacular architecture in these areas. Timber framing was prominent in forested areas like the Weald of Kent and Cheshire; houses were close-studded in the South-East and square-framed in the Midlands and North.

The solid gritstone parsonage of the Pennines is therefore quite different from the pale brick house of the heavy clays of the East. A north Norfolk parsonage of flintstone with red brick quoins and lacings contrasts with a Cotswolds parsonage of glowing soft limestone, which looks part of the landscape if vernacular, grand if of fine ashlar. Parsonages in Kent and Sussex or the West Midlands, of timber-framed wattle and daub or brick nogging, have a rural charm. The areas of Oxford and other clays of the Home Counties have their characteristic brick, ranging from orange reds to buff or yellow clays, to London stocks. The poorest materials, the shales of the East Anglia and Kent coasts, often require weatherboarding, which has a charm of its own. These regional differences of materials, in conjunction with regional building styles, help us to locate a vernacular parsonage just from its photograph.

London and urban parsonages

London is unlike anywhere else and that applies to its parsonages. Firstly, there are surprisingly few, not in terms of geographical density, but pro rata to population. Secondly, they are even better camouflaged, often looking more like other houses or tucked away in terraces in a way that is rare in the country. Next, they are mostly late, mainly Victorian, and nearly always brick, albeit with stone dressings, or sometimes ragstone. In Central London they also differ radically in shape. London was substantially developed in the nineteenth century at the height of the Ecclesiological and Tractarian movements, and is home to many clergy houses, where curates lived together under the aegis of the rector, rather like pupils with their public school housemaster, so these do resemble residential school houses rather than country parsonages. They are often very large, institutional, and of many storeys. The more conventional parsonages are often also tall, normally semis or in terraces, hemmed in by their neighbours, but of narrower frontage. These buildings often also incorporate or abut vestries and have community rooms. There are also more Roman Catholic and Nonconformist houses as a proportion of the whole, which, perhaps untypically, are of equal architectural merit. Finally, the parsonages of Central London have suffered even more alteration, sometimes downright mutilation, than country houses of the same comparatively late date. Some are now flats, some pubs, often quite unrecognisable nowadays to the casual passer-by. The major provincial city centres like Birmingham and Manchester share some of these characteristics.

Evaluating quality

Qualitative judgement is fraught with difficulty. We tend to speak more fondly of old buildings than new. The old part of town is always the most popular with tourists. Is the older parsonage a better house? But what is old? These things are relative: in Houston, Texas, anything before 1930 is old, in Oxford, nothing after the fifteenth century is. I think of the Victorian parsonage as quite a modern house. Theoretically, there are fine, typical, and poor examples of any type of house, style, or method of construction, in any period. The best approach is probably to date a house—the empirical logic of stylistic development often allows pretty accurate dating, sometimes even to within a decade—then to compare it with its peers.

But the passage of time clarifies the consensus of opinion, and here the modern parsonage is at a disadvantage.

There is also a difference between fine architecture and character. A house appeals if it is human and individual. Sometimes a lesser house has a charm that a better one may lack. In a book of this kind, there is a balancing act between selecting obviously "good" houses and those that demand not to be overlooked.

Categorising parsonages

Parsonage Numbers by Period and Style

Broad terms like "Georgian" and "Victorian" tell us little about the style of a particular house, and any such categorisation by period is deficient. My initial research on the best surviving parsonages was simplistic. I used the term "Early" to cover the whole period from the medieval down to the late seventeenth century, "Georgian" to include anything else pre-Victorian, and then Victorian and Modern. Our image of the parsonage may be that of a Georgian or a Victorian house, but those periods together total only two hundred years, and there are existing examples of parsonage houses dating back to the fourteenth and even thirteenth century, possibly even earlier. Even so, before researching this book, I had assumed that very few medieval parsonages had survived. It turned out that I was wrong, and we cannot even guarantee that we have identified many early priests' houses as such. It is true that the surviving early houses are rarely in their original form, and sadly, hardly any are now working parsonages, but their interest outweighs their condition. The result, for the houses recorded in the sources of my research (see Chapter 8), was that 37 per cent were Early, 33 per cent Georgian, 28 per cent Victorian, and 2.7 per cent Modern.

Parsonage Numbers by County

Country parsonages: The top twenty counties on the basis of the overall numbers of notable parsonages in *The Buildings of England* at the time I researched them are listed in Appendix B. Of course, that is only one source, and it is constantly being updated and augmented, so the list cannot be treated as definitive. The results for Gloucestershire and Yorkshire are no surprise. Lincolnshire, which disappoints for its houses in general, more so. Lowest are Cornwall and Cumbria, but parsonages were much less commonly included in these early editions.

Do the parsonages in *The Buildings of England* occur proportionately to the fine buildings as a whole on a county by county basis? In terms of the numbers of listed buildings as a whole, I was given figures by English Heritage showing that Devon is the most favoured county, quite a way ahead of the others, followed by Kent, Somerset, Gloucestershire, North Yorkshire, Greater London, Essex, Suffolk, Cornwall, and Oxfordshire. All but two of those also feature among my twenty counties for the greatest number of good parsonages.

London parsonages: According to *The Buildings of England*, London comes fourth in terms of the number of noted parsonages. But there are six London editions compared with no more than two for any other county. Pro rata to the numbers of buildings featured as a whole, parsonages are fewer than in other leading counties. Furthermore, there are wide variations within the areas of London. North London is parsonage-rich, and so is the much more socially deprived East London, because this area was the prime target of missions by socially conscientious Georgians and Victorians. The central areas are weak by comparison, and considering the exceptional quality of their other buildings. North-West London, the most prosperous sector, is also the most impoverished in terms of its fine parsonages; by the time most of this area was built, the High Victorian missionary age had gone and the Church was in decline.

Parsonage Periods and Styles—Distribution by County

The Buildings of England also shows regional variations in the distribution of the most notable parsonages in terms of their period. Taking my categories, Early, Georgian, Victorian, and Modern again, the greatest number of early fine houses as a proportion of the total is in Cambridgeshire, Cumbria, Devon, Durham, Hertfordshire, Kent, Northumberland, Oxfordshire, Shropshire, Sussex, and West Yorkshire. The Georgian tend to be dominant in Buckinghamshire, Derbyshire, Northamptonshire, Nottinghamshire, Leicestershire, and Lincolnshire; there are also good Georgian houses in Dorset, Essex, Hampshire, and Somerset. The Victorian are dominant in London and the big cities such as Leeds, Liverpool, Manchester, and Sheffield, as we would expect, so many being needed to cope with population explosions; and also in Cheshire, Staffordshire, and East Yorkshire. The few modern parsonages of merit are best represented in Hertfordshire and South Lancashire. Distribution is quite even among the styles in the Cotswolds, parts of the Midlands, and Norfolk (in Suffolk, the medieval and Georgian are equally dominant over the Victorian).

Features, gardens, and associations

Some parsonages are most notable for their setting, or their garden, or for some interesting outbuilding or some feature, such as an antiquity, in their garden, and these are discussed in later chapters.

Now let us see if we can find some examples of the parsonages of all the periods described in Chapter 5.

Notes

[1]   B. Anthony Bax, *The English Parsonage* (John Murray, 1964).

[2]   Arthur Mee, *The King's England, Lincolnshire* (Hodder & Stoughton).

[3]   Anthea Jones, article for *Save Our Parsonages Newsletter*, No. 10, Spring 2005, pp. 26-30.

[4]   R. W. Brunskill, *Vernacular Architecture: An Illustrated Handbook* (Faber & Faber, 1971).

[5]   R. W. Brunskill, *Traditional Buildings of Britain* (Victor Gollancz, 1981), p. 118.

CHAPTER 7

Parsonages Through the Ages

I have selected the houses in this chapter for their particular interest, usually because of the excellence of their architecture, or their typical or noteworthy features, sometimes with the bias of personal knowledge. They are not just rectories and vicarages but include, for example, prebendal houses and those built by an archdeacon or vicar for his private use. I cannot mention more than a fraction of the many tens of thousands of existing houses that have had these functions at one time or another. Even Pevsner's *Buildings of England* series only recorded about 2,200 at the time of my research (see Chapter 8).

I have tried to stick to date order (they are listed alphabetically in the Index), but I have had to exercise discretion in dating because a very large number of these houses, far more than I had previously realised, have many features of more than one period, making a decision necessary as to their most characteristic date. The reason for date order is that I am trying to give the reader a sense of the evolution of parsonage architecture over the centuries.

I have departed from date order in a few cases where houses can only most sensibly be discussed together, by reference to their location, where their setting is convenient for a perambulation. I have handled Central London houses in this way, and a selection of other places where there are parsonages of different periods in close proximity.

Some technical terminology is inevitable as the most succinct way of describing a house. Ashlar is finely cut masonry, rubble is rougher. Bays refer to the horizontal sections of a house usually now best determined by windows: a house with central door and two flanking windows on each side is a five-bay house. Quoins are dressed stone or brick blocks at the corners of the house or its projections. Hoodmoulds are mouldings over windows or doors. Pediments are classical gables. I use the term "Gothick", as is the convention, to refer to Georgian or "Strawberry Hill" Gothic, a quite different style from the later Victorian Gothic.

The earliest surviving rectory must surely be that at Horton Court, Horton, Gloucestershire, a mid-twelfth-century Norman stone ground floor hall. It has a fine ambulatory and is owned by the National Trust. At Bedford, the building that was formerly the Hospital of St John, and inspired Bunyan's Interpreter's House, was also once the rectory. Greatly altered, what looks like a Victorian Tudor building with Gothic casements masks a core said to be as early as about 1216.

The Prebendal Manor House, Nassington, Northamptonshire, is one of the best surviving medieval domestic houses. There was once a Saxon aisled hall, improved after Cnut's visit in the early eleventh century, and in the twelfth century the manor and land were given by Henry I to the Bishop of Lincoln to institute a priest. During the course of the thirteenth century, the house was gradually replaced by a Norman one, a stone building with a great hall and a solar wing. In the fifteenth century, the tithes were producing a big income and improvements were made. The fireplace was moved to the wall, traceried windows and oriel inserted. There was a new gatehouse and a dovecote. From the sixteenth century, the manor was in decline and rented out. In the eighteenth century, the big tithe barn was added and the solar and other unfashionable buildings demolished, the fine lancet windows being replaced by Georgian ones. In 1875, the Church sold the house off, and more recently, features including the lancet windows have been restored. A classic history of the evolution of a house over the centuries.

The Old Rectory, Kingston, Cambridgeshire, is another example of a house with a fascinating history, originally a twelfth- to thirteenth-century aisled hall, with an early-to-mid-fourteenth-century west cross-wing. There were further alterations in the late sixteenth or early seventeenth century. It is timber-framed, with clunch (chalk) walls, on a T-plan. The gable of the original aisle roof is in the east wall of the cross-wing. The north wall of the aisle was rebuilt in the seventeenth century, reusing some of the clunch rubble. The west wall retains four original window openings, one in a two-centred arch with trefoiled head. The garderobe and newel staircase are at the north end of the cross-wing.

Pele towers were defensive houses commonly built around the Scottish border area, where for centuries the borders themselves were disputed (Berwick, for example, changed hands on many occasions) and attack was always on the cards. The great vicars' peles of the Border Country are unlike any other parsonage. In Cumbria, the vicarage at Lanercost has a red sandstone thirteenth-century tower (it is difficult to date any existing house of this kind earlier than this, though no doubt they once existed). Edward I stayed there in 1306–07, during his Scottish campaigns. The parsonage at Boltongate has the remains of a pele, with part of the corner staircase and a slit window. At Croglin, there is another pele tower with the usual vaulted ground floor. It has been Georgianised.

Turning to Northumberland, at Ancroft there is a fortified tower of the thirteenth century at the twelfth century Norman church, like a vicar's pele. The vicar's pele at Corbridge is thought to have been built in about 1300, again as a defence against Scots raiders. The massive stones in the walls are puzzling until we understand that they were taken from the ruins of Roman Corstopitum. The ground floor is stone-vaulted, a useful protection against fire. It is lighted by only two three-inch-wide slits, and a stone stair in the thickness of the wall gives access to the first-floor living room with trefoil-headed windows and wide reveals inside with stone seating space. Another stone stair leads to the second-floor bedroom/ oratory with stone desk for a book. It was owned by Carlisle Priory, monasteries being obliged to provide a manse, and occupied by the vicar till the seventeenth century.

The vicar's pele at Elsdon was recorded as such in 1415, but seems to have been rebuilt in Scottish sixteenth-century manner, with corbelled parapet, machicolations, and caphouse. The Revd Mr Singleton added the house attached in the early nineteenth century, and there seems to be some earlier eighteenth-century Gothick decoration. It was used as the rectory until 1960.

The former rectory at Embleton, a leafy village a few miles from Dunstanburgh, incorporates the ancient early fourteenth-century tower once needed as the vicar's pele. The big new wing was completed in the reign of George IV to the design of John Dobson of Newcastle. The tower may not have originally been a pele, but the solar of an early house, strengthened after a Scots raid in 1385.[1] Peel House, Shilbottle, the former vicarage, is another medieval tower with alterations and extensions of the mid-nineteenth century by F. R. Wilson. He embellished the tower with battlements and a stair turret. Alnham has another vicar's pele, with a vaulted ground floor. It was described as uninhabitable in 1821, but was obviously attractive to the antiquarianism of that period and was rehabilitated, since it was in use shortly after that. At Whalton, the former rectory incorporates part of a pele tower. At Ford, there is another vicar's tower, though not much is left but a vaulted ground floor. At Ponteland, the former parsonage is a pleasant house of the early eighteenth century. Next door is the newer former parsonage, Victorian, by F. R. Wilson. In the grounds lie the ruins of the vicar's pele, and as with other peles, what remains appears to be later than its reputed fourteenth century.

At Ovingham, also Northumberland, the former vicarage was once a medieval Augustinian canonry, and has a fifteenth-century bay, and alterations in the early and the late seventeenth century. It is L-shaped, stone with a slate roof.

Iffley Rectory, Oxon, dates back at least to the thirteenth century, making it one of the oldest of all surviving parsonages, though not continuously inhabited as it was let out for long periods. Next to the ancient church of St Mary the Virgin, it is now part of the suburbia of Oxford, close to the hubbub of the ring road. The Church was bent on selling it in the 1970s, but fortunately had the sense to co-operate with the Landmark Trust to divide it, so that it could both be let out and remain the rectory. It has a manageable four bedrooms, dining room, and panelled drawing room, ideal for parish social occasions, and a good-sized study. There is a compact and manageable garden, dropping in steps to the river, with fine stone walls.

The former rectory at Bishops Cleeve, Gloucestershire, described by *The Buildings of England* as probably the oldest and most splendid in the county, is of coursed limestone, built for the Bishop of Worcester, an H-plan hall house with solar and buttery wings, of about 1250. But it was greatly altered in around 1667 when the front was infilled between the wings, and again in the eighteenth century. It has an Ionic doorway, and bold Venetian windows on the cross-wings.

The old rectory of St Alphege's, Canterbury, next to the church in Palace Street, probably already existed in some form in the late eleventh century. Built about 1250, of two storeys, with upstairs hall with stone-flagged floor, it has huge joists supported by a stone pillar and arches. In the late fifteenth century, a timber front was added and later a third storey. In the sixteenth century, a chimney and two fireplaces replaced the open hearth. It was not sold by the Church until after the Second World War.

Ickham Old Rectory, Kent, incorporates a remarkably complete first-floor hall house of around 1280. There are further eighteenth- and nineteenth-century portions in Tudor style, the former with attractive crowstepped gables.

At Westdean, East Sussex, there is an excellent example of a late thirteenth-century priest's house, of flint with stone quoins and dressings, with first-floor hall and solar. It has staircase and garderobe projections and a fine fireplace, and there is an original two-light trefoil-headed window on the first floor. At Easington, Durham, the former rectory is a large early medieval, perhaps thirteenth- or early fourteenth-century, stone house with hall and cross-wing, buttressed, with second cross-wing of about 1600, of limewashed rubble, with later additions. Surtees called the rear range an oratory. It became the rectory after the Reformation.

Hartburn Old Vicarage, Northumberland, with its heavy and substantial walls, is perhaps sixteenth-century, stone with slate roofs. There is an early vaulted ground floor to one wing, probably a fourteenth- or even thirteenth-century hall house. It also has an eighteenth-century wing. The eighteenth-century vicar, Dr Sharp, was fond of garden features and cut a Gothic grotto into the hillside.

The Treasurer's House, Martock, Somerset, is so named because the rector was treasurer of Wells Cathedral. It is a thirteenth-century and fourteenth-century priest's house of local hamstone rubble, with later additions. It has mullioned and traceried windows, and an open hall with collar beam and wind braces.

The Old Rectory, Loughborough, Leicestershire, consists of the remaining two bays of a ruined medieval hall house of the late thirteenth or early fourteenth century and later, of coursed rubble with ashlar dressings. It has arched doorways with finely traceried spandrels. It was enlarged at various times, particularly after a fire in 1826, with a new Regency frontage. In the late 1950s, its fate hung in the balance. In 1962, all was demolished apart from the medieval parts that remain, which became a museum.

Martley, Worcestershire, is classic timber-frame country. The former rectory is a hall house of around 1300, timber-framed with brick cladding with fifteenth-century and later additions. The front door leads to the screens passage and hall with very fine roof trusses. There are upper and service cross-wings, the former originally separate from the hall, a most important feature.

The former rectory of St Guthlac's, Market Deeping, Lincolnshire, is thought to have been a cell of Crowland Abbey, or possibly the refectory of the priory of Thorney Abbey at Deeping, before the Dissolution. Hiding behind the church, in glimpses of traceried windows and moulded gables, it is a limestone house, dating at least from the early fourteenth century, which has undergone much alteration. In the mid-eighteenth century, the internal medieval hall was reduced, and Thomas Pilkington's symmetrical façade with its Gothick elevations at the incumbent's request dates from the early nineteenth century. *The Ecclesiologist* liked it, observing that it "has lately been enlarged and restored in strict ecclesiastical style".[2] In the early twentieth century, the bishop described it as the coldest house in Lincolnshire. It is now divided. It is said to have had a colourful history, incumbents having been driven out of the house both in the sixteenth century, when the rector had to live in the church tower, and in the seventeenth century during the Civil War.

The former rectory at Cliffe, Kent, originally an early fourteenth-century stone house, was so altered in the nineteenth century by the Revd H. R. Lloyd that it is difficult to trace its history. There is thought to have been a hall and solar. Windows, some of them stone-mullioned and arched, are very irregular, the effect still picturesque.

At Edgmond, Shropshire, the former rectory is an impressive fourteenth-century house with substantial alterations. There are three surviving arched doorways leading from the hall to the kitchen, buttery, and pantry. The north front retains a gabled medieval appearance, while the south is Georgian.

The Old Parsonage, Walton, Somerset, is also largely pre-Reformation. It is thought to have been the courthouse of a monastic manor with attached rectory. Of rubble with ashlar dressings, it has two parallel ranges and cusped stone-mullioned windows.

Alfriston Clergy House, Sussex, was the first historic building acquired by the newly formed National Trust, in 1896. It is a thatched Wealden hall house, dating probably from the mid-fourteenth century or later, after the Black Death. It is oak-framed, wattle and daub-clad, and limewashed, unglazed until the late sixteenth or seventeenth century. It may have been built for a yeoman farmer before it passed to the Church, but its one separate outside door suggests the celibate vicar had a housekeeper. In the nineteenth century, the Ecclesiastical Commissioners wanted to demolish it. It was saved by local amenity groups and the National Trust and bought for £10 following an appeal launched by the vicar, who wanted to restore the house, the Society for the Protection of Ancient Buildings having suggested he approach the trust. The purchase was inspired by Octavia Hill, who worked for the poor, influenced by John Ruskin, as it fulfilled the ideals of simplicity, setting, and rarity, and the mission to preserve old rural England in an era of change. The house is therefore seminal to the whole history of conservation as well as that of the parsonage.

The priest's house in Muchelney, Somerset, is an exceptionally fine house of local limestone with hamstone dressings of the fourteenth century, both simple and decorative. It has a thatched roof, pointed arched doorway, a fine full-height mullioned window of eight lights divided by a transom, the upper lights cusped with tracery, and another large four-light mullioned window, though these are later. It was used by clergy till about 1840. Also at Muchelney is the fine Abbot's House.

At Warton, near Carnforth, Lancashire, the mid-fourteenth-century former rectory, of rubble with sandstone dressings, is now a ruin. It has an interesting arched doorway. The new rectory of 1840, coursed limestone with neat quoins, incorporates an early building of around 1300 with Y-tracery.

Southfleet, Kent, is a fourteenth-century house probably by Thomas of Alkham, rector from 1323, flint, rendered, with hall and cross-wings. It is picturesque, with gables, gabled dormers, and gablet. There are some early windows, some later, mullioned and transomed.

At Ely, Cambridgeshire, the old vicarage of St Mary's is a timber-framed building with a brick and stone wing, sixteenth-century with fourteenth-century parts. A plaque reads: "Cromwell House, the residence of Oliver Cromwell from 1636–1647 when collector of Ely tithes."

The Chantry House at Bredgar, Kent, of c. 1392, is the former chantry college, or living quarters, of flint, with brick dressings and large quoin stones.

Welle Manor Hall, Upwell, Norfolk, the former rectory, is basically a mid-fourteenth-century hall house, with a full-height fifteenth-century porch with stone arched doorway, polygonal stair tower, and another two-storey square tower. The house is mainly brick, significant for this date. The hall still has two arched doorways to the screens passage.

The former rectory at Campsall, Yorkshire, is an early fifteenth-century manor house with additions. It is a late example of a first-floor hall, with chapel and many preserved features, including windows, and some later Gothick features.

The priest's house at Kentisbeare, Devon, perhaps fifteenth-century, was already divided into cottages by 1681. A through-passage house with service end jettied into the hall, it is in fine Devon vernacular of cob, rubble, and sandstone. It has a prominent front external chimney stack.

The Old Grammar School on the north side of the churchyard of St Nicholas, King's Norton, Birmingham, was originally the Priest's House. It is a pretty fifteenth-century building with stone plinth and doorway, ground floor of brick with stone quoins, upper floor half-timbered. It is almost symmetrical, with projecting porch added later as was typical of very early buildings. The windows are mainly plain with mullions.

Shandy Hall, Coxwold, North Yorkshire, was built as an open hall house in about 1450, with gabled cross-wings. Timber-framed, later encased in brick, with seventeenth-century alterations, it underwent more alterations as the home of the eccentric parson Laurence Sterne, who wrote *Tristram Shandy*, from 1760 to 1768.

At Itchingfield, West Sussex, the churchyard contains the charming fifteenth-century pre-Reformation priest's house, timber-framed and part rebuilt in brick. The roof is of attractive Horsham slates.

At West Hoathly, Sussex, there is another fine example of a simple fifteenth-century timber-framed priest's house with plaster infill. It also has a roof of chunky Horsham slabs.

At Maldon, Essex, All Saints' vicarage is a striking timber-framed mid-fifteenth-century house with gables to both sides. *The Buildings of England* rightly calls it "extremely attractive". It is a typical hall with cross-wings, jettied, and gabled with prominent barge boards. The west cross-wing may have been the priest's house of a chantry priest.

Standish Old Vicarage, Gloucestershire, has a fifteenth-century core, enlarged in the sixteenth century, infilled in the nineteenth century, of stone, with buttresses, mullions with hoodmoulds, and a former garderobe projection. Bishop Frampton restored it in the seventeenth century, and there are nineteenth-century additions in the original style.

Claverley, Shropshire, is an interesting fifteenth-century house. The fine end gable has a moulded bressumer and nineteenth-century ornamental bargeboarding.

At Rickmansworth, Hertfordshire, the former vicarage is a picturesque medieval house with fifteenth-century surviving parts, with timber framing, projecting oriel window, jettied upper floor, and gables. It has eighteenth-century and nineteenth-century alterations and additions with Gothick-style glazing bars.

The former rectory at Horsmonden, Kent, is basically a fifteenth-century hall house with first-floor hall in a cross-wing, eccentrically altered and extended in later centuries, with timber framing, tile hanging, red brick, and nineteenth-century bargeboarded gables supplemented by irregular battlemented sections.

At Great Yeldham, Essex, the Old Rectory is a fifteenth-century timber-framed hall house with cross-wings, having very fine roof framing with arched collars and windbraces.

At Haddenham, Buckinghamshire, the Church Farmhouse is a very pretty fifteenth-century Wealden-type timber-framed house, with close-studded projecting and jettied cross-wings. There is a later staircase wing of about 1600 at the back. The former vicarage is a less exceptional eighteenth-century house.

At Twyford, Buckinghamshire, the former vicarage, which belonged to Lincoln Diocese, then Lincoln College, Oxford, is a fifteenth-century hall house with a cross-wing and solar. It is basically timber-framed, with tile hanging, brick and rubble stone, and later additions.

At Sleaford, Lincolnshire, the church of St Denys is fine if much altered. The fifteenth-century vicarage, alas now sold off, also has a bit of everything: half-timbering, rendering, rubble stone, brick, in different styles but an appealing mix with prominent central gable. To the side is a fascinating old stone gate arch with a cross. Completing the styles is a red brick Victorian extension by Charles Kirk Jr, 1861, a little discordant but not offensively so.

Parsonages are usually concealed by a jungle of foliage, but the fine fifteenth-century house at Congresbury, Somerset, is conspicuously visible across open Church land, its stonework mostly now whitewashed but visible on porch and buttresses, mullions and transoms, and dripmoulds with carved head bosses. It has three bays to the left, one to the right of the porch. The Regency "new" vicarage which abuts it is much less remarkable, but good of its kind, with Doric columns inset in a neatly recessed entrance loggia. The two houses, surprisingly but very sensibly, were still at the time of my visit in use as vicarage and church hall, and the old house was apparently still occupied by the vicar until the 1950s, making this the longest continuous Church use found by Savidge.

At Yatton, Somerset, the former prebendal house, of rendered rubble with limestone dressings, is again a mid-fifteenth-century hall with cross-wing, fine buttressed porch, four-centred arched doorway, and transomed and traceried windows.

At Hoxne, Suffolk, the former vicarage has hall and cross-wing, the oldest part dating from about 1470, but much altered. It is surrounded by a delightful moat (moats were mostly of the period 1200–1500), though it is far too big for the house. Parsonage moats were mostly about half an acre, so it is thought that the palace of the Bishops of East Anglia once stood here. It is timbered, with some Victorian imitation timber studding.

The former parsonage at Headcorn, Kent, is a timbered Wealden house. I am told that it was built in 1470, and the date (1516) given in *The Buildings of England* is more likely to be when it, and other lands and properties owned by the Maison Dieu at Ospringe near Faversham, were taken out of the control of the Church in an act of early dissolution by Henry VIII and given to St John's College, Cambridge, to bolster the endowment of Margaret Beaufort. Apparently, it remained in the ownership of St John's until just after the Second World War. The close-studded hall has oriel windows and the solar and service ends are jettied out. There is some fine moulded woodwork.

The rectory at Buckland, Gloucestershire, is described in *The Buildings of England* as "the most complete mediaeval parsonage in the county, though unfortunately no longer used as such". It is basically a late fifteenth-century stone hall house with cross-passage and wings, windows with trefoil heads, with open hall and some subdivided rooms. It was altered in the seventeenth and nineteenth centuries and "gently modernised" in 1932 by Detmar Blow.

The Old Rectory, Cossington, Leicestershire, is a late fifteenth-century house with many later additions, of rubble stone with quoins and an elaborately decorated timber-framed part. There is a central projecting chimney stack next to a very fine battlemented two-storey bay of mullions and transoms, the upper set with Gothic tracery.

At Milverton, Somerset, the former parsonage is a delightful late fifteenth-century hall house of sandstone with glowing hamstone dressings, with a two-storeyed gabled porch with buttresses, and mullioned windows with four-centred heads.

At Gawsworth, Cheshire, the old hall and former parsonage is a fine specimen of the decorative black and white timbering of the West Midlands. The house was built by the priest himself, George Baguley, in about 1480, the end of the medieval era. It represents the hall house in its most sophisticated form (it was once quadrangular), with many features including hall with queen post and carved boss. The substantial nineteenth-century alterations are not unsympathetic. It has a chapel of 1701.

The former rectory at Whitestone, Devon, of local cob, with brick additions, is a good example of the complex evolution of a clergy house. It started off as a late medieval hall house, probably fifteenth-century, and was reconstructed in the sixteenth century, the medieval roof still smoke-blackened. Then came a new Georgian south front of 1775, with five bays and sashes. In the Regency period, further bays and a Tuscan porch were added. It was first the priest's house, then the rectory.

As we get into the Tudor period, we come to Sacombe Green, Herts. This is a timber-framed early sixteenth-century house extended in the seventeenth century. It was originally an open hall, extended with a cross-wing.

Abbey House, Witchampton, Dorset, is an excellent early manor house of brick, perhaps the first in Dorset. Dorset incumbents seem to have been wealthy, rare at the time, and this early sixteenth-century house is connected with parson William Rolle. Gabled, it has irregular mullioned windows with hoodmoulds and ashlar dressings, quoins, plinth, and string course. There is a Victorian range in eighteenth-century style with sash windows.

The former rectory at Cold Ashton, Gloucestershire, is an early stone house of about 1510 said to be by Thomas Key, of rubble stone, a gabled projecting wing with gabled dormers, mullions, and transoms; altered in the mid-nineteenth century by John Clifford, a local builder, still Tudor in appearance.

At Sampford Peverell, Devon, the former priest's house is said to have been given by Lady Margaret Beaufort, Henry VII's mother and a great benefactor. Probably early sixteenth-century. One wing was demolished for the adjacent canalisation of 1830, but a large cross-wing remains. There is a hall, parlour, and solar, but the nineteenth-century restoration was rather heavy and has removed some of the character.

The former rectory at Welwyn, Hertfordshire, was originally an early sixteenth-century moated hall house, and has close-studded timbering and part-jettied upper floor, with later brick infill on the ground floor. It is famed for Dr Young's garden, which Boswell took Dr Johnson to see.

At Great Doddington, Northants, this early sixteenth-century house (though *The Buildings of England* says seventeenth-century) was once the manor house; stately, coursed limestone, entrance front with prominent gabled cross-wings, doorway with four-centred arch.

At Colyton, Devon, the vicarage and Brerewood House are the remaining parts of a 1520 building by Canon Thomas Brerewood, the sixteenth-century chancellor to Bishop Veysey, divided in the 1970s. There is a fine crow-stepped rubblestone porch with room above. The house bears the motto: *"peditatis totum, meditatis totum."*

At Great Ponton, Lincolnshire, Anthony Ellis rebuilt the church tower in 1519, and also enlarged this fourteenth-century house at about that time. Quite simple, of coursed limestone, with crow-stepped gable end and various late medieval and later mullioned windows, it has a series of sixteenth-century wall paintings inside. It was restored in 1921 by Wilfrid Bond (1870–1935). The later, but still former, rectory is quite a plain, dignified stone pedimented house of 1826.

At Great Snoring, Norfolk, is what remains of a house built around a courtyard, with remarkable exuberant brickwork, rather in the manner of Layer Marney, by Sir Ralph Shelton in around 1525. It has many later alterations including sash windows. Early windows have basket arches and four-centred arches, and it is elaborately ornamented with brickwork panels and other motifs, a fine and rare house.

The former vicarage at Methwold, Norfolk, has stylistic similarities to Great Snoring, with its astonishing brickwork and basket arches, though is perhaps even more singular, with its fine early sixteenth-century brick gable end with elaborate polygonal chimney tacked on to a fifteenth-century timber-framed range.

Another unusual stone house, at Chew Stoke, Somerset, was built for the rector from 1524–1546, Sir John Barry, in 1529. Of limestone and sandstone, it has irregularly spaced arched and cusped mullioned windows, with dripmoulds and label stops, and is considerably altered with a much later battlemented parapet as deemed appropriate by the nineteenth-century medievalisers. There is unusual stone detailing of panels with shields. It survived as a working house until 2008, creating local distress when sold off by the bishop. Chew Stoke also has a huge and elaborately Gothic mid-nineteenth-century former rectory.

Savidge says[3] the former vicarage at Brenchley, Kent, perhaps originally a church house, has the date 1320 over the door, but it is thought to have sixteenth-century origins. It is tile hung, weatherboarded, and there is some visible timber studding, and it has a good orange-tiled roof, all very modest and vernacular. The attached former shop is incongruous.

Another good house in Brenchley is the much grander sixteenth-century half-timbered former parsonage with impressive close studding.

At Halesworth, Suffolk, the old rectory is a long, low whitewashed house of sixteenth-century origins, with four very broad bays with an asymmetrically placed barge-boarded porch beneath a steep and deep tiled roof. The big overhanging gable end has vertical exposed timbering.

The former rectory at Longworth, Oxfordshire, of limestone rubble, is again of several periods, part sixteenth-, part eighteenth-, part nineteenth-century, with arch-headed stone mullions, and brick and stone window architraves.

At Bredon, Worcestershire, there is a large, attractive, typically Elizabethan, mainly stone house, a spreading hall house gabled at both ends, with grand stone porch with Renaissance detailing. The Victorian and more recent additions have been carried out in character.

At Kidlington, Oxfordshire, the vicarage is part gabled and mullioned mid-sixteenth-century, of coursed limestone rubble, with arched lights, and part Victorian by Street, who renovated several in the county (1853–4). It also has a recycled fifteenth-century window.

The former rectory at Guiseley, West Yorkshire, is an impressive late Elizabethan sandstone house with nearly symmetrical gabled façade with continuous string coursing, central gabled porch and mullioned windows, more like a secular manor house than a parsonage. There are earlier parts inside, including a timber-framed wall which has been thought to be as early as Saxon.

Barrowby Rectory, Lincolnshire, is essentially late sixteenth-century, about 1588. Superficially, it is eighteenth-century Gothick, with its pointed, mullioned windows, stucco, and Perpendicular-style doorcase. But there is a striking external chimney breast to the left of the door, and bare stone at the side, betraying its age. It bears the initials S. E. G., having been the residence of the Revd Stephen Gladstone, the prime minister's son, incumbent 1904–11.

At Bude, Cornwall, the present house seems to have been a late sixteenth-century hall house, and has later additions. Evidence suggests there was a much earlier manor here which went to the Arundells of Trerice in the fifteenth century. It is of stone ashlar and rubble and granite dressings, with massive chimney stacks. It only became the vicarage from the seventeenth century, and the daughter of a nineteenth-century tenant married the celebrated Hawker of Morwenstow.

At Wath, North Yorkshire, the rectory is basically a sixteenth-century hall with later alterations and windows, of stone with brick entrance range between projecting wings with large stacks.

Northiam, Sussex, consists of two separate houses conjoined, the first, timber-framed, built by the rector in 1593, the second added by a descendant in the eighteenth century, of red brick with eight bays, much more polite.

The church at Barsham, Suffolk, dates from the eleventh century with a round tower and thatched nave. The rectory is later, a vernacular country house of the late sixteenth/early seventeenth century with some timber framing and later ranges including a cross-wing with attractive shaped gable. It is the birthplace of Lord Nelson's mother.

At Stratford-sub-Castle, Wiltshire, the old vicarage has an Elizabethan and Jacobean front with mullioned windows and projecting wings. The garden front, by contrast, is of the early eighteenth century with hipped roof and doorway with segmental pediment.

The vicarage at Waltham Abbey, Essex, is a simple late sixteenth/early seventeenth-century house, timber-framed under plaster. Thomas Fuller, cleric and historian, lived here in the mid-seventeenth century.

The former rectory at Widdington, Essex, is sixteenth/seventeenth-century, timber-framed but much altered in the eighteenth century when it was refaced in red brick with parapet.

We have reached the Jacobean period and at Dagenham, Essex, the vicarage of St Peter and St Paul seems to be an early seventeenth-century timber-framed house part rebuilt in 1665. It has some irregular windows. *The Buildings of England* describes it as "a bizarre concoction". There is also a much grander late eighteenth-century pedimented vicarage.

Silk Willoughby, Lincolnshire, is sadly expanding as a Sleaford dormitory village. The church of St Denys has a fine, ornately decorated steeple and beside it, next to the road, is the Old Rectory, of Lincolnshire limestone, an unassuming but characterful house with a history going back to the early seventeenth century. It has a Venetian window among the sash windows with their neat glazing bars on the south elevation. It was enlarged in 1813 by William Hayward.

There are two good houses at Corby Glen, Lincolnshire, the first a former rectory of coursed limestone with pantiled roof in the local vernacular, long, low, more like a farmhouse than a parsonage, with a tall gable at the garden front, and a strangely grand entrance arch with coped gables and ball finials, and across the road the former rectory dated 1619 and extended in 1697, also of local limestone, with Collyweston slates and coped gables.

At Bushey, Hertfordshire, the former rectory started life as an early seventeenth-century house but was altered and extended in the eighteenth, nineteenth, and early twentieth centuries. The core is still timber-framed. It now looks largely gabled Edwardian.

The former rectory at Edith Weston, Rutland, is an attractive house of 1626, of coursed rubblestone with Collyweston slate roof and coped gables in local style. It has the simple stone-mullioned windows of the time.

At Bemerton, Wiltshire, is the house of the famous George Herbert, flint with stone dressings, quite plain, which he built—or rather rebuilt—himself in 1630, and where he died. Only one original mullioned window remains.

At Coln Rogers, Gloucestershire, the former rectory is an early seventeenth-century limestone house, gabled, with simple mullions and dripmoulds typical of the period, with a new gabled Tudor front of 1842–43 by Daukes and Hamilton.

Herefordshire is timber-frame country, and the former vicarage at Wellington is an attractive seventeenth-century black and white house.

The Old Rectory at Chilmark, Wiltshire, is an impressive seventeenth-century limestone L-plan house with prominent cross-wings, the round-arched doorway set in one of them. There is a separate early nineteenth-century wing.

At Benington, Hertfordshire, the former rectory is of 1637 for the rector, Nathaniel Dod, gabled, typically Jacobean, brick but with plastered front, two-storey porch with Tuscan pilasters, and later features including windows.

At Thorpe Achurch, Northamptonshire, the former rectory, with its delightful seventeenth-century façade with seven symmetrical bays, three projecting, and mullioned windows, is of 1642, rather old-fashioned for that date. The porch leads directly to a traditional hall. The main ranges strongly retain their early ambience, particularly in some upstairs rooms. A landing behind connects the old house with the 1838 extension by Matthew Habershon, which has large, light, Regency-style rooms with period mouldings. There is an annexe reputed to be several centuries earlier than the main house, which may have been an earlier farmhouse later incorporated. Outbuildings include laundry and stabling. The Lords of the Manor and rectors of many parsonages here and in the surrounding villages were Lilfords from the early eighteenth century. There are traces of houses in the front garden and in the field to the side, all now demolished.

The vicarage at Banbury, Oxfordshire, is dated 1649, with mullions and gables, and two-storey porch, remodelled in Victorian days. The former Prebendary House is also Jacobean, ironstone, gabled, with mullioned windows. For good measure there is a fine presbytery of about 1840 attributed to Pugin.

More parsonages through the ages

18: The vicar's pele—Corbridge, Northumberland

19: Tudor—Great Snoring, Norfolk

20: Early with Restoration additions—Bishop's Cleeve, Gloucestershire

21: Tudor—Headcorn, Kent

22: Tudor—Easton on the Hill, Northamptonshire

23: Restoration—Adlestrop, Gloucestershire

24: Restoration—Burford, Oxfordshire

25: Late seventeenth century—Broughton Poggs, Oxfordshire

26: Early Georgian—Preston, Kent

27: Early Georgian—Elkstone, Gloucestershire

28: Late Georgian—Farmington, Gloucestershire

29: Early Victorian—Hallaton, Leicestershire

30: Victorian—Ruan Lanihorne, Cornwall

31: Victorian—Leafield, Oxfordshire

32: Edwardian—St Barnabas, Walthamstow, London

33: Modern—Barnburgh, Doncaster

34: Modern—near Reading, Berkshire

At Dyrham, Gloucestershire, the former rectory is of limestone rubble with some stucco and some ashlar, a seventeenth-century building with the original doorway now inside, altered in the mid-eighteenth century and early nineteenth century.

The Old Rectory, Hamworthy, Poole, Dorset, is a very grand mid-seventeenth-century brick house of about 1650, which *The Buildings of England* calls "complete and remarkable". Red brick, with three dominant curved Dutch gables with triangular and segmental pediments in moulded brick, it has giant Ionic pilasters on high pedestals between each of its seven bays, including the porch. With the now mandatory symmetry, and its prominent moulded chimney stacks, it was built to impress.

The Parsonage House at Lambourn, Berkshire, is a gabled Jacobean house, possibly with sixteenth-century origins, with three prominent gables and much later Venetian and late Georgian windows. The old vicarage is a modest three-bay brick house dated 1791.

At Deddington, Oxfordshire, the former vicarage is a rather stark late seventeenth-century house of bright local marlstone, with three sash window bays and an oculus above the door. The former Rectorial Manor House is a most interesting very early house, rebuilt around 1650. Complicated, of limestone and marlstone, it has a gabled front with three towers behind the main range including a four-storey staircase tower. There are medieval rooms with mullions, including one with no access. There is a first-floor chapel with thirteenth-century arcading. The house was restored in the late nineteenth century. Charles I is reputed to have stayed there.

In Ripon, Yorkshire, the Old Deanery is a fine, large three-bay mid-seventeenth-century house with projecting gabled wings, and canted bays with tall windows on each, much altered in 1799 and later. The Thorpe Prebend House, white rendered, is also seventeenth-century, with a similar layout, though it looks older and is more vernacular, and could be a rebuilding of an earlier prebendal house.

At Staindrop, Durham, the deanery is a vernacular seventeenth-century building with eighteenth-century fabric and later alterations, with pedimented doorcase. The former vicarage is an early nineteenth-century ashlar building with full-height bow windows.

The Restoration period saw fashionable houses of the new compact style emerging alongside more conventional ones. Battle Deanery, Sussex (the vicar is called the dean), bears a date of 1669 but looks earlier and is probably originally sixteenth-century. It is of red brick, with long and short stone quoins, embattled parapet with crow-stepped gable.

Jane Austen visited the former rectory at Adlestrop, Gloucestershire, on several occasions. Theophilus Leigh, the rector, was master of Balliol College, Oxford. It is of about 1670, altered in the eighteenth and nineteenth centuries, of coursed limestone, gabled, slate with dormers. *The Buildings of England* declares it not of particular architectural interest but it certainly has character.

At Hempsted, Gloucestershire, the former rectory bears the inscription: "Whoe'er doth dwell within this door/thank God for Viscount Scudamore." It is dated 1671, with later additions. It is gabled, irregular, rather vernacular, with some roughcast and stucco. There are mullions and transoms, some strapwork and finials. Scudamore was a friend of the notorious Laud.

The vicarage at Great Gransden, Hunts, Cambridgeshire, was built by Barnabas Oley (1602–1685) in the late seventeenth century and remodelled in the early nineteenth century. It is described in *The Buildings of England* as part of an "exceptionally satisfying" group with two farmhouses, but also as a "plain" five-bay house. It is symmetrical, double-pile, red brick.

No history of parsonages would be complete without mention of The Old Vicarage, Grantchester. Its charms are at least fourfold: it is a Restoration house of 1683; it is unpretentiously vernacular; it has a fine garden, with its own island, bounded by a meandering leat of the River Granta; and there is a substantial folly, which every parsonage should have, built by S. P. Widnall, carpenter, photographer, and printer, in about 1854. All modifications to the house over the years have been sympathetic, including the early twentieth-century cross-wing and Mary Archer's own more recent porch. All that is not to mention its fifth charm: it inspired Rupert Brooke, who lodged there, to write *The Old Vicarage, Grantchester.*

Stamfordham Vicarage, Northumberland, is a seventeenth-century house altered in the eighteenth century and with additions by John Dobson in the mid-nineteenth century, of dressed stone. The mid-eighteenth-century part has a Rococo pediment. But, like so many, it seems to have much earlier origins, as a former owner tells me it is alleged to incorporate an original pele tower "which in our day served as dining room with nursery above". Stamfordham also has the early eighteenth-century Presbyterian Manse.

The rectory at Kingham, Oxfordshire, is described in *The Buildings of England* as "one of the finest small houses of this date (about 1688) in the county". It is in classic Restoration style, limestone ashlar with a symmetrical five-bay ashlar front with a doorway with segmental pediment, windows with moulded architraves, dentillated cornice, and roof dormers. It was built by the Revd William Dowdeswell, the rector.

At Islip, Oxfordshire, the former rectory is a William and Mary house built for the Revd Dr Robert South, bearing the date 1689. It is a limestone double-pile house of five bays, sash windows with attic dormers, and a central doorcase with canopy on carved brackets.

Confusingly, there are places called Broughton in many counties, including Buckinghamshire, Cambridgeshire, Hampshire, Lincolnshire, Northamptonshire, Oxfordshire, and elsewhere. Broughton Rectory, Oxfordshire, with a datestone of 1694, was built by rector John Knight, of coursed ironstone rubble, remodelled in the early nineteenth century when S. P. Cockerell added a prominent bay with tall arched windows at the back, and H. J. Underwood added an extension in 1842.

There is another good house at Broughton Poggs, also Oxfordshire, also late seventeenth- or early eighteenth-century, extended by Richard Pace of Lechlade.

The former rectory at North Cerney, Gloucestershire, built by rector John Coxe in 1694, is a fine Restoration house, basically symmetrical, of seven bays with three dormers, and deep sashes, limewashed with hipped roof.

At Weston under Penyard, Herefordshire, the former rectory is a symmetrical sandstone house of the late seventeenth century, with seven bays, boxed sash windows, classical doorcase, and gabled dormers.

Old Court Cottage at Limpsfield, Surrey, incorporates the remains of the timber-framed hall of the abbots of Battle. But we have now reached the William and Mary period, when houses were starting to look more Queen Anne. The rectory is a house of dark brick with red brick dressings and prominent modillion cornice of around 1700, with a brick front of what *The Buildings of England* calls "crowded" bays, with their alternating sash windows.

At Winford, Somerset, the former rectory is a double-pile stone house of around 1700 with hipped roof incorporating some Baroque features, including dressed corner quoins, pilasters, and parapet with prominent cornice and shell hood over the doorway.

Hartlebury, Worcestershire, has a seven-bay house with central projection, brick with stone dressings, doorway with shell canopy, stone window architraves, said to be built by James, son of Bishop Stillingfleet, 1689–99.

St Mary's Vicarage, Lewisham, Greater London, is probably of 1692–93. It is a good house of typical brown brick with red brick dressings, five symmetrical bays, modillion cornice, and doorcase with pilasters and pediment, and its windows still have the wooden mullions and transoms of this important transitional period. It was extended twice in the late nineteenth century using some reclaimed materials.

The former rectory at Inkpen, Berkshire, was built about 1695. It is of red brick, the roof hipped with pedimented and hipped dormers, some windows still with their wooden mullions and cross transoms.

At Lydd, Kent, the rectory has the date 1695 over the door, and a very symmetrical five-bay front with quoins, keystones, and sashes, later stuccoed white, giving a modernised appearance. The doorway has a flat canopy on carved brackets.

At Bywell, Northumberland, the church of St Andrew has a fine Saxon nave and tower. The Old Vicarage is a William and Mary house dated 1698, rubble stone with symmetrical five-bay front, and doorway with broken pediment. Rear wings were rather crudely added in 1901.

Even at the end of the seventeenth century, many parsonages were still based on the old H or E plan. Farrington Gurney, Somerset, sandstone with freestone dressings, is of seven bays with two advanced bays each side making it U-shaped, with very strange side roofs hipped inwards only, and balustraded parapet. There are still some cross-mullion windows.

The rectory at Bolton Abbey, North Yorkshire, was rebuilt in 1700 as a grammar school and looks it. Endowed by Robert Boyle, of Boyle's law fame, it is of coursed stone with slate roof, seven bays, and has some earlier fifteenth century fabric. It is still the rectory for the parish church. Thomas Girtin, friend of J. M. W. Turner and the greatest of the English landscape watercolourists of the turn of the nineteenth century (Turner included), did a number of watercolours of Bolton Abbey. The one I am looking at, of 1801, atmospherically shows the house with its prominent central gable nestling in the foreground of the abbey.

At Shepperton, Surrey, the orderly classical façade of the former rectory conceals an early timber-framed hall house of 1498. It was re-fronted about 1700, and faced with "mathematical tiles", tiles made to look like brick in areas where it was unobtainable. It has a hipped roof, and central range with cross-wings. Grocyn, friend of Erasmus, was rector here from 1504 to 1513.

The former rectory at Chilbolton, Hampshire, is a house of around 1700, elegant, compact, having deep sashes with exposed frames, with "Wrenish" hipped roof, but also side wings with gabled older parts.

At Buscot, in Oxfordshire stone country, the former parsonage is an elegant house of around 1700 on the site of an earlier one, with five regular bays, sash windows, tall chimney stacks. and gabled dormers in hipped roof.

The former rectory at Banningham, Norfolk, is a house of about 1700, of brick with pantile roof, shaped gable in Dutch style and Queen Anne dentil cornicing, and sash windows with gauged brick arches, enlarged later.

The reign of Queen Anne saw the classical style combining the Dutch and the Baroque. At Christchurch, Spitalfields, London, the rectory is an elegant house by Nicholas Hawksmoor, who also designed the church. Early eighteenth-century, of brown brick with red brick dressings, the segment-headed sash windows with glazing bars of the time, it has stucco parapet and dormer windows, and inside, barleytwist-turned balusters in a fine hall.

Another fine Hawksmoor parsonage of the same dark brick, this time detached, is at St George-in-the-East, Tower Hamlets. It has been damaged over the years, but still stands proud in his forceful but restrained and plain Baroque manner.

Whichford House, Whichford, Warwickshire, the seventeenth-century former rectory of coursed limestone and slate, is an elegant house enlarged in the early eighteenth century with Queen Anne features like its pediment with central oculus window. The classical front was only completed in recent years.

At Much Marcle, Herefordshire, the house has a date of 1703, of five bays, brick with stone quoins, steep hipped roof, dentillated cornice, doorcase with open pediment, and is thoroughly "Wrenish". Some windows still have their characteristic mullion and transom crosses.

At Wicken, Northamptonshire, the former rectory is a seven-bay Queen Anne mansion of 1703, of coursed limestone with prominently gabled end bays, described by Savidge as of "Wrenish influence" but rather gabled for that. The upper windows have segmental pediments.

The rectory at Bottesford, Leicestershire, was built in 1708 in coursed ironstone and enlarged on both sides in the late eighteenth century in red brick, giving it a curious hybrid appearance.

The Rectory, Ryton, Tyne and Wear, is a complex house of coursed sandstone, probably late medieval, with projecting gabled side bays, but Georgianised in 1709 with pedimented doorway.

The Old Rectory at Epworth, Lincolnshire, was rebuilt after Samuel Wesley's old house was destroyed by fire in 1709. In good Queen Anne, early Georgian manner, of brown brick with brick quoins, the front has seven slightly uneven bays, modillioned cornice, sash windows, and a doorcase with the flat hood of this period. It was described by Squire William Wright of Wold Newton as the Lourdes of Methodism, as John and Charles Wesley were born here in 1703 and 1707 respectively, their father being rector for 39 years. The Wesley Manse in the High Street is a good, solid, late Victorian structure of rock-faced stone with banded ashlar dressings by Charles Bell. The Warden's House is more modest but in similar style, also by Bell.

The Old Rectory at Tatenhill, Staffordshire, was built for the Dean of Lichfield, William Binckes, in 1710. A simple, delightfully elegant house, red brick with stone dressings, keystones, and rusticated quoins, it is in the country Baroque style of the period.

At West Ashby, Lincolnshire, the former vicarage is "visually satisfying", says *The Buildings of England*. It is of around 1710 with later alterations, five bays, with an ornate bracketed eaves cornice and pedimented dormers. The doorway, said to come from Captain Cook's London house, has Doric pilasters and a straight canopy on carved brackets.

Penshurst Old Rectory, in the curtilage of Penshurst Place, Kent, a medieval manor with a spectacular great hall, is a classic Queen Anne brick house with hipped roof with projecting eaves, seven-bay front elevation with rubbed header bricks over sash windows, and a doorcase with segmental pediment. The diocese of Rochester sold it off in 2004 after a battle with the parish that lasted many years.

At Sible Hedingham, Essex, the former rectory of c. 1714 has a grand seven-bay front with hipped roof and dormers behind parapet and Ionic doorway.

The former rectory at Redmarley D'Abitot, Gloucestershire, is a Queen Anne house, with later alterations, on a moated site. Symmetrical, brick, its three centre bays slightly projecting, it has a large central semi-circular headed window, and a pediment with a Diocletian window, the others typically segmental with rubbed brick arches.

At Leek, Staffordshire, the former vicarage of squared stone is dated 1714, with a later gabled wing. Most of the windows are of late Georgian type with Gothick glazing bars. It was recently sold off by the Church.

At Fairford, Gloucestershire, the house once used as the vicarage is an early eighteenth-century house with later eighteenth-century additions by John Keble, father of John Keble of the Tractarian Movement, who was born here in 1792. It is of rubble stone with stone quoins, and sash windows, very typical of the region.

The Rectory at Wickham, Hampshire, is another typically symmetrical early eighteenth-century house, of blue header bricks with red brick dressings, hipped roof, modillion cornice, and dormers. The later Victorian wings with corner pilasters mask the end elevations.

The former vicarage at Preston, Kent, is an attractive early eighteenth-century red brick house with a prominent parapet and central canted bay window supported by Doric columns to form a porch, very much in local style.

At Kingsland, Herefordshire, the former rectory is a grand early eighteenth-century house, brick with ashlar stone dressings, square plan, five bays with hipped roof.

The former rectory at Chiddingstone, Kent, is an early eighteenth-century tile-hung house of seven bays with pediment over the centre bays, classical and symmetrical, all very neat. Despite that, it incorporates an older framed house.

At Donhead, Wiltshire, the old rectory has an early eighteenth-century limestone façade with quoins and a pedimented central bay, and a doorway with bracketed pediment, but *The Buildings of England* says the house is much older. There are earlier reset features and fragments designed by Robert Adam taken from Bowood, Devon, which was built in the early eighteenth century, altered by Henry Keene and then Adam, and destroyed in the 1950s.

The Old Rectory, Winestead, East Yorkshire, is a red brick house of seventeenth-century origins but basically of the early eighteenth century, with a later Georgian wing and later projecting canted bays. It was remodelled by Francis Johnson in the 1940s, incorporating a number of reclaimed features from demolished houses in Hull and Winestead Red Hall. Andrew Marvell, the poet, was born in the rectory in the 1620s. The thicknesses of the walls suggest the old fabric is part incorporated, though this is not certain.

The former rectory at Forncett, Norfolk, is an early eighteenth-century house with shaped gables in the "East Anglian Dutch" style. It has five broadly spaced bays and unusual rusticated brick pilasters framing the central bays and flanking the door, and a pantiled roof.

At Warborough, Oxfordshire, the former vicarage is a grand early eighteenth-century stone house, of five bays with heavy dentil cornice and dormers, doorcase with triglyphs and Doric pilasters, and an Adamesque fanlight.

At Yalding, Kent, the former vicarage has an early eighteenth-century main range with hipped roof and sash windows added to a seventeenth-century timber-framed house. There is another parsonage here, a mid-Georgian red brick square five-bay house with pedimented doorcase, picturesquely set in a moated site.

The former rectory at Culverhay, Wotton-under-Edge, Gloucestershire, is a strikingly large early eighteenth-century house, but less "polite" than the formal parsonages of the time, with three bays of light, rendered rubble and stone slate roof with dormers visible over a parapet. It has a wide central pediment and grand projecting Doric portico added in about 1830, with a Venetian window above.

The former rectory at Elkstone, Gloucestershire, is a substantial three-storey double-pile early eighteenth-century limestone house. Its prominent central projecting porch, stone quoins and dressings, and round-headed windows with rusticated architraves and keystones give it a formal and Baroque grandeur.

The Buildings of England describes the former rectory at Kislingbury, Northamptonshire, as one of the finest in the county. It is of the early eighteenth century, attributed to Francis Smith, like that at Lamport. Of local ironstone, it has a symmetrical five-bay façade, hipped roof with dormers, fine mouldings, and an open door pediment.

The Priory, in the calm oasis of Church Lane behind bustling Tottenham High Road, London, is a dark brick vicarage with a fine early Georgian front behind a separately listed iron gate apparently brought from a house in the High Road, once also a vicarage. The Doric doorcase has a segmental pediment. The steep roof betrays an earlier house of the early seventeenth century, apparently built for the surgeon Joseph Fenton. Inside, there is fine plasterwork and panelling.

Kirkby-in-Ashfield, Nottinghamshire, is another good house, of 1717, with a five-bay front to the garden and a doorway with hood on scroll brackets, and pedimented dormers on the roof with coped gables.

A former vicarage at Great Yarmouth, Norfolk, has a date of 1718 and an early seventeenth-century rear wing. Its serried ranks of sash windows over eight bays are a little forbidding. Modernised in 1781 with a canted bay, its doorway has a shell hood.

At Staveley, Derbyshire, the former rectory which bears the date 1719 is interestingly different, with two prominent gables. The front was Gothicised in the early nineteenth century. It was the home of the Revd Francis Gisborne, the eighteenth-century philanthropist.

The former rectory at Netherton, Hampshire, is described in *The Buildings of England* as "a very fine house of about 1720". Of brick, it has a hipped roof with modillion cornice, central pediment, and a doorway with pediment on Doric pilasters. It was altered by Raymond Erith in the 1960s.

The former rectory at Therfield, Hertfordshire, is a large and complex early eighteenth-century house, part still fifteenth-century, extended later and in the Victorian period. The early windows are straight-headed, but with pointed and cusped lights. The later parts are brick with sash windows.

At Hampton Lucy, Warwickshire, the former rectory is of 1721, brick with stone dressings and keystones, balustraded parapet supported by piers, big stacks, and prominent doorcase with segmental pediment. It exemplifies the subtle transition from the Queen Anne to the polite Georgian, squarer and boxier but increasingly sophisticated.

At Puddletown, Dorset, the old vicarage is another house with a complex history, originally timber-framed of about 1600, with some fine early eighteenth-century brickwork, aprons below the windows, and blind arcading at the side.

At Croston, Lancashire, with a date of 1722, this is still a Baroque house, with a central bow. The side wings curve up with Dutch gables in a way reminiscent of Jacobean mannerism. The doorway has half columns and open pediment and the first-floor window has pilasters. It has a "ruined" Gothick gateway; to quote the Revd William Gilpin, not everyone can build a ruin.

The stone former rectory at Lamport, Northamptonshire, of the 1720s, was built by Francis Smith for Dr Isham, the rector (Lamport Hall was the Ishams' family seat). It is formal and elegant in Smith's very restrained Baroque, with a parapet, prominent corner quoins, and keystones. It has a pedimented doorway and some fine internal features.

The former rectory at Simonburn, Northumberland, is the northern local sandstone version of the early Georgian of 1725. It has a lingering Baroque influence, with its rusticated quoins and rusticated segmental windows.

Worcestershire is classic vernacular timber-frame country, but the former rectory at Ripple is very much of formal brick, stone quoins, and prominent keystones, a hipped cube. *The Buildings of England* describes it as a "very handsome" house of 1726. Even here there are earlier parts at the back. It was built by Dr John Holte, rector, son of the John Holte of John Thorpe's Aston Hall.

At West Hanney, Oxfordshire, the former parsonage is dated 1727. A red brick six-bay house with mansard roof, its projecting central part is raised in Baroque style, the parapet curving up to it. The windows are segmental with keystones. It has a good staircase. There is also a pleasant, small, early nineteenth-century vicarage here.

Henry Thorold, in his book *Lincolnshire Houses*, says: "There cannot be very many rectories in this volume, or the book would go on for ever."[4] The Old Rectory at Westborough, of 1730 and earlier origin, which he coveted, is a classic early eighteenth-century "doll's house", five bays with central pedimented bay, well proportioned, dentillated pediment and cornice, and hipped roof, with prominent quoins and keystones.

Amersham, Buckinghamshire, has both the rectory of 1985 by Sir Basil Spence, Glover and Ferguson, and the grand house of the 1730s, with projecting open pediment and doorway with Ionic pilasters.

The parsonage at Great Baddow, Essex, is perhaps of the 1730s, classic early Georgian, Doric doorcase with good detailing, but otherwise quite plain, its distinctive feature the parapet swept up at the corners. Symmetrical, it still has the big square-panelled Queen Anne chimney stacks that would become less prominent as time went by.

The vicarage at Castle Hedingham, Essex, is a grand red brick early Georgian house in a fashionable Palladian style with stucco quoins, a Venetian and a semi-elliptical window, stately, with Ionic doorcase.

At Cheveley, Cambridgeshire, the former rectory is an early or mid-eighteenth-century house of brick with stone dressings with five bays, three-bay pediment, and sash windows. The iron gates are said to have been brought from Horseheath Hall, which was rebuilt by Sir Roger Pratt, thus enabling us to mention that great architect in the context of the humble parsonage.

At Lambourne, Essex, the former rectory is a house of about 1740, grand, with seven bays, and quoins also on the projecting three centre bays. It has a good corbelled pediment above the doorway.

A good example of an unusually grand parsonage for a Nonconformist minister is The Old Manse, Bourton-on-the-Water, Gloucestershire, built in 1748. It has a five-bay symmetrical ashlar façade with moulded window architraves and a row of five prominent dormers in the roof.

The Old Rectory at Farnborough, Berkshire, 1749, home of John Betjeman from 1945 to 1951, won *Country Life's* "England's Finest Parsonage" competition in 2008. It is a pleasing house, quintessentially English in its combination of grandeur and informality, despite its rather Dutch manner. It looks Queen Anne with its contrasting dark and red brick and Baroque features, but it seems the parapet and finials are a mid-Victorian addition.

At Astbury, Cheshire, there is a handsome mid-eighteenth-century house of red brick with stone dressings, symmetrical entrance front, five bays with projecting central bays under pediment, and ball finials on the dentillated parapet. The doorway has an open pediment.

At Middleham, North Yorkshire, the former rectory, then deanery, part rendered, is said to be of 1752 with a pedimented doorway, but has medieval origins and probably some seventeenth-century work. Dour, but full of character, it is a very northern house.

The former rectory at Drayton Parslow, Buckinghamshire, bears a date of 1753. It is a pretty house, the symmetrical garden elevation with classic early Georgian Gothick features, ogee windows and a trefoil. It is made of chequer brick, pedimented, with prominent canted bays.

The former rectory at Okeford Fitzpaine, Dorset, is a mid-eighteenth-century house of five main bays, rendered, with hipped roof and prominent flanking stacks, quite unpretentious.

At Somersby, Lincolnshire, the former rectory, mid-eighteenth century, of brick and pantiles with twin later side additions with hipped roof and dormers, is a simple vernacular double-pile Georgian house, its only modest pretension its doorway with traceried fanlight and Doric pilasters. It was the birthplace of Tennyson. His father, George Tennyson, designed the former east wing in a more extravagant Gothic manner. The coachman was the bricklayer.

The vicarage for the grand church of St Mary Magdalen at Newark, Nottinghamshire, is one of several Georgian houses around the close behind, with a good wooden doorcase.

Merstham, Surrey. Originally sixteenth-century, this epitome of the comfortable eighteenth-century parsonage had a new brick house added on in about 1760, stuccoed, but otherwise a classic symmetrical Georgian façade.

The former vicarage at Hunmanby, North Yorkshire, is quite a vernacular version of the five-bay house of about 1760, red brick and pantiled, prominent string course, doorcase with pilasters. The Revd Francis Wrangham is reputed to have had 15,000 books, so his library alone was probably bigger than most modern parsonages.

Wyberton, Lincolnshire, has become an ugly, sprawling suburb of Boston, with huge numbers of modern houses thrown up with no thought for aesthetics. But it has the oasis of St Leodegar's Church and the excellent Wyberton Park, the former rectory, seen across open grounds, of 1689, rebuilt in 1761. It is of red brick with ashlar dressings, with a seven-bay classical façade, Georgian with a local vernacular interpretation, possibly by William Sands Jr of Spalding.

Droxford, Hampshire, has a good mid or late Georgian house, brick, symmetrical, of five bays, the central ones slightly projecting, with sash windows, dormers, prominent cornice, and Tuscan doorcase.

The former rectory at Sandon, Essex, is dated 1765, a stylish house of five bays with a wide broken pediment with oculus window, good mansard roof, and a doorcase with Tuscan columns.

At West Stafford, Dorset, the former rectory is a much earlier house rebuilt around 1767, mainly brick, U-shaped with projecting side gables. Classical features include Venetian and circular windows and pedimented doorcase.

The former vicarage at Coddenham, Suffolk, is of 1770, red brick with an Ionic porch and fine Adamesque interiors.

The long struggle from 1998 to 2001 to save the vicarage at Pinchbeck, Lincolnshire, for the parish, despite a high-profile campaign, ended in failure. *The Daily Telegraph* waxed lyrical about how it had been the centre of social life: "Carol singers sipped mulled wine in the drawing room and girl guides giggled as they camped out on the lawn."[5] It is a red brick T-plan house of 1772, thought to incorporate parts of an earlier house. There are gabled and pedimented dormers, and the rear range has six bays with cornice and parapet. John Betjeman's uncle had been vicar here.

The rectory at Kirkby Lonsdale, Cumbria, is a stone house of the 1780s with later alterations, tall, rising three storeys with sash windows and heavily projecting roof and cornice.

The Old Rectory, Saxlingham Nethergate, Norfolk, of 1784, is by Sir John Soane, elegant, compact, with bowed central bay rising a further storey above the simple cornice. It has a pedimented porch with Roman Doric columns. The ground-floor windows are set within the typical semi-circular-headed arches of the period. Its cool refinement is emphasised by the pale gault brick. "Saxlingham was a cheap house for a country parson where extravagance was neither appropriate nor affordable."[6] Possibly, but many country parsons had much inferior houses.

The Old Rectory, Church Langton, Leicestershire, is a highly sophisticated later Georgian brick house with stone dressings, fine symmetrical façade including dentillated pediment and cornice with Adam detailing, and balustraded first floor, with blind arcading round the windows in the central three bays. William Hanbury built it in the 1780s with his father's money from exotic seed-growing.

Bradwell Lodge, Essex, was once the rectory. A Tudor house with exposed beams, it had a grand new wing added by John Johnson in the 1780s, for the Revd Henry Dudley, a friend of Gainsborough. There is a belvedere with Ionic columns on the roof and it is thought that Robert Adam may have been involved with the plasterwork and Angelica Kauffmann with the painting. Robert Smirke (Smirke's father) did the drawing room ceiling.

At Upton on Severn, Worcestershire, the red brick rectory has the date 1787; it is of three storeys with two-storied canted bays with lunette windows above, and a good doorcase with open pediment.

The Buildings of England says that St Mary's Church, Kinwarton, Warwickshire, with its weatherboarding, makes a "happy group" with the comparatively unpretentious red brick former rectory of c. 1788 and a beech tree.

At Farmington, Gloucestershire, the attractive former rectory is said to have been built in 1788. It is of coursed limestone with a five-bay symmetrical front, with prominent banded parapet, and stone porch with Doric columns.

White rendered, the former rectory at Bigby, Lincolnshire, is a handsome house once attributed to John Carr of York, of around 1790, pedimented, the parapet with subtly balustraded sections.

"Lincolnshire possesses many fine rectories and vicarages, and Beckingham is one of the finest", says Henry Thorold.[7] Beckingham Rectory is early eighteenth-century but, according to Thorold, was refaced in the late eighteenth century with stone quoins and architraves. It is symmetrical, with prominent ashlar quoins and steep central pediment, and projecting ashlar porch.

Brant Broughton, also Lincolnshire, is mainly late eighteenth- or early nineteenth-century, spread out, with prominent side bays and linking arcaded verandah, but the central section with its small pyramidal wings looks much earlier. Thorold calls it "an early victim of the official purge" of rectories by the Church.[8] Rectors included Bishop Warburton.

The former rectory at Addingham, West Yorkshire, is a late eighteenth- or early nineteenth-century classical stone house with three bays and pediment.

The former parsonage at Sedgefield, Durham, with bow windows on the garden front, projecting wings on the entrance front, is said to have been built by Bishop Barrington in 1792.

The former rector's house at Charlton Mackrell, Somerset, is a late eighteenth-century rubblestone house with the Gothick detailing that had then become fashionable, including a battlemented parapet and windows with Y-tracery. It was a 1792 reconstruction of what remained of a very early house that had been allowed to become ruinous, sadly common at this period.

St Albans, Hertfordshire, has had several good houses. The former rectory in Sumpter Yard is a graceful brick late eighteenth-century house with hipped mansard roof with tall central gabled dormer and Venetian and other sash windows, some blank. The late seventeenth-century vicarage of St Stephens was demolished. The former vicarage of St Peter's is of the early nineteenth century, stucco Tudor.

The former rectory at Leadenham, Lincolnshire, has Elizabethan origins but is now mainly of the late eighteenth century, of Lincolnshire limestone.

The former rectory at Spofforth, Yorkshire, is a typical house of several periods. The overall appearance is gabled Georgian of the late eighteenth century, of coursed sandstone, but there are clear traces of medieval features from an earlier fourteenth-century house.

The old rectory at Pertenhall, Bedfordshire, is a Tudor or Jacobean house refronted in the late eighteenth century (it bears the date 1799), red brick, five bays and a three-bay pediment, parapet with hipped roof behind.

The rectory at Eckington, Derbyshire, is a graceful late eighteenth-century sandstone house, with wide centre bays and angled bays with Venetian and Diocletian windows. The Revd Christopher Alderson was a well-known gardener who worked on the grounds.

At Wilton, Wiltshire, the former rectory of about 1795 is red brick with unusual giant yellow brick pilasters on the front elevation. There is also another more conventional mid-eighteenth-century former parsonage here.

The former rectory at Aslackby, Lincolnshire (named after Aslack, a noble in Canute's court), is close by the now sparse ruins of one of the mysterious churches of the Knights Templar. The house was carved out of the grounds of the adjacent Manor House, with its fine Artisan Mannerist wing, in the eighteenth century. The front elevation of red brick has stone quoins, rusticated in local manner, stone string course, and cornice. There are blind arcaded brick arches round the ground-floor windows and wedge lintels on the upper sash windows, each with

central stone keystone. The rear range was demolished and the present owners
have given the back elevation a sash window and stucco Regency look.

The Buildings of England says the Old Rectory, Pulham, Dorset, is "such as few
parsons could boast of". Built around 1800, it is Palladian, with central block and
side wings, but with highly mannered Gothick embellishments, such as pointed
Venetian and four-centred windows, arrow crosses, and battlements.

The former vicarage at Rothwell, Northamptonshire, of around 1800, is a tall
three-storey red brick house with a prominent arch round the central windows,
one of them circular, one round-headed.

The former rectory at Hanworth, Feltham, London, is a formal, symmetrical
early nineteenth-century stock brick house with Greek Doric porch and sash
windows, with typically shallow hipped roof and projecting eaves, attributed by
The Buildings of England to James Wyatt, altered by Teulon in 1865.

At Seaton, East Yorkshire, Wassand Hall is a country house of the 1810s by
Thomas Cundy for the Revd Charles Constable. It is of elegant pale brick, with
hipped roof and sash windows, some set in recessed arches in Regency fashion.
It was restored by Francis Johnson in the 1940s.

The former rectory at Lympsham, Somerset, is a self-consciously picturesque
house in early nineteenth-century Gothick style, rebuilt about 1813, with highly
irregular stone frontage with mullions, traceried windows, turret, pinnacles,
battlements, and buttressed porch.

The former rectory at Wookey, Somerset, is also a classic Gothick concoction.
English Heritage dates it to the mid-eighteenth century, other sources to the early
nineteenth. It incorporates some much earlier stone, and is embattled, with an
embattled projecting central porch. Medieval and Tudor features include arcading
and sculptures.

The former rectory at Goodmanham, East Yorkshire, is a pale brick Regency
house of the 1820s by Charles Mountain, with hipped roof with overhanging eaves,
full-height bow window, and Roman Doric portico. There is a fine hall with Ionic
columns and iron balustraded staircase, and a galleried landing also with columns.
It was restored by Francis Johnson in the 1950s.

Outside, the house at Landbeach, Cambridgeshire, looks a wholly unremarkable
late Georgian sashed box with classical porch, of the local yellow brick that normally
weathers grey, though not here. *The Buildings of England* calls it "unadventurous".
Yet it apparently contains interesting medieval remains.

The Old Vicarage at Bremhill, Wiltshire, is an early house dating back to the
fifteenth century, Gothicised by the Revd William Bowles, rector from 1805 to
1844, roughcast with stone dressings, rather delightful with parapet, turrets, and

tall stacks. He also Gothicised the garden, with grottoes and hermit's cave in the spirit of the period. Bowles was a poet and antiquarian and the house was visited by Lamb and Wordsworth.

The former rectory of 1820–22 at Yaxham, Norfolk, was designed by Robert Lugar for the Revd John Johnson in Italianate style, symmetrical with deeply pedimented outer bays and typically shallow roofline, defiant of the growing Gothic Revival.

At Winterborne Came, Dorset, the former rectory (home of William Barnes, poet and scholar), of the 1820s, is a classic early nineteenth-century example of the *cottage orné*. The thatched roof, thatched verandah, and lozenge-pattern glazing bars are self-consciously pretty, as contrived as stockbroker Tudor, and difficult to take seriously, but the style has charm and is certainly distinctive.

At Kingsteignton, Devon, another *cottage orné* is east of the church, now divided, built as a parsonage for Thomas Whipham by John Rendle of Teignmouth, which he described as "nearly built" in 1821. A typical concoction of artifice, it has a thatched roof, verandah, and Gothick arched windows, glazing bars and detailing but with fine interior, classical with Gothick detailing.

The stone former rectory at Great Brington, Northants, is by Blore, in late Georgian Tudor style of around 1822; tall stacks, with an impressively prominent octagonal tower and a spire.

The Old Rectory at Buckenham, Norfolk, seems to be an 1827 rebuilding of an early seventeenth-century house for the Revd T. W. Beauchamp; of brick with hipped roof, it has a verandah with cast iron columns. A wayside pulpit was added for the Revd William Haslam, the Victorian incumbent, to address the people. There is also a former vicarage here, early with Victorian additions and a curious seventeenth-century crow-stepped brick gable.

At Warboys, Huntingdonshire, the former rectory is an early nineteenth-century house of local gault brick with stone porch. *The Buildings of England* says there is a relic, possibly from Ramsey Abbey, in the garden.

The former rectory at Iron Acton, Gloucestershire, is an early nineteenth-century house in classical style, with hipped roof with modillion cornice. According to Bax, one parson built a tunnel to hide a public footpath through the garden. There are remains of an earlier house.

Didsbury Old Parsonage, Manchester, was restored in the early twentieth century by the eccentric Fletcher Moss, who described himself as an "astonishingly attenuated alderman and absurdly antiquated author". *The Buildings of England* calls it basically seventeenth-century, but it looks about 1830. It had "olde" fittings added by Moss. Also at Didsbury, Emmanuel Vicarage is an impressive double-fronted Victorian house of around 1858.

The rectory at Louth, Lincolnshire, by C. J. Carter, 1828 and 1832, with overhanging oriel, is a good example of the weird reinterpretations of "Old English" architecture made by the architects of this time, often with interesting results. Its elevations are quite complex, and that facing the church, asymmetrical with mock Tudor timbering, is quite different from the rear.

At West Dean, West Sussex (not to be confused with the more famous house in East Sussex), the former vicarage has the date 1833 but looks earlier, with battlements, the Gothick style in transition to Gothic.

At Stainby, Lincolnshire, the former rectory is an eighteenth-century limestone house refaced in the early nineteenth century, with Neo-Tudor gabled porch, to plans prepared in the late eighteenth century, and re-fronted again later.

At Framlingham, Suffolk, the former rectory right behind the church is in Tudor Gothic style, now rather institutional with its whitewashed render. Long, at least nine wide bays, irregular and asymmetrical, with gables, it looks older from the front, with Georgian and earlier features (I was told seventeenth-century, while *The Buildings of England* goes for sixteenth-century).

Wappenham, Northamptonshire. This is a very simple, modest Regency red brick building with 12-pane sashes and gauged brick lintels, but I include it for two reasons: firstly, it is typical of many hundreds, if not thousands, of parsonages built around this time (1833); secondly, it is uncharacteristically by George Gilbert Scott, and his first, built for his clergyman father.

Having spoken of Banningham earlier I must mention Barningham, also North Norfolk, an impressive late Regency house with its three gables and ostentatiously tall chimneys in Tudor style.

We have now reached the beginning of the Victorian period. There was no sudden change of style, classical and Tudor Gothic continuing their rivalry, but the Gothic quickly became much more competent, and would soon be dominant for the parsonage. At Morwenstow, Cornwall, the former vicarage, Tudor, gabled, still rather Gothick windows, 1837, famous for its association with the eccentric Hawker, was derived from a pattern book. The built house can be compared with the pattern and is a little plainer and less detailed (see below and page 113), perhaps for financial reasons, though larger, and undoubtedly eccentric with its famous chimneys in the shape of Hawker's churches and his mother's tomb. Tennyson visited him here.

Figure 4A: The "pattern book" source of the design for Morwenstow Vicarage

Figure 4B: Morwenstow Vicarage

An uncharacteristic—defiantly classical, but in my view pleasing—house by George Gilbert Scott is his 1838 parsonage at Weston Turville, Buckinghamshire; symmetrical, with heavy red brick quoins both at the corners and round the projecting central bay, its only similarity to his Gothic work is its heaviness and solidity. There is a hint of Queen Anne or even earlier about it.

The former rectory of 1839 by William Patterson at Averham, Nottinghamshire, is also still Georgian in style, large, classical, stucco, overhanging eaves, Italianate porch.

The Tudor Gothic former rectory of 1840 at Harnhill, Gloucestershire, stone with gabled bays, windows with dripmoulds, is a rebuilding of a seventeenth-century house with vaulted cellars.

The former rectory at Hallaton, Leicestershire, is a pleasant Neo-Tudor limestone house of about 1840; its projecting outer bays and porch give it the manner of an Elizabethan manor house.

The Old Rectory at Compton Martin, Somerset, is of 1841 by Edward J. Andrews, remodelling a house of late seventeenth-century origin. An unusually interesting stone house in a grand Tudor style, of exceptional height, it has shaped gables with finials, and a tall, narrow projecting centre bay like a tower, flanked by octagonal turrets and some lancet windows. The earlier rear wing is quite different.

At Thorganby, East Yorkshire, Thicket Priory is a very substantial country house by Edward Blore for the Revd Joseph Donnington Jefferson (1844–7). It is a huge Neo-Tudor red brick extravaganza with elaborate stone dressings, traceried windows, towers, turrets, and chapel.

The old vicarage at Swaton, Lincolnshire, hidden behind St Michael's Church, 1844, by Charles Kirk of Sleaford, is more provincial, but still an imposing and dignified, tall, red brick house, with large mullion windows and chunky stone quoins making it look grander.

The 1840s were the crucial years when the great Victorian architects designed their important early parsonages. At Brasted, Kent, the former rectory is by R. C. Carpenter, in his "ecclesiological" style, still Tudor, but more muscular, of rubblestone with mullions. *The Buildings of England* calls it "asymmetrical but not picturesque", but it is certainly impressive, and carries the seeds of High Gothic. It was built for Dr William Hodge Mill, the orientalist rector of 1843–53. The church is by Waterhouse.

Butterfield's Coalpit Heath, Gloucestershire, is another fine and highly important example of the Victorian parsonage, of coursed limestone, "Cotswold Gothic" with prominent external stack, steep gables, mullioned and pointed windows with cusped heads. In 1844, when Tudor Gothic still reigned, it was progressive domestic architecture.

At North Creake, Norfolk, the 1845 former rectory is by S. S. Teulon for the Revd Thomas Keppel. An early work with complicated gabled ranges, its Tudor is said to be uncharacteristic for Teulon, though he did a number like this in the east of England, and the chimney stack is pierced by windows in his favoured manner. This one shows more of his French influence than his Lincolnshire houses.

Glebe House, Exbourne, Devon, is a typical modest former rectory of the 1840s, white rendered with asymmetrical entrance front, still with earlier Tudor Gothic features including buttressed porch, arched doorway, and windows with hoodmoulds.

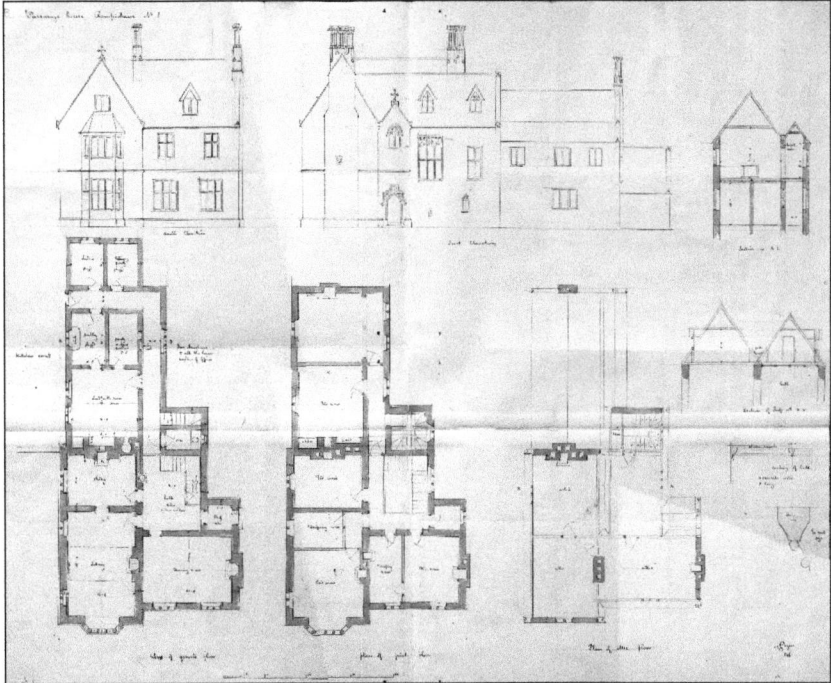

Figure 5: Pugin Hall, Rampisham—plans

Pugin Hall, the former rectory at Rampisham, Dorset, of 1845–6, is an important and influential house by A. W. N. Pugin, one of his two Church of England parsonages. Quite austere but perhaps his most attractive house, it is of coursed rubble, gabled, with mullioned and transomed windows (see Figure 5 and Plate 13). It developed the manner he had started with his homes at Alderbury, Wiltshire, and Ramsgate, Kent.

Woodyer's 1846 former rectory at Marchwood, Hampshire, has "that peculiar character which ought to distinguish a parsonage" (see the discussion in Chapter 13) according to *The Ecclesiologist*, though clearly the Church authorities nowadays would disagree. A Gothic stone house with irregular treatment, it has coupled and cusped lancet windows.

**Figure 6: G. E. Street's first parsonage at Wantage
in about 1895 (above) and 1914 (below)**

G. E. Street's first parsonage, at Wantage, Berkshire (1846–9), is another fine house, with gabled porch, its massive plain limestone walls punctured with small but exquisitely inventive cusped and latticed Gothic windows. It is both convincingly medieval and progressive at the same time (see page 115). These houses by Pugin, Butterfield, Carpenter, and Street would be influential on the coming Arts and Crafts movement.

The Old Manor House at Ingoldsby, Lincolnshire, built as the rectory by Charles Kirk in 1847, must prove to any non-believer that Victorian parsonage architecture can be a delight. It is built of stone with gabled porch and arched doorway, mullioned windows with shaped heads, projecting wing, hexagonal battlemented tower, steep gables, tall staircase window, octagonal battlemented tower; a miniature medieval castle.

At Grendon, Northants, the limestone parsonage by Teulon, 1850, still in Tudor style, is double-pile, with gabled cross-wing, mullions and transoms, and fishscale roof tiles.

The Buildings of England aptly describes the church of St Michael at Llanyblodwel, Shropshire, designed by the Revd John Parker, as "absurd, but individual". The vicarage and school are also "too obviously" to John Parker's design, and the same comment might be applied to the schoolhouse. They are all of his characteristic coursed sandstone and limestone, about 1850.

All Souls Vicarage, Halifax, West Yorkshire, built for the industrialist Edward Akroyd, is the work of Sir Gilbert Scott, as is the very fine church. A typical High Victorian Gothic stone house, mid-nineteenth-century in his mature style, it has steep gables, shaped windows, mullions and transoms, and high stacks.

The Old Rectory at Ruan Lanihorne, Cornwall, is by William White, around 1850. It is in his ecclesiastical Gothic manner, with eccentric exposed trusses at the gable ends, and wilfully asymmetric windows, but has been altered and partly rendered.

There is something about Cornwall that brought out the best in William White, as the slatestone former rectory of 1851 at St Columb Major is another unbridled delight. Medieval Gothic, with traceried windows, courtyard, and moat, it is as good as it sounds. White was another of the major architects who would be influential on future developments of the domestic house.

Creeton is a splendidly remote Lincolnshire village with a sprawling former rectory, which nestles below the lane which rises sharply from the church, hidden apart from its splendid tall chimneys. It started life as an earlier house, but is now quintessential High Victorian Gothic of 1851 with steep gables, by competent local architect Edward Browning, son of Bryan.

Of Sheen Parsonage, Staffordshire, *The Buildings of England* declares: "If anyone wants an example of how Butterfield dealt with a big parsonage, this is it." It then asks whether a Victorian would live there with the same delight as his ancestor in a Georgian house. The answer is yes, unless he is a fool. Stone, of about 1852, it has a half-hipped steep roof with crested tiles, asymmetrical, buttressed porch, and massive stacks. Another house that influenced important architects like Philip Webb.

The former rectory at South Thoresby, Lincolnshire, is by Teulon, 1853, red brick with stone dressings, tumbled gables, polygonal bay, solidly Victorian.

At Culworth, Northamptonshire, the former rectory is of local ironstone, 1854 by E. F. Law, with alterations a little later. It is classic High Gothic Revival with complicated detail including castellated buttressed tower incorporating arched doorway, and inside, a stone staircase, always a bonus for those that way inclined.

The former vicarage at Baldersby, North Yorkshire, 1854, with tiled roof, gabled entrance front, trefoiled mullions, with some timber framing, and half-hipped gables, is recognisably by Butterfield, as is the church of St James. There are also a number of cottages by Butterfield here, which display his important influence on the later vernacular revival.

In Maidenhead, Berkshire, Vicarage Lodge, Boyn Hill, is an early house by G. E. Street in classic "ecclesiastical Gothic", warm red brick with darker brick diapering and banding, reminiscent of Butterfield's polychromatic manner influenced by Venetian Gothic, with segmental arched and pointed windows, 1854–7.

Christ Church and the former vicarage at Fosbury, Wiltshire, are both by Teulon, and *The Buildings of England* considers the vicarage the more original of the two. It is of 1856, of flint and red brick with stone dressings, with an elaborate doorhead with triangular gable corbelled out.

At Steeple Barton, Oxfordshire, the coursed limestone old rectory, also of 1856 by Teulon, still Gothic in massing, has segmental Queen Anne-style window sashes, already a departure from High Gothic, anticipating the domestic revival.

Heydour is a tiny village in Lincolnshire, but has some good houses: to the west of St Michael's Church, Church Lees House looks like a farmhouse but was built as the rectory in 1800, classical, stone, with sash windows. To the south, beyond Priory House (said by Pevsner to be late sixteenth-century), lies the Old Vicarage, of 1857, by William White. Large, tall, asymmetrical, with projecting porch with some timbering, and an expansive roofscape of every conceivable angle, it shows White is by now a sophisticated Gothicist. Arched windows have patterned brickwork in a Venetian manner.

The former rectory at Kings Stanley, Gloucestershire, is a very early house remodelled in about 1720, and then again, in satisfying Neo-Tudor style, by Richard Reynolds Rowe of Cambridge for John Gibson in 1858, limestone, with corbelled oriel window and octagonal turret.

At Hawkchurch, Devon, 1859, there is a classic High Victorian Gothic former rectory by John Hicks, in which Thomas Hardy may have had a hand when apprenticed to him. There is a plan of it in his sketchbook. Of rubble stone, tall with steep gables and high stacks, it has a well modelled two-storey bay and cusped lancet windows in groups.

The parsonage at Alvechurch, Worcestershire, by Butterfield, is a memorable house which has been called the direct antecedent of Webb's celebrated Red House for William Morris, with similar plan. A large, long-gabled house, there is a bold contrast between the stone and patterned brick below and the brightly half-timbered upper storey. There is also a former rectory of the late fifteenth century with later alterations.

The former rectory at Bewholme, East Yorkshire, is by William Burges, 1859, in his eccentric "Northern French fairytale" style. It has a seven-bay front with cross-mullion windows, and steep projecting eaves supported by wooden flying brackets springing out from corbels, anticipating Voysey, and pierced bargeboards. There is a side stair tower rising the whole height under a separate hipped roof.

At Booton, Norfolk, the former rectory is by Thomas Allom for the Revd Whitwell Elwin; Jacobean style, red brick with stone dressings, mullions and transoms, steep roofs with crestings, some good stained glass, of about 1860.

In Oakley Square, off Camden High Street, London, the former vicarage of c. 1861 by John Johnson is a classic High Victorian Gothic extravaganza of yellow London brick, with thick patterned bands of red and yellow brick between the ground and first floors, and also on its free-standing square stair tower with steep spire-like pyramid roof and circular trefoil windows. The ground-floor front window is divided by a thin colonette, supporting plate tracery with quatrefoil, and the gabled porch has red marble colonettes with floral capitals. There are colonettes on the first- and second-floor windows, some arched, some round-arched, some with unpierced quatrefoils.

At Northleach, Gloucestershire, St Peter and St Paul is one of the great fifteenth-century "wool" churches. The solid-looking stone former vicarage is basically of the 1860s, its four serried gabled dormers its prominent feature.

In Hull, Yorkshire, St Mary's Church, Lowgate, was restored by Sir Gilbert Scott for his cousin, and he designed the former vicarage for him in 1864. It is typical red brick High Gothic with stone dressings, its main feature a stone canted oriel window.

The High Victorian vicarage at Swardeston, Norfolk, dated 1865, was built for the Revd Frederick Cavell, father of Edith Cavell. Heavy and solid but also decorative, it has ornamental bargeboards in the gables and ornamental window dressings in Venetian Gothic manner. There is also an older parsonage which has a sixteenth-century range and later eighteenth- and early nineteenth-century additions.

At Shoreditch St Chad, London, church and parsonage are by James Brooks, of the 1860s and 1870s. The latter features a turret and is of his usual red brick and slate. Shoreditch St Michael church and clergy house are again both by Brooks, of the same period, High Gothic.

The vicarage at Polesworth, Warwickshire, is basically a rebuild of a sixteenth-century manor house in 1868, and it still retains that appearance; irregular, largely timber-framed with stone stacks and jettied upper floors.

Sir Gilbert Scott heavily restored the church at Tydd St Giles, Cambridgeshire, and designed the former rectory for his brother, rector here. It is typical red brick Gothic of 1868, with gabled cross-wing and bargeboarded gabled dormers, some brick patterning but otherwise quite plain.

For the former vicarage at Hillesden, Buckinghamshire, Scott, who also restored the church, had progressed to an Arts and Crafts manner. It is of brick with half-timbering, 1870–71 for the Revd Robert Holt, with asymmetrical bays, wooden mullions and transoms.

The Vicarage, Sherborne, Dorset, in the splendid Abbey Close, shows that a convincingly medieval Gothic that blends happily with its very demanding surroundings could still be built in 1878, probably by R. D. Carpenter. Of stone, with two tall front gables and simple mullions and transoms, it was built on the site of a medieval house that was sadly demolished for it. Bax has an interesting footnote that in 1855 a parchment was found between two stones during repairs, with a message saying that the Pope had had a revelation telling him the right medicine for "the seknys that raynyth nowe among the people", probably the sweating sickness first observed in England in 1485.[9]

Barnack, Cambridgeshire, is the site of one of the great limestone quarries. The church of St John the Baptist has a fine Saxon tower, topped by a very early spire, early thirteenth-century. Nearby looms Kingsley House, the old rectory, where Charles Kingsley lived as a small child, grand and elegant, still in Tudor Gothic tradition, an 1880 remodelling of a sixteenth-century house, with a cross-wing of that time. It is of coursed stone with prominent parapets and string courses, with battlemented oriel above the porch, and Gothic windows.

The Vicarage of St Michael and All Angels, Bedford Park, West London, is typical of the Norman Shaw style, domestic revival with coved eaves cornice and Queen Anne chimney stacks. It is of the 1880s by Shaw's protégé E. J. May.

J. D. Sedding's former vicarage for All Saints, Plymouth (1887), is in a remarkable personal Arts and Crafts style, with complex gables and tile hanging, stone with rendered upper parts. Unusual polygonal bays rise up from the basement to a hipped roof over the first floor, the door set in the side. These features and its horizontal window strips presage more modern forms to come.

Liverpool's St Agnes vicarage by Norman Shaw of 1887 is another forward-looking building. Savidge calls it Gothic with a difference,[10] which it certainly is, with its horizontal groupings of casements and bold expanses of red brick. Even the oriel window looks modern.

On the southern perimeter of Hampstead Heath, across the road from the impressive church of 1889–1901 by James Brooks, with later chancel by Giles Gilbert Scott, lies the vicarage of All Hallows, Gospel Oak, also by Brooks, 1889–91, red brick with stone dressings. The Shirlock Road elevation contains the main entrance with Victorian Gothic porch; the other side is a row of offices. The asymmetrical main façade is set back from the abrupt wing to the left, which makes sense only from the side elevation.

Interestingly, the vicarage at All Saints Westbrook, Margate, Kent, is by E. S. Prior, associated with country houses, and indeed its stone and mullioned windows are hardly in local style. *The Buildings of England* calls it "sober for him". It forms a group with the church, also late nineteenth-century but by the local architect T. Andrews, and Prior added vestries in 1897.

Shaw's Corner, Ayot St Lawrence, Hertfordshire, is the former rectory of around 1900, a very Edwardian house of very Edwardian brick, dark mauve with red dressings. It is gabled with segmental headed windows, and has tall stacks. George Bernard Shaw acquired it in 1906 and furnished it in Arts and Crafts style. Many of his plays were written in the revolving hut in the garden.

At St Michael, Aldershot, Hampshire, the former vicarage by Charles Spooner of 1901 is a highly competent domestic revival house with projecting and non-projecting gables, prominent stacks, and Queen Anne features such as leaded casements and dentillations.

By the end of the Victorian and the beginning of the Edwardian period, new parsonages were scarcer, but London was still spreading. St Martin's Vicarage, West Acton, London, is in an enclave of prosperous suburbia, spacious semis with the occasional detached house, and this is one, double-fronted, a similar house next door. In domestic Arts and Crafts manner, it is lower ceilinged but more elegantly detailed than its solid neighbours. Inside, the wide entrance hall has a good staircase and landing. The mysterious and now culverted Bollo Brook flows on its way to the Thames through the back garden, which is of a size ideal for parish activities.

A more substantial introduction to the Edwardian era is St Luke's Vicarage, Kidderpore Avenue, Hampstead, by Basil Champneys, 1902–03. It sits with impeccable manners beside the church of 1897–99, also by Champneys, of similar red brick and scale at street elevation, two peas in a pod. The house looks big with its tall core of three floors plus attic rooms, but has only two bays, with half-height projections at either side, that on the left with hipped turret-like roof, rafter ends subtly suggesting medieval corbelling, that on the right containing the large porch. There are stone-mullioned and transomed front windows with plainer wood-framed casements to the side, all with square leaded lights. The back part is tile hung in vernacular manner.

The Vicarage of St Barnabas, Walthamstow, 1903–04, by W. D. Caröe, in Queen Anne Dutch Arts and Crafts style, red brick, gabled, tile hanging on first floor, with canopied front door, is still a working house, remarkably unaltered. There are outer and inner halls and the main reception room has a view over the garden and the church. Beyond the kitchen is the original cold room for food storage. The rooms, which have all been decorated and furnished in their original manner, have low picture rails with correspondingly deep friezes above—domestic rather than High Victorian. The stairs have a simply moulded mahogany handrail and simple straight balusters. The attic floor has bedrooms and servants' rooms with vertical pine panelling. The first floor has master and other bedrooms and study/library. An intensely practical house, it has the atmosphere of a working parsonage—you can always tell the difference.

The church at Thurlstone, South Yorkshire, is of 1905 by C. Hodgson Fowler and the vicarage of 1906 by Edgar Wood, whose houses are always interesting. Of rubblestone with ashlar dressings, door recessed behind impressive stone doorcase, and wide central bay with mullioned strip windows divided by central transom, it is a consciously vernacular house that at the same time looks forward towards modernism.

The vicarage of St Peter's, Mount Park Road, Ealing, London, is a large Arts and Crafts house by Morley Horder, 1910, of brick with stone dressings, projecting side bays, and gabled porch with chequer pattern. Quite conventional, it has something of both Tudor and High Gothic as well as the vernacular.

St Anselm's Vicarage in Kennington Road, London, of 1913 by Adshead and Ramsey, is straight Neo-Georgian, brick, symmetrical, seven bays, low pitched hipped roof, sash windows with well-detailed brick lintels, and a doorcase with flat canopy. The top floor windows go right to the deep eaves. The chunky pantiles and the window shutters are unusual. It has good vertical railings round the garden facing the street, when they can be seen and are not obscured by gaudy plastic banners.

Set back down a pea shingle drive from Fulham High Street, London, hidden behind tall flats, lies the large Neo-Georgian vicarage of All Saints, with Arts and Crafts church hall nearby. Of three floors, wide front elevation with hipped roof and sash windows and Neo-Georgian doorcase, its good back garden backs onto Bishop's Park. The setting is as important as the house: an oasis off the busy High Street.

The vicarage for St James's Church in Muswell Hill, North London, has a certain elegance. Its foundation stone was laid on the site of the former parsonage in 1915. Its pediment and Adam-style doorway make it a good example of the Neo-Georgian of this period, perhaps by W. B. Collins.

The former vicarage at Clifton Hampden, Oxfordshire, sold off by the Church in 2006 to widespread local opposition, has a provenance going back at least to 1755. It was greatly rebuilt in 1923–24, in a suitably vernacular Arts and Crafts manner that manages to retain the irregular cross-winged look of an early house. The architect was A. S. G. Butler, who wrote books about Lutyens and Bentley; when he built his first house he took out the quantities himself and took satisfaction in having only two bricks left on its completion.

In Shoreditch, Yorkton Street, the clergy house and church hall of 1926–27 by J. Harold Gibbons at St Augustine's almost completely masks Woodyer's only London church. Almost symmetrical, with five bays, the centre bay with tall tower projecting on twin corbels around the porch below, it is quite simple "stripped" Northern Gothic, both fortress-like and friendly. Each bay has tripartite windows with brick mullions. It abuts an earlier Gothic annexe with diapered brick, the two blending politely.

Parsonages varied widely in this interestingly eclectic period between the wars; a few were progressive but many looked back, reflecting Church conservatism. There was the classical pediment of Little Gaddesden, Hertfordshire, by C. H. B. Quennell; the cottage style of Angmering, Sussex, by Morley Horder (1921); the gabled wings of Millbrook, Hants, by J. B. S. Comper (1928); and the giant pilasters of Knodishall, Suffolk, by Munro Cautley (1929). The Arts and Crafts lingered on in Wolverton, Hampshire (Edwin Gunn, 1930), with hipped roofs and dormers, leaded lights and wide Tudor doorway. By contrast, the modern rectory at Prestwich, Lancashire, of 1923 by Taylor and Young, is V-shaped and partly flat-roofed, albeit with Neo-Georgian sashes and two colours of brick giving it a "Wrenish" character. It is a genuinely interesting house. Eaton Socon,

Cambridgeshire, by Stonebridge and Harris (1934), looked forward in its starkness to the typical builders' houses of the 1950s. In Wythenshawe, Manchester, the rectory by N. F. Cachemaille-Day of the mid-1930s, adjoining his church, had a German Expressionist influence.

After the war, rebuildings took some time. Latton, part of Harlow New Town, was by Sir Frederick Gibberd (1951), 1,550 sq. ft, small and rectangular. Holy Apostles, Winchester Street, Pimlico (RC), is a very 1950s church, replacing one destroyed in 1941. The contemporary presbytery (parsonage) called The Priest's House and the church hall are ranged in a planned development round a deep sunken courtyard, typical of its time, the house of three floors having a wide access balcony over the courtyard, contemporary tiling by the front door, and windows with Corbusian architraves, all in the same buff brick. By Hadfield, Cawkwell and Davidson, it is a good try, if not particularly memorable.

St Olave, Hart Street, off Mark Lane, City of London, is a neat, unassuming Tudor-influenced Portland stone parsonage of 1954 by E. B. Glanfield, built right against the reconstructed church. There are four floors plus attic with gable end facing the street. The simple mullioned windows and cavetto doorcase are of the period, though the overall manner of the house looks back. There is a pleasing relief carving of St Olave over the door. It has an institutional feel, like a polite modern infill at an Oxford college.

The rectory and vestry at St James, Piccadilly, London, Wren's famous church, were designed by Austin Blomfield in a Neo-Georgian style. They are a model of propriety, blending perfectly with the church and the Lutyens bank next door, despite being built in 1954–56, symmetrical, with slightly projecting central bay and rising double staircase to the main door. The ground-floor side windows facing Piccadilly have the segmental tops and keystones of the early Georgian style.

The former rectory for St John at Hackney, East London, is a 1950s house thought to be by N. F. Cachemaille-Day, as he worked on the church. It is Neo-Georgian, with fanlight. There is a sitting/dining room and another large room with bay window, and upstairs five bedrooms. Both floors have a through corridor, all rooms leading off. The staircase, with uncarpeted wooden open string treads, wooden ledge, plain white vertical balusters, "Italian" metal scrolls at corner doglegs, and wooden rails with Georgian scrolled ends, is very much of the period.

Most of these post-war houses were quite conventional, but there was some adventurousness. "Open plan" was a symbol of the time, as at Mill Hill, London, John Keble Vicarage by Braddock and Martin-Smith, 1952, with dining dais, apparently able to accommodate 30 people if needed for parish meetings, and Rushmere St Andrew near Ipswich by L. and P. Barefoot, 1959. Even the kitchen had a half glass wall, stair balusters were in classic Festival of Britain style, angled and attached to a thick wooden "ranch-style" rail. The open-plan style could perhaps be seen both as progressive and as harking back to the old medieval hall. It exemplifies the post-war philosophy of transparency, not popular with everyone.

The house at Borehamwood, Hertfordshire, by N. F. Cachemaille-Day (1959) is one of the rare few to be mentioned in three sources, a good design.[11] At Eyam, Derbyshire, the late Georgian rectory built for the Revd Thomas Seward was largely demolished (it has been attributed to James Paine), and part of it incorporated in the plainer new stone house built in 1960. Edmonton St Alphege, London, by Sir Edward Maufe (1962) was built of plain yellow brick, with thick plain window architraves of reconstituted stone, and assertive bargeboards at the gable ends, a corner balcony with thin 1950s-type railings deeply inset.

Two houses that featured in house plan books of the late 1960s and early 1970s (see Plates 33 and 34) are more interestingly modern, and—unlike many of the period—rather successful. The first of these is a rectory at Barnburgh, Doncaster, of 1969 by John Wallis and Associates. The second is in "an expanding parish near Reading" and is part of a complex with church and community buildings, by Colin Oates, 1974.

St Stephen, Canonbury Road, Islington, of 1837–39 by Inwood and Clifton, has a church hall and vicarage by Maurice Taylor, 1968–74. "Quite a bold group behind the church", says *The Buildings of England* of this rather desolate spot. It is an ingenious addition to the end of the church, blending acceptably at the side, but perhaps only pleasing to admirers of those strip windows and that drab yellow brick, echoing the sprawling housing estates and shop precincts of the period.

The archdeacon's house, Sudbury House, just outside Bury St Edmund's, Suffolk, is a typical recent house, designed on traditional lines with no reference to modernism, loosely vernacular, unadventurous, quite a good hall and landing, unfortunate stripped pine doors and architraves, light and insubstantial, of no architectural merit.

Perambulations

The following houses of different styles and periods are more conveniently discussed by location rather than chronologically.

The Buildings of England describes the early sixteenth-century Old Rectory at
Beaconsfield, Bucks, as "important", a house of two storeys round a courtyard.
There is a hall and side wings with jettied gables, a stair turret and newel stair.
There is also a mid-eighteenth-century former parsonage, with Doric pilasters
and detailing.

Burford, Oxfordshire, is one of the country's finest towns. The church of St
John the Baptist at the bottom of the hill was originally Norman but subsequently
much altered, including by G. E. Street, partly prompting William Morris to
found SPAB in his irritation. Across the road is the old vicarage, dated 1672, an
interesting house with mannerist features, stone rather than brick, its unusual
front of Dutch gables containing ornamental medallions instead of windows, the
grand first floor having deep mullioned windows. It shows the transition from
the Jacobean to the Restoration style. The splendidly fearsome gargoyles on the
gate are from an earlier house. Also at Burford, the Old Rectory, about 30 years
later but totally different, is a fine very early eighteenth-century house, said to be
by one of Wren's masons, Christopher Kempster, this time demonstrating a move
from the Restoration to the Baroque and beyond, of ashlar with quoins and sash
windows, and a complicated hipped roofline.

The church buildings next to each other in a group at Easton on the Hill,
Northamptonshire, are a wonderful study in contrasts. The charming medieval,
or at least early sixteenth-century, priest's house is a good example of the early
parsonage, a simple two-floor rubble rectangle with mullioned windows and
external wall staircase, limestone with the odd patching in orange local ironstone
so characteristic of this area. There could be no greater contrast than the glum
new brick rectory with its plastic windows next door. A few paces up the hill to
the east, set back in a fine formal front garden, the splendidly polite Georgian
rectory proudly displays itself, another contrast. To complete the group, Glebe
Cottage, of ancient limestone, nestles opposite.

Leicester has the Chantry House of around 1511, founded by William
Wyggeston for two priests, a three-storey rubble stone building with simple stone
mullions and buttresses; the remains of St Mary's vicarage, probably a sixteenth-
century chantry house; an attractive early eighteenth-century former vicarage in
St Martin's; an early to mid-nineteenth-century former vicarage in Vicarage Lane,
rather grand, stucco and Italianate; and the vicarage of All Souls by Stockdale
Harrison, free Arts and Crafts.

Ludlow, Shropshire, is timber-frame country, and the rectory with its
fourteenth-century core is roughcast over stone and timber with a bold central
gable. Nearby is the timber-framed Town Preacher's House of the early seventeenth

century with twin gables and canted bays. The Reader's House is a church house of the early seventeenth century with earlier origins, an astonishing combination of bleak rubble stone and pretty timber frame.

The Old Parsonage, Marlow, Bucks, fourteenth-century with later, mainly eighteenth-century additions, is very irregular and gabled, both stone and timber-framed, having rare windows with elaborate reticulation. The Deanery alongside is eighteenth-century in appearance but with mullioned and transomed windows. Street's mid-Victorian vicarage completes the architectural mix.

Oxford has a number of parsonages in a small area. St Giles' Old Parsonage, Banbury Road, now a hotel in a very urban environment, has a doorway dated 1659, and looks earlier. It is reminiscent of many Cotswold houses but, alas, at the time of viewing smothered in creeper, all architectural details apart from the tops of the two symmetrical front gables obliterated. Vegetation insults and disrespects architecture. Just up the road is the Roman Catholic presbytery, 25 Woodstock Road, yellow brick, by Wilkinson, 1877–78, very similar to the High Anglican clergy houses of the same period, Gothic, ascetic, and institutional. St Margaret's Old Vicarage, St Margaret's Road, of 1886–87 by H. G. W. Drinkwater, Gothic, is tucked away behind the church, looking part of it. The rectory at St Ebbe's, Paradise Square, is by Street. It is quite early for him, fairly plain in the Ecclesiologists' "Cottage style", 1854, altered in 1886 with an incongruous addition. The school next door, also by Street, was enlarged by Champneys. An oasis in a more anonymous part of central Oxford is St Thomas, Becket Street. The former vicarage north of the churchyard, by C. C. Rolfe, is quite a sumptuous Arts and Crafts-style house. On the other side of the church, undergoing restoration, stands the splendid John Combe's House. An inscription states: "This Parish School House was built in the year of our Lord 1702 and in the first year of the Reigne of Queen Ann at the charge of Mr John Coombes Cityzen and Plaisterer of London borne in this parrish and free of this city. For the benefit of as many poor children as the rent of the house will pay for their teaching to read and write the teacher to be ye Clerk of this Parrish", adding "if duely qualified"—clearly written by a lawyer. Later a vestry house, it looks seventeenth-century, and not what one thinks of as Queen Anne.

Southwell, Nottinghamshire, has several fine church buildings apart from the splendid Norman minster. They include the Bishop's Palace and the remains of the Archbishop's Palace, the Residence and Vicars Court, and a large number of prebendal houses including the fine Cranfield House, textbook Queen Anne, built for a member of the Mompesson family like the house of that name at Salisbury.

Stamford, Lincolnshire, is one of the finest stone towns in England, ranking with Bath and Burford, and the oldest house on Barn Hill is the former vicarage of All Saints, in use as the vicarage in the mid-fifteenth century and probably earlier, with its two-storey rubble façade with Tudor-style two-light windows with dripmoulds, and four-centred arched doorway. It was drawn by William Stukeley when it still had its tall hall windows. It is surrounded by grander Georgian buildings. The Victorian Tudor later parsonage, much more formal, is on the north side of St Peter's Hill, another splendid street with much to see. The rectory of St Mary's in St Mary's Street is again a delightful vernacular house of obviously very early origins. It has the form of a small medieval hall house with gabled cross-wing, so attractive that the later Georgian sashes hardly annoy. *The Buildings of England* says the two-light window with tympanum set into the front left side is twelfth-century, though reset. The rectory for St George's, of 1881 by Edward Browning, is in St George's Square, another good street, otherwise Georgian and earlier; for a Victorian house it blends well and interestingly, its projecting central bay giving it an appropriately early appearance.

There are several good houses in Thame, Oxfordshire, including the sixteenth- or seventeenth-century Church House in the High Street, the stone early Victorian Tudor vicarage on the site of a much earlier one, and the once-moated Prebendal House. The prebend was established in the twelfth century, the house is very early (thirteenth-century) and was listed as ruinous in 1661.

Apart from the splendid Bishop's Palace, Wells, Somerset, has the Old Deanery, the Vicars' Close, St John's Priory, late fourteenth/early fifteenth-century, a doorway in Priest Row reputed to be from the fifteenth-century priest's house, the early seventeenth-century Dean's Lodging, St Cuthbert's Vicarage of the early-to-mid-eighteenth century, and the former St Thomas' Vicarage by Teulon, about 1860. The Old Deanery is of twelfth-century origins, now mainly late fifteenth-century with new late seventeenth-century windows by Bathurst, president of Trinity College, Oxford, very early sashes, and buttresses and corner turrets. The houses in Vicars' Close are a very rare example of planned medieval terrace housing. They could claim to be twenty-seven parsonages all in a row, but these were the cathedral vicars.

At Wingham, East Kent, there is a fifteenth-century Wealden house that was occupied by the vicar at one time or another. Wingham was one of the Archbishop of Canterbury's important manors in the early medieval period, providing considerable income. There are other good clergy houses here, including the Old Canonry and Canon Cottage, of timber frame with flint base dating from the late thirteenth century, the Old Manse of the seventeenth and early eighteenth century, timber-framed Canon House and Canon Villa, probably sixteenth-century, the former Vicarage House of the late seventeenth century with a row of moulded brick pilasters on a brick string course, and a large, grand nine-bay mid-eighteenth-century vicarage with pediment.

Central London

The parsonages of the West End, West Central, and City areas of Central London are largely Victorian or later, and just one morning or afternoon walk in any of the areas below can accommodate several of these houses with ease.

Westminster

In Dean's Yard, The Deanery, the abbot's house till the Reformation, set round a small courtyard, has been called the most complete medieval house left in London. It has good round-headed Elizabethan windows in the north range, and large medieval traceried windows to the west. There are various canons' houses dotted around Dean's Yard, two of them by Pearson, 1882. Here we also find the very *raison d'être* of many a parsonage house, the offices of Queen Anne's Bounty by Blore, 1846–47. There are two offices here, both well-mannered Tudor Gothic, one with a two-floor canted bay, the other with a two-floor battlemented oriel.

In complete contrast, 43 Palace Street is a fine Arts and Crafts former presbytery (parsonage) to St Peter and St Edward Chapel (RC) by J. B. Bentley, 1880. Unlike the monstrous post-war development opposite, it is human in scale and ingenious. Irregular, tall, of stock brick with red brick banding and dressings and some mullioned windows, it has Queen Anne touches in a free and adventurous style.

Westminster Clergy House, behind Westminster Cathedral (RC) and also by Bentley, is Queen Anne rather than the Byzantine of the cathedral. An interesting feature is the oriel window supported on a single pier, partly lighting the apse of the Archbishop's Chapel. In Carlisle Place, just round the corner, Manning House, about 1897, is a huge palazzo-style extravaganza, its light brick contrasting with the red and white of the surrounding Edwardian blocks, massive yet almost self-effacing in their garish company. It was built as the Guardsmen's Institute by H. A. Darbishire but served as the Archbishop's Palace in the late nineteenth/early twentieth century. There is some Church Commissioners' housing in Regency Street, 1901, Tuscan-style pilasters flanking triple windows, ornamented but pleasant.

In Great Peter Street, St Matthew's Church, by Sir Gilbert Scott, was reconstructed after damage. The clergy house of 1891, immediately recognisable as such, is by John Oldrid Scott, red brick, gabled, lancet windows, pointed on ground floor, flat-topped on the rest. The red brick relieving arches above red sandstone lintels, if a decorative feature, are so self-effacing as to be barely visible. This is sparse, stripped Gothic from which all life has been stamped out, polite but charmless. The red sandstone niche above the door, though totally empty, seems positively florid.

Belgravia and Pimlico

The brick church of St Paul, Wilton Place, is by Thomas Cundy, and the clergy house a towering pile of 1871 by Withers. Of five floors and basement, it has wide irregularly spaced bays, the central three slightly projecting, their tall gable looking less Victorian than the Gothic smaller side gables. It has stone bandings on yellow stock brick, some windows arched, some grouped, some rectangular, all sliding sashes with Georgian glazing bars, no casements. There are Gothic stone embellishments on the porch and on the corner where a canopied statue projects. Despite the strange mix, a High Victorian feel prevails.

St Mary, Bourne Street, is a Byzantine church with round-arched windows, and on the corner is the even odder former clergy house, in an almost rural vernacular surrounded by the stucco of Belgravia; five main bays, four floors, the top three tile-hung with small grey slates; central mansard gable with sub-Venetian window with "Gothick" glazing bars. The hipped roofs make it look as though it should be on the waterfront at Bergen, or perhaps the Devon coast, explained by the fact that it was formerly a pub.

Cundy's group of school, church, then clergy house at St Barnabas, Pimlico, of mannered random rubble stone that Disney would have admired, manages to please in its incongruous setting of terraces of various periods just off Pimlico Road. The neo-medieval clergy house has towers and a hidden garden with statue, irregular from St Barnabas Street. The school is less quaint, more four-square to the road. Round the corner in Ranelagh Grove, the clergy house presents a long, more integrated façade, like almshouses, with pointed windows, more obviously Victorian. The later Church Rooms of 1900 blend well.

An oasis of civilisation in an urban jungle, 162 Buckingham Palace Road is exposed to the full hubbub of this major road, across from the bus station; formal, terracotta-dressed, fussy late Victorian Arts and Crafts, already looking Edwardian, canted bay, much deeper at the side along Elizabeth Street, church hall back extension; terracotta cartouches with labels blank, never engraved. By R. W. Edis, completed in 1892, it was formerly the parsonage of the Church of St Philip, Belgravia.

Mayfair

In Down Street, Christ Church, 1865, is of ragstone by F. and H. Francis, and across the road, No. 21, dated 1892 on a wall plaque, is the former vicarage. Dark red brick Tudor Revival, on a corner site, with side entrance through terracotta ogee-arched doorcase, it is a typical Central London townhouse, tall and narrow with three floors plus basement and attic. It has only a two-bay front, the bays linked by an arch, plush terracotta dressings, good railings, and balcony. On the roof, two gabled dormers flank a smaller central pyramidal dormer with a finial.

Farm Street boasts the Church of the Immaculate Conception (RC), the English headquarters of the Jesuits. The Victorian ragstone church by J. J. Scoles, in what *The Buildings of England* describes as "Decorated-cum-Flamboyant" style, is flanked by the massive former Church House by Goldie, Child and Goldie, 1886. A great monolith, a bit like a railway hotel, it dominates the church, in very contrasting red brick, of five tall floors and a basement, five wide bays, a stone arched blind arcade above each of the upper bays. A string course divides the two upper from the two lower storeys. Each window has a stone lintel and sill and the doorway has a modest Tudor arch.

A presbytery of the same church, by A. E. Purdie of 1886–87, 114 Mount Street is another vast building that would look wildly extravagant anywhere else, but here less flamboyant than the surrounding High Edwardiana. It has very fine detailing, big, deep two-transom windows on the main front, and smaller ones at the side, all in dark red brick, stonework exactly colour-matched. It is Italianate Gothic, with some good stained glass.

St Mark's, North Audley Street, by J. P. Gandy Deering, of the 1820s, his only church, has a Greek Revival façade whose crumbling stonework makes it look Greek Survival! Alongside is the former vicarage, 1887–88 by Sir Arthur Blomfield, a total contrast, "gabled and Netherlandish", in dark red brick. With three bays, four floors and an attic in the Dutch gable, the ground-floor front is recessed behind a central arch and a projecting porch to the side. Each first-floor window has a pedimented gable and there is one side canted bay. The third floor has a pedimented central bay. Its complex "asymmetrical symmetricality" and rich detailing make it grander than the church.

Duke Street, south of Oxford Street, harbours the Ukrainian Catholic Cathedral, originally the King's Weighhouse Chapel, 1889–91 by Waterhouse, brick and terracotta in an eastern style. Waterhouse's former school and minister's house round the corner in Binney Street, the latter less ethnic, are still strongly red brick and glazed terracotta, with chunky balcony and corbelling.

Marylebone

North of Oxford Street, the vast and impressive St James's Spanish Place (though in George Street) (RC), has its minimally Gothic clergy house built into its side, four floors plus slit windows in the gables, only two bays wide, stock brick with limestone dressings. Closer to Holborn lies the celebrated symbol of the Ecclesiological Movement, All Saints Margaret Street, and its remarkable Clergy House and offices, 1849, all by Butterfield, set round that small courtyard with its delightful miniature garden. It is quite austere, despite its banded and diapered bricks, a curious Butterfield effect. The windows have his typical angled heads under segmental arches, but it importantly already begins to look forward to Webb and the Domestic Revival.

Soho

The Welsh Presbyterian Church in Charing Cross Road and its vicarage in Shaftesbury Avenue are integral, ingeniously conjoined behind the alien edifice on the corner of the block. God is now Mammon in the form of an Australian drinking house. Modest for a house with stately detailing, and not very wide, the full width hall, with two entrances, one at each side, perhaps for office and domestic use, leading to rooms above and below, makes it seem wider. The staircase has iron balusters, simple uprights with curving tops. A corridor at the back leads right into the church, giving the vicar little excuse for late arrival. The former church is a rotunda by James Cubitt with arcaded side aisles.

Holborn

St Alban, Brooke Street, Holborn, is of 1856–62 by Butterfield, and the adjacent Clergy House is also by him, 1859–63, a typically assured composition in characteristic muscular Gothic, quite austere despite polychrome brickwork. It is of four asymmetrical bays with an entrance arch which leads right through the building to the church behind. The windows are in clusters of two and three with arched mouldings and decorative spandrels above, some with plate tracery of quatrefoils and some with rays of alternate stone and brick. Some of the smaller windows have cusped arches. As at All Saints Margaret Street, it makes full use of the restricted site.

St Andrew, Holborn, was remodelled by Wren in his typical Portland stone. The vicarage (combined with vestry clerk's office and court house in a large complex) is a total contrast of Victorian stock brick Gothic with stone dressings. The courtyard side to the west presents the appearance of a medieval castle in miniature, L-shaped with its circular tower at the street end, corbelled under the turret. There are gables and another turret. From Shoe Lane, behind, it looks different: plain and institutional, like a dormitory block or hospital, windows grouped in pairs with cross-mullions and transoms. Needless to say, it is by that so-called rogue Teulon, 1868–71.

City of London

The grand and imposing former St Bride's vicarage is in Bridewell Place, Fleet Street; elegantly sophisticated, by Basil Champneys in eclectic Queen Anne Revival style, it stares boldly down to Tudor Street. Of five symmetrical bays of dark red brick, with finely cut brick architraving round the door, triangular and segmental pediments on the row of five dormers, it is both imposing and graceful. The delicate composition is marred by a greedy top floor for which permission should never have been granted.

The present vicarage of St Bride's, difficult to find and then to see, is approached by narrow alleys and hidden away between the church and a raised walkway, simple Georgian Revival with good sash windows and glazing bars. *The Buildings of England* says it was built in 1958, by J. R. Stammers.

At St Vedast, the clergy house at 4 Foster Lane to the north looks Georgian or early twentieth-century Georgian Revival, but is apparently by Dykes Bower, 1960. There are still a couple of interesting old side alleys amid the otherwise modernist devastation of this area. In Martin Lane, off Eastcheap, the former rectory by John Davies for St Clement Eastcheap, 1851–53, is an imposing house with tall, elaborate campanile with striking round oculus window. The heavy dressings include busy stucco quoins with deep channelling, Italianate bay to south, arched porch, chunky stucco architraves to all windows, and a large clock. The dark red brick goes well with the cream stucco work. There is one vertical bay of incongruous Tudor slit windows.

At St Mary-at-Hill, south from Eastcheap, what Pevsner calls "Savage's gaunt brick rectory of 1834", by James Savage, faces the street; Wren's church, which may be at least partly by Hooke, who never gets his due, is hidden behind. "Rectory AD 1834" is written on a stone plaque right at the top of the five-floor building, with tall, narrow, pedimented porch bearing a skull and crossbones. There are tripartite "Wyatt"-type sash windows and an intriguing barrel-vaulted tunnel goes right under the house through a porch.

In St Andrew's Hill, one of the fascinating old streets between St Paul's and the river, lurks No. 35, the rectory of about 1766, an elegant Georgian house of dark stock brick and sashes, nice pedimented doorcase with fanlight, and polygonal oriel window at the south-east corner. Two side windows, one arched, have elegant "wheatsheaf" iron bars. Early meetings of the Church Missionary Society were held here.

The Old Deanery, St Paul's, further east, is a good Restoration house of seven bays, boldly dentillated cornice, dormers, fine doorcase, with double flight of steps up to the door. Edward Woodroffe signed the building contract so it is unlikely to be by Wren, though he may have been consulted. The Chapter House of 1712–14 to the north is, however, by him and another gem.

Some working parsonages

Here are some of the houses that continue to do the job for which they were intended, though all under threat. Many parsonages in this gazetteer have been stately houses, some rivalling the manor house. These are smaller, generous but homely ones that the Church can ill afford to lose.

The Rectory, Trent, Dorset, is of Tudor origin, but much of it is now of about 1750 with Venetian windows at the garden front with central canted bay, in bright local stone, with later Regency additions on both sides, one at right angles to the main house, by Mr Turner, who became rector in 1835. He collected German stained and painted glass, and inserted fragments in one impressive window on the landing (the east window of the church has more of his collection). Divided since 1951, it has good stairs, landings, and rooms, but is not huge. There is a large oil portrait of Archbishop Fisher, who lived there for ten years (1962–72) after his retirement and worked as curate. One pane of the stained glass is still broken, damaged by Fisher's grandson playing with a ball. Upstairs there are big square Georgian bedrooms with shutters, and a Venetian window overlooks the garden.

Marlesford, Suffolk, still very rural, has a delightful medium-sized rectory, the core apparently square Queen Anne, enlarged in the late eighteenth/early nineteenth century, and an impressive Regency bow of pale gault brick added on to one side of the front door. The garden extends all round with lawns and trees. There are traces of an even older house, since a window in the kitchen with its deep reveals looks as though it once had mullions. The fine doorcase is pedimented with pilasters and good architraves and fanlight. At the back of the house there are five widely spaced bays. There is a large, pleasant hall, sitting room, dining room, study, and service rooms on the ground floor, and upstairs bedrooms and an attic room. The ground-floor sitting room and the master bedroom above it, in the bowed wing, have elegantly curved sashes.

The Vicarage, Torrington, Devon, is an attractive late Georgian building, the front added in the early nineteenth century to a late eighteenth-century back. The elegant hall and staircase have characteristic Regency curves, the rooms are spacious, the dining room large enough for a dozen or so to sit round the table. At the time of my visit, the interior, with its smoking logs in the fireplace, breathed atmosphere, like stepping back into the world of the Regency parson. The back ranges are unspoilt; above, bedrooms and bathroom, and two cellars below. Outside, there is an acre or so mostly of lawn round the house, and a further acre of walled gardens, well laid out with paths and beds. It is ideally situated a hundred yards from the church, across the road.

The Vicarage, Dedham, Essex, is a Regency house, but there are medieval traces in the cellars. From the garden at the back, it can be seen to be on two levels, the more imposing early nineteenth-century part added to the earlier, with a fine drawing room with graceful deep sash windows. The Regency section has Neo-Gothic battlements and buttressing, and the front door, with circular lantern above, leads to a long hall which subtly separates the formal offices and drawing room from the inner private rooms, the morning room and kitchen, and passage to the back garden. The back hall has a fine staircase with simple scrolled balusters leading to the bedrooms, study, and store on the first floor, then the second floor with more bedrooms and guest suite. The churchyard runs up to the vicarage windows. The exterior render may be playful in colour but blends with the traditionally bright village and surroundings. The architect Mark Thompson had a hand in the house.

Figure 7: The Vicarage, Dedham, Essex—a sketch by Constable

The rectory at Bishops Nympton, Devon, was built in 1839 to replace an earlier one near the church. It is a modestly spacious and very pretty building, square with iron verandah to west and south, stucco with Soanian incised patterning. It has nicely proportioned rooms, the ground floor, three reception rooms and kitchen giving onto a service wing; a gracious staircase and upstairs, large bedrooms, bathroom, and dressing room, and more in the back part. Outside, there are one and a half acres of garden, stable block, and walled garden. One recent visitor laughed and exclaimed: "Absurd! Brighton sea front in deepest Devon."

The vicarage at East Coker, Somerset, is another of the simple but elegant houses of this period, ideal for its purpose but now looking vulnerable to sale, of characteristically symmetrical front elevation and low-pitched hipped roof.

The vicarage at Lastingham, North Yorkshire, has a delightfully vernacular quality, like a farmhouse, appropriate for its remote setting but architecturally unusual for a parsonage, stone with a pantiled roof.

Sadly, since the first edition of this book, the following two erstwhile surviving traditional parsonages have been sold off. Ilminster Rectory, Somerset, is mainly late eighteenth/early nineteenth-century, probably replacing an earlier building to the south. Steps lead down from the front of the house to a public alley that goes round the churchyard. The lower part of the garden abuts on the churchyard, at a higher level across the alley. There are steps down to the front door, rather fine (late medieval Gothic, of thick oak, studded). An arched stone frame has been contrived to house it. There are high ceilings in the main part, and on four floors, principally ground and first, but with cellars under part, and attics above. The drawing room and dining room are spacious. The study is near the front door. The kitchen is approached through a back hall. There are good offices, larder, storeroom, utility, and cloakroom. The windows are large Georgian sashes. Outside, there is a south-facing terrace commanding a view of the church and over the town roofs to the country beyond, giving a great sense of historical continuity.

The fact that there was no perceptible change in style of the compact classical late Georgian "box" parsonage in the early Victorian period is well illustrated by Ridgewell, Essex, of around 1840, typical of so many built earlier, of three bays with shallow hipped roof and overhanging eaves. Formerly the vicarage but later the rectory, it is a simple central corridor house, extremely manageable, but that has not saved it. The front façade of polite gault brick, with typical pilaster-like lesenes at the corners to give some modelling, unusually turns its face from the village and obediently salutes the church. The red brick at the sides and back is harshly different. The sash windows are deep and generous in late Georgian manner. The typical vicarage garden is lawned and mostly at the front. The square wide rooms each side of the hall look Victorian but still have simple Regency layout. The staircase with its slim, square balusters curves up to the square upper rooms. There could be no more typical house of this type.

Notes

1   R. B. Dawson, *A Short History of Embleton Church and the Fortified Vicarage* (British Publishing Company, 1933).

2   *The Ecclesiologist*, Vol. ii, June 1843, p. 147.

3   Savidge, *The Parsonage in England*, p. 22.

4   Henry Thorold, *Lincolnshire Houses* (Michael Russell, 1999), p. 177.

5   *Daily Telegraph*, "Parish Heritage Goes to Highest Bidder", 28 December 2000.

6   Ptolemy Dean, *John Soane, Architect* (Royal Academy), p. 69.

7   Thorold, *Lincolnshire Houses*, p. 116.

8   Thorold, *Lincolnshire Houses*, p. 124.

9   B. Anthony Bax, *The English Parsonage* (John Murray, 1964), p. 47.

10   Savidge, *The Parsonage in England*, p. 146.

11   Nikolaus Pevsner and others, *The Buildings of England*, 54 volumes (Yale University Press, 1951); Bax, *The English Parsonage*; Savidge, *The Parsonage in England*.

CHAPTER 8

The Finest Parsonages

This book is not "A Thousand Best Parsonages". It might be a lifetime's work to see all existing parsonages and, besides, I lack the tenacity of Nikolaus Pevsner, or even that of Sir Simon Jenkins. Also, interiors are important, and vicarages, however hospitable their occupants, and they vary, are not open to the public. In any case, assessing merit by awarding stars is surely a ludicrous practice, unworthy of any book about architecture.

Even so, in an attempt to be as objective as possible, I must admit I could not resist shortlisting the best parsonages based on the available sources. If a house has been mentioned in earlier research, there may be good reason for that. This chapter gives the result. The detailed method I used is set out in Appendix E. The gazetteer in Chapter 7 was not done on this basis, though, being a collection of notable parsonages, it includes these.

Of the 252 parsonages shortlisted by my method set out in Appendix E, the following 13 had four mentions in the sources cited:

Alfriston, Sussex; Bemerton, Wiltshire; Bolton Abbey, Yorkshire; Church Langton, Leicestershire; Corbridge, Northumberland; Gawsworth, Cheshire; Grantchester, Cambridgeshire; Great Snoring, Norfolk; Market Deeping, Lincolnshire; Morwenstow, Cornwall; Muchelney, Somerset; Ripple, Worcestershire; Winterborne Came, Dorset.

Are these the best English parsonages? If so, most are early houses. Three are Georgian, and only one Victorian (and that very early). Note that no county is duplicated.

In *England's Thousand Best Houses*,[1] Simon Jenkins chose houses that must be open to the public, and so mentions few clergy houses: only Shaw's Corner, Hertfordshire; The Old Rectory, Epworth, Lincolnshire; Wesley's House, East London; and the Prebendal Manor House at Nassington, Northamptonshire. The Anker's House, Chester-le-Street, Durham, is an anchorite's, or hermit's, cell. He also mentions some posher residences: Bishop Auckland Palace, Durham; the Archbishop's House at Knole; the Archbishop's Palace at Maidstone; Lyddington Bede House, Rutland, part of the summer palace of the Bishops of Lincoln; Lambeth Palace and Fulham Palace, London. The Priest's House at Wimborne Minster, Dorset, is apparently not a priest's house but an ironmonger's shop. The Rectory Mansion at Brading, Isle of Wight, is now a nightmarish but fascinating tourist shop. He also includes the Prior's House which survives at Castle Acre Priory, Norfolk. The Landmark Trust also has some interesting properties (see Chapter 10), including Iffley Rectory, Oxfordshire.

If these are factored into my analysis, Epworth and Iffley join the finalists with four points, bringing the total up to 15.

In *The Buildings of England*, there are 73 parsonages for which the entries are much longer than the others. These are listed in Appendix D, together with their counties. Comparing these 73 parsonages with the 84 in Appendix C, only the following are duplicated: Bradwell, Essex; Bremhill, Wiltshire; Church Langton, Leicestershire; Coalpit Heath, Gloucestershire; Congresbury, Somerset; Corbridge, Northumberland; Cossington, Leicestershire; Elsdon, Northumberland; Embleton, Northumberland; Great Snoring, Norfolk; Guiseley, Yorkshire; Iffley, Oxfordshire; Market Deeping, Lincolnshire; Marlow, Buckinghamshire; Martock, Somerset; Shilbottle, Northumberland; Tottenham, London; Twyford, Buckinghamshire; West Dean, East Sussex. By this method of evaluation, these 19 are the best parsonages. They are certainly very good houses. Most again are early, and only one is Victorian, though certainly outstanding. Northumberland is the top county here, but that is because of its vicars' peles.

I must caution that neither of these can be a definitive list of the best parsonages, and my research shows that there are many good houses not recorded in any of the above sources. The listings alone make that clear: there are about 4,000 listed parsonages.[2]

I should add that the *County Guides* edited by Arthur Mee refer to a number of parsonages, though often very briefly. There is little consistency between these and those in *The Buildings of England*; Mee contains only a fraction of the number, but also mentions quite a few different ones: *The Buildings of England, Buckinghamshire* has only eight out of Mee's 16, *Hertfordshire* five out of Mee's nine, *Nottinghamshire* only two out of 15, *Somerset* only seven out of 22, *Gloucestershire* 11 out of 17, *Norfolk* ten out of 22, *Wiltshire* ten out of 23, *Yorkshire, West Riding*, only four out of 19; *Worcestershire*, however, has all five of Mee's five. Many of the parsonages in Mee are not noted primarily for architectural reasons but for their gardens and their other associations. Mee has a liking for early priest's houses and Georgian parsonages.[3]

Bad parsonages

The Buildings of England is sometimes critical of a parsonage, but that does not mean it is a bad house in the sense that a 1960s bungalow is a bad house. It is likely to be a house of character. Still, aspersions are rather fun. In Barnston, Cheshire, Christ Church is by G. E. Street, but the vicarage is by J. Francis Doyle, "a less happy design". In Birkenhead, a rectory rebuilt in Victorian times "in a Streetish parsonage manner", was part demolished in 1961: "the architect responsible for destroying this important example of Victorian decorative art was Felix Holt". At Aston Clinton, Buckinghamshire, the old rectory of 1850 is "by E. B. Lamb but quite harmless externally". In Cornwell, Oxfordshire, the vicarage of 1875 by Lewis Stride is "dull" (this adjective occurs a lot). In Countisbury, Devon, a house built by the Revd W. S. Halliday in about 1830 is "undistinguished neo-Tudor". The Old Rectory, Tarrant Gunville, Dorset, is "an extraordinarily bald and stolid block of c. 1798". The Gothic Church House at Wimborne Minster, Dorset, of 1905–06, is "spiritless". The Georgian rectory at Winston-on-Tees, Durham, is "very plain and rambling". The Old Rectory at Rodmarton, Gloucestershire, rebuilt 1872 by A. W. Maberley, is "drab rock-faced Tudor Gothic". The vicarage at Bitton, Gloucestershire, is "built in glaring red brick and clumsy concrete porch". The Old Rectory at Horsmonden, Kent, is "unbeautiful". In Denton, Lancashire, "everything is odd about the church" and the rectory of 1882 by J. Medland and Henry Taylor is "exactly as strange". The manor house at Clifton Hampden, Oxfordshire, built as the parsonage by G. G. Scott, is "undistinguished". The old vicarage of St Margaret's Church, Oxford, by H. G. W. Drinkwater, is "cumbersome". At Climping, Sussex, the parsonage of c. 1833 by W. F. Pocock has a "gimcrack stucco Gothick front". At Lower Shuckburgh, Warwickshire, the church, by Croft (one of Goodhart-Rendel's "rogues", see page 177), is "ugliness", "wildly improbable", the vicarage "evidently Croft also". The vicar called the Old Vicarage at South Cave, Yorkshire, 1845, to designs of William Denton of Hotham, "railway architecture". The St Clement Danes, Westminster, parish house by H. and P. Currey, 1897–98, is "niggardly".

Notes

[1] Simon Jenkins, *England's Thousand Best Houses* (Allen Lane, 2003).

[2] About 3,800 Grade II and close to 400 of exceptional significance (35 Grade I and over 330 Grade II*).

[3] Research by David Shacklock.

CHAPTER 9

The Architects

We know little about Georgian architects when compared with Victorian, and very much less still about Tudor and Jacobean ones. We might expect, therefore, that of those mysterious medieval architects we know virtually nothing. In fact, John Harvey, in his book *English Mediaeval Architects*, names no fewer than 1,300, of whom 20 are known to have had high status.[1] Many were associated with the exceptional buildings of those times, our great cathedrals, monastic buildings, castles, manors, and halls. They include John De Cranswick (born in 1311), who undertook repairs to the mansion of St Andrew's prebend for the minster authorities in Beverley; John Mason (mason), who may have done work at Vicar's Close, Chichester; Richard Horssale (mason), who contracted to build a church house, 60ft by 19ft, for £10, which still exists, though part rebuilt, in Sherston High Street, Wiltshire. Thomas Bele (fl. 1521–33) (mason) repaired Hockham Rectory for the Cluniac Priory of Thetford, which had impropriated it.

James Nedeham (carpenter) was ordered by Thomas Cromwell on 17 December 1534 to survey the parsonage at Bishops Hatfield, Hertfordshire.

Henry Yevele was a master, and developed the perpendicular style. In Westminster, the Abbot's House by Yevele is "one of the finest mediaeval houses left, and the only one of comparable interest anywhere near London".[2]Built in the 1370s, it has very fine window tracery.

How many of these men built simpler priests' or clergy houses? William Wynford (mason) is considered second only to Yevele, and he probably designed the important houses in Vicars' Close, Wells, built for the vicars attached to the cathedral.

Of Tudor builders there is limited knowledge, but in Elizabethan and Jacobean times a number emerge, though there was still no such thing as an architect; most of those to whom buildings have been attributed are surveyors or master masons who were eminent in their trade. They supervised the construction of their buildings as craftsmen rather than architects, though the distinction is to some extent academic, as many prepared detailed drawings of their proposed buildings.

Moving on to the seventeenth century, it would be nice to think that Inigo Jones designed parsonages, or even his great pupil John Webb, who produced designs for country houses, all of them too grand for parsonages. Amesbury Abbey was perhaps closest as being built on the site of an earlier priory, and one of the most intimate of his designs. Ashburnham House was owned by the Dean and Chapter of Westminster.

It would also be nice to have a parsonage by the great Sir Roger Pratt (1620–85), architect of the sadly demolished Coleshill House in Oxfordshire, that greatest of Restoration houses designed in the 1650s. At least his gates can be seen at the former rectory at Cheveley, Cambridgeshire.

We are now in William and Mary and Queen Anne territory. Francis Smith (1672–1738), with his brother William (1661–1724), was based in Warwick. Attributed to him are the fine rectories at Hampton Lucy, Kislingbury, and Lamport, Northamptonshire. From time to time we read tantalising reports of parsonages, or at least parts of them, being of the design of Wren, Vanbrugh, and Hawksmoor. Well, we know that Hawksmoor (c. 1661–1736) designed the rectory of 1726 at Christ Church, Spitalfields, and that also of the 1720s at St George-in-the-East, Tower Hamlets, and, it seems, also the one at St John Horsleydown in Bermondsey, of 1733–35. His rectory at St George, Bloomsbury, of 1726–28, was demolished, but the vestry, with its delightfully chunky pilasters, keystones, and architraves, and the sweeping curve of its main elevation, cleverly tucked into the small yard to the north, survives, as a tribute to him by Street. And one of Wren's masons, Christopher Kempster, is thought to have designed the fine Old Rectory at Burford.

Surely Colen Campbell, that grandly seminal figure of Palladianism, did not design any parsonages? It seems probably not, and Waverley Abbey, a villa of the Newby/Stourhead kind, near the abbey ruins, probably built around 1725 for John Aislabie, who was expelled from the Commons, is the nearest we can get. It was described by Bishop Pococke in 1754 as a fine Palladian house. William Kent did some work for Queen Caroline at Richmond Lodge after 1727, namely the hermitage of 1732 and Merlin's Cave of 1735, the former classical, but romantically ruined, the latter wildly Gothic. He also did the hermitage in the Elysian Fields at Stowe in the later 1730s, but no doubt mock hermitages are cheating.

We do know a number of eminent architects who were involved in the design of parsonages or worked on them during the long Georgian period. They include

Paine, Carr, Adam, the Wyatts, Dance, Soane, Nash, Smirke, Cockerell, and Burton. The first half of the eighteenth century brought a new spirit of research and enquiry about so many things, including architecture. Batty Langley (1696–1751), by trade a garden designer, arguably got the Gothic Revival really under way with his tome on *Gothic Architecture*, published 1742, and Isaac Ware (1704–66) was the pioneering author of *A Complete Body of Architecture* (1756–57). Their ideas would have their impact on the future shape of the parsonage.

James "Athenian" Stuart (1713–88) and Nicholas Revett (1720–1804) were founders of the Greek Revival style, which would also affect parsonage design, and published their influential studies of Athenian antiquities in 1762.

James Paine (1717–89), the noted Palladian, did the unexecuted design for the rectory at Kedleston in 1759. He designed the interesting St Anne's Parish Workhouse in Manette Street, Soho, London (1770–71), where a naughty churchwarden who was a carpenter suppressed tenders and appropriated materials for his own use. He worked on the medieval Old Deanery at York in around 1750. The rectory at Eyam, Derbyshire, of about 1768, for the Revd Thomas Seward, attributed to Paine, was demolished, though parts were incorporated in the new parsonage.

James Essex of Cambridge (1722–84), who studied under Sir James Burrough, was a remarkable architect and the first to take a detailed interest in true medieval Gothic. He knew more about early construction methods than anyone before Thomas Rickman and the much later revivalists of the early nineteenth century. His observations on King's College Chapel were made in the mid-eighteenth century. He did alterations to Cole's House, Milton, Cambridgeshire, for William Cole, rector and antiquary.

John Carr (1723–1807), son of Robert Carr, mason, who practised in York, was the principal architect of Yorkshire and the North in his day, developed Buxton and Harewood House, Yorkshire, and designed rectories at Aston, near Rotherham, Alderton, Suffolk, and possibly that at Bigby, Lincolnshire.

Robert Adam (1728–92) was born in Kirkcaldy. He was associated with the rectory at Kedleston Hall, Derbyshire; drawings suggest he did not design it but proposed improvements to the garden façade. He proposed the hipped roof without dormers, the large pediment, and the tall relieving arch round the central of the three bays of that elegant house. Fragments by Adam are incorporated at Donhead, Wiltshire. He may also have been involved with the interior plasterwork at Bradwell Lodge, Essex.

The new building at Bradwell Lodge, with its elegant classicism and fine belvedere, was added to the existing timber-framed house for the Revd Henry Bate by John Johnson (1732–1814), who was born in Leicester and worked in London.

In an era of limited mobility, there was always scope for talented architects to build up a practice known in their region of the country, and many of these were associated with parsonages. They included John Carr of York, Joseph Pickford of Derby, John Langwith of Grantham, and Joseph Rowe, who designed Kentisbury Rectory in 1779 and refronted Cornworthy Vicarage in 1784, both in Devon. William Sands Jr. was a Spalding architect active in the later eighteenth century. A little later came Jeptha Pacey, architect and builder of Boston, who worked on the assembly rooms, churches, and plans for rebuilding Wigtoft Vicarage in the 1810s and 1820s, Richard Pace, who did a number of parsonages in the Cotswolds and Oxfordshire, and Bryan Browning, again in Lincolnshire.

Joseph Pickford of Derby (1734–82) did a fine parsonage in the 1770s at Edensor, Derbyshire, Chatsworth Estate, sadly demolished in 1838 for "improvements".

Samuel Wyatt (1737–1807), son of Benjamin, builder and architect, of the great Wyatt dynasty, was engaged by Robert Adam. He worked on Kedleston Rectory, Derby, in 1771, moving it to a new site, as well as St Mary's Rectory, Holkham (1801–03), for the First Earl of Leicester, Wrotham Rectory, Kent, for the Revd George Moore (1801–02), and Lutterworth Rectory, Leicestershire, for the Hon. and Revd Henry Ryder (1803).

George Dance Jr (1741–1825) developed the Prebendal Manor of Finsbury, owned by St Paul's Cathedral, and did the plans for John Wesley's new dwelling houses there, as well as Wesley's own house in City Road, stock brick with scrollwork band between floors, good doorcase and fanlight (about 1780), now the Wesley Museum.

James Wyatt (1746–1813) was one of the most celebrated of all the classicists who also understood Gothic. He designed Bidborough Rectory, Kent (later called "Wyatts"), around 1790, and also Stoke Poges, Buckinghamshire, in a Gothic style. He was also apparently responsible for the former rectory at Hanworth, Hounslow, off Park Road, altered by Teulon.

John Carter (1748–1817) was another important figure in early Gothic Revival, doing the drawings for the *Builders Magazine*. He was a passionate but impractical character.

William Hayward (d. 1825), related to William Hayward of Shrewsbury (c. 1740–82), son of John Hayward, surveyor to Lincoln Cathedral, did work on the parsonages at Silk Willoughby and Metheringham, Lincolnshire.

Sir John Soane (1753–1837) joined Dance's office in 1768. He designed the elegant rectory at Saxlingham Nethergate, Norfolk, 1784, and did designs for alterations at others including Bemerton, Wiltshire, and Ringwould House, Kent, for the Revd John Monins (1813).

John Langwith (c. 1753–1825), son of the Grantham builder (c. 1723–95) of the same name, designed the vicarage at Grantham, and Barkston Rectory, Lincolnshire. His son Joseph (1787–1854) did parsonage alterations at North and South Stoke, Great Ponton, Haceby and Barkston in Lincolnshire, and Knipton, Leicestershire, in the 1820s.

John Nash (1752–1835) was apprenticed to Sir Robert Taylor and became one of the most influential of all English architects thanks to his association with the Prince Regent. The potency of his classical and Italianate stucco style bridged the Georgian and Victorian eras, but he was also a pioneer of the new Gothic. St Mildred's Rectory, Whippingham, Isle of Wight (1804), anticipates the High Gothic of Butterfield and Street, and even the Arts and Crafts, with its hipped gables and oriels. He planned the new clergy buildings north of St Martin in the Fields after the Royal Mews clearances in 1825.

Samuel Pepys Cockerell (c. 1754–1827), father of the better known C. R. Cockerell, did alterations to Broughton Rectory, Oxfordshire.

The late Georgian period I loosely call Regency was the twilight of the long classical era and the birth of the eclecticism that was to characterise architecture right through to the early twentieth century. The explosion of parsonage architects and builders happy with the Greek Revival, the Italianate, or the blossoming Tudor Gothic Revival included, in order of date of birth, Richard Pace (c. 1760), Bryan Browning (1773), Robert Lugar (c. 1773), H. E. Kendall (1776), W. H. Ashpitel (1776), Thomas Rickman (1776), George Moore (c. 1777), Sir Robert Smirke (1781), C. J. Carter (1784), Edward Blore (1787), C. R. Cockerell (1788), H. M. Wood (1789), Thomas Cundy (1790), Francis Goodwin (1784), Henry Harrison (c. 1785), John Dobson (1787), John Green (1787), Thomas Cubitt (1788), William Burn (1789), R. D. Chantrell (1793), R. H. Sharp (1793), William Patterson (c. 1793), Charles Dyer (1794), William Parsons (1796), Sydney Smirke (1798), A. W. Maberley (c. 1798), W. J. Donthorn (1799), Decimus Burton (1800), and William Railton (c. 1801).

The spirit of architectural enquiry and debate continued unabated and was flourishing by the late eighteenth century. Writers included James Malton (1761–1803), a pioneer of the *cottage orné*, who published two works on cottages and "rural retreats" and his amazing design for a small house. This, with its combination of classical and Gothic features, gable end, and porch, seemed to anticipate the Edwardian suburban semi, and must surely have been highly influential on parsonage design. The authoritative John Britton (1771–1857) was not an architect, but from 1807 for 20 years wrote with a mission to put architecture on the right course. Joseph Gandy (1771–1843) was a prolific designer, exhibiting his drawings from 1800 for almost 40 years. He might have been a good architect, but was hopelessly impractical and few of his designs were built. Robert Lugar (c. 1773–1855) was another writer, also an architect, who liked the *cottage orné* and the Gothic. He did the Italianate Yaxham Rectory, Norfolk, in 1820–22. John Buonarotti Papworth (1775–1847) was a prolific architect who designed Woolwich Rectory, Kent, in the early 1800s. He published his *Rural Residences* in 1818 and took the view that the design of the parsonage should reflect the character of the church. J. C. Loudon (1783–1843), primarily a landscape gardener (he helped transform London squares by replacing evergreen trees with planes and sycamores), produced his *Encyclopedia* in 1834, and did parsonage designs in extravagant pattern-book styles. Authorities differ about Loudon's importance: John Gloag found him "earnest and often boring" and said "his copy books assisted the general decline in taste". But he was one of the first to be concerned about "dishonest" features, for example the practice of adding dripmoulds for decoration where overhanging eaves now rendered them otiose, the sort of revulsion that Pugin shared, though he had no time for Loudon.

These writers were important not only for their theories and designs, but because for the first time they were less preoccupied with the grand mansions of the gentry and were beginning to focus their concerns on the concept of the smaller domestic house that was needed for the burgeoning population; here the parsonage would be a key template.

Richard Pace of Lechlade, Gloucestershire (c. 1760–1838), designed or altered a number of parsonages from the 1800s to the 1830s and his practice was continued by his son Richard. They included Coxwell and Shrivenham, Berkshire; Coln St Dennis, Lechlade, Oddington, Coberley, and Hatherop, Gloucestershire; Broughton and Broughton Poggs, Chinnor, and Shipton-under-Wychwood, Oxfordshire; and Little Hinton, Wiltshire.

Daniel Harris (c. 1761–1840), of Oxford, was an architect and builder as well as keeper of the County Gaol. He did parsonage rebuildings at Bampton (1799), Swyncombe (1803), and Stoke Talmage (1820), all in Oxfordshire.

Sir Jeffrey Wyatville (1766–1840) probably thought himself too grand for parsonages, but he did a design for a rectory at Kelmarsh, Northamptonshire (1815), three bays, with Doric porch, estimated to cost £4,915, a huge amount at that time. His Kempstone Lodge, Norfolk, looks exactly like a country parsonage but is in fact a farmhouse.

Of Henry Hakewill (1771–1830), who did Exning, Suffolk, and South Weald, Essex, Howard Colvin wrote: "His Tudor Gothic buildings are of little interest." John Plowman (c. 1773–1843) was an architect from Oxford. He won second prize for his design for the Ashmolean Museum, and worked on six or seven rectories.

Bryan Browning (1773–1856) was born in Thurlby, Lincolnshire. In 1817, he made designs for Ringwood Vicarage, Hampshire. From about 1820 to 1830, he was with George Woolcott in Doughty Street, London. He worked on parsonages at Stoke Dry, Rutland; Alwalton and Fletton, Cambridgeshire; and Greatford and Deeping St James, Lincolnshire. Charles Mountain (c. 1773–1839), the Greek Revivalist, designed Goodmanham, East Yorkshire.

Thomas Rickman (1776–1841) was an important figure. He was of a Quaker family, qualified as a doctor, became an insurance broker, but studied church architecture and began practice in 1818, working in Liverpool and then Birmingham. With his "minute observations",[3] he wrote the first detailed study of the Gothic styles of architecture and was the first fully to understand the evolution from Norman to Early English, to Decorated, to Perpendicular, as he called them, and as they have been known ever since, as early as 1811. He designed Soham Vicarage, Cambridgeshire, in 1833–4 and Great Oakley Rectory, Essex, in 1834–5.

W. H. Ashpitel (1776–1852), who specialised in maritime dock structures, did additions and alterations at Shenley Rectory, Hertfordshire.

William Bilby (1776–1848) was from Suffolk and designed or altered parsonages at Dallinghoo, Bredfield, Martlesham, and Boyton.

Thomas Hopper (1776–1856) declared: "It is an architect's business to understand all styles, and to be prejudiced in favour of none", which summed up current thinking—not a message to appeal to Pugin. Hopper apparently designed the Old Rectory at Little Leighs, Essex, for the Revd John Green. *The Buildings of England* describes it as Tudor Gothic. It looks to me like an earlier house remodelled, so if correct he was certainly competent.

H. E. Kendall (1776–1875), apprenticed to Thomas Leverton, did Tillington Rectory, Sussex, and Fishtoft Rectory, Lincolnshire.

James Trubshaw (1777–1853) was from a family of architects, and designed Walkeringham Vicarage, Nottinghamshire, 1825.

Sir Robert Smirke (1781–1867) was a pupil of Sir John Soane in 1796. He began his practice in 1806, and became very successful with his Greek Revivalism, going on to design the British Museum. He designed Offley Rectory, Hertfordshire, in 1810, and Markham Clinton Vicarage, Nottinghamshire, for the Duke of Newcastle.

Mark Thompson (1783–1852), born in Woodbridge, Suffolk, did a number of parsonages in East Anglia, including those at Lound, Boxford, Bures, Hartest, and probably Dedham, which *The Buildings of England* says he built in 1815 and Colvin says he rebuilt in 1825 (it was extended in 1841 and again later). Thompson's plain classical boxes post-dated his early Tudor Gothic work at Boxford, showing that there was no simple transition from classical to Gothic. His Gothic, as at Boxford, tended to be of the "Frankenstein" mould (see page 67).

Francis Goodwin (1784–1835) was born in King's Lynn, Norfolk, and designed Commissioners' churches, as well as the parsonage at Bilston, Staffordshire (about 1822).

C. J. Carter (1784–1851) lived in Louth, Lincolnshire. He designed Eastville church, school, and parsonage in 1839–40. He remodelled The Sycamores, Louth, for the Revd Augustus Hobart-Hampden, with shaped gables, "a kind of latter-day Artisan Mannerism"[4]. He designed parsonages for Louth, Gayton-le-Marsh, Burgh-upon-Bain, and Little Carlton, Lincolnshire, and Milton Ernest, Bedfordshire, in the 1830s and 1840s.

Henry Harrison (c. 1785–c. 1865), son of John Harrison, London builder, did quite a few parsonages, including Barming, Kent; Bexhill, Sussex; Bletchley, Buckinghamshire; Feltwell, Norfolk; Great Hampden, Buckinghamshire; Oakham, Rutland; Steeple Ashton, Wiltshire; Ware, Hertfordshire; Wisbech, Cambridgeshire; and Hadleigh Deanery, Suffolk (1831), perhaps his best work, with the help of William Whewell's designs, though Colvin calls it "poorly detailed"!

We are now getting to the architects of a period when a certain competence in revived Tudor Gothic was considered more or less essential, though classical expertise was still demanded. John Dobson (1787–1865) studied under John Varley and became friendly with Smirke. He is noted for his practice in Newcastle. He did alterations and additions at a number of parsonages, including Stamfordham and, in 1828, the vicar's pele at Embleton, Northumberland.

Edward Blore (1787–1879) was surveyor to Westminster Abbey and an antiquarian. He designed the offices of Queen Anne's Bounty in Dean's Yard, Westminster, in a dutiful and studiously observed Tudor Gothic with simple mullioned and transomed windows, canted bay and oriel, brick with stone dressings. He was also responsible for the major residential wing of Lambeth Palace. He designed the immensely complex Thicket Priory, Thorganby, Yorkshire, and the picturesque rectory at Great Brington, Northamptonshire. He was unfairly scorned by Pugin, since he and Rickman were probably the first two architects since James Essex with deep knowledge of medieval architectural detail.

Christopher Cockerell (1788–1863) trained under his father S. P. Cockerell (see earlier), a pupil of the great Sir Robert Taylor, and became assistant to Robert Smirke. He designed some very fine buildings and championed Neo-classicism rather than Gothic or even Greek Revival. Goodhart-Rendel wrote that there had never been a more accomplished English architect, but he was unfashionable and Pugin described his Ashmolean Museum as "another unsightly pile of Pagan details". Even so, he designed a parsonage in Tudor style for his brother, the Revd Henry Cockerell, at North Weald Basset, Essex, at a cost of £2,060 in 1827; Enstone Vicarage, Oxfordshire, and Sackford Almshouses, Woodbridge, both also Tudor; and Caversfield House, Oxfordshire, for the Revd R. B. Marsham (1842). This was a classical house, of five bays with pedimented gable on a deep cornice, and projecting two-floor central bay, rather severe.

Thomas Cubitt (1788–1855) developed huge areas of Central London in the period of building growth between the Battle of Waterloo and the Great Exhibition, putting it on the international map. He built the vicarage for Christ Church and St John near Island Gardens on the Isle of Dogs, London, and the Revd James Hammond's house in Belgrave Place, now Buckingham Palace Road, about 1845; but H. E. Kendall Jr designed the house, in the style Cubitt favoured, all three floors and basement stuccoed, prominent long and short corner quoins, with balconies and round-headed windows in Italianate manner, grouped in threes with thick masonry mullions. Cubitt was a pioneer of big subcontracted building projects, and did construction work for architects. His son Lewis Cubitt trained under Kendall and designed many of his houses. The Prince Regent and Cubitt may have designed the Italianate Osborne House together; Cubitt would not build Gothic.

William Burn (1789–1870), son of architect Robert Burn, trained under Robert Smirke. He could do anything from Greek Revival to Scottish Baronial, Italianate to Tudor Gothic. He is widely admired for his country houses, and designed the impressive deanery at Lincoln (subsequently the cathedral school), advanced for its time.

H. M. Wood (1789–1867) was based in Nottingham from around 1810. He did parsonages at Sawley, Derbyshire, and Clifton, Colston Bassett, and Radcliffe-on-Trent, Nottinghamshire.

Fuller Coker (fl. 1820–45) was an architect and builder at Shipdham, Norfolk, from about 1820 to 1845. He did designs for parsonages at Cranwich, Cranworth, Harpley, Ryburgh, and South Raynham.

Matthew Habershon (1789–1852) practised in Bloomsbury. He studied Gothic architecture but was also happy in the classical style, in which he did a new wing at Thorpe Achurch, Northants. His parsonages included that at Aston Sandford, Buckinghamshire. In his pioneering book *The Ancient Half-Timbered Houses of England*, 1836, he attacked Pugin.

Thomas Cundy (1790–1867) worked for his father who did the classical Wassand Hall at Seaton, East Yorkshire, for the Revd Charles Constable. He did the group of buildings with parsonage at St Barnabas, Pimlico, London.

Charles Fowler (1792–1867), born in Cullompton, Devon, became renowned for his Covent Garden Market but did parsonages such as the Archdeaconry of Cornwall in Exeter, in Tudor Gothic with a strong medieval feel, and, much later, the more Puginian vicarage at Bovey Tracey, Devon.

R. D. Chantrell (1793–1872) was a classically trained pupil of Sir John Soane who designed Commissioners' churches and Bramley and Kirkstall parsonages near Leeds.

William Patterson (c. 1793–1875) of Nottingham did parsonages at Averham (1838), and Stapleford (1876).

Sydney Smirke (1798–1877), best known for the British Museum Reading Room, was the classically trained younger brother of Robert. He did the parsonage at Halsall, and probably also that at Bickerstaffe, North Lancashire, in the 1840s.

Anthony Salvin (1799–1881) worked for John Nash and began his own practice in 1828. He was prolific and designed more than twenty parsonages. His style has been called "Manorial Gothic". His vicarage at Northallerton, Yorkshire, was castellated Tudor, but he was versatile. His rectory at Denton, Lincolnshire, was in Italian style.

William Donthorn (1799–1859) was born in Swaffham, Norfolk. He was a pupil of Jeffry Wyatt (later Wyatville) from 1817 to 1820, and designed country houses, workhouses, and many rectories, mainly in Norfolk and Sussex. His two totally different styles were a very austere and almost featureless Greek Revival and a Wyatville Tudor Gothic.

Charles Parker (1799–1881) published *Villa Rustica* in which he tackled the challenge of the early Victorian Italianate style for smaller houses.

Decimus Burton (1800–81) trained under his father, the builder James Burton, who developed much of Bloomsbury, London, and George Maddox. He has several parsonages, including the rectory at Sevenoaks (1831), that at Great Brickhill, Buckinghamshire (1834), alterations at Stapleton House, near Bristol, for the Bishop of Gloucester (1841), a house for the Revd J. Linton at Hemingford

Abbots, Huntingdonshire (1842), the rectory at Calstock, Cornwall (1853), and alterations to the vicarage at Isleworth (1865).

Peter Thompson (c. 1800–74), designer of Sutton Rectory, Norfolk, was described as "ingenious but dubious" by Colvin. He entered the competition for the new Houses of Parliament and was an antiquarian forger.

William Railton (c. 1801–77), pupil of William Inwood, was dull but designed one of the world's most famous monuments—Nelson's Column. He was architect to the Ecclesiastical Commissioners from 1838 to 1848 and practised in either a basic Gothic or Italianate style disapproved of by *The Ecclesiologist*. His Italianate was little more (or less) than his Gothic stripped of its dripmoulds and Gothic dressings, favoured by the Commissioners because without the frilly bits it was cheaper. His many parsonage designs include those for St Barnabas, Bristol, and Upleadon nearby. Although he is considered no more than competent, his influence as one of the Commissioners' triumvirate that included Christian and Ferrey, discussed below, was great for a time.

Joseph Paxton (1803–65) is famous for his advanced glass buildings, but he was competent in several conventional styles. He did alterations to the parsonage at Mothel in Ireland for his daughter Blanche in 1854.

Henry Roberts (1803–76), a pupil of Fowler and Smirke, was a pioneer of workers' housing. He was also responsible for parsonages, for example at Norbiton, Surrey, and Brampton, Cambridgeshire, in the mid-nineteenth century. As a Nonconformist, he was happier with the classical style.

Thomas Allom (1804–72) designed the rectory at Booton, Norfolk, in his Tudor Gothic style.

E. B. Lamb (1805–69), dubbed a "rogue" by Goodhart-Rendel (see page 177), was in the Tudor Gothic tradition but original, as at Copdock, Suffolk (1858). *The Ecclesiologist* called him "inartistic" and "presumptuous",[5] but in some ways his free style put him ahead of his time.

John Johnson (1807–88), best known for his work at Alexandra Palace, designed the High Gothic St Matthew's vicarage at Oakley Square, Camden, London.

T. H. Wyatt (1807–80), a later member of the Wyatt dynasty, was prolific and competent, designing more than 23 parsonages, specialising in Tudor and Jacobean Revival styles but influenced by Pugin. He designed a number in Wiltshire and Dorset. Those at Alderbury, Wiltshire, and Weston Patrick, Hampshire, are good examples (see Figure 8 on page 168).

Arthur Ashpitel, son of W. H. (1807–69), who became a writer, did some East London churches including St Barnabas, Homerton High Street, Hackney, and the vicarage.

Figure 8: The Rectory, Weston Patrick, Hampshire

The architects we have just been looking at were all born in the late eighteenth century and the very early years of the nineteenth century. Many architects we think of as Victorian were, of course, born in the Regency period, and that is important for our understanding of the development of early Victorian architecture and the Gothic Revival. We must now turn to the architects who thought mostly in Gothic from the start, and were the most influential on the development of the mature Gothic style. The relative chronology of the Gothic architects is helpful in getting them in context. Scott was born in 1811, Pugin in 1812, as were Teulon and Carpenter, Butterfield in 1814. Others were Woodyer (1816), Pearson (1817), Devey (1820), Brodrick (1822), Street (1824), White (1825), Brooks (1825), Burges, Bodley, and Seddon (1827), and Waterhouse (1830). The earliest of these architects are thus in fact as close or closer in date to Sydney Smirke (1798), Donthorn (1799), and Decimus Burton (1800)—all classicists—than they are to the later ones, and this gives a clue to the rapidity of the process of change from Classical to Tudor Gothic, to High Gothic Revival, that was taking place.

George Gilbert Scott (1811–78) grew up in an intensely clerical family; his father was perpetual curate of Gawcott, Buckinghamshire, and several of his brothers were clergymen. Articled to James Edmeston, London, he worked with W. B. Moffatt (1812–87) and practised with his son J. O. Scott. He became Sir Gilbert in 1872, due to his work for the Crown. He had nearly 1,000 commissions and designed more than 30 parsonages. His first parsonage was at Wappenham,

Northamptonshire, in 1833, very unpretentious, but he rapidly blossomed. There is no space here to do justice to all his parsonages, but that at Leafield, Oxfordshire, is typical. Several are described in Chapter 7. They were usually highly competent.

S. W. Daukes (1811–80) practised in Gloucester and Cheltenham. In 1846, he designed the old vicarage at Tewkesbury, where the "scraping and scouring" of the abbey by Sir Gilbert Scott had partly prompted William Morris to found SPAB. His Tudor Gothic could be convincing, as for example at Toft, Cambridgeshire, and he did alterations and additions, for example at Coln Rogers, Gloucestershire.

A. W. N. Pugin (1812–52), son of A. C. Pugin (1762–1832), began his practice about 1833. Although he was so influential, he only designed two Anglican parsonages, both in the 1840s, after his two celebrated houses for himself at Alderbury, Wiltshire (St Marie's Grange), and The Grange, Ramsgate. These are the former rectory at Rampisham, Dorset, now called Pugin Hall, and one at Lanteglos, Cornwall. As a Catholic he designed more presbyteries, the first at Derby in 1837, others at Birmingham, Nottingham, Uttoxeter and Brewood in Staffordshire, and Fulham and Woolwich in London.

We talk of Pugin as the great pioneer of the Gothic Revival, but we have seen that Teulon and Carpenter were of the same age, and the hugely prolific Ewan Christian was born only two years later in 1814. A number of those born earlier, for example Scott, born in 1811, and going back in time E. B. Lamb (1805), Railton (c. 1801), Salvin (1799), Cundy (1790), Burn (1789), and Blore (1787), were all primarily Gothicists. James Essex was doing competent Gothic work far earlier still. Lamb's mannered style (see earlier) may have been described by *The Ecclesiologist* as "uncouth and grotesque"[6] (his was also the rectory at Aston Clinton, Buckinghamshire), but Salvin and Scott were very well regarded and Burn, who bridged the Georgian and Victorian, was held in great esteem. Christian, born only two years later, if a plodder, was an important plodder. In that light, Pugin cannot be seen in simple terms as the pioneer of Neo-Gothic. He was scholarly and idiosyncratic, but then so had Essex, Blore, and Rickman been. However, he had an innovative genius and his writings were very influential.

Scott, Butterfield, and Street must be regarded as the three core Church of England High Gothic Revivalists, in general rather than parsonage terms. We tend to be rather sniffy about Scott, perhaps because of his disregard for ancient fabric, but he was prolific and enormously successful. Butterfield and Street symbolise the High Gothic to many, though they also paved the way to the Domestic Revival.

Teulon, Carpenter, Pearson, White, and Bodley give those three stiff competition. Teulon (1812–73), whose practice began about 1840, is the most controversial of these. His style was idiosyncratic, an "acrobatic Gothic" as Mark

Girouard has it,[7] with a French influence, in my view always interesting. Our image of Victorian High Gothic is one of turrets, towers, and spirelets. In fact, houses of this much criticised yet magical and archetypal kind are quite rare. They are more often the creations of the inventiveness of Teulon or Wilkinson than the comparative solemnity of Pugin, Scott, Butterfield, and Street. Yet Teulon could also often be perfectly conventional, if complex in his detailing, and he was fundamentally Tudor Gothic, as at Harrington or Welton-le-Wold, Lincolnshire. The vicarages at North Creake, Norfolk, and St Andrew, Holborn, are typically picturesque, the latter with the rounded French forms he liked.

R. C. Carpenter (1812–55), like Butterfield, was firmly associated with the Cambridge Camden Society and epitomised the High Church. There is something monumental about his great stone double-ranged wedges, like his fine house at Brasted, Kent. His Monkton Wyld, Dorset, is also typical with its parallel ranges and towering blank gable end, the front door in the smaller subsidiary gable; Kilndown, Kent, again has twin gabled ranges, the front door even more oddly placed. He is more orthodox than Teulon, but like him he has the capacity to surprise.

William Butterfield (1814–1900) also worked for the Ecclesiologists. He had his own practice by 1844. Although known for High Gothic, with pointed arches, steep roofs, gables, and patterned brick, he could also be quite simple in more vernacular mode, his half-hipped roofs looking ahead to the Arts and Crafts movement. At the same time he was a traditionalist, often favouring stone for church and parsonage, brick for humbler dwellings. His groups of church, parsonage, and school include Cowick, Hensall, and Pollington, Yorkshire. His early parsonage at Coalpit Heath, Bristol, 1844, is important and very progressive, being 15 years before Webb's Red House, which developed its manner. His Alvechurch, Worcs, is quite different but also considered progressive, and the brick banding of his All Saints, Margaret Street, London, particularly well known, is one of his trademarks. Pevsner liked his Sheen, Staffordshire, and his Great Woolstone, Buckinghamshire (1851), with its inventive massing, clever gables, modern bay window, and rich brickwork, which again anticipates Webb and later Arts and Crafts styles.

Benjamin Ferrey (1810–80), from the office of William Wilkins, the celebrated architect of the National Gallery, became Diocesan Surveyor for Bath and Wells, starting as a Tudor Gothicist but becoming closer to Pugin. His influence on parsonages was important and extended beyond his diocese because he did work for the Commissioners as well, after Railton had fallen from favour. He designed about 30 parsonages. His rectory at Wavendon, Buckinghamshire, is typical.

Ewan Christian (1814–95), articled to Habershon, first worked in the office of Railton, then John Brown, beginning in the late 1830s, and is no doubt best known for his late and uncharacteristic National Portrait Gallery. But it was as consultant to the Commissioners that he became highly influential over parsonage design. Influenced by Pugin, competent rather than inspired, he was nevertheless better than Railton and perhaps as good as Ferrey, and is underrated. He designed a staggering number of parsonages, about 380, enough for a book by themselves.

J. P. St Aubyn (1815–95) was a pupil of Thomas Fulljames of Gloucester, and is held in suspicion of church "over-restoration". His parsonages include those at Stoke Canon, Devon, and Horsley and Siddington, Gloucestershire.

Significant regional parsonage architects in Lincolnshire, one of the best counties for parsonages, included Edward Browning (1816–82), son of Bryan, whose brother was a vicar in Stamford, and he designed St George's Rectory. He remodelled the rectory at Creeton in 1851, in a competent High Gothic manner.

Henry Woodyer (1816–96) was for a time a pupil of Butterfield. His individual style of Gothic was generally liked and approved for parsonages by *The Ecclesiologist*, as was specifically his rectory at Marchwood, Hampshire, a good example of his work. Another fine parsonage of his is that at Highnam, Glos. There is also a good one at Caldicot, Monmouthshire, and another in Shanklin, Isle of Wight, and his contribution to the development of the Gothic style was considerable.

John Loughborough Pearson (1817–98), who began his practice in 1843, was another outstanding ecclesiastical architect. His best work covers a long period from the 1850s to the 1880s. Anthony Quiney considers All Saints' Vicarage, Hove, of 1882–3, "the best of Pearson's red brick gothic houses for the clergy".[8] His houses were often of brick with stone dressings, favouring half-timbered sections, windows with trefoils, and plate tracery in the Early English style. But he could range from the simple (Braintree, Essex, 1855) to the complicated (Ayot St Peter, Hertfordshire, where only the arched entrance is ecclesiastical, though of 1866), to the advanced: Whitwell, Derbyshire (1885), anticipates Voysey, though rather a hotch-potch with Edwardian-style bays vying with early mullions. Freeland, Oxfordshire, of the 1860s, with its complex roofline, Crowton, Cheshire (1871), and Clifton, York (1870s), were also looking towards vernacular revival.

Joseph Clarke (1819–88) did the complex at St Barnabas, Soho, with its French Gothic-style chapel.

Edward Andrews did the very unusual Tudor rectory at Compton Martin, Somerset, in 1841.

John Ruskin (1819–1900), though not an architect, was a hugely influential figure, a powerful adherent of the Gothic style who influenced Butterfield and many others. He differed from many, including Pugin, in disliking modern English and "Northern" Gothic, rating the continental and Venetian, and advocated polychromy. He detested the rationalism of classicism, which he saw as inhuman. He saw architecture as a total experience, hardly seeing it in pure architectural terms, and liked the effect of weather on stone. His study at Brantwood, his house near Coniston, was just like that of an educated country parson.

William Wilkinson (1819–1901), the Oxford architect of the Randolph Hotel and the presbytery of St Aloysius, Woodstock Road, Oxford (RC), was an archetypal High Gothicist of country and town houses and parsonages, the latter including those at Godington, Ramsden, and Upper Heyford, Oxfordshire, and Swanbourne, Buckinghamshire.

Sir Matthew (Digby) Wyatt (1820–77), another of that dynasty, designed Aldingham Hall, Lancashire, for the Revd John Stonard in the 1840s, Gothic with a tower.

George Devey (1820–86), whose practice began about 1840, was an individualist who did a number of country houses, many now demolished. He designed the former vicarage at Chearsley, Buckinghamshire, for the Revd William Gilbert in the late 1860s, and Wickwar Parsonage, Gloucestershire, in around 1870.

Cuthbert Brodrick (1822–1905) studied under Henry Lockwood. His fine buildings include Leeds Town Hall, and his parsonages included the vicarage, later manor, at Paull, and the former vicarage at Thorpe Bassett (both 1857), both rather ordinary brick late Georgian-style houses, less interesting than his major works. He liked to work on a grand scale.

G. E. Street (1824–81), an architect of major importance, was born in Woodford, articled to Owen Carter of Winchester in 1841, and went to Scott and Moffatt in 1844, setting up his own practice in 1848. He made a spectacular start with the medieval Gothic of his parsonage at Wantage, Berkshire, and became architect to Oxford Diocese before going to London. His Boyn Hill, Maidenhead, of the 1850s, typified his patterned brick Venetian influence. In the later 1850s, he became more austere, as for example at New Bradwell, Buckinghamshire, with its simple segmental sash windows, like Webb. Then in the 1860s, ecclesiological Gothic took hold and meant more polychromy and stone dressings, and from the 1870s came some remarkable parsonages in Yorkshire, including those at Wansford, Thixendale, East Heslerton, and Helperthorpe, some in more vernacular manner, for Sir Tatton Sykes. Street's office was the most influential breeding ground of all for important later architects.

Richard Reynolds Rowe (1824–99) was the successful Cambridge architect who did a good job on the rectory at Kings Stanley, Gloucestershire, in 1858.

William White (1825–1900) was another architect of major influence who worked for Scott before starting his practice around 1847. He was a leading exponent of Butterfield's "parsonage style" and produced a number of subtle parsonages, including Stow-cum-Quy, Cambridgeshire; St Ive and St Agnes, Cornwall; Beaminster, Dorset; Little Baddow, Essex; Heydour, Lincolnshire; and Milcombe, Oxfordshire. His domestic manner is attractive, assured and inventive, and despite his liking for polychromy his houses could be quite vernacular, in "cottage" style, with his favoured broad, rather than vertical, windows. His early work had been more Gothic and fanciful, as at St Columb Major, Cornwall.

James Brooks (1825–1901) began his practice in 1852. A good solid Gothicist, he did many churches and parsonages in North and East London, including several in Shoreditch. His own Arts and Crafts-influenced house of 1861–2 is in Stoke Newington.

J. P. Seddon (1827–1906) was articled in 1847 to Thomas Leverton, and Voysey was a pupil. He practised with John Pritchard from 1852 to 1862, producing many churches and well over 20 parsonages, many in the West of England and Wales. Highly competent, he developed a range of Gothic forms, and increasingly turned his attention to furniture, metalwork, tiles, and stained glass.

G. F. Bodley (1827–1907) was a pupil of Scott from 1845–50 for his training in ecclesiastical buildings and parsonages. He designed both the church and the parsonage at St Martin's, Scarborough, the latter in Norman Shaw Queen Anne, to which he graduated after his assured and new interpretations of Gothic.

F. R. Wilson did work on Peel House, the pele tower at Shilbottle, Northumberland, in 1863.

William Burges (1827–81) studied under Blore. His was the late wave of true Gothic and his inventive parsonages included Bewholme, East Yorkshire, with French-style gabled dormers (1859), the rectory at Apsley Guise, Bedfordshire (1864), and the vicarage at Chevithorne, Devon, in the 1870s for Sir J. Heathcote-Amery, with its flat grid of mullions and transoms. He called the Georgian era "the dark ages of art" and even his private houses could have been vicarages in their medieval manner—Tower House, Melbury Road, Holland Park, London, for example.

James Fowler (1828–92), articled in Lichfield, but of Louth, was an admired Lincolnshire architect of churches and parsonages. He did the rectory at Amcotts, Utterby, and that of St Matthew, Skegness.

Also of Lincolnshire, Charles Kirk, who, with his son Charles, seems to have built everything in Sleaford, was also obviously very competent, as his parsonages at Ingoldsby and Swaton amply demonstrate.

John Hayward was a skilled Devon architect who was largely a Gothicist, but his vicarage at Halberton (1847) is Italianate.

John Hicks was the architect who designed the rectory at Hawkchurch, Devon, to whom Thomas Hardy was apprenticed in the mid-nineteenth century.

Sir Arthur Blomfield (1829–99), son of the Bishop of London, articled to Philip Hardwick, began his practice in 1856, his competence shown by his Netherlandish vicarage of St Mark's, North Audley Street, London.

Alfred Waterhouse (1830–1905), unlike the other great Victorian architects, did only a few parsonages, which makes his Minister's House in Binney Street, Mayfair, all the more interesting.

John Douglas (1830–1911) designed some of Chester's best-loved buildings, and several parsonages in Cheshire and neighbouring counties. He liked half-timbering and vernacular features.

The middle and late years of the Victorian period gave rise to a remarkable new style: the Arts and Crafts, more a movement than a style and more appropriately called the Domestic or Vernacular Revival as applied to houses. It grew from long gestation in High Gothic, where tantalising hints can already be seen, and some of the architects we have discussed were the real pioneers. Philip Webb and Richard Norman Shaw, both born in 1831, were the key early practitioners of the full style. William Morris, founder of SPAB and visionary promoter of English crafts, born 1834, was also a great influence on this new architectural philosophy, though he never designed a building. A number of these architects designed or worked on parsonages, and their birth chronology is helpful: T. G. Jackson (1835), J. D. Sedding (1838), J. F. Bentley (1839), Basil Champneys (1842), E. S. Prior (1852), Temple Moore and Ernest Newton (1856), W. D. Caröe (1857), Edgar Wood (1860), W. H. (Walter) Brierley (1862), Sir John Ninian Comper (1864), M. H. Baillie Scott (1865), Detmar Blow (1867), Edwin Lutyens (1869), and Morley Horder (1870).

Philip Webb's Red House for Morris at Bexleyheath, Kent, is considered groundbreaking as the first flowering of the Domestic Revival. He also designed The Vicar's House, Brampton, Cumbria, in 1877, a red sandstone house based on a farmhouse, projecting wings on the entrance front, but simple at the back. He pioneered this "stripped", less ornamented style, Gothicism without Gothic detailing, influenced by and developed from Butterfield, whose parsonages he studied, Street (he had been Street's assistant), and White. Importantly, while firmly based on the earlier "parsonage style" of those architects, his manner could even more naturally be used for any house. Webb abandoned Gothic windows and mouldings, and hastened the return to the sliding sash window.

More parsonages through the ages

35: Early medieval—Iffley, Oxfordshire

36: Iffley interior

37: Medieval—Sleaford, Lincolnshire

38: Later medieval—Hoxne, Suffolk

39: A contrast in styles—Northiam, Sussex, Tudor east wing

40: A contrast in styles—Northiam, Sussex, eighteenth-century west wing

41: Dryden's house—Aldwincle, Northamptonshire

42: All Saints, Stamford, Lincolnshire

43: Restoration—Grantchester, Cambridgeshire

44: Restoration—Southwell, Nottinghamshire

45: Georgian—Bampton, Oxfordshire

46: Georgian—Bampton, contrasting rear elevation

47: Regency—Dedham, Essex

48: Early Victorian—Exbourne, Devon

49: Late Victorian—St Michael and All Angels, Bedford Park, London

50: Edwardian—St Peter, Ealing, London

Norman Shaw (1831–1912), articled to William Burn, assistant to Salvin and Street, partner of W. E. Nesfield from 1862 to 1868, though of the new philosophy, did not much like traditional sash windows in his parsonages (though Holy Trinity, Bingley, Yorkshire, had them), thinking them inflexible, as they dictated a vertical rectangular window shape which did not particularly suit the vernacular style. At Bingley, he used local stone and also designed the church and school buildings. He designed the outstanding St Agnes vicarage and church hall in Liverpool (1886–87), and for Harrow Mission, Latimer Road, London W11, he did a new mission room, church, clergy house, and club room in 1895–7. His Bishop's House, 5 Kennington Park Place, London SE11, was a new house and chapel for the Ecclesiastical Commissioners, and he rebuilt the rectory at Low Bentham, Yorkshire, in stone, typical Domestic Revival style, in 1884–85. He also did alterations at the fine house at Gawsworth, Cheshire.

E. W. Pugin (1834–75), the awkward son of A. W. N. Pugin, continued his practice after 1852 and, like his father, designed Catholic buildings. His two churches, All Saints and St Ann at Stretford, Lancashire, both have linked presbyteries.

T. G. Jackson (1835–1924) was articled to Scott in 1858. His first work was the former rectory at Send, Surrey, in 1861, good mature Gothic, and he is known for his scholarly and contextual interpretations of Tudor and Jacobean styles in Oxford.

J. D. Sedding (1838–91) was articled to Street, practised with his brother, and designed most interesting houses, including the parsonage for All Saints, Plymouth, in a progressive style.

J. F. Bentley (1839–1902) was a pupil of Henry Clutton and, of course, the architect of Westminster Cathedral. He also designed the interesting presbytery there, and another good one nearby at 43 Palace Street.

John Oldrid Scott (1841–1913), second son of Sir Gilbert, designed the "stripped Gothic" clergy house of St Matthew, Great Peter Street, Pimlico, London.

Basil Champneys (1842–1935) was a late exponent of Gothic who also had a picturesque brand of Queen Anne Revival. He designed the satisfying vicarages for St Bride, Fleet Street, and St Luke, Hampstead.

C. C. (Clapton Crabb, since you ask) Rolfe (1845–1907), a nephew of William Wilkinson, and son of a clergyman, was—like Wilkinson—a highly competent Oxford architect who designed the former parsonage at St Thomas, Oxford, in Arts and Crafts style.

Charles Bell (1846–99), was a Lincolnshire architect who specialised in Wesleyan chapels (see Epworth, Lincolnshire, in Chapter 7).

E. S. Prior (1852–1932), one of the most brilliant of the Arts and Crafts practitioners, designed the parsonage at All Saints, Westbrook, Margate.

E. J. May (1853–1941), disciple of Shaw, designed the parsonage at the influential Bedford Park estate, West London.

Temple Moore (1856–1920) was articled to George Gilbert Scott Jr in 1875. Rather underrated, he did major alterations to the seventeenth- and early nineteenth-century former rectory at Walkington, East Riding, and designed "Holmwood" at Redditch, Worcestershire, for the Revd Horace Newton, Cotswold Jacobean with mullioned windows; also a rectory at Roos, East Riding (1892–3), Queen Anne with hooded canopy, and a vicarage at Helmsley, North Yorks, for the Revd C. N. Gray (1898), among others.

Waller and Son were active around 1900 in Gloucestershire, restoring churches and building vicarages, with complex roof shapes, as at Newnham-on-Severn, and making alterations, as at Duntisbourne Rouse (1880).

Ernest Newton (1856–1922) was articled to Norman Shaw in 1873 and founder of the Art Workers' Guild in Bloomsbury. His parsonages include St Barnabas Vicarage, Beckenham (1888); Bollington, Cheshire (1898); and St Nicholas Rectory, Stevenage, Hertfordshire (1919).

Sir Reginald Blomfield (1856–1942), son of the Revd G. J. Blomfield, was skilful at restoration work, and could create a convincing Jacobean staircase for a Jacobean house, as at Apethorpe, Northants, even if SPAB might not approve. He did Newstead Vicarage, Lincolnshire, in 1919. Sir Arthur Blomfield was his uncle, and his grandfather was Bishop of London.

W. D. Caröe (1857–1938) joined Pearson's office in 1881. Son of the Danish consul in Liverpool, he became an architect to the Commissioners when Pearson's brother-in-law, Ewan Christian, was chief architect, then became chief architect himself. His buildings, in his Arts and Crafts style, apart from the remarkable Swedish Seamen's Church in Liverpool, and the magnificently detailed 1 Millbank, London, until recently the headquarters of the Church Commissioners, included vicarages at Walthamstow and Stamford Hill, London.

Edgar Wood (1860–1935), articled in Manchester, began his practice in 1885 and with J. Henry Sellers did some very progressive work with concrete and flat roofs. He wore a black cloak and carried a silver-handled cane. He retired early to live in Italy and paint. Both a traditionalist and fascinated by Art Nouveau, he produced remarkably modern forms, such as the amazing "Upmeads" at Stafford, unfortunately not a parsonage. He did St Saviour's Vicarage, Thurlstone, Yorkshire, in 1906. His work reveals the importance of Arts and Crafts and Art Nouveau to the infant modernist movement.

Walter Brierley (1862–1926) was articled to his father in York and in 1885 joined James Demaine there. He designed vicarages at Huntington and Sancton, Yorkshire. His versatility embraced Neo-Classical and Gothic as well as Arts and Crafts, and he was meticulous in his detailing, believing small elements of a composition vital, and insisted on good materials and workmanship. He wanted a revival of craftsmanship. He favoured tile-hanging and Shaw's signature arched window transom motif, supposedly from Sparrowe's House, Ipswich.

M. H. Baillie Scott (1865–1945) designed White Lodge, Wantage, Berkshire, for the chaplain of St Mary's Convent (1899), gabled, roughcast, small windows, generally Voyseyan, its sparse absence of eaves creating a sculptural shape that anticipated the continental work of the great Adolf Loos.

If Wood heralds the dawn of modernism, so do Parker and Unwin, the socialist architects of Hampstead Garden Suburb. Barry Parker (1867–1941) was concerned in his reconstruction of Thornthwaite Old Vicarage, Cumberland, with preserving its charm while avoiding "imitation old". Raymond Unwin (1863–1940) is inextricably linked with Parker. Unwin was a socialist who still strongly believed in links with the past, reflected in their Arts and Crafts designs, influenced by the theories of Ruskin and Morris about unified design.

Detmar Blow (1867–1939) was heavily influenced by Webb. He made alterations to the Old Rectory at Buckland, Gloucestershire.

S. D. Adshead (1868–1946) did St Anselm, Kennington, South London, in his traditional Neo-Georgian style.

Sir Edwin Lutyens (1869–1944) designed a number of famous houses, and the two parsonages at the highly regarded Hampstead Garden Suburb in the first decade of the twentieth century before he turned to classicism after about 1912.

Morley Horder (1870–1944) designed the noted vicarage for St Peter in Ealing.

C. H. Reilly (1874–1948) was an influential traditionalist who worked for John Belcher. He did the rectory and vestry at St Michael, Cornhill, City of London.

Sir Edward Maufe (1883–1974), one of the three modern cathedral architects, purveyed a Swedish-influenced, simplified Gothic in his churches and a simple modernism in his parsonage at St Alphege, Edmonton, London.

H. S. Goodhart-Rendel (1887–1959) has been described as an architect of "rational eclecticism", capable of Neo-Georgian, Victorian Revival, and modern styles. He called others "rogue architects" and was a bit of a rogue himself;[9] he apparently worked on the unusual clergy house at St Mary's, Bourne Street, Belgravia.

Taylor and Young were responsible for the interesting V-shaped rectory at Prestwich, Manchester (1923).

We are now into the post-war period. Sir Basil Spence and Sir Frederick Gibberd, with Maufe and Giles Gilbert Scott, were the four modern cathedral designers. Spence (1907–76) worked in Lutyens' office before becoming one of England's most eminent modernists. His practice designed several parsonages in his characteristic "Festival of Britain" style, and that at Amersham, Buckinghamshire, in a later manner.

Sir Frederick Gibberd (1908–84) did a number of blocks of flats in the dreaded modernism of the 1950s, and his parsonage at Latton, part of Harlow New Town, 1951, was small and rectangular.

Parsonage architects included Guy Pemberton, Austin Blomfield, Kenneth Mackenzie, N. F. Cachemaille-Day, active from the 1930s through to the 1960s, who did the noted St Michael and All Angels, Manchester Wythenshawe (1937), and St Nicholas, Manchester Burnage, and G. G. (George) Pace.

Pace (1915–75), who designed the rectory at New Middleton, Lancashire, in 1957, did vicarage alterations and subdivisions in a comparatively sensitive modernism that did not turn its back on the past. His startling dictum was: "Modern architecture is not and cannot be naturally in the service of the Church." Despite that, he fervently believed that new churches must give expression to the Church as it is now. While he admired the continental modernism of Gropius and others in that it reflected the world of its day, he believed that the industrial revolution had ended the "organic culture" of the past, in which spiritual faith had led to buildings beyond human scale. The modern architecture was part of a "dissolution" of faith that had been going on for two centuries, and that meant both rampant individualism and dehumanisation. Loss of faith had brought architecture's demise. Though he believed that the past held the key to the future and that the Church architect must "strive with integrity" against modernist principles because they were in conflict with the faith, his dilemma was that he did not think a church could be revivalist either.

Pace believed that the Church architect must reflect the state of the Church. He admired earlier architects such as Temple Moore ("great but unsung"), Street, Bodley, Goodhart-Rendel, and, of the modernists, N. F. Cachemaille-Day. Street had wanted to become a clergyman and Bodley was an Anglo-Catholic, but the Victorians had also been profoundly affected by industrial growth. The philosophy of Pace perhaps helps us understand the difficulties experienced by the parsonage architects of the modern era.

S. E. Dykes Bower (1903–94) designed some excellent houses in the Arts and Crafts tradition and the parsonage at St Vedast, Foster Lane, City of London.

Raymond Erith (1904–73) did church alterations and almshouse designs, but apparently no complete parsonages, though he did some work at Netherton, Hampshire. He would have been very good at them. Perhaps the Church could no longer afford architects of his stature. Quinlan Terry, born 1937, once his partner, has done some parsonage modifications.

Francis Johnson (1911–95) did a number of restorations of medieval houses in Yorkshire in the 1940s and 1950s for wealthy clergy.

We can now see that Victorian and modern architecture are not totally opposed, as the early modernists insisted. While in form they differed greatly, both were born of great change, and strong architectural dogma, and the concept of "honesty" of form was as much a Victorian as a modern one. The word honesty when applied to architecture can be meretricious, but I note that a Victorian rectory is even now not so readily described as "attractive" by estate agents as an earlier one, even when its merits are obviously greater. It was not necessarily intended to be, and that is quite a modernist trait.

Notes

[1] John Harvey, *English Mediaeval Architects* (Alan Sutton, 1984).

[2] John Harvey, *Henry Yevele c. 1320–1400: The Life of an English Architect* (Batsford, 1944).

[3] Arthur Stanley's funeral sermon for Sir George Gilbert Scott, 6 April 1878. Reproduced in George Gilbert Scott, *Personal and Professional Recollections* (Cambridge University Press, 1879), Appendix B, p. 387.

[4] Nikolaus Pevsner, John Harris and Nicholas Antram, *Lincolnshire: The Buildings of England*, second edition (Penguin, 1989), p. 543.

[5] *The Ecclesiologist* 16 (1855), p. 150.

[6] Ibid.

[7] *Country Life* 148 (31 December 1970).

[8] Anthony Quiney, *John Loughborough Pearson*, (Yale University Press, 1979).

[9] H. S. Goodhart-Rendel, "Rogue Architects of the Victorian Era", in RIBA Journal, Vol. 56 (April 1949).

CHAPTER 10

The Curiosities

Hermitages and follies

With Hawker of Morwenstow, we can speak not only of his eccentric parsonage, its chimneys modelled on church towers and his mother's tomb, but of the little hut that was his own hermitage. Along the cliff path from the house, built of wrecked ships' timbers and driftwood, it perched above the rugged and hazardous North Cornwall coast, and he could sit there in quiet contemplation, or in refuge from the strong winds, or even looking out for wrecks, something of a Cornish occupation.

There are much earlier equivalents of Hawker's Hut. St Guthlac of Croyland, Lincolnshire, set up his hermitage in the fens. St Pega was his sister and St Pega's Church, Peakirk, is a unique dedication. East of the church is the hermitage, a chapel on the traditional site of St Pega's Cell. Guthlac came to Croyland as a hermit in 699, so if these can be called parsonages they are certainly among the earliest!

One mile south-east of Areley Kings, in Worcestershire, in the parish of Astley, there is a hermitage. This is architecture with a difference—apartments and cells on two levels, cut into the sandstone cliff by the Severn. Bishop Latimer in 1538 said it could house 500 men. The hermit's cell at Roche, Cornwall, is situated on top of a granite chapel which is built into a granite tor. The chapel dates back to 1492 and access is given by a 30ft iron-runged ladder.

We discussed William Kent's hermitages, in an excuse to claim him as one of our architects. There are others. In the eighteenth century, the hermitage was reborn in a quite different way, as a folly, in the new spirit of wistful romanticism that accompanied the Enlightenment. This was an era in which Christian clergy happily saw no contradiction in building pagan temples in their grounds, if they could afford them. Gilbert White, who had a cut-out of Hercules (cheaper than marble) in his at Selborne, not only built a hermitage there but made his brother dress up as the hermit for the benefit of young ladies taking tea. Another hermitage of this new "rustic" type is at Bicton Park, East Devon. It is built of wood, with a stained glass window. William Stukeley's Temple of Flora at Stamford, and his Hermitage, were renowned. William Cole had a hermitage in his garden at Bletchley, also mid-eighteenth-century. Midford Castle, Bath, by John Carter, late eighteenth-century, has a rustic hermitage, now restored. In Chapter 7 we noted the garden at Bremhill.

The tradition continued in the Victorian period. At Farringdon, Hampshire, the rector Thomas Massey built his own rectory in Gothic style, then spent 30 years erecting the vast red brick and terracotta edifice with elaborate patterning known as Massey's Folly. Nobody knows why it was built, including Massey himself. When asked, he replied that it would be a tea room with a red globe that would turn green when the tea was brewed. It is wild Victorian Gothic with a touch of Indian Mughal thrown in.

The old rectory at Claydon, Suffolk, has a folly of two towers and a wall, and an underground grotto, "exceedingly pretty" according to *The Buildings of England*.

At Marshchapel, Lincolnshire, the Norman House near the church is a Victorian folly built for the curate, in the shape of a Norman church, with a corbel table and windows with chevron and roll mouldings, in red brick, and arched fireplaces.

Churches and porches

We saw that the earliest parsonages were sometimes the church itself. A number of churches have rooms over the porch. At Croyland Abbey, the splendid Lincolnshire church, the parvise chapel, over the porch, was provided as living quarters for the parish priest after the Dissolution. It is cruciform and has windows looking into the church.

In the interesting Smithfield area of London is the church of St Sepulchre without Newgate, Giltspur Street. Here we have a fine Tudor porch, looking rather nineteenth-century Tudorbethan, but apparently dating back to 1450 or so, a survivor of the Great Fire. John Rogers, the vicar, was the first Protestant martyr. There are two floors of fine ashlar above the porch, the first with a broad and ornate oriel window, the second with two smaller windows, and again at the side elevations. The vicar is reputed to have lived in these rooms right up to the twentieth century, and if so, I envy him. They look cosy. The roof is crenellated and flanked by crocketed pinnacles.

Very close is St Bartholomew, Smithfield, the fine surviving portion of a twelfth-century Augustinian priory, and the Priory Gatehouse, renovated in the 1930s but still medieval in appearance. It too has rooms above, also recently inhabited by the parson.

Parsonage towers

Pentlow Tower, near Sudbury, is a folly, almost 100ft tall, built by the Revd Edward Bull, in the grounds of his rectory. He built it in 1859 in memory of his parents, in what can loosely be called Tudor Gothic style. It is mainly of red brick, and has an oak spiral stair with 114 steps. At the top it has battlements and machicolations.

The Revd Edward Bull was apparently the father of the Revd Henry Bull, who built Borley Rectory, so perhaps was prone to eccentricity. It has been suggested that when he built his own rectory at Pentlow he destroyed an early seventeenth-century house of great interest, with gabled wings in the Tudor style and a bell tower. It had been on a moated site and there is likely, therefore, to have been an even earlier house.

At Hadleigh, Suffolk, also near Sudbury, adjoining the Deanery, there is a turreted gateway tower known as the Rector's or Deanery Tower, of brick, built in the late fifteenth century by Archdeacon Pykenham to display his wealth, but leading to nothing except the old parsonage, before the existing Deanery was built.

The former rectory in Martin Lane, City of London, itself has a tall bell tower with a clock.

Whitton Tower is a vicar's pele house for the vicars of Rothbury, Northumberland. Thomas Sharp, vicar in the 1720s, and son of the Archbishop of York, built yet another tower, a stone folly tower, on a hill near the gardens; it is round, with classical doorway, windows, and cornice, but battlemented. It was said to be to help local employment, but he used it for his astronomy and astrology.

The church house

Travelling down to Devon on the south coast main line, you pass right through the spectacular red sandstone cliffs at Dawlish. As you emerge, you see the weird rock formation known as the Parson and Clerk, named after the ambitious vicar and his clerk who lost their way in the fog on a visit to their sick bishop, were waylaid by an old man who offered a bed for the night, woke up and found they were in the open air. The old man revealed himself as the devil and cast them over the cliff. The old vicarage at Dawlish is of some interest, being probably late seventeenth-century with some mullioned and transomed windows, but this is our introduction to Devon and Dartmoor. I said in Chapter 4 that most of the church houses are down here.

My notes showed 57 Devon church buildings recorded in *The Buildings of England* that were not parsonages, and I found that a great many were church houses. The fascinating ones found in these Devon villages include that at Widecombe, Dartmoor, of around 1540, a fine stone building with gablet and granite arcading, still in use today, facing the village green with the Sexton's House, church and delightful Church House Inn nearby. That at Braunton is probably also sixteenth-century, altered when it became a school in the eighteenth century. Rectangular, of whitewashed rubble, it is less architectural but has interesting detailing. The former church house at Manaton is also typical of the Devon church house, again early sixteenth-century, long and low, of granite rubble with granite dressings. The Priest's House, Holcombe Rogus, was in fact also a church house, part village hall, part inn, of around 1500. One of the longest thatched buildings in Britain is the former church house alongside the churchyard at Cheriton Fitzpaine, Devon.

Other West Country church houses include The Parish House at Baltonsborough, Somerset, built in about 1500, with a parish meeting room and guest rooms above, and the spectacularly long former church house at Sherborne, Dorset, built in the 1530s for All Hallows parish. Of stone, now with more recent shops below, it has a series of four-light mullioned windows on the first floor with arched heads.

I also noted church houses in Shropshire, and one or two in Essex. Herefordshire villages are known for their timber-framed cottages near the church and some of these may have been church houses, as well as priests' houses. Finally, the church house at Boston, Lincolnshire, is quite different, a good Jacobean Mannerist example.

Not quite parsonages, but . . .

In Beverley, Yorkshire, are the remains of the Minster Bedern, or lodging for the vicars of the minster, nine bays in a stone wall with a carved medieval hand.

At Mere, Wiltshire, there is both a Chantry House, a hall house with two-storey solar end and large service end, and a Charnel House, with a fifteenth-century window.

Bishop Morton of Ely (1478–86) built, on the cusp of the Tudor period, a palace of brick, very sophisticated at the time, at Hatfield, before he went on to Canterbury. It was described in *The Buildings of England* as the best domestic building in the county and "one of the foremost monuments of medieval brickwork in the country". His later brick gatehouse at Lambeth is a London landmark.

The Prior's Lodging at Much Wenlock, Shropshire, is not exactly a parsonage but a magnificent example of refined religious house building of the end of the fifteenth century. It has a busy but ordered façade of multiple buttresses framing serried rows of segmental headed windows, almost modern in their repetitive style, with a deep roof of neat stone tiles. Another prior's house is that at the Cluniac priory at Castle Acre, Norfolk, which continued to be inhabited after the Dissolution, and still exists, a fine patterned flint-gabled building with many medieval features.

Of the several good stone buildings in Trent, Dorset, the Chantry is the closest to the church. It was probably the house of a chantry priest and is a very good example. A simple building with fine mullioned windows, hoodmoulds, cinquefoils, and other late medieval details, it has a big chimney breast beside the hoodmoulded doorway.

The Little Castle at Bolsover, Derbyshire, designed by John Smythson for the Duke of Cavendish, is said by Simon Jenkins[1] once to have served as the rectory— surely a contender for the number one parsonage in terms of splendour!

The house at Leighton Bromswold, Huntingdonshire, which looks so splendid in Savidge's drawing, is not identified as a parsonage in *The Buildings of England*, though the original castle is described as having been a prebendal manor house. It is worth mentioning that John Thorpe apparently designed a modern house here in the early seventeenth century, but it was never built—as with many Thorpe houses, it seems—though the gatehouse of 1616 was.

Bishopthorpe, York, is an archbishop's palace, but Thomas Atkinson's Gothick range of the 1760s for Archbishop Drummond could so easily be the ideal rectory of that style, and alas, there are few others. It is a wedding cake from Venice, and a harbinger of the way parsonage architecture would be developing later on in the Regency period.

The splendid Mompesson House in the fine Cathedral Close at Salisbury was occupied by the bishop from 1946 to 1951. There are several good houses here—The Wardrobe was once the bishop's storehouse, later used as lodgings, and The Canon's House has a fine open-timbered roof in the hall with good panelling. Cathedral precincts up and down the country contain all manner of fine medieval and seventeenth- and eighteenth-century houses connected with the Church, and would be the subject of a fascinating book in themselves—perhaps I should write one myself.

We can hardly omit mention of A. W. N. Pugin's own houses. His first, built for himself in the Gothic style of which he was a pioneer, St Marie's Grange at Alderbury, Salisbury, is the image of a Victorian parsonage, if an eccentric one, with its spiral staircase accessible only by a drawbridge, influenced by Sir Walter Scott. Its impracticality reveals Pugin as an incurable romantic and not at all as he is often portrayed. His other house, The Grange, Ramsgate, though again not technically a parsonage, can hardly be distinguished from one, and embodies the architectural principles of his parsonages. It is next to the church of St Augustine and has a tower from which he surveyed the Goodwin Sands looking for ships in danger, as I used to do as a child from the Bank House in nearby Deal.

The Landmark Trust has an interesting selection of properties associated with the Church. Tewkesbury Abbey Gatehouse is an early Tudor building—may it possibly have housed a priest or church official? It also has the gatehouse of Cawood Castle, North Yorkshire, once owned by the Archbishops of York; Church Cottage, Llandygwydd, Cardiganshire, of bold Welsh slate, for the caretaker of the now demolished church; and eight cottages in Coombe, Morwenstow, Cornwall, the home of the Revd Stephen Hawker, who was immortalised, albeit it seems inaccurately,[2] by Sabine Baring-Gould. As well as The Grange, Ramsgate, which I have just discussed, the Trust also has the extraordinary Methwold Old Vicarage, discussed in Chapter 7; Monkton Old Hall, a fine monastic guest house; and Iffley Rectory, Oxfordshire, which it calls the Old Parsonage, though it is still in part a working parsonage. The new wing was added in 1500. Warden Abbey, Bedfordshire, has only a fragment of a house on the site which may have accommodated one of the last abbots. Finally, it has the Parish House, Baltonsborough; The Priest's House, Holcombe Rogus; and rooms at The Wardrobe, Salisbury Cathedral Close, all discussed earlier.

Vicars' private houses

Mountsorrel, Leicestershire, was built not as a rectory but as a private house by a vicar, and described as "exceptionally elegant" in *The Buildings of England*, very similar to the parsonage at Church Langton. Others included Ditchingham House, Ditchingham, Norfolk, a brick Georgian house built for the Revd William Buckle about 1780, later inherited by H. Rider Haggard, author of *King Solomon's Mines*. Kirkshield, a house near Simonburn, Northumberland, was built as a shooting lodge for the Revd James Scott, in the Georgian Gothick style with crocketed pinnacles. At Ditcheat, Somerset, The Abbey is said to have been built about 1475, albeit now largely Victorian. The Manor House at Meare, Somerset, was a fourteenth-century summer house of the Abbots of Glastonbury. At Shadingfield, Suffolk, Shadingfield Hall was built in 1814 by the rector, five bays with a Greek Doric porch. At Hemingbrough, Yorkshire, Hemingbrough Hall was built in 1842 for the Revd John Ion, a large Tudor-style gabled house by Weightman and Hadfield. At Middleton-on-the Wolds, Yorkshire, Horsewold Farm was built about 1810, probably by Peter Atkinson Jr for the rector. The warden of Croft House Settlement, Sheffield, the Revd William Blackshaw, had a large upmarket suburban house specially designed by Edgar Wood. Edith Weston Hall, Rutland, was designed in Tudor style by Lewis Vulliamy for the Revd C. H. Lucas in 1830, but was demolished in 1957. At Exminster, Devon, Spurfield, with its mullions and half-timbered gable, was built by Pearson in the 1880s for the Revd S. Willoughby Lawley. Another much earlier Pearson house, Quar Wood of the 1850s, French Gothic with saddleback stair tower, was built for the Revd R. W. Hippisley, but subsequently ruined with unsympathetic 1950s alterations. Other good private vicars' houses, including those at Seaton and Thorganby, are described in Chapters 7 and 9.

Fragments

A number of parsonages have, or have had, fittings from other houses incorporated in them, or fragments taken from churches or other buildings, or interesting follies in their grounds. At Horningsea, Cambridge, the staircase incorporates a communion rail from St John's College; at Great Asby, Cumbria, there is a fourteenth-century window-head from the old church; at Berry Pomeroy, Devon, two doorways and a fireplace from the castle; at Holy Trinity, Ilfracombe, Devon, a late medieval framed ceiling with carved bosses; at Stoke Rivers, Devon, a polygonal thatched building with Gothick windows; at Powerstock, Dorset, decorated window-heads and Norman shafts in the garden; at Sydling St Nicholas, Dorset, a medieval fragment showing a bow and arrow in the garden; at Thorncombe, Dorset, fourteenth/fifteenth-century window-heads in the garden; at Heighington, Durham, door surround and lintels of the early vicarage; at Staindrop, Durham (deanery), a dovecot, a five-seater closet, and a mullioned summer house.

At Kempsford, Gloucestershire, there is a seventeenth-century parapet with a ruined building containing an octagonal stone called the Castle Pillow; at Weston Sub Edge, Gloucestershire, fourteenth-century stained glass in the porch; at Hill, Gloucestershire, ruins of a fifteenth-century tithe barn; at Crewkerne, Gloucestershire, Abbey House, a preserved fifteenth-century window, all that remains of the priest's house on this site; at Fownhope, Herefordshire, a barn with cruck trusses; at Grafton, Herefordshire, an old ruined church; at Tretire, Herefordshire, a Norman window in the garden; at Weston Under Penyard, Herefordshire, some of the stone from the medieval Penyard Castle is thought to be incorporated in the former rectory (c. 1700), an elegant house of post-Restoration type.

At Yarkhill, Herefordshire, Norman trumpet-scallop capitals; at Ayot St Laurence, Hertfordshire, seventeenth-century heraldic glass; at Much Hadham, Hertfordshire, a seventeenth-century dovecote, later a cottage; at Tewin, Hertfordshire, a timber-framed barn and stables; at Carisbrooke, Isle of Wight, the remains of a Roman villa of basilican type; at Owston, Leicestershire, two fifteenth-century door arches are incorporated in the walls; at Caythorpe, Lincolnshire, a Gothic building with crenellations in the garden; at Horbling, Lincolnshire, a thirteenth-century arch with polygonal responds and capitals in the garden; at Louth, Lincolnshire, there was once a thatched "hermitage" and other early Victorian rusticities in the garden; at Sleaford, Lincolnshire, to the left of the house is a stone gateway with four-centred arch; at Stainby, Lincolnshire, a fragment of an early cross shaft, probably eleventh-century, in the garden; at St Mary's, Stamford, Lincolnshire, set in the wall a twelfth-century two-light window and inside, much later than the house, nineteenth-century Gothic panelling; at Wootton, Lincolnshire, in the garden, a folly with a tower with blind windows, and a screen with blind arches, nineteenth-century.

At Barnwell, Northamptonshire, several thirteenth-century fragments in the boundary wall; at Helmdon, Northamptonshire, in the porch, the lintel of a sixteenth-century fireplace with a carved dragon; at Birtley, Northumberland, a ruined tower in the garden, with slit windows with splayed reveals; at Longhorsley, Northumberland, a ruined building in the garden with arched doorways and a mullioned window; at Stannington, Northumberland, fragments from the old church in the garden; at Ducklington, Oxfordshire, medieval tie-beams with heraldic devices said to be from Minster Lovell Hall; at Eynsham, Oxfordshire, stone pier and capital fragments, arched spandrels with carved beasts, cinquefoiled window and gargoyles in the garden; at South Newington, Oxfordshire, a former farmhouse, with fourteenth-century stone arch inside and in the garden wall; at Pishill, Oxfordshire, a fine barn of flint and stone, part weatherboarded, behind the rectory. At Bishop's Castle, Shropshire, an early thirteenth-century doorway with shafts and stiff-leaf capitals, and a sedilia, in the garden wall. At Wells, Somerset, in Priest Row, all that remains of a former priest's house is a fifteenth-century doorway; at Selworthy, Somerset, there is a fourteenth-century tithe barn in the grounds of the former rectory; at Stoke Ash, Suffolk, a brick dovecote of 1600; at Polesworth, Warwickshire, the Victorian vicarage incorporates the arch-braced roof of the former hall and an Elizabethan fireplace, with a column in the garden; at Cricklade, Wiltshire, a Norman arch fragment in the garden; at Broadway, Worcestershire, the 1608 cupola of the church in the garden; at Harvington, Worcestershire, the east window of the church in the garden; at Kirkbymoorside, Yorkshire, Anglo-Saxon sculptures in the porch; at Melsonby, Yorkshire, ruins of a former tower house; Guiseley, Yorkshire, has the north wall of the medieval hall inside, and a timber-framed wall, possibly Saxon, and within the grounds, a "Roman bath"; in Eastgate, York, near the minster, medieval stonework and the seventeenth-century gate from the friary, in the old vicarage wall; at Catwick, Yorkshire, Norman shafts in a gateway in the garden wall; at Dunnington, Yorkshire, in the garden, a medieval shaft with a polygonal sundial on top.

Not purpose-built

At Hockley, Essex, an existing farmhouse had front rooms added in about 1820 to turn it into the vicarage. At Malton, Yorkshire, the parsonage north-east of the church, once that of a Gilbertine priory of around 1150, has an inscription recording that it was built as the school house in 1786. At Rodborough, Gloucestershire, the Old Rectory was converted from seventeenth-century weavers' cottages, and later adapted as the parsonage in 1842–43, the great era of building and conversion. In

Alnmouth, Northumberland, the vicarage was built as a granary and converted in the nineteenth century. In Stroud, Gloucestershire, Rodney House with its gables and mullions was built in 1635 for the Webb family of clothiers and used later as a vicarage. The later vicarage, built by Thomas Falconer in 1929, was also built as a private house.

Not what it seems

In outer Sheffield, to the south, lies the so-called Bishop's House, a very fine L-shaped timber-framed house with cross-wing of about 1500. It is heavily restored and now looks a little Neo-Tudor with its bold studding. But there is no evidence that a bishop ever lived there. Bishop Latimer was born at Latimer's House, Thurcaston, Leicestershire, in 1475, though he does not appear to have lived there.

Something old, something new

Rarely are both old and new parsonages worthy of mention in *The Buildings of England*. One case is Dymock, Gloucestershire, where the old rectory, an early eighteenth-century house, is near the new, by H. Stratton Davis, of around 1950.

Other curiosities

A house by Ernest Newton was built in 1911–12 in Kettleshulme, Cheshire, as the parsonage for a church that was never built. The rock-faced parsonage at Haydon, Dorset, by P. C. Hardwick (1857), is bigger than both the church and the school. At Kelloe, Durham, there is a deserted medieval village with the remains of the vicarage with a blocked doorway with four-centred arch.

Perhaps the rectory at Bishopstone, Herefordshire, could be described as the earliest parsonage. It was built in 1812 as the new rectory, but a Roman pavement was found when the foundations were dug. A later rector described how several barrow-loads of tesserae were used to fill up a pit in the garden. Wordsworth wrote about it.

At Wold Newton, Yorkshire, there is a vicarage of chalk in the grounds of another former vicarage of 1839. At Blackpool, North Lancashire, the church of St Wilfred is connected at the east end with the older vicarage. At Rendcomb, Gloucestershire, the new rectory, a seventeenth-century farmhouse, was older than the former one, a Georgian cube of 1832-33. At Harwood, Lancashire, a fragment of the demolished old vicarage stands in the churchyard. In Chorlton-on-Medlock, Manchester South, the priest's house is attached to the Armenian church. At Blymhill, Staffordshire, the eighteenth-century rectory was enlarged by Street, who also designed the school in his typical manner, and rebuilt the church, but his work was demolished.

A rectory at St Anne's, Soho, the bombed out Wren/Talman church, was built as part of a modern complex including a chapel and flats. At Denton, East Sussex, there is a ruined priest's house, with one trefoil-headed window preserved, of around 1300. In Kinwarton, Warwickshire, the Crown Hotel was built as the vicarage and opened as a hotel as early as 1815. At Knightwick, Worcestershire, the small chapel is of only two bays, while the old rectory is a five-bay Georgian house.

The former rectory at Warton, Lancashire, had become ruinous by the early eighteenth century, and a cottage was built into the northern end. It was built by the sons of the splendidly-named Marmaduke Thweng.

The former parsonage at Chailey Moat, near Lewes, East Sussex, is encircled by a moat, from which you might think the moat dated from the medieval origins of the house in about 1540. However, it was apparently dug by the vicar from 1713-53, by himself. He certainly defaced the house with an incongruous new extension.

The site of the Iron Age hill fort at Mellor, Greater Manchester, is partly in the garden of the Old Vicarage there, and a ditch close to the house has recently been excavated.

Imber, Wiltshire, was already the loneliest village on Salisbury Plain before its people were removed in 1943 so that it could be used as a battle-training area. It was in a valley prettily occupied by a medieval church, a vicarage, a manor house, a school, a Baptist chapel, a pub, a few farmhouses and cottages, and fewer than 200 people. The church is still intact, but the rest of Imber, including the ruins of the Tudor-style Victorian rectory, is a battle-broken mess once described as "mercifully covered by a summer shroud of nettles".[3]

Ghosts

You might expect there to be ghost stories about pele towers. Legend tells of a subterranean passage from the dungeon at Embleton, Northumberland, where captured reivers were imprisoned, to Dunstanburgh Castle. A secret chamber was also discovered in a wall between a passageway and a room. The priest who hid there would have to crawl between two floors and drop into the chamber, lit only by a crack. Its doors have "chatieres", holes to let a cat through for ratting. There may be a ghost: "a certain door resisted all efforts or appliances to close it. It is now bricked up."[4]

At Epworth, Lincolnshire, the timber and thatch rectory of Samuel Wesley was destroyed in a fire in 1709. The young John Wesley was spotted looking out of a window, and was snatched to safety. The new house (see Chapter 7) has "Old Jeffrey's Chamber" in the attic, the scene of the famous hauntings in Wesley's journal. The ghost was apparently a Jacobite sympathiser, who groaned, rapped and tapped, and walked about in leather boots. A bed levitated. These phenomena were witnessed by his servants and children before Samuel was himself assailed by them and had to perform exorcisms.

At the part-medieval Southfleet, Kent, the Bishop of Rochester had to exorcise the spectre of a woman in 1874. This did not stop later sightings of a dwarfish little figure, dressed like a nun, thought to be the mistress of an excommunicated monk who had been walled up.

There is a tale of a remote fenland vicarage on the Lincolnshire/Cambridgeshire borders believed to have been built on a site once occupied by a monk's cell, and haunted by a monk called Ignatius. The wife of a vicar who lived there for 20 years got to know him and he told her that he had been the monks' watchman, whose task had been to ring a bell when the floods had made it necessary to move to higher ground. This he had failed to do, and the island was flooded, with much loss of life. He had been denied a burial. One night the wife awoke from a nightmare to find a tendril of ivy had crept into the room. Then a light shone and two hands suddenly gripped her throat. Ignatius appeared, pulled the hands away, then vanished. When he returned, he told her the assailant was the ghost of a man who had died in her room. His appearances are now less frequent, perhaps because he has been partly released from his penance. Later owners merely heard footsteps occasionally.

Lark Hall was a farmhouse at Alwinton in the Coquet Valley, Northumberland. In 1800, it was invaded by a poltergeist. When the Revd Mr Lauder, minister at Harbottle, visited, the Bible on the window recess made a series of gyrations in the air, and landed at his feet.

At the back of Amen Court, London, home to the Dean and Chapter of St Paul's (with houses by Ewan Christian), there is a dark wall. Newgate Prison, demolished in 1902, used to be behind. The "black dog of Newgate" slithers along the top of this wall, slides down into the courtyard and melts away. There is a nauseous smell. In the reign of Henry III, a sorcerer had been imprisoned and cannibalised by his fellow inmates. His dog exacted its revenge, but continues to patrol. Another mystery here is the medieval stonework at the foot of the wall; it is not the city wall proper.

Talking of St Paul's, the ghost at the Old Deanery is of a less romantic kind. A toilet roll holder was often reported to the Dean as "decidedly wonky", but had always righted itself by the time he got there to repair it. Anyway, he found himself philosophically unable to accept the concept of a haunted toilet roll holder.

St John's Library, Blackheath, was formerly the vicarage, and the childhood home of Elsie Marshall, who was murdered in 1895 while a missionary in China. Her spirit continues to haunt the library.

Charles Kingsley lived in the impressive rectory at Barnack, Cambridgeshire, when he was five. The house was reputed to be haunted by the ghost of a former rector who cheated a widow of the parish. Kingsley is said to have seen the ghost, in a flowered dressing gown and nightcap. The haunted room is called "Button Cap".

The Chantry, Berkeley, Gloucestershire, is the house that Edward Jenner (for more about him see Chapter 14) owned from 1785 until his death in 1823. In 1885, it was sold to the Church as the vicarage, replacing the one where he was born. In the 1980s, it became the Jenner Museum. There has been paranormal activity there for 300 years, with the ghost, perhaps of Jenner, entering his study. There have been footsteps on the stairs, and a dog running up them with claws clattering. The graves of Saxon nuns are on the property. A photograph was taken showing the ghostly image of a man sitting on a chair in the attic.

It's that parsonage of M. R. James at Goodnestone, Kent (see Chapter 14), this time in the hands of Joanna Lumley. When she was in the cellar on the first day of living there, a man in a flat cap approached and said: "Leave this place." She found out that a tunnel led from the cellar to the graveyard. A fresh grave was dug by the tennis court, then disappeared overnight. There were the usual paranormal activities, footsteps, lights, temperature changes, and so on.

The old parsonage at Warblington, Hampshire, on Pook Lane (which no longer exists), was haunted. The story had been recorded by an investigator, and was published in 1897. In August 1695, all were gone to bed except the maid, who raked the fire, took a candle, and turning, saw someone in a black gown walking through the room, and out of the door into the orchard. Later, the investigator was there when a man saw the apparition, which walked into his room, stood at the bed's foot, whistling, then came to the bed's side, drew the curtain, and looked on him. The investigator also saw it, and asked it, "In the name of God, what it was that made it come disturbing of us? I stood some time expecting an answer and, receiving none, I put out my arm to feel it, and my hand seemingly went through the body of it, and felt no manner of substance till it came to the wall." It seemed to have "a morning gown of a darkish colour, no hat nor cap, short black hair, a thin, meagre visage of a pale swarthy colour, the eyes half shut, the arms hanging down." A vicar there had previously murdered his illegitimate children.

On All Hallows' Eve, at midnight, 12 blue lights rise from the mound that is the site of the old church at Horsington, Somerset, then divide, and three go to a barn at the back of the Old Rectory, which served as a temporary church. A Great Dane rears up in fright.

Victorian Gothic architecture raises thoughts of the spirit world, and none more than Borley Rectory, Essex. This house was a classic unmanageable Victorian parsonage, being astonishingly massive for a rural village with a population of 121, with its 11 bedrooms and chapel on the first floor. On the other hand, the Revd Henry Bull, who built it in 1863, did have 14 children. Later, the Revd G. E. Smith, despite all the alleged paranormal manifestations, is said to have found it difficult to live there mainly because of the cold, the difficulty of heating it, and the lack of mains water. It was not architecturally distinguished, Gothic without conviction, though it had two fine marble chimneypieces. The symmetrical garden front presented itself as the main façade, though the main entrance leading to the central hall was in the long side elevation, quite typical of the complex large house of this period. It was built either on the site of an earlier rectory or a Benedictine monastery. The cellars had to follow the irregular footings of the old building.

There was a Nun's Walk in the grounds (surely all proper rectories should have one, together with a stone staircase and a folly) and a story of an eloping monk and nun who were caught. The monk was executed and the nun bricked up alive in the convent wall. The nun's ghost was regularly seen, an expression of intense grief on her face. The house was disfigured by a bricked-up window in the dining room, right beside the main porch, reputed to have been done by the first vicar to stop the nun peering in.

There were numerous other manifestations. The "screaming girl" was observed clinging to the window sill of the Blue Room, yelling at the top of her voice until she had to let go, crashing through the verandah roof to her death. Another upstairs window was seen lit up on dark nights, but the maid was in the kitchen and said she had not been up. When investigated, the room was in darkness. The newly arrived vicar's wife found a neatly wrapped parcel in the library, which she unwrapped to discover a human skull. A headless man was seen in the garden. The vicar's daughter woke at night to find an old man in dark clothes wearing a tall hat, by her bed. A black coach, its lights ablaze in the darkness, but silent, was often seen approaching the house, or sometimes just the sound of clattering hooves was heard. A chauffeur, sitting in the kitchen reading the paper, saw a black hand moving slowly up and down between the door and the jamb before disappearing.

The "strange coat", old and torn, was one day found hanging on a bedroom door. There was a "cold spot" near an arch on the landing. A lady who came to paint the house from the garden encountered the "strange insect with goggle eyes" (it had a large head and tapering articulated body) flying at her. A bramble thicket at the bottom of the garden was found to have a hole torn into it and a buried cat was dug up. There was constant poltergeist activity, including ringing from the bell system, flying objects, whispering noises, and keys being expelled from door locks.

Then there was the story of a French nun said to have been strangled in the seventeenth century and buried under the cellars. Voices were heard calling "Marianne" (the name of the vicar's wife). A number of scribbled pencil messages appeared on walls, such as "Marianne please get help".

In short, the house comfortably acquired the reputation of being the most haunted house in Britain. It finally burnt down in 1939, but even afterwards the paranormal activities, including galloping horses and the appearance of a girl in white in a burnt-out upper window aperture, continued. There is a photograph allegedly showing a brick from the rubble levitating. Finally, a jaw bone and part of a skull were dug up from below the cellars—and yes, it was that of a woman.

Gone, drowned, never built

The destruction of Borley leads to the subject of demolished parsonages. About 40 of the parsonages thought worthy of inclusion in *The Buildings of England* are either demolished or derelict. This is particularly regrettable when the demolitions include houses by eminent architects, such as the rectory at Seaton Carew, Durham, by Salvin, that of St Mary's (RC), Derbyshire, by Pugin, and the rectory built around 1768 at Eyam, also Derbyshire, by James Paine for the Revd Thomas Seward.

Great Lever Hall, in outer Bolton, Lancashire, rebuilt by Bishop Bridgman in 1631–34, a lost timber-framed house, served as a rectory and was demolished in the vandalising years of the mid-twentieth century. It is now buried under the A666. That's progress!

Some of the parsonages mentioned in *The Buildings of England* were never built. They include that proposed for Duggleby, Yorkshire, by G. E. Street for Sir Tatton Sykes; plans for another proposed Street house at Fimber, Yorkshire; two Leicester schemes commissioned from Basil Spence and Partners, incomplete, and at St Aidan, "neither church nor vicarage built"; and one designed by Pearson for Eastoft, Lincolnshire.

On the side of a remote valley in the Yorkshire Wolds lies the deserted village of Wharram Percy. It is mentioned in the Domesday Book, but was finally abandoned in the early sixteenth century. Among the many medieval foundations there are the sites of two vanished vicarages.

Finally, dropping in on the vicar presents an unexpected challenge at Haweswater. The church and the vicarage, drowned by the reservoir, can only be reached in diving gear.

Notes

[1]   Simon Jenkins, *England's Thousand Best Houses* (Allen Lane, 2003), p. 141.
[2]   Piers Brendon, *Hawker of Morwenstow* (Jonathan Cape, 1975).
[3]   Geoffrey Grigson, *The Spectator*, 31 August 1961.
[4]   R. B. Dawson, *A Short History of Embleton Church and the Fortified Vicarage* (British Publishing Company, 1933).

Part Four: The Present

"But now I only hear its melancholy, long withdrawing roar"
Matthew Arnold

C H A P T E R 1 1

Church Law and the Parsonage

The law on parsonages

The Church of England exercises its powers in relation to parsonages under Church law, embodied in what are called Measures, approved by General Synod and agreed by Parliament.

Dilapidations had always been a problem, but for centuries had largely been dealt with at the bishop's discretion. The setting up of Queen Anne's Bounty in 1704, the beginning of the centralisation process, helped augment clergy incomes, and was to lead to funds being made available for new parsonages, if only after another century had passed. Maintenance problems when one vicar succeeded another continued to be settled privately, often unsatisfactorily. The Ecclesiastical Dilapidations Act of 1871 created the new phenomenon of the Diocesan Surveyor, and set up quinquennial inspections, but this was still on a voluntary basis for those who deemed them useful. The 1923 Ecclesiastical Dilapidations Measure made quinquennial inspections compulsory, and for the first time required the vicar to pay a levy for dilapidations based on estimated repair costs, in effect a tax. In subsequent years the vicar's burden was lightened by funding, then the Repair of Benefice Buildings Measure of 1972 brought another significant change. Responsibility for maintenance and repairs to parsonage houses now passed fully to the dioceses, and the diocesan parsonage boards which were newly set up. The boards are required to undertake such repairs as are specified in the surveyor's report. The incumbent must consent but in any case has a general duty of care for the building, and is required to get approval for any additions or alterations of his or her own. The diocesan synod can ask the parish to pay additional contributions or directly pay the cost of repairs itself; the dioceses are largely funded by the parishes anyway. Repair funds were no longer "ring-fenced" and could now be pooled.

The other important matter is that of the sale of the parsonage. In 1838, the incumbent was for the first time empowered to sell his house with consent. Under the 1866 Parsonages Act, Queen Anne's Bounty was also empowered to sell parsonages, though the vicar was still lord of his vicarage. Nowadays, the terms of the Parsonages Measure 1938, revised but still in place, govern the sale of the parsonage, and allow this where the residence, including outbuildings and appurtenances, "shall be inconveniently situate or too large, or where for good and sufficient reasons it shall be thought advisable to sell and dispose of the same or any part thereof". The wording applies whether the vicar or the bishop instigates the sale. In practice it is normally the bishop, not the incumbent in residence, who does so. During the incumbency, the bishop needs the vicar's consent, but in a vacancy he does not. The Parochial Church Council (PCC), which represents the parish, must be consulted, but the bishop does not have to act in accordance with its wishes, and often in practice does not. The proceeds of sale are "ring-fenced" for the parish only if a new house is to be built in replacement for the old, and only to the extent of the funding needed, and otherwise go to the Diocesan Board of Finance or Diocesan Parsonages Board. So far as the parish is concerned, not only does the house go, but so does the money.

The Endowments and Glebe Measure 1976 was the next piece of centralising legislation. Endowment income for a benefice, or benefits under any other private schemes, which until then had been available to help finance the parish, and thus support the parsonage, were all now placed under the control of the Church Commissioners. The income or benefit was commuted to an annuity payable towards the incumbent's stipend, but the passage of time speedily eroded its value. All future gifts in trust for the endowment of a benefice, including land and houses, were to be transferred by the Commissioners to the diocesan boards of finance. Not, it might be thought, a way of encouraging gifts to a parish from well-meaning benefactors. In the past, parsonages had often been provided and repaired by means of such philanthropy.

Glebe lands and all rights over parsonage land belonging to the benefice were also all transferred at a stroke to the diocesan boards of finance. *Country Life* commented:[1]

> This transfer of glebe resulted in nearly 21,000 properties with about 112,000 acres of land being transferred from the clergy to the diocesan boards of finance. This was expropriation on a grand scale. Even if it could have been justified in terms of financial prudence, it was a terrible move

psychologically, seen as it was by the parishes as the draining away of their life blood.

The dioceses also had power to acquire parish property for glebe, and were given powers to sell, lease, or mortgage glebe land in order to bring in revenue. Money from sales and rents was to be paid to the board's stipends fund accounts, not to the parishes. The measure allowed the dioceses to sell the parsonage where the board was "of the opinion" that it was not necessary for the convenient occupation of the incumbent or not required.

The Pastoral Measure 1983 was the next vital piece of legislation. Though not primarily about parsonages, it has had a devastating effect on them. It is the duty of the diocesan pastoral committees to review arrangements for pastoral care in the diocese, and under a "pastoral order" made by the bishop, or a "pastoral scheme" made by the Commissioners, following consultation with interested parties, a wide range of arrangements can be made, such as the creation, alteration, or dissolution of benefices and parishes, including sharing agreements for parsonage houses, holding of benefices in plurality, establishing team ministries or group ministries, and so on.

In practice, most schemes or orders are for the combining of parishes. A scheme may designate any house as the residence of the incumbent, and transfer a house to the diocesan board of finance to be held as glebe land, or for disposal. Any parsonage not occupied by an incumbent is usually sold. Funds generated, except where specifically allocated, again go to the diocesan stipends fund capital account or pastoral account, not to the parishes. It is under the powers in this and the 1938 Measure that the bulk of the sales of rectories and vicarages have taken place.

All this centralisation has strained relations between diocese and parish. The sale of an old house may be eminently justifiable, but parishioners want the capital to be put back into their community. If the house is not to be replaced, the parish usually gets no tangible benefit at all. Once that pot of money has gone, the common lament of parishioners is that they are never told and cannot even find out where, specifically, it has gone or on what precisely it has been spent.

The parishes have a right of appeal to the pastoral division of the Church Commissioners. The Commissioners say they are an impartial appeal body. They are certainly separate and distinct as a corporate entity from the dioceses. However, they are not perceived as truly impartial and independent by parishioners, nor can they be. They have a long history of funding the dioceses. They devised the whole modern policy of selling off parsonages in order to house vicars in much smaller parsonages, and developed the "Green Guide" in order to implement that policy. They normally adjudicate in favour of the bishop—it is thought that about 85 per cent of appeal decisions by the Church Commissioners favour the diocese, not the parish. Representatives of the Commissioners say it would be surprising if this were not so, because the diocese has the broad picture, and the parish is less well informed. For all these reasons they could never be an independent third party in the sense that a lawyer would recognise that term in any arbitration or conciliation process. Having said that, it is difficult to see how any truly objective appeal system would work.

In this way, the dioceses administer the parsonages. The churches, by contrast, remain the responsibility of the parishes, so church and parsonage lie within quite different command structures. Would so many parsonages have been sold off if those at local level had had control over them?

Abolition of the freehold

Although the clergy freehold has always been a central tenet of the Church of England, it has regularly been under threat. The rector or vicar with the freehold has no heritable interest in the parsonage, but owns it and can veto its sale by the bishop, while he is in residence. Upon an incumbent's retirement, increasing use has been made of priests-in-charge, who do not have this right, which makes the process of selling the parsonage easier.

In 2002, the Archbishops' Council recommended that the clergy freehold should be abolished and replaced with a new form of tenure, "common tenure", closer to a relationship of employment. Under these proposals the ending of the freehold would also have ended the ownership of the parsonage by the incumbent; it followed that ownership would have to be transferred to some other body. The review group suggested various possible alternatives: the diocesan board of finance (or diocesan parsonages boards), the PCC, or a new Benefice Corporation. It has not in the past been thought meaningful to debate legal title to Church buildings for which there may be no deeds. Parishioners tend to regard the parsonage, if "owned" by anybody, as belonging to the parish. After all, a lot of parsonages were expressly given for the incumbent or parish in perpetuity by a wealthy patron or benefactor. In the end, there was sufficient opposition to force the proponents of the new measure to abandon their plan to expropriate the parsonage. Common tenure is a reality, ending 800 years of the freehold of office, but, for the time being anyhow, the incumbent (but not the priest-in-charge) keeps the parsonage.

The direction of the Church

As well as centralisation, the twentieth century could be characterised as one of politicisation. The report *Faith in the City* (1985), which suggested that the problems of the inner cities were being ignored by government policy, was disliked by the Conservative government of the 1980s. *Faith in the Countryside*, the booklet from the Archbishops' Commission on Rural Areas in 1990, was better. It acknowledged that parishes had sometimes been combined without adequate consultation and that the transfer of glebe from benefice to diocesan ownership "hit rural people hard", and that the replacement of older, larger vicarages with smaller, modern ones "deprived villages of a meeting place for community and other church activities". It said that "dioceses should regard parsonage houses as part of the Church's overall missionary strategy". The care and presentation of buildings was of prime importance to the mission of the Church. But then it said: "The replacement of older parsonages with modern ones can usually be justified economically and often has the support of the clergy." Yet it added: "The policy has been criticised in rural areas, however, because whereas older larger houses provided a meeting place for church and community activities the newer parsonages are too small." And: "Diocesan parsonage boards and the Church Commissioners are asked to look more sympathetically at requests in rural areas for larger houses with additional rooms." Many parishioners agree with all that, but it is not Church policy.

The "interim report" requested by the archbishops from the Resourcing Mission Group (2006) acknowledged that the Church was suffering from "poverty of vision". Yet it concluded that "mission should determine how the Church's riches are used—rather than the buildings, which are often a hindrance". But the fact is that, without its buildings, the Church cannot survive.

The role of the clergy

The Church will always say there is no overall diocesan policy and each diocese forges its own. But there is a widespread move to change the role of the clergy. They are encouraged to seek more privacy. Specifically, they are discouraged from having large rooms where parishioners can meet. Parsonage houses are to be perceived as a private domain, and it is now thought that no vicar should be required to open his or her house to parishioners unless he or she wants to. I have several emails from diocesan secretaries firmly declaring that to be their policy.

It is a pretty fundamental change. The parsonage has for centuries been regarded as a focus for parish ministry. In *Bishop of Gloucester v Cunnington*, Lord Greene, MR said:

> The reasons for this special treatment [of a parsonage] are of a spiritual nature, and are based on the necessity for ensuring that the cure of souls is conducted by the incumbent residing, not only in the benefice, but in the parsonage house itself which is provided to enable him to perform his spiritual duties and (what is important) the duties of hospitality connected therewith.[2]

In *Phillips v Minister of Housing and Local Government*, Lord Denning, MR said:

> A rectory of the Church of England has for centuries been recognised to have special attributes connected with the Church. It is vested for the time being in the incumbent as a corporation sole. It is a house set apart, not merely as his residence, but so as to be used by him for his spiritual, pastoral and procedural duties.[3]

Policy towards churches contrasted

There is a growing awareness of the value of our built heritage to our culture, manifested in the growth of building preservation trusts, amenity societies, and conservation and campaigning groups. Even within the Church, a group called the Church Heritage Forum was set up in 1997, and in 2004 this produced a "statement" entitled, in the prevailing jargon, "Building Faith in our Future". Inside the glossy cover, which showed a group of laughing schoolchildren in a modern classroom, some of its quotes were telling: "A Church which sells its church buildings is selling its own history and forfeiting its future", said an admittedly German church official. It refreshingly acknowledged that the legacy of buildings is of value, with promising pronouncements, such as: "The mere presence of the church building contributes at a very deep level to . . . sense of place." It waxed lyrical about the importance of churches to the community, and rightly referred to churches as part of the "landscape of the settlement". So far, so good. But there was a problem. Nowhere was there any reference to rectories and vicarages. They were not even within its remit.

I am told that it was a major leap even to get this initiative off the ground. It seems to be a fact that many of those with influence in the Church do not believe that concepts such as history, heritage, environment, and aesthetics, the essential qualities of the English parish, should play any part in the strategy or mission of the Church.

The National Churches Trust is a national, non-denominational charity set up in 1953 (as the Historic Churches Preservation Trust) to provide finance for essential repairs to churches and chapels (there are more than 20,000 churches in England and Wales, of which 16,000 are Anglican and 14,000 listed), but it does not deal with parsonages. The Churches Conservation Trust is concerned only with redundant churches. The Cathedral and Church Buildings Division of the Archbishops' Council is responsible for national policy on churches and serves the Church Buildings Council (previously Council for the Care of Churches) and the Cathedrals Fabric Commission for England, and there are other committees concerned with various aspects of church care. But none of these bodies deals with parsonages.

In an article in *Church Times*[4] the then chief executive of English Heritage rightly said that churches are not just about the cure of souls but communal focus, identity, and memory. Again, no mention of our traditional rectories and vicarages, of which those that remain can be described in exactly the same terms. They were once the hub of the community in every parish in the land.

Notes

[1] "More parsonages to become redundant", *Country Life*, 9 November 1978; "Of churches parsonages and glebe", *Country Life*, 7 July 1983.

[2] *Bishop of Gloucester v Cunnington* (1943) K.B. 101, per Lord Greene, MR. Research by David Harte.

[3] *Phillips v Minister of Housing and Local Government* (1965) 1 Q.B. 156, per Lord Denning, MR. Research by David Harte.

[4] Simon Thurley, "Keeper of the Purse Strings", *Church Times*, 26 November 2004.

CHAPTER 12

Why the Great Sell-Off?

Throughout its history the English parsonage has been in some kind of crisis. There has always been scarcity, superfluity, vacancy, neglect, dilapidation, and a perceived need for modification or replacement. History is no confirmation of wisdom, but does put the "great sell-off" in perspective. The recent story of the Church of England has been one of decline in churchgoing and in the stipendiary clergy, and pressure on funds.

The parishes are the grass roots of the Church. They are where the worship, the ministry, and most of the fundraising are done. Cynics might say that if all the bishoprics were to be abolished, the work of the Church would go on in the parishes, and a great deal better. They have their own administrative organisations, the parochial church councils. Many are now combined in group benefices, but each parish retains its own PCC. There is little slack in these parish organisations. Unlike the diocesan bureaucrats who talk of "outreach" in conference rooms, they mow the churchyard, clear the church gutters and drains, plant the hedges, change the lightbulbs, and get the church repairs done. They increasingly finance the diocesan offices, which neither would nor could exist without them. The cost of the central Church institutions is a problem. In 1994, for example, it was equivalent to that of a thousand clergy, their housing, pensions and all else included.

The two main reasons given by the dioceses for selling parsonages are consistent with the two major pieces of legislation, the Parsonages Measure 1938 and the Pastoral Measure 1983. The first is unsuitability, the second redundancy. Taking the second first, benefices are reorganised and parishes continue to be combined into group benefices. Normally, there is one church in each parish. One vicar now has to serve all of them, perhaps with a curate or lay reader, or there may be a team or a group ministry. Logic dictates that a disused parsonage house is what is termed "redundant". It is then concluded that it should be sold. That does not sound unreasonable. But might it not be useful in future? Retained, and let out, its substantial capital value is not lost and valuable income is gained. The dioceses will say they are not property companies. But agents exist to handle lettings and they could be instructed to do so if the will was there.

The concept of unsuitability, by its nature, is much more debatable. It is more subjective. When houses have been sold because they are deemed unsuitable, new ones have had to be built or bought, and the older ones, being in the main much better houses, have become valuable assets in the hands of their private buyers. There are three major perceptions that have contributed to the argument that new houses make life better for the clergy. The first is that they simply do not like living in traditional parsonages, because they see them as too old-fashioned and no longer suited to life "as it is today". In more specific terms, it is said that they want, or need, the practical benefits of modern conveniences. The cost of maintaining and repairing large houses is a burden, and the clergy don't have the money to heat large and draughty rooms. Clergy often have working spouses, want privacy, and find large gardens too time-consuming.

Another potent perception is that the clergy are embarrassed to live in houses that are better than those of their flock. This seems a sort of inverted snobbery or perhaps a political correctness. But are parishioners envious of a vicar with a bigger house than their own? Most people surely understand the system. The vicar does not own the house in any normal sense, and it is a place of work, dedicated to mission, as well as a home.

"If the Church proposes, as it often does, that the parsonage is only the private dwelling of the parson, then this view fails. But if the vicar uses it for work, has a study/office in it, if hospitality is exercised, if the house becomes a place for the social enrichment of the body of Christ, and for activities of different age groups that it builds up, then the parish, whether rich or poor, accept it as the appropriate house, and make no inappropriate comparisons."[1]

The pastoral argument is that by putting the vicar in a house more like his neighbour's, he is brought nearer to the people. The fact that larger houses can be used for PCC meetings, parish meetings, pastoral care, community fêtes, garden parties, and car boot sales seems to carry no weight. There are certainly vicars who agree with their diocese. One response to a survey of traditional parsonages was:

> I regret that in my case your request for help . . . is as seed falling on
> stony ground. There can be little or no mileage in preserving the notion
> that the Church is in any way museum-like. The very existence of huge
> parsonages speaks nothing of the Gospel . . . I would dearly love to sell
> all the parsonages . . . and thus enable clergy to live in . . . less alienating

circumstances. "Live in an old parsonage and maintain the depressingly drab status quo" hardly commends the Gospel, does it? Here endeth my reply—I need to lift the black cloud occasioned by your letter and will therefore do some parish work as an antidote.[2]

By contrast, the former vicar of Pinchbeck said after his beloved vicarage was sold off:

> Our family loved living in the vicarage—it was one of the great bonuses of the job. We used it for parish suppers, council meetings and garden parties, so everyone benefited.[3]

Money is not a permitted statutory reason for selling a parsonage. Despite that, financial justifications are frequently made. The argument is at first sight straightforward. The Church must be cost conscious and efficient, as any modern organisation has to be. Sale of old parsonages releases money which can be used either for the financing of other Church liabilities, such as clergy pensions, which are of course a huge concern, or new, smaller houses that are cheaper to run. But the statistics suggest that the capital raised from parsonage sales has not always been preserved and reinvested.

The cost of maintenance is certainly a headache to any institution. It is repeatedly said that old, large parsonages are quite simply too expensive to maintain. This remains an obsession despite the much reduced number of old houses in the Church's care, and despite the maintenance problems created by some of the new, more shoddily built houses. Dioceses are obliged by law to send their surveyors out to each house at least once every five years, but even when this is adhered to, the recommended maintenance is not always carried out. Eventually, dioceses tend to use the poor state of repair of the house as a reason for selling, resulting in a depressed market price.

One diocese demolished the elegant chimney on a Regency parsonage. This prevented the rector from using the fireplaces for the fires he needed in the winter, quite apart from the fact that it had damaged a fine house. A diocesan officer said: "We have on a number of occasions informed the incumbent that the chimney stacks were in very poor condition and . . . [they] were removed rather than rebuilt at the time the parsonage was re-roofed." A classic case of failure to understand a traditional house or to do normal maintenance.

"We bought our house straight from the Church nine years ago", says [Ms. X]. "It was in a terrible condition, with almost no plumbing. The poor rector was reduced to living in three rooms on the ground floor—there was no heating at all." Even so, the stunning looks of the eighteenth-century Grade II Old Rectory at Coberley, near Cheltenham, Gloucestershire, drew 20 bidders.[4] The retiring rector himself was unimpressed by such whingeings.

The unofficial reasons

Official reasons given by bureaucracies are rarely the whole story. There are underlying motivations. Like short-term income. Money is liquidity and a cash injection may help avoid embarrassment in the year-end accounts. For every sale, the diocese gets a capital windfall. Then there is the "change" syndrome. The idea that every organisation must be in a state of constant change is a modern obsession. There is change all around us, so we must change just to stand still. The cynic might observe that this frenzy of change has not equated to progress. "Heritage phobia" is another problem. There is a detectable "mind-set" in the Church which says that no value must be placed on its heritage, except perhaps where money can be made from tourism. This may be linked to the "change" culture. The Church sees its traditional buildings as a burden, an encumbrance. There is a widespread perception both in General Synod and in the diocesan offices that buildings have nothing to do with "today's Church". It is an odd notion, and completely out of step with mainstream sentiment. But it is difficult to supplant. It is reflected in the extraordinary dictum of the Archdeacon of Leicester, intent on selling the rectory at Scalford, Leicestershire, no matter what, who said: "The mission of the Church is not about vicarages."[5] In General Synod there was even considerable opposition to the Church Heritage Forum, which simply, and belatedly, acknowledged the importance of churches. The Church hierarchy seems to have little time either for its buildings or for its history.

Then there is bureaucracy itself. At the end of the thirteenth century, at the height of its power, the Catholic Church had 17 dioceses and 40 archdeaconries. Today, with far fewer clergy to serve nearly 20 times the population, there are 41 (down from 43) English Anglican dioceses and about 150 archdeacons. A bureaucracy seeks to justify its existence. It becomes self-serving, just as our vast modern state sector now exists mainly to preserve its own jobs. Study groups must therefore be set up and recommendations made. This is not just useless; it can be positively dangerous: silly decisions can be made. Centralisation also leads to a "control" culture, and this does not care for too much individuality or initiative at parish level, unless authorised, channelled, and directed. Fixed ideas develop into firm policies: whenever an older parsonage becomes vacant it must be disposed of. If there is an incumbent in the way, removal or relocation of the incumbent becomes an obsession. If parishioners express their fears at proposed diocesan action, they are seen as an obstacle, either to be ignored, or if they persist, flattened. Many a PCC secretary has resigned after the enforced sale of the parsonage.

The book *Parsonages: A Design Guide*, colloquially known as the "Green Guide", which lays down recommended specifications, dimensions, configuration, and square footage for parsonages, is a symbol of that centralisation of control. It has become the Bible (if that expression can be pardoned) of diocesan staff. It is advisory, not mandatory, as it expressly states, yet it is widely used by diocesan officers to require an older parsonage of, say, 3,000 sq. ft to be sold, because it exceeds the recommended 2,000. The use that has been made of it has proved a disaster for the traditional parsonage.

The sceptics

"There are those . . . who . . . argue that the sale of our former rectories and vicarages has exacerbated the Church's drift from the centre of the community, and deprived parishioners of what was a parish resource."
Jackson-Stops and Staff, UK Market Review 2005/2006

Parishioners, land agents, journalists, conservationists, and campaigners have been expressing worries about the sense, financial or otherwise, of these sales for many years now. It is widely recognised that many early sales were justifiable. Some of those rectories were very large. The doubts crept in when those that were much more modest, and ideally situated, started being sold off in large numbers, their only apparent crime being their age.

Save Our Parsonages (SOP) was born in 1994 in response to disquiet, not to say distress, in the parishes. Its founder director, Noël Riley, got a ready press from the outset. Typical was the article in *Perspectives* (January 1995) which commented:

For years the Church of England has been selling off its historic parsonages on the grounds that they are too old, too large and too expensive to maintain. In place it has built new vicarages, often in the large gardens of the older buildings, which are then sold for a handsome fee. Sadly, the good intentions to cut costs are proving too optimistic, as badly built vicarages of the 1960s and 1970s are soaking up large repair bills—and the cramped rooms of the new parsonages are turning out to be too small for parish meetings. Now a body has been launched to campaign against the Church's compulsive shedding of its historic buildings, arguing that vicarages can be successfully modernised . . . Save Our Parsonages is appealing for support to convince the Church that its ruthlessly 'rational' policy is an expensive mistake.

The supporters of SOP believe that the traditional parsonage is a focal point for the local community, even for those who are not churchgoers, and gives meaning to the life of the village both on a symbolic and a practical level with garden parties and community activities; that it is also the most effective tool for advancing the Church's mission, and if the house is lost to the Church, its congregations diminish.

Some of the more recent work of SOP has been directed towards trying to improve the appeals procedures we discussed in Chapter 11. This led to the development of its "code of practice" as a tool in the effort to mediate between the parishes on the one hand and the centralised Church bodies on the other. The purpose of the code was to improve consultation, and it proposed that there should be a meeting between the diocese and the parish at the time when the sale of its parsonage is first mooted by the diocese. Not only did no diocese agree to implement it, none even took the trouble to comment on its wording.

Mervyn Wilson, a committee member of Save Our Parsonages, explained:

SOP has set out the importance of satisfying three parties: The bishop and his staff, the priest/incumbent, and the people of the parish. Each must respect the other, as our faith teaches. One cannot act on his own, even though in the past the vicar came near to it, though he always needed diocesan permission, and sometimes his patron's. There have also been many instances since the 1938 Parsonage Measure of bishops acting on their own (generally through archdeacons and parsonage boards). There is considerable evidence that when one is allowed to act alone, or overmuch deference is given to one, the mission and pastoral ministry of the church is adversely affected.

He added:

It is important that lay people should be brought in early . . . It is important that the diocese should be open and fair in its presentation of figures to the parish. Generosity responds to openness and reality withers wherever there is suspicion of hidden agenda or special pleading.

In 1989, Gervase Jackson-Stops, recording the battle with the Diocesan Parsonages Board to save the seventeenth-century vicarage at Towcester,[6] lamented the poor standard of design of new parsonages, concluding that there must be a sociological as well as a financial motive behind parsonage disposals. He pointed out that in recent years there had been a revolution in thinking about agricultural and industrial buildings, with warehouses and barns now making fantastic sums, and with all that going on "it seems nothing less than mad that the Church should still be divesting itself of one of its prime capital assets". He wisely pointed out that to attract the right candidates for the ministry, that is, those who intend to become part of the community and not be "unseen within it", the Church must offer them houses that are "not only distinctive but also represent the Anglican tradition at its best". He concluded: "These buildings are in every way as meaningful as churches and cathedrals."

Of course, if the clergy really are happier in their new abodes, and the old ones really are unsuitable, perhaps we are all happy. After all, the public demand for old rectories always exceeds supply, though the Church never acknowledges that. Perhaps diocesan secretaries are from Mars, implanted into the bodies of Earthmen, in a sort of "invasion of the parsonage sellers".

Notes

[1] Mervyn Wilson, from *Save Our Parsonages Newsletter*.

[2] A quotation by a vicar from J. Hummerstone, *Historic Parsonages in Devon* (1995, survey report).

[3] Another vicar, quoted in *Save Our Parsonages Newsletter*.

[4] "Simply Divine", *Sunday Telegraph*, 10 July 2005.

[5] *Save our Parsonages Newsletter*, Summer 2004, p. 14.

[6] "A Parsonage to be Proud Of", *Country Life*, 31 August 1989.

Part Five: The Legacy

*"In my beginning is my end. In succession houses
rise and fall, crumble and are extended"*

T. S. Eliot

CHAPTER 13

The House

The parsonage has been with us for a thousand years. For much of that time it has been at the centre of English life. The legacy of the parsonage is architectural, cultural, and sociological as well as spiritual. It is a snapshot of the state of the Church at any one time. It is, or once was, and should still be, central to the life of the town or village as a whole. The presence of the house in the parish is as important as that of the vicar.

Sadly, the story of the parsonage is also one of neglect; the Church has never been good at looking after its property, whether due to poverty, pluralism, irresponsibility, political upheaval, disputes about legal responsibility, or lack of funds. At Stoke, in Staffordshire, the historic moated parsonage was abandoned by the nineteenth-century rector and it was demolished in 1891. At Harlton, Cambridgeshire, the former vicarage, recorded in the fifteenth century, was ruinous in 1783 and had been demolished by 1807. At Eastling, Faversham, Kent, the interesting much earlier rectory (see Figure 9 on page 218) that preceded the new house of the 1840s (now itself sold off) no longer exists.

In other ways the house was treated like the vicar. Just like him, the new one was formally welcomed to the parish. The population in the Cardiff area was rapidly expanding in the late nineteenth century and in 1879 a school was built at St German's, Roath, Cardiff, to the design of G. F. Bodley. In 1884, a new permanent church, also by Bodley, was opened. Then his new clergy house went up. The Benediction of the New Clergy House took place on 24 April 1894. We can see from the Order of Service that it started in the church with psalms, collects, the vicar's address, a hymn, and a collection for clergy house funds; that was followed by a procession to the clergy house with a hymn. Then at the house there were prayers for it and its occupants, followed by prayers "at the door"; "at the dining room"; "at the vicar's room"; "at the studies"; "at the oratory"; "at the waiting room";

"at the kitchen"; "at the sleeping rooms", and "at the guest chamber". A final hymn
was sung on the way out.

**Figure 9: The demolished rectory at Eastling,
Faversham, Kent, in an 1827 print**

The ideal rectory

"Though a stranger to the village I knew at once that this was the parsonage"
William Addison, The English Country Parson

In the western part of York lies Acomb, its village character now preserved
only round the green. In that setting is a mid-Victorian red brick house with
timber-framed gables. *The Buildings of England* calls it "an unmistakeable former
vicarage". What makes it so? Plato said that a work of art is merely the imitation
of perfection. My research has made me wonder whether there is such a thing as
the essence of a parsonage.

The early parsonage was next to the church. The Georgian parsonage was
often, though by no means always, in a prosperous new road a little way away,
like the manor house. The Victorians once again tended to see proximity to the

church as desirable. The setting gives a clue to how the vicar saw the role of the parsonage in his time.

The size and relative sophistication of parsonage houses changed over the years. They were small when the social status of clergy was low, grew in size when it was higher or the town was more prosperous, and shrank again when money was scarcer or, in recent years, when the Church began signalling its modern faux humility, something without earlier parallel. But even with all those changes, at least before the twentieth century there was something about it that marked out the parsonage.

We noted in Chapter 6 that, according to Brunskill, the parsonage is neither in the "great house" nor the "cottage" category, nor in many cases and in later times, the "small house" either. It is most often a "vernacular large house". This usefully narrows the field for what in a given town or village may be the parsonage. The widespread disappearance of the vernacular in Victorian times means that there are few truly vernacular Victorian parsonages, but they continue to fit that broad picture.

Parking opposite the church in any village, I have many times seen at least three possible candidates for the old rectory. In Horbling, Lincolnshire, one was the manor house adjacent to the churchyard, with its own private access door through the garden wall, as might be expected of the rectory. One was a good Victorian house in Tudor style across the road, but this seemed the wrong shape, too long and low, and only of one and a half storeys. The third, gaunt and early Victorian, tall with arched doorway, hidden behind the manor house, now boxed in by a private road with modern houses at the back, proved the best candidate. Setting proved its worth. Owners of old parsonages also seem adept at keeping their charms concealed from the prying eye by barrages of vegetation, so this, perversely, becomes a clue. Finding the parsonage you seek, incidentally, is fraught with other pitfalls. If you ask somebody local where the old parsonage is, they will often direct you to a completely different house from the one in *The Buildings of England*, but that is merely a function of the number that exist.

These are all useful clues in our search for the essential parsonage. But even more pertinent are form and style. To what extent can a parsonage be identified as a parsonage from its appearance, and how? Does it have special characteristics, or is it just like any other house of its size, status, and period? Then there are wider questions. To what extent is the theory that the form of a building should reflect its function relevant to the parsonage? How relevant is its identifiability as a parsonage to its suitability for the mission of the Church? What is the interface between the function of a parsonage and its aesthetics? Is a parsonage better suited for its job if it is of fine architectural quality?

Form and function

The theory that form should reflect function could almost be said to be the battlecry of modernist architects. But it is not a new theory. It has a very long history. Since Vitruvius, shortly before the birth of Christ, theorists have tried to establish links between the functionality of a building and its appearance. Traditionally, English architects have not been as obsessed by theory as those in continental Europe. Palladianism, coming after the Baroque, might be thought comparatively purist, but James Stuart and Nicholas Revett saw its non-load-bearing pillars and pilasters as corrupt by comparison with their favoured Greek Revival. Loudon was also prone to theorising, and the whole nineteenth-century reaction to classicism encouraged it. Pugin was as dogmatic, and as ideological in his way, as any Le Corbusier. He believed that all ornament should be derived from practicality, even though he did not go so far as to say that any ornament or decoration was anathema, as the modernists of the 1920s did. Their view was to a considerable extent a reaction to the Victorian manner, a great irony considering Pugin's theories were not dissimilar and led him to conclude that the Gothic was the only true style. That alone is enough to show that what is essentially the same theory can be interpreted in different ways, and can lead to very different results.

Part of the difficulty is what is meant by functionalism. A building may reveal its structure and the functions its parts play, and display its core materials. That is one type of functionalism. A building may illustrate by its form the function it performs, since a church, a castle, a barn, a factory, and a house all have their own forms. That is a quite different type of functionalism. In the first sense, conscious design, style, or ornamentation are irrelevant, while in the second, they may be very relevant, even dominant. In between, perhaps, is the theory that the form of a building should allow it to serve efficiently, as a place in which to live, or as a factory, or whatever. In the first sense, the theory is better served by the medieval and Victorian parsonage than the Georgian, since they were built from the inside, the rooms dictating the external shape, whereas in the case of the Georgian, external symmetry was dominant and the interior had to comply with that. But that was true of all houses, not just parsonages. In the third sense, the

Figure 10A: The Rectory, Upper Heyford, Oxfordshire

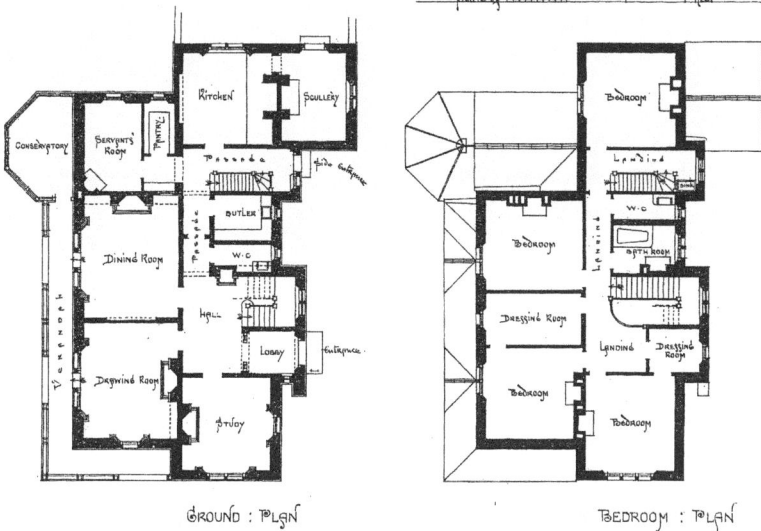

Figure 10B: Plan of the Rectory, Upper Heyford, Oxfordshire

theory is of limited use in distinguishing the parsonage from any other house, there being no need to discriminate between a religious or a secular function. But parsonages were built for the specific purpose of serving the Church, and it seems inevitably likely that some are more successful in that role than others. It is also true, I think, that many of us have a mental image of a parsonage, perhaps even of what we think a parsonage ought to look like. So, does the architecture of a parsonage have, or ought it to have, any distinguishing characteristics?

The first inconvenient fact is that not all parsonages were purpose-built. The medieval priest was often happy to use any hovel for his home. A number of parsonages were converted from other Church buildings, for example monastic offices, and throughout history, houses never built for the Church but for secular use have regularly been acquired for use as parsonages. In Georgian times, the squire, or lord of the manor, was sometimes the vicar, and used or gave his house as the vicarage. Bungalows or boxes on modern estates are regularly acquired by the Church as parsonages. It must follow that, by their nature, these have at least no necessary relationship in form to their new function; any such relationship must then either be a matter of accident or of how they may subsequently have been adapted (*pace* those who may say that a house becomes holy through mere clerical occupancy!).

But what about the purpose-built houses? Something more akin to the theory in the second sense above was widely believed by the early nineteenth-century theorists, even before Pugin: the parsonage should look as if it is inhabited by a clergyman, whether by making use of the physical characteristics of the church or by some other means. Most English churches were built in the thirteenth to fifteenth centuries in Gothic rather than classical style, and the Victorian Gothic was a conscious endeavour to make the house as fitting as possible for an ecclesiastical purpose. The Victorian parsonage is accordingly the easiest to recognise from its architecture. With its lively roofline and window tracery, it sometimes almost looks a smaller version of the church alongside it. The medieval priest's house, though otherwise plain, also had arched or segmentally moulded, and often cusped, windows, in the same manner as the church, from which we might conclude that the medieval builder had the same intent. But we must remember that most stone medieval houses of any type, with any kind of pretension, had similar windows.

As to the Georgian parsonage, it looks little different from the gentleman's house next door. It may be argued that the Georgian church was built in the classical style, and so was the Georgian parsonage. But the parsonage looks markedly more like the squire's house than any church. Without those ecclesiastical references it looks more secular than its Victorian equivalent, more worldly, elegant, and urbane. The footpath from Greatford to Barholm, Lincolnshire, leads through flat, peaceful fields, empty apart from a rare Leyland tractor, to the church, and beside it the old rectory by Edward Browning, son of Bryan Browning, of 1850. Despite its late date, it is a simple but elegant three-bay ashlar limestone house still in Georgian style, more irregular at the back. Only a hundred yards or so away is Manor Farmhouse, about the same size and shape, a little more Regency in style with long sash windows down to the ground, but for all the world also the rectory. The two are indistinguishable as to their function, except that one is beside the church, and that, for Georgian houses, is unreliable evidence.

Yet Nikolaus Pevsner's comment in his introduction to Savidge, "The Georgian rectory could be any Georgian gentleman's house, the Victorian rectory could not possibly be anything else",[1] is not quite right either. When we look at a Georgian parsonage, we can often say it has the appearance of one. It could perhaps even be argued that its more secular appearance is appropriate for the Georgian clergyman in an age of enlightenment, unable or even unwilling to rival his assiduous Victorian equivalent in his study of scriptures or sermon, the port decanter in his dining room his priority. Equally, and more controversially, the idea that the Victorian High Gothic parsonage is distinctive can also be overdone. Large numbers of Victorian houses were built in the Gothic style, not just the parsonage. William Wilkinson produced a book of house designs in which his large country houses, with their banded brickwork, steep gables, mullions, and turrets, are just scaled-up versions of his High Gothic parsonages, quite indistinguishable from those at Linton, Herefordshire, Swanbourne, Buckinghamshire, and Upper Heyford, Oxfordshire (see Figure 10A on page 221).

As for the modern parsonage, it is easy to conclude that it rarely attempts to display any characteristics that may associate it with the Church, and it is more or less impossible to distinguish it from any other house.

Is there a distinction between the urban and the rural parsonage? We saw in Chapter 6 that the Catholic and Anglo-Catholic clergy houses differ very much from the normal parsonage in their massing, and are usually identifiable by their form, though even these can look like seminaries, vestry houses, or other institutions.

If the house is a working parsonage, there are more clues, but these are nothing to do with the form of the house. Its condition will help identify it—its privatised fellow in the next village will look much less dilapidated. Then there is the garden, which is likely to be satisfyingly unkempt. The interior provides even stronger clues. My experience of those I have visited is that they have a special character and atmosphere markedly different from that of any other house, especially their counterpart in private hands, albeit rather hard to define. There is a certain informality, an individuality, a scholarly and sometimes unworldly air, and a sense of timelessness. In physical terms there is an absence of gadgetry, a greater likelihood of a proper fire in the grate. Former parsonages have lost that atmosphere.

The culture of the parsonage is exemplified in a catalogue of Bonhams, the auctioneers, in my possession entitled "Books, Manuscripts, and Photographs from the sale of the Contents of The Old Rectory, Banningham". The sale was on 22 March 2004 and was of a wonderful collection of over 350 items at the Norfolk house, including antiquarian books and bindings, music scores, diaries with drawings, bibles and theological works with wonderful woodcuts and engravings, nineteenth- and twentieth-century illustrated books including Charles Kingsley and M. R. James ghost stories, natural history books including Bewick, books and magazines on art, architecture and country houses and gardens, books of etchings of East Anglian buildings and antiquities, albums of early photographs, manuscripts and estate maps, and other ephemera. It is so very much what you expect to see assembled from the shelves and drawers of the library of a country parson.

Richard Wellby, a conservation architect,[2] has considered the whole question of whether a parsonage has particular characteristics; the background to his thesis was the sale by the Church of its traditional parsonages to private buyers and the question of their ability to adapt to this change of use. He asked whether the fact that a house was a parsonage could be determined by inspection. Can the theories of semiotics be applied to the parsonage? He agrees that context is important: proximity to church and graveyard, for example. Symbolic trees: oak, ash, and yew. Affinity with farming: most country parsons had to be farmers too. What about the nineteenth-century Gothic style? This was not totally conclusive. Many early nineteenth-century writers of the pattern books saw Gothic as a style that could be applied to other houses just as readily as to parsonages. It was just a style. If pressed, however, they did tend to see the Gothic as the most appropriate. T. F. Hunt thought the classical style always "out of harmony" when adjacent to the church. J. B. Papworth thought the parsonage should reflect the church. The High Gothicists very much took that view. Here Mr Wellby notes the contrasting modern view of the Church Commissioners that "a parsonage is essentially a normal family house as well as a base for the incumbent's work . . . " How Pugin and the Tractarians would have railed against that statement! It reveals how differently the Church now sees itself. Mr Wellby's broad conclusion is that the

Victorian purpose-built parsonage was much more obviously a parsonage in terms of its style than those of other periods, and in the case of both the medieval and the modern house it is more difficult to determine its function.

It is worth noting that the most "ecclesiological" of the High Gothic parsonages, with their turrets and stair towers, which convey such a powerful image of the parsonage, are by no means as common as might be thought. Most Victorian parsonages were not of that type. The evidence overwhelmingly suggests that parsonages have conformed to the wider formal and stylistic developments over the years that have been applied to any house of their size. To understand the architecture of the parsonage it is sufficient to understand architecture. The most distinctively Victorian parsonage is unmistakeably dateable by the same stylistic rules as its secular equivalent, and its form is defined by its period rather than its peculiar function. That is not to say that it is not identifiable, far from it, but we must primarily look to factors such as setting, massing, the status of the house, the quality of its detailing, its garden, and its scale relative to the other houses in the town or village to identify the parsonage.

The ideal parsonage

Where does that leave us in our search for the ideal parsonage? The concept of aesthetics is out of fashion among our opinion formers today, almost frowned upon. But you do not have to be an architectural historian to understand there is something about a "good" house that we are aware of when we see it. The more parsonages we see, the more we are likely to conclude that aesthetics are an important factor. They have often been designed with a little more care, and it shows. Associated qualities such as quality of materials, lack of ostentation, and a sense of tradition, venerability, and dignity are all rather subjective and intangible, but we may observe that parsonages, as a general rule, have these in greater measure than their secular equivalents. The greater complexity of the larger parsonage often gives the architect more scope to display his skills. I can see that many of the qualities I admire in a parsonage are those that the Church nowadays most dislikes.

There is no one architectural style, no one period of history that summarises the ideal parsonage, but it is unlikely to be the modern parsonage in which the qualifying criteria will be recognised. The last war represented the end of an era and the beginning of a new one, both in cultural and in architectural terms. The early post-war years symbolise the demise of the concept of the "fine" house, and of the concept of elegance, even in terms of architectural aspiration. "A parsonage is essentially a normal family house as well as being a base for the incumbent's work" are weasel words, which may be translated as "the Church has lost the courage of its convictions". By contrast, a mere glance at many an earlier parsonage suffices to show it to be a good house, to some degree irrespective of its architectural significance or integrity; most of the older parsonages, even with bits and ends having been added, or when truncated or defaced, look well for it, and allow us to read their history, as we can with our ancient churches.

Does better architecture make a better parsonage? Does its appearance make it more effective? Does an aesthetic house confer unquantifiable benefits on its town or village? In my view, the quality of a house and its appropriateness for its function and its setting create a better environment. A better environment gives rise to contentment, and a contented community is a better one.

So, what is the ideal parsonage? There is probably no such thing. If we try to create one with pencil and paper, or on our computer, by taking our favourite feature of this, and our favourite feature of that, and putting them together, it will certainly not work. But it must have both substance and character. My own mental image is one of gables, steeply pitched roof, chimneystacks, a generous doorway, and an appealing combination of local stone, brick, or timber. I am tempted to add the mullioned window to that list. I suppose I am thereby revealed to have ruled out Regency classicism. It can excel, but it has too much competition. I even have worries about the coveted Palladianism. A classical pediment stuck on an English house is of course elegant, but it works even better in Italy, particularly if by Palladio. I am obviously closer to the romanticism of the English tradition.

The analysis in Chapter 8 is supposedly a more objective one, but if correct, it is a blow both to the Victorian and the more recent parsonage. I tried to jot down my own favourites for comparison. I also found I was mostly listing early houses, but some Victorian ones as well. My own top 20 (at least on the day I did that exercise) was as follows: Muchelney, Somerset; Wantage, Berkshire; Methwold, Norfolk; Coalpit Heath, Gloucestershire; Cossington, Leicestershire; Great Snoring, Norfolk; Congresbury, Somerset; Iffley, Oxford; Market Deeping, Lincolnshire; Bridewell Place, London; Corbridge, Northumberland; Chew Stoke, Somerset; West Hanney, Oxfordshire; Great Brington, Northamptonshire; Burford, Oxfordshire; Oakley Square, Camden, London; Bredon, Worcestershire; West Ashby, Lincolnshire; St Columb Major, Cornwall; Easington, Seaton Holme, Durham.

Ten of these houses are medieval or Elizabethan, six are Victorian, one (Market Deeping) is medieval but encased in a Victorian skin. The other three are Restoration, Queen Anne, and early Georgian. On another day, the choice might have been different, but I note with interest and some surprise that there is no parsonage here from the popular late Georgian and Regency era of parsonage building.

The parsonage as a focus for learning

The history of teaching in England, from the earliest times of Christianity until the nineteenth century, was inextricably bound up with religion. The clergy were prominent founders of Oxford and Cambridge and the other universities, for a long time fellows and teachers had to have clerical training, and clerical education was their most fundamental task. There was no state involvement in education at all until 1833 and it was in the hands of the Church. The strongest association and most important function of the traditional parsonage, after the Christian mission, has been that of teaching and education.

University staff remained celibate even after the Reformation. The colleges were patrons of the parishes and had the right to present incumbents. Religion was inextricably bound up with Latin. Grammar schools, as they were named, taught Latin grammar, a vital skill for the educated classes and clerics alike— the first English Bible was not introduced into churches until 1539. After the reign of Elizabeth I, things were no less stringent—on the contrary, teachers had to be mainstream Protestants and not Dissenters. There was an initial fall in students after the dissolution of the monasteries, which had been major teaching institutions, but this was only temporary and the university student numbers rapidly increased in the seventeenth century. It was not until 1854 that religious tests finally ceased to be a requirement for a degree, and by the late nineteenth century fellows were no longer required to be in holy orders. Despite that, the Church continued to have a vital role in education.

A good Victorian rector or vicar thought it his duty to provide education for the local children, whether of the prosperous or the poor. If he could not afford a school building, tuition took place in his house, which was usually big enough for the purpose. Here the Victorian parsonage proved itself of great worth. For the parson and his family, education was another form of income. The Brontës sketched out a prospectus for a school to educate young ladies at the parsonage, at £35 a year for board and education. Nothing came of it; Miss Branwell, their aunt, would not pay for the necessary alterations to the parsonage. In 1858, government grants became based on standards achieved. The role of the parish clergy was vital, but they now had to have good teachers. To appease Dissenters, the 1870 Education Act which finally set up publicly maintained schools, the Board Schools, made them non-denominational.

Then there was Sunday school, started by Robert Raikes and Thomas Stock, still an indelible part of the memory of many of us who grew up in post-war Britain, but first invented for the labouring children of the poor, who were at work all week and could only attend school on Sunday. Sunday school was often held in the rectory. Only later did it sometimes switch to the church or the hall. The parsonage was more and more a central part of the everyday life of the village.

The vicarage garden

The clergy have always been associated with gardening, indeed the phrase "the vicarage garden" has become a cliché, conjuring up indelible images of croquet, cucumber sandwiches, and tea on summer lawns between intermittent showers. Vicarages have usually had notably fine and spacious gardens, even in areas of comparatively high density. For many of us, the vicarage garden has been the English version of the Garden of Eden, the nearest place to paradise in East Sheen.

Medieval monks were gardeners, and their traditions survived the Dissolution. The medieval garden, square to reflect the cloister, was a practical affair, consisting of the herb garden and the vegetable garden, and later the flower garden. Nicholas Colnet, who was Henry V's physician during the Agincourt campaign, grew herbs at the Prebendal Manor House, Nassington, Northamptonshire, where the gardens recreate those of the thirteenth to fifteenth century. Some plants were grown for medicinal purposes, others for their symbolism, others for their fragrance.

Fishponds survived at the parsonage even when the need to eat fish had gone. Hutchins, in his *History of Dorset* (1774), noted that at the parsonage at Nether Compton the trout "seem to have forgot their natural shyness" and followed the rector to be fed.

William Lawson, vicar of Ormesby, Yorkshire, wrote a very early gardening book, *The New Orchard and Garden*, in 1618, with a chapter on tree management.

George Herbert, in *A Priest to the Temple*, or *The Country Parson, a Spiritual Guide for Parsons* (1652), wrote that the clergy should teach their parishioners gardening, because gardens were places of healing and delight, and also dispensaries, because of their herbs. It was part of the job of the parish priest to grow herbs for medicinal purposes. Robert Herrick, the Royalist clergyman, was not so keen on his farm and garden on the edge of Dartmoor in around 1630, and longed to be in London, despite his poetry about wild flowers.

Over the centuries, fashion in garden design swung between the formal and the free. Tudor and Jacobean gardens were still formal, but more recreational, and after the Restoration they became more sophisticated, emulating the pomposity of the French style or the precision of the Dutch. In those days nature was something to be tamed, not celebrated. The eighteenth-century opposition to the formal French garden began in England. The ideas of Capability Brown brought in a new conceit—that wild landscape could be improved by artifice, a man-made wilderness substituted for a real one, idealised with vistas. Then around 1800, the romantic garden became tamer again with the influence of Repton, then Loudon and Decimus Burton. There was a move to more formality in prim Victorian times, but greater eclecticism as well. Gardeners such as Paxton had a taste for spectacular and surprise effects. The Edwardian era favoured grand gardens based on the Baroque and French Renaissance influences, but the flower garden movement of William Robinson, and later Lutyens and Jekyll, was bringing informality back. The Arts and Crafts garden favoured local materials, traditional plants, freedom of growth, and naturalism, but up to a point—Jekyll realised freedom had to be controlled in the new smaller gardens of the day.

The vicarage garden has rarely had great pretension, but has usually been special nonetheless. The vicarage garden is as necessary to the parsonage as the house, and evolved as befitted the material means and the spiritual aspirations of the parson and in the way he interpreted his calling. Until Victorian times the vicar was usually also a farmer, and much of his land was working land. In the eighteenth century, if he was wealthy he developed a love of antiquarianism, and built hermitages and grottoes. In the nineteenth century, he could afford gardeners and had time himself to grow plants and cultivate vegetables.

The parsonage itself can even sometimes be identified by its garden. If it is in the centre of town it is often, even now, a survival of a more generous plot from earlier times when the population was low and there was more space. It often has a large grassed area. The lawnmower was invented in 1830. I wonder if the parsonage lawn immediately got neater as a result?

Of notable parsonage gardens, those mentioned in *The Buildings of England* include the "hanging gardens in terraces" at Winston-on-Tees, Durham; that at Bury, Lancashire; Finmere, Oxfordshire, where the grounds had been landscaped by Capability Brown, but no trace remains; and that at Bremhill, Wiltshire, where William Bowles was said to have "frittered away its beauty with grottoes, hermitages, and Shenstonian inscriptions".[3] At Sydling St Nicholas, Dorset, the mainly Tudor parsonage is near the old market cross, and yews in the garden are thought to be 1,000 years old.

It is worth considering the history of one fairly typical vicarage garden. At Bulwick, in Northamptonshire, the oldest part of the house, dating from the seventeenth century, was that of a yeoman farmer. After the enclosure, in this case in the 1770s, the rector got about 300 acres, including 20 acres adjacent to the house. In 1817, the rector, John Tryon, a cousin of the squire, added a "gentry front" to the house and planted park trees in the fields opposite. At the back he had his farm buildings. He lived like a gentleman farmer. In his day an area of garden was walled. In 1862, he was succeeded by John Holdich, who kept a diary, from which we learn how he cleared away the farm buildings, and added to the house a new range, consisting of butler's pantry, larders, WCs, a garden entry, drains, a wash room, a stable, and carriage block. He planted Wellingtonias and other trees of interest. There is no record in his diary that he used the garden for other than his private needs and pleasure. In his day the walled garden of about half an acre would have provided food for the family and staff. He also planted fruit trees and had an orchard. He would probably have kept a house cow, and carriage horses.

A tennis court was added in the early twentieth century and probably made available to the village. Not much is known of this period. The rectors were still living as minor gentry, but things had begun to change. Clergy had less money. The stipend had decreased in real value and the tithe had become valueless. The glebe farm produced less in the depression of the 1930s. The new vicar had less money, but still a social conscience. The full-time gardener went, and was replaced by a jobbing gardener, at least until 1939. In the war the now underused walled garden was made available to a village pig club. In other places it provided allotments.

After the war many such vicarages were sold, but many still had gardens of one or two acres, and often housed elderly clergy, who could not maintain them personally and had not the means to pay for help in the garden. Gardens became neglected; areas of them were sold, and in due course the house went too. But some continued to be cherished and even improved, Bulwick among them. The rector re-created the garden in the 1970s as a resource for his ministry in the parish. There were social events on lawns; places for games for the youth club, places where the elderly could meet, and where the occasional service could be held. It was also open to the public and provided a venue for garden retreats. In the 1990s, the rector began to develop a Journey of Life garden. It was appreciated as a spiritual place, and it had its roots strongly within a tradition that goes back to Eden. Now the parsonage at Bulwick has been sold, and the story has come to an end.

Parsonage garden plants

Research shows a certain tradition in planting. A spreading tree on the lawn; fruits such as mulberries, quinces, medlars, apples, walnuts, pears, plums, cobs, and hazel; the Gloire de Dijon rose, carpets of aconites and snowdrops in spring. The parson's garden reflected his taste and education, and his social position, in a long tradition, continuing from the Middle Ages. The new protestant clerics tended their gardens as well as their flocks and made the English rectory or vicarage garden into one of the great mythic images.[4] Clergy up to the eighteenth century were active in promoting herbal remedies.

Dr William Turner, Dean of Wells from the 1550s, had studied botany and medicine in Italy. He wrote a herbal, and presumably planted specimens in the deanery garden. He describes the plants and where to find those that can be used to cure complaints. It was the time when Cranach and others were painting their views of paradise. In the seventeenth century, protestant clerics, so conscious of sin, looked to a prelapsarian world, and identified the fault which had destroyed its peace and tranquillity. Meanwhile, many sought to recover it in their private domains. Apples, above all: there was a view that apples reproduced without fertilisation, and so were spared the sin of concupiscence.

The *Ailanthus altissima*, or Tree of Heaven, was popular for its reminder of the afterlife. There is one at Harlton, Cambridgeshire, where the drive sweeps round it, planted by the Revd James Fendall, for whom the house had been built in 1843. Parsonages have some of the oldest cedars. Lombardy poplars were also a favourite.

This enduring mix of learned enquiry, practical action, and an eye to beauty in varying ways also distinguished many later clergy, and some of them are discussed in the next chapter. The clergy have taken a wide interest in natural history in all its forms, and it has often been through the experience of their garden that their interest has been kindled.

Of course, the parsonage garden has a less flattering image. When Edith Olivier accompanied Rex Whistler to a run-down rectory in the hope of buying it, she noted: "The garden was a wilderness. Sombre yews and laurels had encroached onto the white gravel path; and in the untidy grass patch in front of the house could be seen the ghosts of flower beds . . . " William Addison, arriving in a village, noted:

> It was not so much the unpretentious charm and quiet dignity of the house itself as the garden that distinguished it from the manor house. Some might say it was a neglected garden. No doubt the parson lacked the means to keep his lawns as trim as those of the squire. And yet . . . there was a graciousness about its borders that made this kind of neglect seem almost a virtue.[5]

Bax talks of the parsonage garden in terms of "the choked alleys of its evergreen walks", but adds: "Even when the flower beds are hidden by nettles, when the lawn is pied with tickets flung over the wall from a bus stop, or fowls scratch among the runaway laurels by the gate, even then the parsonage retains its proper atmosphere."[6] At Orwell's fictional rectory, "the front garden was choked with ragged fir trees and a great spreading ash which shadowed the front rooms and made it impossible to grow any flowers".[7]

The parsonage garden today

"The garden is too large; it will be a burden to the vicar"—so a parsonage board sells the parsonage.

There are still clergy who see the parsonage garden as an asset to ministry. Vicarage teas, fêtes, space for the scouts and guides, for youth clubs, a place for the elderly to meet on summer afternoons; a place for barbecues and church social gatherings, held wherever the vicar is willing, the parish compliant, and the garden suitable. But nowadays, research suggests that clergy are more likely to find their gardens a burden than a blessing. They are encouraged to see gardening as irrelevant to their parochial work and the mission of the Church. Too often the diocesan concern is narrowly bounded by cost and financial liability. Today, open days for private gardens are popular, and parishioners are more likely to be invited into those than into the vicarage garden.[8]

Town and country

*"The old squire is dead . . . He has moved in most cases to the place of
business . . . the big house is sold to a rootless stranger who had succeeded in
that business world, or to an institution, or it had fallen derelict . . . Wider
education and a broader mental outlook among the parishioners have reduced
in their eyes the stature of the parson. To a great extent the parish has lost
its identity . . . its problems are not discussed among and solved by the chief
figures within its community. Self-government of its own small affairs is
nearly lost. The county councils, town-based and urban in their approach, run
the rural areas . . . Those far-off parish puppets with a low density of voters
to the square mile, traditionally unvocal, suffer the worst inattention."*
Thomas Firbank, born 1910

The parish system was rooted in rural life, but when the towns and cities grew so
fast in the late eighteenth and nineteenth centuries, it had to adapt. In Victorian
times, the clergy house for accommodating all the curates needed for a busy urban
parish under one roof became necessary. Now many have become conference
centres, hostels, or other institutions. The urban parsonage has been through the
same periods of strength and decline.

Population growth and immigration have changed urban culture. Most
communities have become more fragmented, less settled. The neighbourhood
values of the war and immediate post-war period are now best recalled by Ealing
comedies. The role of the urban church has changed accordingly. Traditional
Anglican latitudinarianism has declined, and evangelicalism has become more
important. Migration, travel, and commuting mean that people spend a lot of time
in a place of work different from where they live. The parish system has become
more fluid. The ethnography of a community and the diversity of religions within
it also have a crucial impact on the role the parsonage is expected to fulfil. It will
not be perceived as so central to the community in an area of ethnic and religious
diversity and will need to adapt. That is the challenge for the urban parsonage
of today.

Some with influence in the Church seek to end the parish system altogether,
both in town and country. Instead of that, they should surely be stressing its
importance, and redoubling efforts to create stability. Nevertheless, changes
in urban life have led to a concern among the clergy about the message their
parsonage gives, and to some an unease about a house that can be distinguished
from those of its neighbours. There is a paradox here. A high profile in the

community has always been important for the vicar. Yet city clergy now often feel they should have nothing more than a flat.

With the huge growth in population, there is also a problem of definition. What is a rural area? The Church sometimes uses terms like "urban, semi-urban, suburban, semi-rural, rural, and remote" as a basis of categorising its parishes, but these are difficult to define precisely. What is regarded as a mere village in Sussex or Surrey may be an important market town in Lincolnshire or Cornwall. Directions I was given to a wedding in Forest Row, near East Grinstead, gave the alarming warning "this is a fairly rural area"; an inhabitant of Hexworthy, on Dartmoor, would be unlikely to agree.

Truly rural churchgoers tend to remain dedicated to their own group of parishes; even just to their own parish within the group. To them, abolition of the parish system would be a heavy, perhaps terminal, blow, breaking up the only remaining sense of community they have. Whether by accident or design, the country vicarage has a high profile. It is physically more conspicuous than its urban equivalent. If it has a more than averagely welcoming vicar, it still has a strong role in village life. If it has been the parsonage for a long time, it contributes to a sense of permanence. If that traditional parsonage is replaced by a new one, the profile of the Church is likely to suffer, particularly if the new house is indistinguishable from the growing suburban sprawl on the village outskirts. Its symbolic value is then lost.

Here, the nature of the particular house is crucial. Its impact depends on the size and type of village it serves and its location in the village. Just as important, it depends on how long it has been in the service of the Church, and on less quantifiable factors that the pragmatism of modern Church officials does not allow them to value, such as its age, appearance, style, and setting. It depends on its suitability, not in the narrow sense used by diocesan officials of its appeal to its temporary incumbent, but for the people of the parish. The real value of the traditional parsonage may be much greater than its perceived value in a parish of declining church attendance. It may be the last thread holding a poor village together, giving rise, when sold off, to demoralisation and deprivation.

Density of population can have a complex effect. Tiny villages may have no sense of community if they merely serve as dormitory or holiday settlements; conversely, there are areas of London which are urban villages with a strong community spirit, even if most of the inhabitants are commuters. In these areas, whether they be a Shropshire parish of one hundred souls or a parish in suburban Ealing, the vicar, the parsonage, and what goes on there may be under great scrutiny. As Jane Austen observed: "A fine preacher is followed and admired; but it is not in fine preaching only that a good clergyman will be useful . . . where the parish and neighbourhood are of a size capable of knowing his private character, and observing his general conduct."[9] The parsonage contributes to the profile of the vicar. As the number of parsonages declines, so does that contribution.

The Church's mission

There is nowadays much talk about the Church not needing buildings at all. Some of those in influential positions see buildings as an encumbrance, and say all gatherings should be conducted in private rooms, as they were in the early Church. We can be certain that if that comes to pass there will be a Church of England no more. But even our Church officials have not yet seriously contemplated destroying or even divesting themselves of our great cathedrals, which so comprehensively demonstrate that modern builders will never rival the achievements of the past, and single-handedly vindicate the Gothic style. The other churches may have fared less well, but a surprisingly large number are still in use. Parsonages have not been so fortunate. Yet traditional rectories and vicarages are as much a part of the heritage of the Church as its churches. They are also intensely practical buildings for meetings, garden parties, and other local activities. Sold to a private owner whose life is not focused on the community, their *raison d'être* is lost. "In some cases I suspect that it would have even been better to keep the parsonage than the rather unremarkable hundred-year-old church!"[10] All the people, including those who are not active churchgoers, understand the role and importance of the parsonage. The traditional parsonage and the church are the nucleus of the village. The relationships between the buildings create their own harmony of space. These things are vital to the mission of the Church.

THE OLD RECTORY

Heritage, conservation, environment, community

"Bishop's palaces have either been pulled down, and rebuilt on a mean
and reduced scale, or their grandest features left to decay . . . and
the inhabited part repaired in the worst possible taste. Nor have the
rectories and canonries escaped even worse treatment. Many of the
old buildings have been entirely demolished, and some ugly square
mass set up instead; and all have been miserably mutilated . . . "

A. Welby Pugin[11]

"Heritage" is in many ways an irritating word, conjuring up visions of jousting, heraldry, armorial bearings, and striped pants. But it means more than just old things and old architecture. The concepts of stability and order, qualities the traditional clergy in their traditional houses symbolised, are out of fashion in the twenty-first century. But they cement the relationship between the clergy and their parishioners. Despite our apparent glorification of change, people, particularly in rural communities, are conservative. They prefer continuity.

Our built environment is an important part of our heritage. Nowadays we take more interest in it. The reasons for that are complex. One is that we realise we have disregarded it. The early modernist architects wanted to erase history, so they delighted in spurning traditional stone and brick in favour of concrete, steel, and glass. Despite what we are told about modernism having matured, it remains in thrall to those now outdated theories of utopianism. It is the only movement in architecture that has turned its back on the past. This vandalism of tradition has reignited our interest in it. English parsonages represent tradition.

The Church of England has divested itself of most of them, and there will always be those who say it is better off without them. That cannot alter the fact that it once owned a great architectural heritage. It is obvious to anyone just by looking at these houses what an enormous loss the Church has suffered.

The parsonage in literature

The world's longest-running play is Agatha Christie's *The Mousetrap*, in its 57th year at the time of writing the first edition of this book, and in its 65th now. It is set in a vicarage. Other plays which feature parsonages include *The Holly and the Ivy* by Wynyard Brown, also a film, and *See How They Run*, a farce by Philip King written in 1944 which has been popular ever since. The action takes place at the vicarage of Merton-cum-Middlewick. Everyone waits for the bishop's immortal line: "Sergeant, arrest most of these vicars."

Fiction that features parsonages includes *The Warden* and *Framley Parsonage* by Trollope, and George Eliot conveys the atmosphere in *Scenes of Clerical Life* and *Adam Bede*. In her *Middlemarch*, the rector of Howick has a mansion and land while the wife of a poor rector has to pray for her coals. In *Northanger Abbey*, Jane Austen writes of Mr Tilney's new-build substantial stone parsonage, describing it as "at the further end of the village, and tolerably disengaged from the rest of it . . . " *The Way of All Flesh* by Samuel Butler and *The Vicar of Wakefield* by Oliver Goldsmith are largely set in the parsonage, if with little detail of it. In her *Life of Charlotte Bronte*, Mrs Gaskell called Haworth "a small oblong stone house with not a tree to screen it from the cutting wind". Flora Thompson's *Lark Rise to Candleford* portrays the effect of the agricultural depression of the 1870s on the tithe, the new, less squirearchical vicars such as Mr Delafield, and the villagers becoming less servile. In *A Clergyman's Daughter*, George Orwell, writing in 1935, says: "The rectory . . . was a house of the wrong age, inconveniently large, and faced with chronically peeling yellow plaster."[12]

Other books include *The Rector's Daughter* by F. M. Mayor, who also wrote ghost stories, and Sheridan Le Fanu's mystery novel *The House by the Churchyard*. As for poetry, Herrick, Wordsworth, and Rupert Brooke write of the parsonage.

Fictional crime takes place in parsonages in Conan Doyle's *The Devil's Foot* and Agatha Christie's *Murder at the Vicarage*. And in an uncharacteristically literary reference, the vicar in *Hammer House of Horror*, the television series, speaking of the need for an exorcism, says: "It happened to John Wesley's father in his rectory, you know."

The wider influence of parsonage design

The "great rebuildings" as they have been called, the modernisations of the Elizabethan and Restoration periods, have for some time been recognised as the results of the emergence for the first time of a more prosperous middle class keen to display its wealth. The first rebuilding brought the beginnings of the concept of the modern house, doing away with the open hall in favour of private rooms, parlour, and bedchambers, which could now be afforded by the yeoman class, albeit in their case still with mullions and thatch. The second rebuilding brought more sophistication: the double-pile house, the grander hall, the desire for Italian and French features such as Tuscan porches and dentil cornices. The model these upwardly mobile yeomen took for their farmhouses was the smaller manor house—or the local rectory. The parsonage had become a template for the way of life they sought.

The history of the architecture of the English medium-sized house, of the kind the yeoman aspired to, continued to be embodied in the Queen Anne, Georgian, or Victorian parsonage, in updated form. By the Queen Anne and Georgian periods, architects were using the parsonage more and more as their model. In the eighteenth and early nineteenth centuries, when architects began to turn their attention for the first time in history to the smaller house, the beginning of a genuine democratisation of architecture, it was the parsonage that was making the running. There was an urgent need for more parsonages, which helped. The parsonage was now centre stage. In Chapter 9 we discussed the importance of the pattern books. The parsonage was smaller than the grand or manor house and larger than the vernacular cottage, and therefore greatly significant for the pattern-book writers and other theorists. It embodied what the growing middle classes aspired to, whether they were clergy or not, and its design embodied what the architects were trying to achieve.

It was a logical progression that, by the Victorian era, for the first time, it was not beneath the dignity of the very greatest architects to turn their attentions to the parsonage. Scott, Pugin, Butterfield, White, Street, Teulon, Carpenter, Bodley, Lutyens—the list goes on—all designed parsonages. The parsonage was increasingly a test of their competence, and *The Ecclesiologist*, the magazine of the Cambridge Camden Society, founded in 1839, exercised judgements over the propriety of parsonage design that were influential and perceptive, and also sometimes harshly critical. The idea of the planned environment was also now taking a greater role in building science and the parsonage was often part of a

Changes and rebuildings, the parsonage in its setting, porches and gatehouses, London parsonages, some smaller parsonages, curiosities

51: The ancient site—the moat at Hoxne, Suffolk

52: Changes over the years—Bulmer Tye House, Essex

53: The parsonage in its setting—Stanton, Gloucestershire

54: The parsonage in its setting—Combe, Oxfordshire

55: Rebuildings—Barnack, Cambridgeshire

56: Rebuildings—Clifton Hampden, Oxfordshire

57: The porch parsonage—St Sepulchre, City of London

58: The gatehouse parsonage— St Bartholomew, Smithfield, City of London

59: The reduced Victorian parsonage—Aldwincle, Northamptonshire, today

60: The London parsonage—St
Mary at Hill, City of London

61: The London parsonage—
St Olave, City of London

62: The London parsonage—St Michael, Shoreditch

63: The practical nineteenth-century parsonage—Torrington, Devon

64: The practical nineteenth-century parsonage—Ridgewell, Essex

65: The practical nineteenth-century parsonage—Harlton, Cambridgeshire

66: The practical nineteenth-century parsonage—Egloskerry, Cornwall

67: Curiosities—The Wardrobe, Salisbury

68: Curiosities—The Priest's House, Holcombe Rogus, Devon

planned group of buildings. Victorian piety saw the parsonage as a model for the type of house the middle classes should aspire to.

The skill of the Georgian and Regency architects in such devices as the modelling of the staircase hall and the layout of stairs, landings and half-landings, back stairs and access to the attics, and so on, had created elegance in comparatively modest houses. The High Victorian architects excelled in carrying on this tradition by creating some of the subtlety and grandeur, the quality and complexity of the great house in the shell of something much more modest in scale. The qualities deemed most desirable in the parsonage over the years could now be seen reworked in the ordinary mid-Victorian villa.

Because of these qualities, the fixed idea of the Church today that the Victorian parsonage has become outmoded needs to be challenged. A good example of a simple, small, eminently practical such house at Egloskerry, Cornwall, mercifully still in Church use, is shown in Plate 66.

The huge population growth of the Victorian era now gave rise to the concept of the garden suburb, as an antidote to the cramped back-to-back housing of urban industrialisation. Sir John Betjeman has pointed out[13] that the new idea of the planned suburb gave rise in its turn to the need both for medium-sized houses in their own grounds to cater for the newly prosperous, and for cottages that looked private rather than institutional. It was here that the designs of parsonages that had been built in earlier times proved to be so influential. The opportunity was taken to study the history of the parsonage, which, in most of its earlier manifestations, was seen as an archetype for the middle-class house.

The High Victorian parsonage had paved the way for the Arts and Crafts parsonage. For the first time, English architecture was also now highly influential on the continent. The Germans, in particular, inordinately admired the English Domestic Revival.[14] Architects like Baillie Scott were at their best working on small buildings. The style was truly a populist one, versatile enough to satisfy all classes in the way the international modernists claimed for themselves, but failed to achieve. As Frederick Etchells[15] remarked, there is a difference between architecture and "utilitarian construction". Parsonages were architecture. And they influenced the rest of domestic architecture.

Notes

1 Savidge, *The Parsonage in England*, paperback edition (SPCK, 1969), p. xv.

2 Richard Wellby, *Parsonage Houses—an analysis of change of use* (unpublished thesis for Plymouth University School of Architecture, 1995).

3 Tom Moore, diary entry 1 September 1818, quoted in *Tom Moore's Diary*, ed. J. B. Priestley (Cambridge University Press 2015, originally published 1925).

4 Jane Brown, *The Pursuit of Paradise: A Social History of Gardens and Gardening* (HarperCollins, 1999), p. 61.

5 William Addison, *The English Country Parson* (J. M. Dent & Sons, 1947).

6 Bax, *The English Parsonage*, p. 5.

7 George Orwell, *A Clergyman's Daughter* (Victor Gollancz, 1935).

8 This section also draws on the notes of Mervyn Wilson and his sources, *Vicarage Gardens; The English Vicarage Garden* (1988), *A Parson in the Vale of White Horse* (1982); George Woodward's letters, 1753–61; John Holdich's diary, 1862–92.

9 Jane Austen, *Mansfield Park* (1814).

10 The Revd Michael Johnson, vicar of Wroughton, Wiltshire.

11 A. Welby Pugin, *Contrasts: or, a Parallel between the Noble Edifices of the Middle Ages and the Corresponding Buildings of the Present Day; Shewing the Present Decay of Taste* (Charles Dolman, 1841).

12 Orwell, *A Clergyman's Daughter*.

13 John Betjeman, *A Pictorial History of English Architecture* (John Murray, 1972).

14 Stefan Muthesius, *The High Victorian Movement in Architecture, 1850-1870* (Routledge and Paul, 1972).

15 Frederick Etchells, "Le Corbusier: A Pioneer of Modern European Architecture", in *Studio* No. 96 (1928), pp. 156-163.

CHAPTER 14

The People

The parsonage is part of our landscape, and has a symbolic as well as a physical presence. The same could be said of the vicar. The parish clergy have always been central to community life and of great importance to education and learning. But they have not always fared well themselves. Before the Reformation, they were mostly very lowly, even though the Church was central to society; they were rarely any more than on a par with the yeomanry, a step above the peasantry perhaps, sometimes not even that. What they had was the aura of priesthood, setting them above others as sole mediators with God, and that conferred respect or at least importance. A few were wealthy. Even in Saxon times there was a wide social mix: nobles as well as serfs were parish priests. Some were educated in monastic schools. Under the Normans it was loyalty that counted. Parishes were handed out irrespective of education, country priests rarely being educated. In late medieval and Tudor times education expanded, and a theology degree became important.

After the Reformation, the aura of priesthood was gone. They were little more financially secure either. As prices rose rapidly between 1540 and 1600 through growth of trade, they lost their medieval dues, and their outgoings increased with the demands of their lay patrons. The seventeenth century followed, a period of great upheaval, clerical uncertainty, and danger. By the end of the century the parish clergy were above the labourer but not yet on terms with the squire. Most were local grammar school boys who had somehow survived Oxford and Cambridge.

With the eighteenth century came a more stable and relaxed environment, coinciding with increasing prosperity, as incomes increased with the enclosures, the growth of agriculture, and the aid of Queen Anne's Bounty. The impoverished vicar slowly gave way to the more prosperous one of Jane Austen. But there were still thought to be far fewer gentlemen than plebeians among the clergy, though there were conspicuous exceptions. Even in 1848, supposedly the height of clergy prosperity, Macaulay was recording that the clergy were "on the whole" a plebeian class.[1] In fact, in the nineteenth century far fewer clergy were plebeians than before; indeed most were from Oxford and Cambridge. By this time Kelly's directories placed gentlemen and clergy ahead of the "commercial" inhabitants of their district who were the successors of the old yeomen. The clergy were now almost on a par with the squires, and what was more they now actually had to live in their parsonage. After centuries of absenteeism, the Gilbert Acts, the William Scott Act of 1803, and the Pluralities Acts had finally seen to that. The most prosperous parsonage was the Victorian one. But patronage was still all-important. If he had no connections, the poor curate might not even have a house in his benefice.

At that time every remote village had an incumbent, overeducated for his flock, and he was often there till death. The Revd P. H. Ditchfield, in his book *The Old-Time Parson*, wrote: "When the new rector on his induction takes the key . . . and tolls the bell, it is his own passing bell that he is ringing."[2] Sydney Smith had said the countryside was "a kind of healthy grave".[3] The bishop and archdeacon usually lived a long way away and had no wish to visit such wastelands, and in those days they had less power.

The idea that a clergyman must be a gentleman was now starting to be characterised as the "gentleman heresy". Hurrell Froude, a key member of the Oxford Movement, who coined the phrase, spoke for those who believed that the lower classes were vital to the Church if it were to prosper. Theological colleges were founded in the early nineteenth century to cater for those unable to get a university education. History thus began to repeat itself and there was now increasing talk of the clergy being "ill-educated peasants". Trollope subscribed to this view: the clergy from the theological colleges were "less urbane, less genial".[4] The decline of graduate clergy was in any case fairly inevitable since the great growth of industry and commerce meant more and more graduates were doing better in secular careers. Despite that, Tindal Hart thought the clergy at the height of their power between 1868, the abolition of the church rate and decline of the vestry meeting, and 1921, the coming of the Parochial Church Council.

Although neither police nor magistrates, clergy saw themselves as the guardians of law and order through their pastoral work. The clergy also had an important role in helping the poor. They sometimes found them allotments on the glebe, on condition that if convicted of poaching they must give them up. "What spectacle so delightful", asked the Revd John Sandford, "as that of a healthy, industrious, contented and religious peasantry, men . . . whom you found rude, lawless and estranged . . . but whom the sympathy of the superior has reformed and won?"[5]

They also took an interest in housing. Canon Barnett at St Jude's, Whitechapel, bought sites and rebuilt houses, becoming interested in drains: "Sanitary improvements come very naturally within a clergyman's province." But Richard Jefferies observed that most agricultural labourers "stood aloof" and "cleaned their boots on a Sunday morning".[6] They had no quarrel with the Church, but no affinity with it. Clergy were identified with the rich. When a Devonshire vicar invited a group of loafers to go to church with him, they retorted: "No, and you wouldn't go unless you were paid for it."

By the later years of the nineteenth century, the Church was starting on its longest period of uninterrupted decline. The incumbent had been part of civic life as chairman of the vestry, which was the parish administration, secular as well. The vestry at Walmer, Kent, organised sewage arrangements and the cricket match on the Goodwin Sands, and had rivalry with that at Deal. But in 1894, parish councils were set up. The vicar was no longer automatically chairman, and might not even be a member. The vestry was now a wholly Church body. After the First World War, the rigid hierarchy began to crack. The freehold was being eroded. The power of the PCC increased. Clerical eccentricities were being curbed, though socialism gained ground, leading to the observation that the clergy were more interested in Karl Marx than Jesus Christ.

At first the vicar had been celibate. Later, he was married. The duties of the clergyman's wife increased in importance, until in Victorian times she was no less vital than the vicar himself to the mission. She was a cultivated woman, with an indispensable role in community life. She was church organist, in charge of fêtes and charity fundraising, and ran the parsonage at the same time. Nowadays, the role of the spouse (male or female) has declined again; he or she has a career to pursue.

The clergy and their parsonages

One image of the clergyman is that of the railway enthusiast. These gentlemen cheerfully fixing derailments on their attic layouts are well represented by the Revd W. Awdry, born in 1911, rector of Elsworth with Knapwell, Cambridgeshire, who was author of *Thomas The Tank Engine* and the 25 subsequent books. Practically every child growing up in post-war Britain collected these strange-shaped volumes, with their hauntingly bright illustrations of locomotives with sinister faces. He also lived and wrote at the vicarage at Emneth, Norfolk, a gabled Gothic pile of 1850.

Sir Henry Baker, largely responsible for compiling *Hymns Ancient and Modern* (1861), served as vicar in the village of Monkland, near Leominster. He wrote "The King of Love My Shepherd Is" and "Lord, Thy Word Abideth".

Richard Barham, born in 1788, was better known as Thomas Ingoldsby of *The Ingoldsby Legends*, its material collected among the smugglers of Romney Marsh. He was ordained in 1813, was at Snargate, Kent, then became a Canon of St Paul's and had a living in the City.

Sabine Baring-Gould, whose family home was Lew Trenchard Manor near Okehampton, Devon, appointed himself to the living as squarson. He lived in the Georgian rectory at Lew Trenchard, and designed and built a new rectory there in an Arts and Crafts style in 1902, a good design apart from the mean staircases, and it is thought he had forgotten about them in his original plans. He recorded the story of many of the vicars we here discuss, and his bibliography extends to well over a thousand publications, more still being discovered. His subjects included religion, folklore (including werewolves, cannibalism, ghosts, and medieval superstitions), topography, and archaeology. He wrote 30 novels, lives of the saints in 16 volumes, and hymns including "Onward, Christian Soldiers". He regarded his collections of West Country folk songs as his major achievement. Conan Doyle read his *Book of Dartmoor* (1900) for *The Hound of the Baskervilles* (1901).

He was not interested in promotion and generally averse to Church affairs outside his own parish. He said of the Archbishop of York, William Thomson, "he possessed an autocratic . . . temper, such as was naturally bred in a man advanced from a breeches-maker's shop in a small provincial town." He had the privilege of reading his own obituary in *The Times*, his cousin's death being mistaken for his own, and was pleased with it, commenting that he had more friends than he had thought. Tales of his eccentricity can be exaggerated, but at a party he bent down and said to a child: "And whose little girl are you?" Bursting into tears, she replied, "Yours, Daddy." And he did have a pet bat.

William Barnes was a nineteenth-century rector at the classic *cottage orné* at Winterborne Came, Dorset. He wrote hundreds of poems, many in Dorset dialect, despite being fluent in Greek, Latin, and several modern languages. He was eccentric with his white hair and patriarchal beard, and eighteenth-century dress, but he was visited by Tennyson, Gosse, Palgrave, Kilvert, and Manley Hopkins.

Richard Baxter (1615–91), the theologian, served in Bridgnorth and Kidderminster. A Nonconformist, he fought for Parliament in the Civil War but supported the Restoration. He was a prolific writer and his devotional works were influential.

John Bloxam, ceremonialist and ecclesiologist, was Newman's curate at Littlemore, near Oxford. He made services more formal with candles and alms dishes, controversial at the time but now accepted practice.

In the 1960s, the Revd Teddy Boston installed a short length of track, wagons, and a full-sized locomotive in the garden of his rectory at Cadeby, Leicestershire, continuing to add to the rolling stock of the Cadeby Light Railway.

Thomas Bray served in a country parish in the late seventeenth century before establishing missions in America and parish libraries in England and America, which led to the SPCK (Society for Promoting Christian Knowledge), then to the SPG (Society for the Propagation of the Gospel in Foreign Parts). Later, he was rector of St Botolph, London.

Joseph Butler was rector of Stanhope in the early eighteenth century before becoming Bishop of Durham (1750-1752). He was famous for his theological and philosophical writings, including his critiques of Hobbes and Locke, and he influenced later philosophers.

An Oxford clergyman of great fame was Charles Lutwidge Dodgson (Lewis Carroll), who was ordained deacon because all dons had to be in holy orders, but never became a priest. He was obsessed by draughts, and placed thermometers all round his room, constantly checking them. When he preached the university sermon, people came in flocks expecting witticisms, but were treated to a solemn sermon about reverence. Carroll, or rather Dodgson, was born in 1832 at Daresbury Parsonage, near Warrington, in rural Cheshire, which burned down in the 1880s. But long before then, in 1843 when he was 11, his father had become rector at Croft-on-Tees, Yorkshire, a much richer living, where Carroll photographed the large Georgian rectory with its symmetrical classical façade, pedimented doorcase, pantiled roof, and tall chimneystacks. He wrote private magazines, and even a family publication called "The Rectory Magazine", which had nine issues and a serial story called *Crumble Castle*. Under the floorboards was found a thimble and a white glove. Later, when he was 18, he wrote *The Rectory Umbrella and Mischmasch*. He attended Cuddesdon College and was ordained as a deacon in 1861.[7]

Hugh Clark was a sixteenth-century Puritan who struggled to save the sinners of Oundle. His sermons were clearly not boring—after hearing one of them a member of the congregation came to his parsonage with a dagger, intent on killing him.

Cole's House at Milton, Cambridgeshire, is so called because it was let to William Cole, the antiquary and rector of Milton in 1768. It is an early timber-framed house and alterations were done for Cole by James Essex, the early Gothic Revivalist.

Miles Coverdale, Bishop of Exeter, published the first complete translation of the Bible, making use of Tyndale, very controversial in 1535. He had a palace at Paignton, Devon, the tower and ruins of which can still be seen.

George Crabbe, born 1764, was trained as a doctor, became a writer, and was ordained as a clergyman, becoming chaplain at Belvoir Castle, Leicestershire, then rector at Trowbridge, Wiltshire. In his poems like "The Village" (1783) he spoke of the poor wages and insanitary conditions of the lower classes, and the tyranny of the squires.

The parsonage at Milverton, Somerset (discussed on page 105), now called The Old House, was in fact the residence of the archdeacons of Taunton and was occupied by Thomas Cranmer and Stephen Gardiner, before Cranmer supplanted Gardiner in the patronage of Henry VIII.

Lord Grey lodged as a pupil of Dr Mandell Creighton at the Vicar's Pele at Embleton, Northumberland, in the late nineteenth century. Creighton would sit in his library working on his *History of the Papacy*. When disturbed by Grey, he would "parade with him up and down the terrace for ten minutes, explaining and expounding".[8]

Percy Dearmer, poet, hymn writer, and liturgist, author of *The Parson's Handbook*, served as the vicar of St Mary the Virgin, Primrose Hill, London, at the turn of the twentieth century. He worked with Vaughan Williams on *The English Hymnal, Songs of Praise,* and *The Oxford Book of Carols.*

John Donne, the Jacobean metaphysical poet, born a Catholic, became Dean of St Paul's. He hung on his wall a bizarre portrait of himself rising from the grave at the Apocalypse.

Erasmus was the illegitimate son of a Dutch priest who came to England and stayed with Sir Thomas More in 1509. He is regarded as one of the most influential of all theological writers, satirising the excesses of the Catholic Church but never leaving it. He was "nominal rector" of Aldington, Kent, and criticised English buildings, complaining that glass excluded wind, but admitted thin, pestilent air which was long stagnant. Floors, of clay and rushes, were carelessly renewed, harbouring "spittle and vomit and urine of dogs and men", beer and remnants of "fishes and other filth unnameable"; "a vapour exhales which . . . is far from wholesome".[9]

Nicholas Ferrar bought the manor of Little Gidding and restored the abandoned church. He founded an Anglican community there which much impressed Charles I, but was not popular with the Puritans, and after his death it was broken up and destroyed. He helped publicise George Herbert's work. T. S. Eliot visited Little Gidding in 1936, and it was the subject of one of his *Four Quartets*. There is a community there again, based at the parsonage.

J. W. Fletcher was a contemporary of Wesley and a theological Methodist. He became vicar of the humble parish of Madeley, Shropshire. Robert Southey, who wrote a lot about religious men, greatly admired his piety and charity.

In the sixteenth century, Bernard Gilpin attacked the clerical vices of his time but got away with it and was given the wealthy living of Houghton-le-Spring, where his house surpassed many bishops' palaces. He remained controversial and was charged with offences, but was saved by Queen Mary's death. He kept open board on Sundays, founded a grammar school, refused a bishopric, and would not accept tithes in bad harvests. He went on journeys, preaching, giving away money, going through Yorkshire and Northumberland where the people "sat in the darkness of ignorance". When his horses were stolen, there was such an outcry that the thief gave them back.

James Granger was the eighteenth-century vicar of Shiplake, Oxfordshire, and published his *Biographical History of England* in 1769. He had a collection of 14,000 portrait engravings.

J. R. Green, born 1837, was a London clergyman who became librarian at Lambeth, and a celebrated historian.

William Grimshaw was the evangelical perpetual curate at Haworth, Yorkshire, in the mid-eighteenth century, where Patrick Brunty (Brontë) was later incumbent. He used a riding crop on the indolent and was frequently physically attacked himself. He invited Whitefield and Wesley to preach, and infuriated other clergy by preaching in their parishes.

William Harrison, rector of Radwinter, Essex, from 1577 until his death in 1593, published his *Description of England* in which he recorded the great house rebuildings that were taking place in the Tudor and Elizabethan periods.

Reginald Heber, born in the fine rectory at Malpas, Cheshire, in 1783, started as a parish priest at Hodnet, Shropshire, becoming Bishop of Calcutta in 1823, representing the whole of India. He wrote "From Greenland's Icy Mountains" and "Holy, Holy, Holy! Lord God Almighty!".

The Revd Samuel Henshall, rector of Bow Church, East London, from 1802–7, was the first to patent the corkscrew. It was manufactured by Matthew Boulton, who pioneered steam engines with James Watt. It must have been a relief to be able to get wine out of the bottle!

Herbert Hensley Henson, born 1863, the theologian and writer who became Bishop of Durham in 1920, first served as a parish priest in Barking. He was controversial in his castigations of both Catholics and Dissenters, and got involved in politics.

George Herbert (1593–1633), the devotional poet and writer influenced by Nicholas Ferrar, was ordained in 1630 and served as rector of Fugglestone, near Salisbury. He wrote "The God of Love my Shepherd is". He was highly talented but unambitious. At Bemerton, near Salisbury, he rebuilt the parsonage himself, with its gables and mullioned windows. The house was extended in the nineteenth century for the then rector, his wife, four daughters, ten servants, gardeners, and stablemen.

Robert Herrick's verse is a reminder that there were still many poor parsonages in the seventeenth century:

> Lord, thou hast given me a cell,
> Wherein to dwell

He became fond of his remote parish of Dean Prior, Devon, with its still semi-pagan customs, was ejected as a staunch Royalist during the Civil War, but later returned. The present vicarage is early nineteenth-century, but may incorporate some of the remains of his modest thatched property.

Richard Hooker, the great sixteenth-century theologian and writer who upheld Church tradition and refuted the ideas of fundamentalist Puritans, even though he married one (his landlady's daughter, in fact), served the parishes at Drayton Beauchamp, Buckinghamshire, Boscomb, near Salisbury, and Bishopsbourne, Kent. To Hooker, the true end of human life was the enjoyment of God "which being once attained, there can rest nothing further to be desired".

John Hopkins became rector at Great Waldingfield, Suffolk, at a house which dates back to the fourteenth century, in 1563. Hopkins, with Thomas Sternhold, produced *The Whole Book of Psalms*. The site goes back to Roman times, there are springs around the garden and in the cellar, and there was a Roman temple nearby. The study has panelling from the church.

The theologian John Howson, Dean of Chester, who took holy orders in 1846, and in 1866 had the vicarage of Wisbech, was a pioneer of the ordination of women.

Michael Hudson, a royal chaplain, fought for the King in the Civil War and was the original of Dr Rochecliffe in Sir Walter Scott's *Woodstock*. Woodcroft Castle, Etton, Cambridgeshire, was his parsonage, where he had his chapel.

John Keble, theologian, writer, author of *The Christian Year*, and a founder of the Oxford Movement, born 1792, was the son of the clergyman John Keble, vicar at Coln St Aldwyns, Gloucestershire, who did not live at the eighteenth-century vicarage there, Tudorised with later additions, preferring the family house at Fairford. The Keble family held the manor at Eastleach Turville, Gloucestershire, and John Keble was non-resident curate at the two Eastleach churches, taking on Southrop as well, where a white owl lived at the parsonage he occupied there. A sermon of his in 1833 caused Newman to declare it the start of the Oxford Movement, which Keble led with Pusey, aimed at restoring High Church ideas. He became curate, then vicar at the gabled Tudor Gothic parsonage at Hursley, Hampshire, where he stayed for the rest of his life. He wrote "New Every Morning Is The Love" and "Blest Are The Pure In Heart".

Thomas Keble, his brother, was incumbent at Bisley, Gloucestershire, where the church was restored by W. H. Lowder, Thomas Keble's curate and pupil of Butterfield.

John Kettlewell, author of several devotional books of instruction, was parish priest in Coleshill, Warwickshire, but was deprived of his living because he opposed the Glorious Revolution of 1688 which embedded Protestantism.

Francis Kilvert, famous for his diary of parish life, became vicar of Bredwardine, Herefordshire, in 1877. He had been curate at Clyro, Radnorshire, where he records visiting a vicar who lived in a hut built of dry stone without mortar. Invited to preach in Wales, and assured that the pulpit would reach to his chin, he found it scarcely above his waist, so had to crouch diagonally to read his sermon. Visiting the sick, he had to climb to a tiny room in the roof of a hovel too low for him to stand upright, and was almost overcome by its shattered window almost empty of glass, its horrid smell, the wailing of children below, and the ceaseless moaning of the dying man, "Lord have mercy upon me". He tells of an acquaintance's aunt who had a frog's eyes, mouth, legs, and feet and hopped, wearing a long dress to cover her feet. He had a distinctly Victorian obsession with females, and his diaries record him spying on young girls bathing in the nude. He was excited by bare bottoms, speculating as to whether they were formed in that way so that they might be whipped.

The parsonage at Langley Burrell, Wiltshire, where Kilvert was brought up, a symmetrical Georgian house with central pediment built in 1739, was put on the market in 2001 at £1.25 million.

Charles Kingsley, author of *Westward Ho!* and *The Water Babies*, was born in the vicarage at Holne, a picturesque little Dartmoor hamlet, then went to Clovelly, Devon, as a child, where his father was rector for four years. The mansion has twice been destroyed by fire and rebuilt. He lived at the old rectory in Barnack, now Kingsley House, from the age of five, his father again rector. After that he found himself at St Luke, Chelsea, where his father was rector, and died there in 1860. From 1844, he was himself rector at Eversley, Winchfield, Hampshire. Kingsley wrote *The Water Babies* in the study at Eversley Rectory, timber-framed with later alterations, the parsonage with the study chimney climbed by poor Tom in that book.

Kingsley found his archdeacon too inquisitive. He did not like Nonconformists either, calling the Baptist pastors "muck enthroned on their respective dunghills, screeching on their scrannel pipes of ragged straw".

Cosmo Gordon Lang, who became Archbishop of Canterbury, was from a Scots Presbyterian family but served as a "slum priest", then as Bishop of Stepney. He got involved in the 1936 crisis by vociferously supporting Edward VIII's abdication. He was born in 1864 at the Manse in Fyvie, Aberdeenshire, a Scottish parsonage of "heathen" stone.

Thomas Leigh, of the Leigh family who owned Adlestrop Park, Gloucestershire, was the early nineteenth-century rector at Adlestrop and uncle of Jane Austen, who was his guest on at least three occasions at the rectory, which dates back to the seventeenth century.

John Lemprière was author of a Victorian classical dictionary which Keats is said to have known by heart. As vicar of Abingdon, he neglected his duties, and his various teaching posts at grammar schools were scarcely more successful. He was finally deprived of his stipend, then became headmaster of Exeter Free Grammar School, before effectively retiring to be rector of Meeth, deepest Devon.

The Diary of John Longe, Vicar of Coddenham, 1765–1834, published by the Suffolk Records Society, is an account of an affluent clubbable gentleman parson, the occasions he hosted and was guest at, his training of young curates, the marshalling of parishioners under the threat of Napoleon's invasion, and his work as a magistrate. Nothing profound, just a valuable contribution to our understanding of life and culture in rural England.

Henry Lyte was born in 1793 in Scotland and educated in Ireland, but became minister in Brixham, Devon, where he wrote "Praise, My Soul, the King of Heaven", then "Abide With Me" as he watched the sun setting over Torbay.

Thomas Robert Malthus, political economist, born 1766, warned about the dangers of population growth, presciently but unheeded. He was a country curate at Okewood, Surrey.

Henry Edward Manning was a nineteenth-century Anglican minister who became a High Churchman allied to the Tractarians. He defected to Catholicism, and built Westminster Cathedral. He was rector of Lavington-with-Graffham, Sussex.

Henry Martyn, born in Truro in 1781, intended a career at the Bar but by chance heard Charles Simeon speaking about missionary work and became his curate at Ely, then took charge of the parish at Lolworth. He went to India and translated the New Testament and Prayer Book into Hindustani, Urdu, and Persian. He died of a fever in Turkey and his epitaph was written by Lord Macaulay, the historian and politician who, as a toddler, gazing at a factory from his cot, had said to his mother: "Does the smoke from those chimneys come from the fires of hell?"[10]

The rectory at Aston, Yorkshire, was built by John Carr of York for the clergyman poet William Mason, quite plain. In the summerhouse is a commemorative urn to Thomas Gray. He was chosen by William Pitt the Younger for Poet Laureate, but refused.

Frederick Denison Maurice, the nineteenth-century educationalist and theologian, born 1805, son of a Unitarian minister, became an Anglican priest in 1834, served at Bubbenhall, Warwickshire, and Guy's Hospital, then became an academic and founder of the Christian Socialist Movement with Kingsley.

John Mitford, contemporary and friend of Reginald Heber and Sydney Smith, was related to Lord Redesdale, and so got the living at Benhall, Suffolk, where he built a parsonage and was a keen gardener. He had a cedar from Lebanon and many rare shrubs. He is known for his "commonplace books". In the 1840s, he edited *The Gentleman's Magazine*. He was an ornithologist, a fanatical cricketer, art enthusiast, and editor of *The English Poets*. Charles Lamb called him "a pleasant layman spoiled". At the parish of Farnham, between his two, the church was built over a Neolithic site, where there was witchcraft in the fourteenth century. According to Tindal Hart, "to this day it seems to breathe an evil atmosphere and some people are scared to enter it". There is a rumour that he officiated at a coven there.

William Mompesson was rector of Eyam, Derbyshire, when in 1665 the Black Death broke out from a flea in contaminated clothing from London. He closed the church and ordered possessions to be burned, including the contents of his own rectory, persuading the villagers to stay. Most died, including his wife, but he prevented the spread to the rest of that part of the country.

The Revd Marcus Morris, born 1915, was vicar of St James, Birkdale, Lancashire, and an RAF chaplain. He founded the popular comic *Eagle*, which he created to wean schoolboys off the new American horror comics. *Eagle*, with the attractions of its innovative layout and Dan Dare versus the Mekon, was far ahead of its time.

The former rectory at West Torrington, Lincolnshire, was the home of T. W. Mossman of the Oxford Movement, who added the chapel in 1863. He used the rectory to train the poor as priests, causing local consternation.

John Mason Neale, born 1818, helped found the Cambridge Camden Society, later the Ecclesiological Society, in 1839. Ordained in 1841, he was Warden of Sackville College, the fine Jacobean almshouse in East Grinstead. His hymns and carols include "Good King Wenceslas", and "O Come, O Come, Emmanuel" was his translation.

John Henry Newman studied at Trinity College, Oxford, and was made vicar at St Mary's, the university church, in 1828. He was a leading figure, with Pusey, in the Oxford Movement. In 1842, he withdrew to Littlemore, and defected to Catholicism in 1845. Following a feud with Manning and an attack by Kingsley, he became a cardinal. He wrote "Praise to the Holiest in the Height".

At Olney, Buckinghamshire, the former vicarage was built by Lord Dartmouth for John Newton, the slave trader, born 1725, who eventually became curate there. He had worked on slave ships and turned religious after being saved from a storm. At Olney, his sermons were popular. He collaborated on the *Olney Hymns* with William Cowper, published in 1779, including "God Moves In a Mysterious Way", "Glorious Things of Thee Are Spoken", "How Sweet The Name Of Jesus Sounds", and "Amazing Grace!". Cowper, poet and fervent evangelical, lived at Orchard Side in Olney, a red brick Queen Anne house in the High Street. He wrote the poem "John Gilpin".

Titus Oates, whose father was rector of Marsham, Norfolk, concocted a non-existent plot to replace Charles II with the Catholic James II, and was the Anglican vicar of Bobbing, Kent. He became a Catholic convert, but from then on attacked Catholicism, like his father, who had reverted to the Baptist doctrine. For his perjury he was pilloried and flogged, but survived.

William Paley, born 1743, was a philosophical theologian who had the rectory of Musgrave, Westmorland. His *Natural Theology* argued for "intelligent design".

In the 1920s, Father (Alfred Hope) Patten famously restored the shrine of Our Lady at Walsingham and rekindled interest in the pilgrimages that had taken place in pre-Reformation times.

John Coleridge Patteson, born 1827, was a curate in Alfington in the parish of Ottery St Mary, Devon, before going to Melanesia as a missionary. He was murdered by natives in the Solomon Islands.

Francis Peck (1692–1743), born in Stamford and rector of Goadby, Leicestershire, wrote a number of works, including *Desiderata Curiosa* about English history, and memoirs on Oliver Cromwell and Milton.

Henry, the son of Spencer Perceval, the prime minister who was assassinated in the lobby of the Commons in 1812, was rector of Elmley Lovett, Worcs, from 1837 to 1883, living in the attractive rectory with its Queen Anne façade, dentillated cornice, quoins, and keystones.

John Prince was vicar of Totnes, then Berry Pomeroy, Devon, the latter for 42 years, where he seems to have done much building work on the vicarage. Between 1681 and 1723, he compiled *Worthies of Devon*, a sort of Who's Who. His indiscretions in a Totnes alehouse with a young girl scandalised the locals. The language used by witnesses at his trial was so coarse that it caused the records to be suppressed.

Hugh Sheppard, known as Dick, who conducted the first service ever broadcast on the BBC, was made an Anglican priest in 1907 and vicar of St Martin in the Fields, London, which he turned into a social centre. The parsonage next door is a stucco John Nash "wedding cake". He founded the Peace Pledge Union in 1936.

Charles Simeon, born in 1759, was a leader of the evangelical movement in the late eighteenth century and had the living at Holy Trinity, Cambridge, where his sermons were controversial and frequently interrupted.

John Skelton, born about 1460, was ordained in 1498. He was Poet Laureate and tutor to Henry VIII. He retired from court circles to become rector of Diss, where his sermons were derided for their histrionic and sarcastic nature.

The Revd Charles Slingsby was a classic nineteenth-century squarson, lord of the manor at Scriven, Yorkshire, as well as parson, patron, magistrate, and sportsman. He inherited the estate from his uncle who, like him, died while out hunting. Unlike some squarsons, he was well liked because he did not leave his clerical offices to underpaid curates.

John Smythe, born in Lincolnshire about 1570 and educated at Gainsborough, was ordained an Anglican minister in the sixteenth century, but he was too radical to become vicar of Gainsborough, as often suggested, and therefore probably never had his own parsonage. He then went off to Amsterdam and formed his own Baptist Church.

Laurence Sterne was born in Ireland. His uncle procured him the livings of Sutton-in-the-Forest and Stillington, North Yorkshire. At a time when he, his mother, and his wife were all seriously ill, he wrote *Tristram Shandy*, an immensely light-hearted book. It was criticised by Samuel Johnson, but praised by Voltaire and Goethe. He also published his sermons. He was perpetual curate at Coxwold from 1760 till his death eight years later. He named the house Shandy Hall after his book. It is an attractive vernacular parsonage, like a farmhouse. He invented the idea of holding confirmation classes in the vicarage rather than the church, a common practice later on. He was addicted to hunting and when he saw a covey of partridges on his way to church he went back for his gun. His infidelities made his wife ill and for a time she thought herself to be the Queen of Bohemia. He was asked by the squire to read the draft of *Tristram Shandy* at Stillington Hall, only to find the guests all went to sleep, so he threw the papers into the fire. His grave was violated after his death and his body sold for dissection, his features being recognised by a friend.

K. T. Street, minister at Aslackby and Kirkby Underwood, Lincolnshire, fancied himself as a poet. Of the Robin Hood Inn at Aslackby, he wrote:

> Gentlemen, if you think good
> Step in and drink with Robin Hood!
> If Robin Hood abroad is gone,
> Then take a glass with Little John!
> But if perchance you come when they
> With the wild deer are far away
> In Keisby say, or Temple Wood –
> Still, step inside. The ale is good.[11]

(There is more, but . . .)

Geoffrey Anketell Studdert Kennedy, born in 1883, was a curate in Rugby and a vicar in Worcester. As a First World War chaplain helping the wounded, he was known as "Woodbine Willie". He wrote poetry about his wartime experiences.

William Stukeley, antiquarian and architect in the Gothick manner of Batty Langley, was vicar of All Saints, Stamford, from 1730 to 1747, then rector of St George the Martyr, Queen Square, London, from 1747 to 1765. He is known for his researches on, and detailed drawings of, Avebury and Stonehenge, and on Roman sites, and his interest in Druidism. His friends included Sir Isaac Newton. In 1738, he built a Temple of Flora in his vicarage garden in Stamford. His family home was Stukeley Hall in Holbeach, Lincolnshire.

Jonathan Swift, the early eighteenth-century satirist, was a Church of Ireland minister.

Thomas Teasdale, curate of Luckington, Wiltshire, spent ten years working on his *Greek Dictionary* but was pipped at the post by Liddell and Scott, who were both Oxford students born in 1811, whose *Lexicon* became the standard work.

William Temple, Archbishop of Canterbury in 1942, was president of the Workers' Educational Association, highly esteemed by Winston Churchill. He was the first primate to be cremated.

Thomas Tenison, seventeenth-century rector of St Martin in the Fields and subsequently Archbishop of Canterbury, was a fine preacher and established the first public library in London.

The Revd Roger Thacker was a very active minister appointed to St Paul's, Hammersmith, in 1974, who restored the church and rebuilt the vicarage. He found a large figure of Christ in a skip with the hands cut off, and put it in the hallway at the vicarage to remind us that Christ has no hands but ours.[12]

Augustus Toplady, born in 1740, Calvinist and opponent of Wesley, wrote "Rock of Ages". He served in various parishes in Somerset and Devon.

Charles John Vaughan was headmaster of Harrow School and became vicar of Doncaster in 1859 after refusing a bishopric. He was an evangelical.

The Revd Charles Voysey, born in 1828, father of the celebrated architect C. F. A. Voysey, was curate, then vicar, of Healaugh, Yorkshire, where the family lived in the stone rectory built by his predecessor, the Revd Edward Brooksbank, and had held curacies in Whitechapel and North Woolwich, London, before being defrocked from the Church for his unorthodox preaching and founding his own church, the Theistic Church, in 1871. Voysey's son, the architect, refurbished Woodlawn House, Dulwich Village, for his father and also designed Annesley Lodge, in Hampstead, for him. The name Annesley came from his ancestor, Susanna Annesley, who was John Wesley's mother.

Brian Walton, born in 1600, was made rector of St Martin's, Ongar and Sandon, Essex. The "Life of Brian" involved being a supporter of Archbishop Laud, and he was imprisoned for a while. He edited a *Polyglot Bible* in nine languages, including Chaldee, Samaritan, and Syriac.

John Wesley, son of the rector of Epworth, after ordination became an itinerant preacher and founded the Methodist conference in 1744. He was shouted down when preaching in the church of John Milner, his friend and a minister at Chipping, Lancashire, in 1752, and had to continue in the vicarage. Charles, his younger brother, followed the same course and wrote hymns, including "Hark, The Herald Angels Sing" and "Love Divine, All Loves Excelling". Samuel Wesley, their father, was accident-prone and was disabled after being thrown from a waggon. His rectory was twice burnt down and haunted by a poltergeist (see Chapter 10).

George Whitefield became a minister in 1736, shared in the Wesley brothers' mission, but later developed differences from them as an adherent of Calvin. He was a great orator, but too itinerant to be confined to a parsonage.

At Burton Agnes, Yorkshire, the chancel was rebuilt by, and the Georgian vicarage much enlarged for, Archdeacon Wilberforce, vicar in the mid-nineteenth century, son of William.

At Upper Slaughter, Gloucestershire, Francis Edward Witts, the rector from 1808 to 1854, has a canopied tomb in the church. His *Diary of a Cotswold Parson*, originally extending to 107 volumes, was published in 1978. The Witts' home became the Lords of the Manor Hotel. There are two good old parsonages here, including the Way's End, the rectory from 1914 till 1955.

Many country clergy kept diaries, but that of James Woodforde is the most complete account we have of a typical eighteenth-century parson. It extends to 74 volumes, and runs from the age of 19 to his death. The archetypal Latitudinarian, not a holy but a kindly man, he was mainly interested in food, cards, and hare coursing, but also his parishioners, the very spirit of Georgian England. He fed the farmers on tithe days, entertained, introduced prayers on Ash Wednesday, and lived, a bachelor, with his manservant, in a house replaced by a later and finer one at Weston Longville, Norfolk. He provided vegetables for his table from his grounds, as well as sheep meat. His diaries record in great detail his preoccupation with his cuisine, not omitting its liquid accompaniment. He wrote:

> Brewed a vessell of strong Beer today. My two large Piggs, by drinking some Beer grounds . . . taking out of one of my Barrels, got so amazingly drunk by it, that they were not able to stand and appeared like dead things almost . . . [13]

John Wycliffe was a seminal figure of the early Church, and deeply controversial, as he translated the Bible into English in 1382, so long before the Reformation, and the Lollards, its precursors, were his followers. He was forced to retire as Master of Balliol and was lucky to be allowed to retreat to his rectory at Lutterworth.

Parsonages with important Church associations included H. J. Rose's fine vicarage at Hadleigh, where the historic meeting of the Puseyites, after John Keble's sermon on "National Apostasy", led to the inauguration of the Oxford Movement; Radley, where Charles Gore founded the medievalism of the Community of the Resurrection; and Longworth, Oxfordshire, where J. R. Illingworth was incumbent and hosted the "Lux Mundi" group at his rectory, and also where Roger Lloyd wrote *The Church of England in the Twentieth Century* in 1946.

Slindon, West Sussex, was a residence of the Archbishops of Canterbury and there are remains of their palace at Slindon House, rebuilt around 1560. Stephen Langton died there not long after mediating in the Magna Carta negotiations.

The clergy as architects

Not only were the Victorian clergy learned in so many fields, but many were even their own architects—and indeed architects for others. It could be argued that this tradition started with Richard Poore and William of Wykeham, bishops of Salisbury and Winchester in the thirteenth and fourteenth centuries, though they are now seen more as project managers than architects, who were then usually master masons. Even before them, the medieval London Bridge was built by Peter, the priest at St Mary Colechurch, in 1176. The Chapel of St Thomas-on-the-Bridge was built at the centre of it and dedicated to the martyr Becket.

There have been plenty of later clergy-architects. Canon Basil Clarke (1903–78) identified 151 of them, not counting those based overseas, as well as eight architects who became clergymen. We have already seen that Sydney Smith built his own rectory in the early nineteenth century, and Hawker of Morwenstow designed his a little later. John Predden rebuilt his vicarage at Caddington, Bedfordshire, in 1812.

The Pluralities Act of 1838 merely gave a boost to these activities, with so many new parsonages having to be built. William Grey, on his return from the diocese of Newfoundland, designed the church, clergy house, and schools at Rownhams, Hampshire, 1855, and, with R. J. Jones, the clergy house at Swanmore, Isle of Wight, 1860–2. Bishop John Medley sent his son Edward to study under Butterfield for three years. William Henry Lowder, brother of the Ritualist C. F. Lowder, was also a pupil of Butterfield. Herbert Woodward, who became a canon of Zanzibar Cathedral in 1930, had been articled to Teulon.

John Hanson Sperling, rector of Wicken Bonhunt, Essex, from 1856, built the rectory there, described by Pevsner as "gruesome", though it is not too bad. William Haslam, curate at Perranzabuloe, Cornwall, wrote, in his book about his ministry: "In this district, schools were not built nor parsonage-houses enlarged without sending for me." Francis Charles Hingeston-Randolph designed the vicarage and schools at St George's, Truro, and wrote:

> . . . I am practically a Professional Architect and have been always recognised
> as such by the Bounty Board and the Ecclesiastical Commissioners under
> whom I have built several large Parsonage Houses.[14]

The architectural writer and curate at Bradfield, Essex, J. L. Petit, critic of the
Gothic and advocate of the Queen Anne Revival, designed one church at
Caerdeon, Gwynedd, which *The Ecclesiologist* was scathing about, describing
it as "the Swiss chalet on the Barnet road".[15] It is certainly extraordinary and
unlike any other church I have seen. William Carus Wilson, author of *Helps to the
Building of Churches, Parsonage Houses, and Schools* (1835), built two churches,
and parsonages at Casterton, Holme, and Grimsargh, and others on the same plan
as Holme at Silverdale, Preston Patrick, Austwick, and Hurst Green (Cumbria,
Lancashire, and Yorkshire).

Ernest Geldart was perhaps the best example of the nineteenth-century
clergyman-architect. He trained in the office of Waterhouse in 1864, and besides
his other design projects he was responsible for 43 structural works, including
the vicarage at Sparkwell, Devon, which, however, with its diagonal bay, looks
as though no architect has been near it. He also added a chapel to the rectory at
Little Braxted, Essex, where he was incumbent from 1881. Unlike the others, he
started charging for his services. He also designed stained glass.[16]

The following further parsonage architects are listed in alphabetical order of
place:

The rector at Ashley, Northamptonshire, from 1853 to 1874, the Revd Richard
Pulteney, did building work in the village, remodelled the manor house, had a
school by Scott and cottages built, and made additions to the rectory.

At Bloxham, Oxfordshire, the vicarage was designed by the vicar, George Bell,
in 1815 and built by E. Randle, later enlarged in 1858 by Street.

Wriothesley Russell of the Bedford family built the Regency estate housing
at Chenies, Bucks, including the Regency-style rectory where he lived as rector.

The former vicarage at Cleasby, Yorkshire, is inscribed to the effect that it was
built by Bishop Robinson of London, 1717.

The Revd Thomas Scott, father of Sir Gilbert Scott, was born at Gawcott,
Buckinghamshire, in 1811. He designed Holy Trinity Church, and also designed
his own vicarage, which was demolished in the early 1960s. But Gilbert designed
the parsonage at Wappenham, Northamptonshire, for him.

The vicarage at Mapledurham, Oxfordshire, was built by Lord Augustus Fitz-
Clarence, son of King William IV and the actress Mrs Jordan. He was vicar from
1829 to 1854.

The vicarage at Swalcliffe, Oxfordshire, was rebuilt by Canon Payne in 1838 from his own designs.

At Ulceby, Lincolnshire, the former rectory called The Peacocks is said to have been designed by the vicar of that name in 1850. The centre bay has giant columns with Norman-type lattice work.

The naturalist clergy

Clergy have made a fine contribution to the study of our birds, animals, and plants, including such arcane aspects as mycology, the study of fungi. Gilbert White (1720–93) was born at Selborne, Hampshire, where his grandfather was vicar. He had curacies in Hampshire and Wiltshire, including Farringdon, and became perpetual curate of Moreton Pinkney in Northamptonshire. He moved to the family home, The Wakes, Selborne, which his father bought as a house for his widow, after his father's death, where he became curate once again. It dates back to 1500, and is now a museum devoted to him and Captain Oates, of Scott's expedition. It is scarcely an exaggeration to say that the work of White and his collaborator Thomas Pennant brought a revolution in the way we view nature. Before *The Natural History and Antiquities of Selborne*, 1789, birds and other wildlife were not subjects to study but creatures to avoid, ignore, or eat. His effect on our perception was second only to that of Darwin.

Back in the early seventeenth century, Charles Butler, who lived in a thatched cottage in Wootton St Laurence, Hampshire, for 47 years, was the father of British beekeeping. Stephen Hales, FRS, born 1677, vicar of Teddington, Porlock, and Faringdon, was a pioneer of plant and animal physiology. Octavius Pickard-Cambridge, born at his father's rectory in Bloxworth, Dorset, was a world authority on spiders. Francis Rosslyn Courtney Bruce bred mice. Keble Martin wrote *Concise British Flora* (1965). The nineteenth-century parson John Mossop of Covenham, Lincolnshire, was a noted ornithologist and John Henslow of Hitcham was the botanist and close friend of Darwin who recommended the latter for *The Beagle*.

To bring the story up to date, Andrew Linzey is an ordained priest and member of the theology faculty at Oxford who importantly upholds the rights of animals against the traditional humano-centric Christianity derived from Aquinas.

The gardening vicar

Gilbert White was a gardener as well as naturalist. He had met Alexander Pope, an enthusiast for the new romantic movement in landscape gardening, and set out to create his "Arcady" at Selborne.

George Woodwards, vicar of East Hendred in the mid-eighteenth century, took pride in his strawberries, his peas and beans, gooseberries and currants, plums and lettuces. He also grew auriculars and apricots. He was typical of the clergy of his time, living like yeoman farmers, with gentry connections, but also Oxbridge-educated.

Christopher Alderson, rector of Eckington in the late eighteenth century, was also chaplain to Queen Charlotte and had a hand in the design of gardens at Windsor. He laid out his own garden with a small temple and water features, recalling the paradise garden.

A well-known Victorian gardener was Samuel Hole (1819–1904), rector of Caunton, Nottinghamshire, and later Canon of Lincoln and Dean of Rochester. He wrote of gardens and was founder of the Rose Society. Of Lamorran rectory, he wrote:

> Believing in Eden as thoroughly as though I had seen it . . . believing that
> our love of horticulture and our happiness in a garden are reminiscences
> of our first glorious home, and longings to reproduce it . . . I shall never
> forget the garden at Lamorran.[17]

His own garden was at Caunton Manor, and he was an expert on roses.

Charles Kingsley (1819–75) at Eversley was deeply sensitive to the beauty of flowers and at Eversley Vicarage made sure churchgoers could see from the churchyard the flowers of his garden, to uplift their souls as they entered the holy place. He filled the garden with flowers and planted rhododendrons.

The rose gained popularity in late Victorian times and the Revd R. A. Foster-Melliar at Sproughton Rectory, near Ipswich, and the Revd J. H. Pemberton both wrote about roses. Canon Henry Ellacombe (1822–1916), rector of Bitton in Gloucestershire from 1850 until his death, was a prolific gardening writer of the palmy years that preceded the 1914 war. He loved his flowers and plants and knew the character of each intimately. He brought new plants into fashion and described his garden in 1900 in his book *In My Vicarage Garden and Elsewhere*. He succeeded his father (1790–1885), whose ideas he continued.

After Victorian formality, the philosophy of the Arts and Crafts movement brought a return to simplicity. In 1883, William Robinson (1838–1935), who was apprenticed to an Irish vicar, published his influential book, *The English Flower Garden*. He abhorred the stiff formalism of terracing, stonework, and gravel, like Versailles and the Crystal Palace.

The Revd William Wilks (1843–1923) was vicar of Shirley, now in the London borough of Croydon but then only a hamlet between farms and the estates of large houses. He became secretary of the RHS in 1888, greatly increasing its membership, and was a driving force behind the first Chelsea Flower Show, and the society's gardens at Wisley. He also bred the Shirley poppy. In his parochial work he gave the lie to those who claimed that gardening clergy neglected their parishes. He started clubs to help the poorer people in the parish and introduced a special service book for children's worship. He invited parishioners to walk in his garden from 2pm to 4pm every Sunday. The vicar of Shirley in 1988 said of the now truncated garden, "we see it as a parish asset".

The Revd George Herbert Engleheart (1851–1936), vicar of Chute Forest, Wiltshire, experimented with daffodils. The Revd Joseph Jacob of Whitewell Rectory, Shropshire, was famous for bulbs and apples in the early twentieth century. Canon Horace Rollo Meyer (1868–1953), with his gardener, Izzard, grew daffodils and irises and was founder of the Gardens Guild movement.

Many parsonage architects were also garden designers. Sir Reginald Blomfield (1856–1942) specialised in the formal Edwardian garden, while the influential Gertrude Jekyll, a pupil of Robinson, saw the garden more as an informal extension of the house, albeit less wild than Robinson's, and worked as a team with Sir Edwin Lutyens.

At Great Witley, in Worcestershire, Canon Carnegie dammed a stream to make a small lake, and had a broad grass walk backed by yew hedges leading down to it. Up to 1945, the garden of four acres or so was maintained, the rector employing two gardeners. The garden had a flat lawn for games, a rose garden, herbaceous borders, many fine trees, and a productive kitchen garden. There were bees, a house cow and a pig, and many fruit trees. It breathed the mythic air of Eden, that air so potent in moving people of all ages to pleasure and delight.

Artists and scientists

Edmund Cartwright, born in 1743, inspired by visiting Richard Arkwright's cotton mills, invented the power loom. A Manchester company bought 400 of his looms, but the factory was burnt down. He was incumbent of Goadby Marwood, Leicestershire, and became a prebendary of Lincoln Cathedral. He wrote poetry much admired by Sir Walter Scott.

J. W. E. Conybeare of Barrington, Cambridgeshire, was a late Victorian high churchman of many accomplishments. He invented a temperature chart used at Addenbrooke's Hospital; he was a mountaineer, archaeologist, and writer. He was a pioneer cyclist and covered huge distances at night. Finally, he left his vicarage, turned Catholic, and wrote for the next 30 years. He was a bit of an eccentric, with a gunpowder flask on his bike for firing sweets at children. The class structure of the times is revealed by his wife referring to Holman Hunt's new painting of Christ while in discussion with the lady of a grand house, who frostily replied: "I do not like having forced upon me that our Lord was a working man and his Mother a peasant woman."

The Revd William Davy of Moretonhampstead and Lustleigh, Dartmoor, also born in 1743, wrote a 26-volume *General System of Theology*, which he sent to the bishop without acknowledgement. When he visited the palace, the bishop said: "I cannot be supposed to notice every trifle that appears in print." He also invented a diving bell.

The Revd George Garret, born in 1852, who was a curate in his father's Manchester parish, formed a company to make the first mechanical submarine. He then made a better one. Both were called *Resurgam*. More submarines followed in partnership with a Swedish industrialist.

The Revd William Gilpin (1724–1804), vicar at Boldre, New Forest, Hampshire, was one of the originators of the idea of the picturesque. Of the Gothic Revival, he said, "it is not every man who can build a house that can execute a ruin" (Essays, 1792). His drawings of ruins in wild romantic landscapes are always recognizably his.

The Revd Henry Moule (1801–80) was vicar of Fordington, Dorset. His speciality was drainage and refuse and, shocked by the cholera outbreaks of the mid-nineteenth century, he patented a dry earth system for flushing the lavatory in 1860. He was an early "green", writing on such matters as the safe and economic disposal of waste.

Adam Sedgwick (1785–1873), clergyman and geologist, reinterpreted Britain's rock strata and was a mentor to many, including the young Charles Darwin, though he rejected Darwin's ideas. He was born at the vicarage at Dent, Yorkshire, a modest vernacular house, into a family with three generations of vicars. He was Woodwardian Professor of Geology at Cambridge, and President of the Geological Society of London.

The warrior clergy

In medieval times, many bishops led armies in the battlefield. Archbishop Scrope of York raised a rebellion and attempted to overthrow Henry IV, and was executed. John Wycliffe, Master of Balliol College, Rector of Lutterworth, who attacked the clergy and their power and influence, was friendly with John of Gaunt. Odo, Bishop of Bayeux and brother of William I, helped organise the Norman invasion and fought the Saxon rebellions (he famously wielded a club, because it was against Canon Law to draw blood). Henry le Spencer, fourteenth-century Bishop of Norwich, helped crush the Peasants' Revolt. In 1412, Robert Newby, rector of Whitchurch, Oxfordshire, left his best sword to his brother in his will; and that of the vicar of Gainford, Durham, bequeathed his best suit of armour and arrows.

The political reformers

The reputation of the nineteenth-century Church may have been that of "the Conservative party at prayer", but socialism was growing. Charles Kingsley called himself a Chartist and preached a sermon equating the Kingdom of God with the socialist millennium. His brother-in-law, Sidney Godolphin Osborne, fought for the labourers against the farmers; his view that a cholera epidemic was caused by germs was scorned, but was later proved to be correct by T. H. Huxley. The Revd F. W. Tuckwell, rector of Stockton, Warwickshire, was ashamed at "the painful contrast between my own comfortable rectory and the squalid pigsties in which many people live"—those called "the dearly beloved brethren" on a Sunday but "the masses" the rest of the week. But while the comfortable rectory made the parson conscientious in his charitable works, it usually confirmed his satisfaction with his place in society. He could teach poor children to be content with their lot.

The aristocrat Conrad Noel at Thaxted, Essex, was violently anti-capitalist and hung the Red Flag and the flag of Sinn Fein in his chancel. He walked out of a meeting with the bishop, saying he could not sit at the table of a heretic. He inaugurated the "Thaxted Movement" with its folk dancing and singing.

John Groser, a supporter of Noel and vicar in Stepney, received a permanent injury from a policeman in the General Strike. Another supporter, Charles Jenkinson, advocated women for the priesthood, a heresy in 1936. He became chairman of Stevenage New Town Development Corporation.

The sportsmen

There were many sporting clerics and they flourished in the early nineteenth century. The Revd W. B. Daniel made a study of the possibility of the interbreeding of dogs and foxes. The anti-hunting lobby of the evangelicals gained ground, but the hunters persisted. One Devon clergyman, asked to view his potential new church, said information as to the meets of the hounds would be more to the point. Twenty Devon vicars kept hounds, the most celebrated being Jack Russell of Swymbridge, who gave his name to the well-known terrier. He had hounds while just a pupil at Blundell's School and was still riding very long distances in his old age. He had the hides of his favourite horses made into armchairs in his rectory.

John Froude, the Devon parson whose family included Hurrell Froude the Tractarian, was vicar of Knowstone-cum-Mowland, a remote moorland hamlet. Shunned by the gentry, he had a crowd of dubious characters living at his vicarage, poachers and beaters, ready to do his bidding. He would say "what a terrible thing it would be if the rick of Farmer Greenaway were to burn" or "there's Farmer Moyle going to sup with me at the parsonage tonight. Shocking thing were his linch-pin to be gone". He told his bishop he was unable to attend a visitation because he would be hunting, but if the fox ran in the right direction he'd be delighted to dine with him. When the bishop said he'd heard many queer tales about him, he replied: "So have I of your lordship, very unpleasant and nasty tales. But when I do, I say it's a parcel of . . . lies." He teased guests by leading them to expect good food, then serving hard cheese, sour cider, and unsweetened plums. He had a reputation for inflammatory speeches.[18]

William Moreton, vicar of Willenhall, Staffordshire, was a cock-fighter and drank three bottles of port a day. The Revd Edward Stokes was blind but would hunt with a servant who rang a bell at the jumps.

Among the more placid sports, archery became popular, and in the late nineteenth century, croquet ruled. "There is something infinitely attractive in . . . sedate tea and croquet parties on the spacious lawns of many a Lincolnshire rectory", observed Canon P. B. G. Binnall. It helped to make the vicar human against all appearances to the contrary. Cricket was also popular with the clergy. The Hon. Edward Bligh, vicar of Birling, Kent, represented an England XI against Kent; David Sheppard (later Bishop of Liverpool) was a recent Test batsman and not long ago I recall my own vicar being clean bowled by Ted Dexter on Ealing Common.

All clergy, of course, rely on gambling. Where would the garden fête be without raffles and prize draws?

The drunk and the incontinent

The medieval clergy, often ill-educated peasants with no spiritual or pastoral training, could do what they liked in remote, isolated villages. The pattern was to spend the day in the alehouse and get into fights. The rector of Thornton turned his rectory into an inn. William Amswyth, rector of Lowick, entered the home of Robert Merbury, assaulted his servants and stole his livestock. In Norwich, ten priests in 1333 were accused of incontinency. Robert, incumbent of St George-at-the-Gates, "keeps incontinently Beatrice of Brok". The rector of Drayton was "ill-famed with the same woman". Roger Pecke, vice-dean of Rockland, was "ill-famed with the same Beatrice" and others. Wiliam Phillipes of Cantley "doth not catechise the yowth, is often overtaken with drincke". At Ribchester, Lancashire, the church records the drowning in the hazardous River Ribble of the first recorded rector Drogo, in the thirteenth century.

In the seventeenth century, William Frost of Middleton, Essex, was always drunk and "came whooping and hollowing home . . . in the night". The vicar of Frodingham, John Leeke, told a woman "he had carnall knowledge of many women, why should I be soe difficult". He threw a mug full of beer in someone's face in his own house and broke people's windows. Robert Large, curate of Hoo, was "so drunke that he fell into the fire and afterwards into a bush". Lionel Players, rector of Uggeshall, was a glutton and parishioners complained of his "eating custard after a scandalous manner" (see also Chapter 3).

The eighteenth century was a time of more relaxed discipline. Jeremiah Bolton, vicar of Bawtry, was happy to tell the Archbishop: "I ever took care to avoid . . . unnecessary journies to the alehouse, and those I resorted to were no tippling houses, they were the best inns in the town." One clergyman of the period was so drunk that while taking a funeral he fell into the grave himself. Another, protesting that he was never drunk on duty, asked by the bishop when a clergyman is not on duty, replied: "True, I never thought of that."[19]

In the nineteenth century, the clergy had more freedom and prosperity. When a visitor asked for the vicar in a Devon village, he was asked if he'd seen a man on a white horse, blind drunk, cursing and swearing. When he said he had, he was told: "That's our parson. And a dear good man he be."[20]

The vicar of Carlton, North Yorkshire, the Revd George Sanger, stood trial for arson when the church burned down in 1881, allegedly deranged by putting a local girl with child.

The eccentrics and the offenders

Having already discussed Baring-Gould, Lewis Carroll, and Kilvert, the line between normal and eccentric is obviously fine in the case of the clergy. The astrologer John Dee, absentee rector of Leadenham, Lincolnshire, and Upton on Severn, Worcestershire, was never ordained, refusing to be, but happily living off benefice income, indulged by Archbishop Parker and the Queen. From 1579, he devoted himself to the occult sciences. He had a crystal ball and mediums, including one who had had his ears cropped for making counterfeit money. He went on a quest for the Philosopher's Stone. At a séance, a nude spirit directed him and his medium to share their wives.

Melchior Smith, vicar of Hessle and Hull, was indicted in 1567 for having "spoyled, taken down and letten down a great peece of the vicar mansion house in Hull called the vicarage". The sermons of Robert Blackwood of Kirton were like "the roaringe of an oxe in the toppe of an ashe tree". Roger Broadhurste of Freethorpe let his vicarage fall down and preached only one sermon in four years. At Stanford-le-Hope in 1591, there was a row between the rector Martin Clipsham and a Puritan lecturer, Tristram Blaby. When Blaby started to preach, Clipsham shouted, "Come down thou prating Jack, thou foamest out thine own poison", and Blaby attacked him in the churchyard.

In the seventeenth century, Edward Wallis, vicar of Capel, Kent, denounced the Scots from the pulpit as "dogs and divells", adding "if ever Scote goe to heaven, the divell will goe toe". The rector of Burgh-next-Aylesham, Norfolk, fancied his Latin, and when one John Crow was buried he wrote in the register "*aquila caelestis factus*". In the revolutionary period before the Restoration, there were many eccentrics who invented cults; Roger Brearley, curate at Grindleton, Yorkshire, founded the Grindletonians. His successor, John Webster, demanded that astrology and magic should be studied at university in place of theology. Henry Compton, Bishop of London, told the Archbishop of Canterbury, of a wayward curate, "If your grace can do nothing with him, I will have . . . his ragged habit taken off his back and have him whippt from constable to constable, till he comes to his last abode".

The Revd Mr Jones, curate of Blewbury, Berkshire, wore the same hat and coat throughout the 43 years he was curate. When the hat grew threadbare, he was observed hovering about a scarecrow. He stole its hat and bound the brim to his own crown, preserving it for the rest of his time.

A Shropshire rector habitually argued on some obscure theological point in the pulpit until all the villagers were gone and the clerk had to whisper, "Sir, when you're done, blow out the candles, lock the door and put the key under the mat".[21]

The Revd Samuel Parr used to visit slaughterhouses and help poleaxe cattle. He became headmaster of Norwich School, where his reputation for strictness spread panic through the city. Dr Nathaniel Bridges, as his team parson, declaimed from his pulpit: "I am going to discourse upon a person seldom if ever named in this place—I mean of course Jesus Christ." He was a strong adherent of the Whig cause, a supporter of Charles James Fox, and a great opponent of the monarchy, describing George IV as "uniting the insolence of a profligate, the coarseness of a blackguard, and the ferocity of a brute".

The revival of evangelicalism in the later eighteenth century produced eccentrics like William Grimshaw of Haworth, who turned from a life of hunting, cards, and drinking into a mentor who forced all parishioners to attend all Sunday services and stay inside their cottages all day. He patrolled the parish, causing parishioners in the local pub to leap from the windows and over the wall. George White, curate of Colne, was a notorious absentee who had to conduct 20 burial services for those who had died in his absence, dying of drink himself. The rector at Bingham, Nottinghamshire, Henry Stanhope, went mad and rode around on a white mule. But he did at least live in his parsonage house.

John Coleridge of Ottery St Mary was the father of Samuel Taylor Coleridge; he was so unworldly that when given clean shirts for a stay away from home he just put one on top of the other. Julius Hare of Hurstmonceux had a habit of turning the pages of his prayer book with his nose. When the rector of Willian, Hertfordshire, found that one of his men had impregnated a woman, he booked his passage to Canada and invited the whole village to his rectory lawn, where he thrashed him. One squarson of the Lincolnshire wolds married his cook. When she said she should be buried in the family vault, he replied that so long as they were man and wife they'd go on as they were, but after that he would go into the vault and she would be outside, with no bricks.

"Never ask a man if he comes from Yorkshire. If he does, he will tell you without asking. If he does not, why humiliate him?" Sydney Smith was a journalist, social reformer and Canon of St Paul's. He disliked the patronage system of his day and told Gladstone, "Whenever you meet a clergyman of my age, you may be sure he is a bad clergyman". He was made rector of Foston-le-Clay, Yorkshire, where there had been no resident vicar for 150 years. He was presented in 1806 but never lived there, until the new Archbishop of York, Vernon Harcourt, tightened up on residency. Still Smith only moved to Heslington, near York, but finally decided in 1814 to build his own house in his parish, at a cost of over £4,000, with the help of Queen Anne's Bounty, replacing an old hovel. He told his architect, "you build for glory, I for use", sacked him, tried to make bricks himself, and built the house. He installed air tubes for his fires, a speaking trumpet at his door for directing his labourers, and a telescope to spy on them. He installed a "universal scratcher" for his cattle. The house, though celebrated, escaped my architectural shortlist, despite Macaulay calling it "the very neatest, most commodious, and most appropriate rectory I ever saw". *The Buildings of England* calls it "plain, normal", which it is.

Smith fitted antlers to two of his donkeys, but removed them when they were said to be "typical of the neighbouring squires". He made a girl he called Bunch his butler, complaining of her slamming doors, spilling gravy, and bluebottle fly-catching (standing with her mouth open). In 1831, he became a canon at St Paul's Cathedral, and rented No. 1 Amen Court (see Chapter 10) to Richard Barham, author of *The Ingoldsby Legends*. He opined: "There are three sexes: men, women, and curates." Asked if he believed in the Apostolic Succession, he said: "Certainly, Bishop . . . is directly descended from Judas Iscariot." In 1839, he went to Combe Florey, Somerset, where he rebuilt the rectory. He defined heaven as "eating fois gras to the sound of trumpets".

R. S. Hawker was a true nineteenth-century character. Born in his grandfather's Plymouth vicarage, he went to be incumbent at Morwenstow, Cornwall, where no vicar had lived for a century. As a boy he had dressed himself in seaweed and sat on a rock at Bude combing his long hair; a farmer took a shot at him but missed. Halfway through his time at Oxford he heard that his father could no longer support him, so he immediately proposed marriage to a lady twice his age, who had "taught him his letters". As rector, he would not wear clerical attire, instead favouring a long-tailed claret coat with a yellow poncho and blue fisherman's jersey with a cross on one side, high seaboots, and a beaver hat, saying he had no wish to look like an unemployed undertaker. He went everywhere with a pig, which he took into parishioners' drawing rooms. If he entered a cottage where he knew there was an unbaptised child he would sniff the air loudly and say: "I smell brimstone." However, he allowed Catholics, Anglicans and Dissenters to hold discussions at his parsonage. "I thought it best, they will never meet in the next world."

When asked for his views and opinions he took his interlocutor to the window and said: "These are my views. As to my opinions, I keep them to myself." He told guests he would give them the "costliest liquor in Cornwall", then offered a jug of water, his well having cost him a lot of money in litigation with Lord Churston. He could be short-tempered: when he was trying to throw out old pews, and a farmer refused to leave his, he demolished it with an axe and threw the wood into the churchyard. He took the panels out of his pulpit, maintaining the congregation should be able to see the preacher's feet. He spent a lot of time meditating, in the church or in his little hut out on the cliffs, where he saw many shipwrecks. He is said to be the originator of harvest festivals in 1843. He was fond of carrots and to bless his crop he burnt all the old sermons on a bonfire; when the crop failed, he observed there were too many of his grandfather's among them. He excommunicated his cat for mousing on Sundays. His "Song of the Western Men" had the famous line "and shall Trelawney die". A lesser known, but obviously influential work is his *The Quest of the Sangraal*, acknowledged by Tennyson as superior to his own treatment of the Arthurian legends.

John Mavor had a small living at Forest Hill, near Oxford, but also the rectory of Hadleigh, Essex, where he had a good stipend. But he built a huge vicarage at Forest Hill and, despite his grant, said it had ruined him. He got into disputes, was arrested at least twice, was deprived of the living in 1848, and died in the debtors' prison. Charles Rose, rector of Cublington, Oxford, never got up before midday on Sunday, and had eight servants in his rectory. He threw the bacon at his wife and the stains were still on the wall when the next rector arrived. John Skinner, rector of Camerton, Somerset, was unkind to his children at the rectory, so they sought refuge in Bath. The bishop liked him, but he was a troubled man and shot himself in a woodland near his rectory in 1839.

Joshua Brooks of Manchester would quietly leave his seat while the choir was singing and chat with friends in the aisles. In the middle of a burial service he would break off and go for a bag of sweets. Once he performed a number of weddings at the same time and got the names mixed up, saying "sort yourselves when you go out".

Baring-Gould, in his *Old Country Life* (1890), records an old rector who, after visiting a parishioner's home on duty, would stay there all night after playing cards, returning to his rectory in the morning. He was sometimes found asleep in his flower bed, unable to get in. When invited to stay at the great house by the squire for a couple of nights, he would sometimes simply go to the servants' quarters and stay on a couple of nights more. Once, the lady of the manor discovered him there. Unabashed, he said that, like Persephone, he spent half his time in the nether world.

Anthony Cass, a mindreader, broke into conversations saying, "What you are really thinking about is this . . . " A curate called Davies was made incumbent of a tiny Suffolk hamlet where his rectory was moated, breeding mosquitoes, and was infested with ants. His antipathy developed into an obsession, pouring pepper onto the floor, driving visitors away. Benjamin Philpot, rector of Walpole, Suffolk, considered himself a medical expert, doctoring parishioners, and once offered to bleed the bishop when he fell from his horse. Parson John Lucy, of Hampton Lucy, born in 1790, had such a notable wine cellar that guests were often obliged to stay the night. The vicar of Disserth, Mr Thomas, started his sermons with no idea what to say, rambling on with "ah, yes, here we are, and it is a fine day indeed".

Despite all the legislation culminating in the Pluralities Act 1838, there were still some absentees. William Elford of Lew Trenchard, Devon, lived at Tavistock, asking of his bishop how he could be expected to live in a parish where he could not get his wig curled. One absentee from remote Lincolnshire justified himself with: "Satan himself couldn't get there in winter and I am always before him in spring."[22] A Cornish vicar would not visit his own church, merely chatting to parishioners in his dressing gown at his garden gate only a few yards away, after the service, which had been conducted by a visiting priest.

The Revd Benjamin Lovell of Milton, Surrey, read from a Bible in Hebrew to a Methodist, scoffing his ignorance of Hebrew. When he had gone, his nephew said he was afraid the Hebrew would be lost on him, to which Lovell replied that he was no more reading Hebrew than Double Dutch.

Some West Country clergy were in league with the wreckers of ships along the coast. A Cornwall vicar, after being informed of a wreck, walked from the pulpit to the font by the door, then announced to his congregation: "There's a wreck in the cove—let us all start fair", and rushed off.

Canon William Buckland, Devon clergyman and geologist, boasted that he had cooked and eaten mice, moles, crocodiles, and bluebottles. As a house guest of Lord Harcourt, Archbishop of York, at Nuneham Courtenay, he was shown the heart of Louis XIV, preserved in a casket as was the custom. In one version of the story, he remarked that he had eaten his way through the entire animal kingdom, but never the heart of a king, and popped it into his mouth. He discovered the Megalosaurus, and, in a limestone cave on the Gower Peninsula, Wales, a human skeleton which he called the Red Lady, supposing it to be that of a prostitute.

Canon Spooner, warden of New College, Oxford, was of course famous for his "spoonerisms", but also had a habit of giving the answer rather than the question when interviewing undergraduates. He also poured wine on spilled salt, rather than vice versa.

The Anglo-Catholic movement bred some notable characters, none more so than the Revd Leycester Lyne, better known as Father Ignatius. He was obsessed with his attempts at reviving the monastic life in the Church of England. He claimed to have performed miracles, though mostly retributory ones, and set up a Benedictine monastery in a wing of his rectory at Claydon, Suffolk, imposing strict discipline on the monks. After various scandals the bishop had to debar the monks from the parish church. He got into financial difficulties and retreated to a site near Llanthony in Wales, building his own abbey with donations, but his notoriety continued.

The twentieth century brought some lingering eccentricity: another odd Anglo-Catholic was Benjamin Fearnley Carlisle, who became Father Aelred, Abbot of the Benedictines on Caldey Island, Pembrokeshire. Despite being recognised by Archbishop Temple, he was self-elected and a rebel, claiming his abbey was beyond episcopal jurisdiction. A charismatic figure with great and hypnotic charm and good looks, he dabbled in the occult. He imposed penances and dubious practices, the monks having to bathe and sunbathe in the nude, and to flagellate. He defected to Rome.

The Revd Harold Davidson, the rector of Stiffkey, caught his daily trains to London to work with prostitutes. This gave rise to allegations of immorality, particularly when he was photographed with a naked 15-year-old girl. After his inevitable defrocking he raised money by such means as variety acts and exhibiting himself in a barrel on Blackpool promenade. He died at the claws of a lion named Freddy in Skegness.

Hard drinking was still a tradition despite the increase in evangelicalism. The vicar of Herne, Kent, was asked after Dunkirk in 1940 for empty bottles that could be filled with petrol in the event of invasion. In his cellar he found many hundreds of wine bottles. "I don't know what the village thought", he said.

Henry Montgomery Campbell, vicar of West Hackney, then of Hornsey in the 1920s and 1930s, became rector of St George's Hanover Square, and finally Bishop of London. When asked about his children, he said: "My son never does anything today that could be done in a fortnight; so he's a solicitor. My . . . daughter can neither read nor write, so she is a teacher." He bumped into a student on retreat in the town, who said: "The Holy Spirit has told me to do some shopping." He replied: "One of you is mistaken; it's early-closing day." He reportedly found the Guildford clergy amiable but stupid. "At least I cured them of the former", he remarked. When a churchwarden expressed surprise that he was visiting Pentonville Prison, he replied: "It's much the same as anywhere else, except that there I'm preaching to *convicted* criminals." At the Athenaeum Club, someone asked him to speak at his village debating society, saying, "We need a wit". "Try those two members over there," said Campbell. "They are halfwits." When Mervyn Stockwood arrived at Lambeth as new Bishop of Southwark clad in purple cassock, cloak, and socks, he greeted him: "Hallo, Mervyn—incognito, I see." He told the Archbishop: "If a man can't get on with anybody, make him a bishop." He said to an ordinand visiting him: "Take a chair, Clinton." "It's Fiennes-Clinton, my Lord." "Take two chairs, then." Before his death, he penned the lines:

> Tell my clergy when I'm gone
> For me to weep no tears
> For I shall be no deader then
> Than they have been for years.[23]

For many of these stories I am indebted to Tindal Hart, who notes rather sadly that the vicar today cannot survive as an eccentric. He is busy, not very effective, but at least respectable.

Famous children of clergy

Joseph Addison's father was Dean of Lichfield and he lived in the Cathedral Close. A man of letters, born in 1672, he founded *The Spectator* magazine with Richard Steele, in 1711. He also had a political career.

Matthew Arnold's uncle and tutor was a minister at Laleham, Middlesex, and his godfather was John Keble. He attended Newman's sermons in Oxford. He was a poet and critic and son of Thomas Arnold of Rugby School.

Jane Austen's father, William George Austen, was of the lower ranks of the landed gentry, and his wife Cassandra was of the wealthy Leigh family. George Austen was rector of Steventon, Hampshire, as well as a farmer and teacher. Jane lived at the rectory until she was 25, when she moved to Bath with her family, then to Chawton, Hampshire, part of her brother's estate. She stayed at the rectory at Adlestrop, Gloucestershire, now Adlestrop House, three times, with the rector, the Revd Thomas Leigh. The core of the house was built in 1672 and it had eight hearths (see Chapter 7).

R. D. Blackmore, author of *Lorna Doone*, was born in 1825 at Longworth, Oxfordshire, meeting place of the *Lux Mundi* group, where his father John was rector before going to Combe Martin, Devon. He went to live at the rectory at Elsfield, near Oxford, before returning to Devon. The Devon vicar John Froude was the feared Parson Chowne in his *The Maid of Sker*. During his schooldays he liked to stay at his uncle's "large and commodious rectory" at Charles. In old age he wrote of "the ancient parsonage, where the lawn is a russet sponge of moss and a stream trickles under the dining room floor, and the pious rook, poised on the pulpit of his nest, reads a hoarse sermon to the chimney pots below".

Andrew Bonar Law, the shortest-serving British prime minister and the only one born outside the British Isles, was the son of the Revd James Law of Portrush, Antrim. He also at one point lived in a Presbyterian manse in Coleraine, Londonderry.

The novels *Jane Eyre*, *Wuthering Heights,* and *Agnes Grey* were written by Charlotte, Emily, and Anne respectively, daughters of the Revd Patrick Brunty, who had changed his name to Brontë, at Haworth Parsonage. A couple of years later, the last two were dead. For their books, they assumed the surname Bell. Their work is imbued with the atmosphere of the surrounding moors. In 1854, Charlotte married Arthur Nicholls, the curate at Haworth, then died in pregnancy. The girls wrote their works in the dining room of the bleak parsonage, hewn from the grim local millstone grit. It is a severe five-bay house of 1779, with quite an imposing entrance hall, and a north and west wing added by John Wade, the successor incumbent, in 1872.

Samuel Butler was brought up in a parsonage in the mid-nineteenth century and was unhappy there. Canon Thomas Butler, rector of Langar, Nottinghamshire, was beloved by parishioners but a bully at home, and was immortalized by Samuel in *The Way of All Flesh*. His fictional character was Thomas Pontifex, who punished his infant son Ernest for saying "tum" for "come", his screams being heard from the dining room. Ernest later said of his father, "As soon as his back was turned the air felt lighter".

Edith Cavell was born in 1865 in Swardeston, Norfolk; the parsonage where her father, the Revd Frederick Cavell, was minister for 45 years is described in Chapter 7. In the First World War, she helped hundreds of soldiers to escape from Belgium and was imprisoned, court-martialled, and executed for her pains.

Samuel Taylor Coleridge, poet and philosopher, was the youngest son of the Devon country vicar of Ottery St Mary. Besides his famous literature he was a forerunner of the Broad Church movement.

Richmal Crompton, author of the visionary *William* books, which even managed to entertain my own children, was the daughter of a late Victorian clergyman.

John Dryden was born in a thatched rectory at Aldwincle, Northamptonshire, across the Nene from Rockingham Forest.

Eric Gill was the son of a Methodist minister and was ordained in the Anglican Church, then became a Catholic and Dominican. He was a prolific twentieth-century artist, illustrator, and sculptor, whose fine draughtsmanship is instantly recognisable, and he was architect of the church and presbytery (parsonage) of St Peter the Apostle at Gorleston-on-Sea (RC) in the 1930s.

Looking at a Christie's catalogue, I saw a reproduction of Harold Gilman's *In the Nursery, Snargate Rectory* and read that his father was parson at this house on Romney Marsh, Kent, and that it was Gilman's family home. The painting atmospherically depicts a classic Victorian rectory interior with gilt overmantel.

Frances Havergal, the poet and hymn writer of "Take My Life and Let It Be", born 1836, was daughter of the rector at Astley, Worcestershire, and spent the first nine years of her life at the rectory. Her father, the Revd William Havergal, was also a prolific hymn writer (and composer).

Thomas Hobbes, born in 1588, political philosopher, was the son of the curate at Westport, Malmesbury, Wiltshire, whose "ignorance and clownery" was remarked on by John Aubrey. He abandoned him after getting into a fight with another clergyman, and Hobbes was educated by his uncle. He became tutor to William

Cavendish, Bess of Hardwick's grandson. He wrote *Leviathan* in 1651, in which religion was seen as less important than civil society, and got into conflict with the Church, accused of being an atheist and heretic, causing him to investigate the law and nature of heresy. The house at Westport was "stone-built, and tiled, of one room (besides a buttery, or the like, within) below, and two chambers above" (Aubrey).

Robert Hooke was a natural philosopher, as scientists were then called, a contemporary of Wren and Newton. Like Wren, he was also an architect, historically much underrated, probably because he fell out with people. He was born at Freshwater, Isle of Wight, where his father was curate at All Saints. His three brothers were ministers and he was expected to go into the Church. He spent his first 13 years at the parsonage at Freshwater. He designed many fine post-fire London buildings. His book masterpiece was his *Micrographia* (1665).

The former rectory at Dinton St Mary, Wiltshire, was the birthplace of Edward Hyde, first Earl of Clarendon, grandfather of Queens Mary and Anne. Intended for holy orders, he studied law, became a historian, politician, and Charles II's Lord Chancellor. Parts of the house may date to before the Reformation, including the dovecote.

Antiquary and medieval scholar M. R. James, who was born in 1862 in the parsonage at Goodnestone, Kent, lived in the rectory at Great Livermere, Suffolk, the childhood home of another eminent antiquary, the eighteenth-century "Honest Tom" Martin. He is famous for his ghost stories, several set in Suffolk, like *Oh, Whistle, and I'll Come to You, My Lad*.

Sir Gerald Kelly, the prominent artist who became president of the Royal Academy, was the son of the curate for Camberwell St Giles, who lived at Camberwell vicarage. His sister Rose married the notorious occultist Aleister Crowley.

C. Day Lewis, Poet Laureate, was the son of the Irish clergyman the Revd Frank Day Lewis, who moved to London, and "could not express warmth and affection".[24]

Louis MacNeice was one of the Thirties Poets who included W. H. Auden, Stephen Spender, and Day Lewis, also son of a Church of Ireland clergyman. His poems explore his background both as an insider, as the rector's son, and an outsider, as pupil at an English public school.

The father of Field Marshal Lord Montgomery was the Anglo-Irish vicar of St Mark's, Kennington, London. When his father became Bishop of Tasmania he was away much of the time, and he detested his childhood.

There is a plaque near Burnham Thorpe, Norfolk, marking the site of the rectory where Lord Nelson was born in 1758. After his father died in 1802, the house was demolished and the new rectory built on the site. Nelson's illegitimate daughter Horatia married the vicar at Burnham Westgate, the Revd Philip Ward, and the family took the name Nelson Ward. They moved to Tenterden, Kent, but the vicarage was so dilapidated that they had to live in temporary accommodation for 18 months. She became a classic vicar's wife.

Laurence Olivier lived as a child at the rectory at Letchworth, Herts (where his father was rector), which he described as "the glorious Queen Anne rectory in Old Letchworth". But then his father moved to the "decent but jerry-built" (as he described it) new house in Letchworth Garden City.

The father of Robert Baden Powell, founder of the world Scouting movement, was a clergyman, mathematician, and liberal theologian at Oxford.

At Shirley, Derbyshire, the old vicarage was the birthplace of the novelist brothers John Cowper Powys and Theodore Francis Powys in the 1870s. The books of the former contain obscure references to Welsh mythology and he has been described as "an irresistible long-winded bore".

Sir Joshua Reynolds was the son of a clergyman and village schoolmaster at Plympton, Devon.

Cecil Rhodes, born 1853 in Bishop's Stortford, Hertfordshire, was the fourth son of the Revd Francis Rhodes, who gave up his large vicarage in Bishop's Stortford for a school while a new schoolhouse was being built, but had constant rows with his churchwardens. He took pride in never having preached a sermon for longer than ten minutes.

Dorothy Sayers, the twentieth-century crime writer and playwright who also wrote about Christianity, was daughter of an Anglican clergyman who had the living at Bluntisham, Cambridgeshire, and her description of Lord Peter Wimsey's family seat may be based on her elegant rectory there. Her involvement with an unemployed car salesman resulted in a pregnancy that she kept secret.

There were many clergymen in the family of George Gilbert Scott, the prominent nineteenth-century architect, including his father, and he was grandson of Thomas Scott, Buckinghamshire clergyman and Calvinist author of a *Commentary on the Whole Bible*. His vigorous over-restorations of Gothic churches offended William Morris and contributed to the founding of the Society for the Protection of Ancient Buildings.

The broadcaster John Sergeant was brought up at the seventeenth- and eighteenth-century vicarage at Great Tew, with its distinctive off-centre porch, a parsonage still at the time of writing occupied by the vicar.

George Tennyson had the living at Somersby and Bag Enderby, Lincolnshire, and lived at the rectory at Somersby. His younger brother inherited the family estates, rebuilding Bayons Manor in fanciful medieval style. George was embittered. Alfred Tennyson, one of his 12 children, was brought up at Somersby in a repressive atmosphere. His first book of poetry was published at nearby Louth. In 1837, the family had to move from Lincolnshire. He never went back, but always retained his memories of the idyllic Wolds. The rectory at Halton Holgate, near Spilsby, mainly nineteenth-century, was the home of the Revd Thomas Rawnsley, much visited by Tennyson.

Sybil Thorndike, the actress, born in 1882, was the daughter of a canon of Rochester Cathedral. Her house, the former rectory of St Margaret's (1781), is now known as Thorndikes.

Rex Warner's father was a Gloucestershire clergyman. A writer and translator, he associated with the Thirties Poets at Oxford.

Gordon Welchman (1906–85), the son of a former vicar of St Mary's Fishponds, Bristol, was a key contributor to Second World War codebreaking at Bletchley Park and abroad. He was born and brought up in the former vicarage at St Mary's. This would have been the normal place for his blue plaque, had the house not been misguidedly demolished. Placing the plaque on the church required permission of a Consistory Court "in the unique circumstances".[25]

Ralph Vaughan Williams, who was related to the Darwins, wrote the melody of "Come Down, O Love Divine", a hymn tune he called Down Ampney after the Gloucestershire village where his father, the Revd Arthur Vaughan Williams, was vicar.

Richard Wilson, the most important pioneer of eighteenth-century British landscape oil painting, was the son of a clergyman at Pengoes, Montgomeryshire, Wales.

Sir Christopher Wren, astronomer, physicist, and architect, was born at East Knoyle, Wiltshire, and lived at the rectory where his father, Christopher, was rector, then at the deanery at St George's Windsor, due to his father's rapid rise in Laud's Church, then the rectory at Bletchingdon, north of Oxford. He designed 53 London churches after the Great Fire of 1666 but, alas, no country parsonages.

Parsonages and the famous

Both the grandfathers of W. H. Auden were clergymen and he was brought up an Anglo-Catholic.

Douglas Bader's father died as a result of war wounds and his mother was remarried to the Revd Ernest Hobbs. Bader was brought up in the rectory at Sprotbrough, Doncaster, South Yorkshire.

Charlotte Bronte wrote *Jane Eyre* after visiting the eighteenth-century vicarage at Hathersage, Derbyshire. She based the "Norton" in *Jane Eyre* on Hathersage.

Rupert Brooke, born in 1887, rented the Old Vicarage, Grantchester, in 1910. He had a group of friends known as the Neo-Pagans. The house summarised England for him and he wrote much of his immortal poetry there. In *The Old Vicarage* he wrote: "Stands the church clock at ten to three? And is there honey still for tea?" He died in Lemnos in a wartime hospital ship in 1915. The house at Grantchester had long been abandoned by the Church, the reason this time being that it was too small. Samuel Widnall, photographer and printer, had bought it in 1853, and built the splendid Widnall's Folly in the garden, for his photography and printing business. Today it belongs to Jeffrey and Mary Archer.

John Bunyan, born in 1628, author of *The Pilgrim's Progress*, was a Nonconformist preacher who was arrested after the Restoration. His charming birthplace and cottage at Harrowden and Elstow, Bedfordshire, are both gone, the former (it seems) through negligence since it was reported as in danger of collapse in 1906, the latter demolished in 1838. A cottage in Hertfordshire where he is thought to have lived was demolished in 1877. According to one source, another cottage where he lived at Elstow was also demolished in 1968, as it was thought to be a traffic hazard. If that is correct, it is an utter disgrace. Anyway, Bunyan does not seem to have had much luck with his cottages. The Moot Hall contains his relics. St John's Rectory, Bedford, was the scene of many discussions between Bunyan and John Gifford, the pastor. It is reputedly the "House of the Interpreter" in *The Pilgrim's Progress*.

Edward Browning's fine rectory at Lowick, Northants, home of the Revd William Lucas Collins, was the scene of meetings between many literary luminaries between 1872 and 1888, including Anthony Trollope, who wrote there, and George Eliot, whose *Middlemarch* is centred on a village called Lowick.

Former prime minister David Cameron lived in an old rectory in Berkshire, where his family moved when he was three. He described it as "a very warm, happy, family home. The privilege of it was the warmth and happiness rather than anything else".[26]

Charles Darwin, when he moved out of London, went to live at Down House, Bromley, Kent. Darwin had been intended to be a clergyman and, appropriately, the house had been a parsonage—Down had bought it from the Church. Gwen Raverat, his granddaughter, who specialised in wood engravings, wrote about the house and was tenant at the parsonage at Harlton, Cambridgeshire, in the 1930s. Darwin is reputed to have started on *The Origin of Species* while staying at Hitcham House, Ipswich, rebuilt by James Spiller, friend of Sir John Soane, in an elegant classical manner. It was the rectory of his friend and mentor, the Revd John Stevens Henslow (1796–1861). He was a botanist and geologist who worked with Adam Sedgwick.

T. S. Eliot was an agnostic who converted to Anglo-Catholicism. He commemorates East Coker and Little Gidding in his *Four Quartets*, and knew the parsonages. It was from East Coker that his Puritan forebears migrated to New England. His ashes were buried there.

The seventeenth-century vicarage at Clether, Cornwall, was where Thomas Hardy drove off in his trap with his lover, Emma Gifford, embracing her triumphantly in the sight of his love rival at an upstairs window, as the other was dying of tuberculosis there, something he recalled with regret.

Augustus Hare (1834–1903), travel writer and memoirist, lived at his uncle's rectory at Hurstmonceux, Sussex, "as much a palace of art, from its fine collection of pictures and books, as a country rectory could be", as Hare wrote. But he was not happy there. He was regularly thrashed by his uncle with a riding-whip. His grandmother wore white, rode on an ass and went to church with a white doe which stood at the pew door. He used to stay at Stoke Rectory, Shropshire, childhood home of his mother. He was a pupil at Kilvert's Hardenhuish Rectory, Wiltshire.

Ted Hughes's friend Lucas Myers lived for some time at the rectory of St Botolph's, Cambridge, and they and a few others launched *Saint Botolph's Review* on 26 February 1956. It was at the launch party that Hughes and Sylvia Plath met; her poems had already appeared in Cambridge publications, and she quoted Hughes's own verse to him as they danced.

Edward Jenner is credited with discovering the idea of vaccination at the end of the eighteenth century, which led to the eradication of smallpox. He was born in a rural vicarage in Berkeley, Gloucestershire, in 1749: a gabled, vernacular house with mullioned windows. At the Chantry, Berkeley, Gloucestershire, a vicar built a Temple of Vaccinia, thatched and rustic in the prevalent romantic style, and Jenner vaccinated villagers there. Jenner was also a naturalist and student of bird migration.

Josh Kirby, the popular fantasy artist who illustrated Terry Pratchett's books, lived in the Tudor rectory at Shelfanger, near Diss, Norfolk, which has been described as a place where time stood still, and where you were never sure whether you had reached the end of the house or not, because there always seemed to be rooms leading away from rooms, passages, corridors, stairs.

Cleo Laine (formerly with the late John Dankworth) owns the vicarage at Wavendon, Buckinghamshire, built in 1848 of local greensand and limestone, and uses it for music festivals. It is said in *The Buildings of England* to be by Butterfield, though Thompson says it is by Ferrey.[27]

Barbara Lyall (Webb), the patron of Lutyens who introduced him to his influential clients, was born in 1845 at her father's rectory at Godmersham, Kent.[28]

The novelist W. Somerset Maugham, often credited for being the precursor of Ian Fleming's "James Bond" books, was orphaned at the age of ten and sent to live with his cold and cruel vicar uncle and straight-laced aunt at their gloomy vicarage at Whitstable, Kent. His miserable life there is reflected in his book *Of Human Bondage* (1915). The house has been demolished.

A. A. Milne lived in a rectory, Broadgate House, Steeple Bumpstead, Essex.

Deborah Mitford, who became the Duchess of Devonshire, moved from Chatsworth to the Old Vicarage, Edensor, Derbyshire, of which she wrote:

> The house has no architectural merit, but its atmosphere makes it a happy place—the influence, I believe, of the devout men who occupied it for two hundred years.[29]

She had half of the house and was fond of calling it her "semi".

The First World War poet Wilfred Owen lodged in the vicarage of All Saints, Dunsden, near Reading, a large Victorian house, with the vicar who lived alone with servants. The experience disillusioned Owen, and he lost his faith.

Anna Sewell, author of *Black Beauty*, may not have lived in a rectory, but was a very active evangelical, as was her mother, both as Quakers and later in the Church of England. Her brother gave Sewell Park to Norwich.

The old rectory at Ayot St Laurence, Hertfordshire, is a seventeenth-century house. George Bernard Shaw moved into the new one in 1906, renamed it Shaw's Corner, gave it to the National Trust in 1944, but continued to live there till he died aged 94 in 1950.

Both of Trollope's grandfathers were clergymen. He stayed with the Revd Lucas Collins at Lowick Rectory in Northamptonshire. His mother Frances, or Fanny Trollope, was the daughter of the Revd William Milton, who had vicarages near Bristol and at Heckfield, Hants, the latter half-timbered.

J. M. W. Turner's uncle by marriage was vicar of Tonbridge, Kent, where the Georgian vicarage was replaced by a Victorian one, partly on the plan of the earlier one, itself demolished in the 1960s when the present one replaced it.[30]

Charlotte Mary Yonge was a novelist, author of over 250 works, heavily influenced by John Keble, her neighbour, and was known as the poet of the Oxford Movement. She taught at Sunday school for 71 years.

Parsonage associations and visits

Edward I stayed at Lanercost Pele several times in his Scottish campaigns, as with less certainty did Robert Bruce. The adjacent priory was attacked by William Wallace and David II. The old part of the vicarage at St Alfege, Greenwich, is said to have been part of Placentia, the fifteenth-century palace that was the birthplace of Henry VIII, added to the building by him for his cook.

Castle House, Deddington, Oxfordshire, the former rectorial manor house, dates from the thirteenth century, though mostly seventeenth-century. Charles I is said to have stayed there in 1644 after the battle at Cropredy Bridge. He is also said to have favoured the former vicarage at Inkberrow with a visit in May 1645 before Naseby, leaving some rare maps there. The existing Old Vicarage is a nineteenth-century brick building in Tudor style.

At Odstock, Wiltshire, the early nineteenth-century rector threw away the church key after gypsies had cursed anyone who locked the door and there were two deaths. There is a seventeenth-century house called The Parsonage, once an inn where Oliver Cromwell is said to have stayed.

Bonnie Prince Charlie visited Leek, Staffordshire, and slept or held council in the bedroom over the front door of the parsonage on 3 December 1745 on the way to Derby. The vicar's wife died of fear in sheltering the Pretender.

Richard Cromwell died at Cheshunt vicarage in 1712. James Wolfe, hero of Quebec, was born in Westerham vicarage in 1727. It has a Georgian façade, but is earlier.

William Huskisson died in Eccles vicarage in 1830 after being knocked down by one of Stephenson's engines after stepping out to greet the Duke of Wellington.

At Bunny, Nottinghamshire, Sir Thomas Parkyns (1662–1741) collected stone coffins. A lawyer, he also wrote a Latin grammar and was an amateur wrestler and architect. He drew up the building plans for his estate and designed and built the hall, school, and vicarage in the early eighteenth century.

Parsonages associated with the famous include Ecton House, Northamptonshire, built in about 1640, which was visited by a number of eighteenth-century luminaries, including William Hogarth and Benjamin Franklin, who came to research his ancestry.

Notes

1   Thomas Babington Macaulay, *The History of England from the Accession of James II* (1848).

2   Peter Hampson Ditchfield, *The Old-Time Parson* (1908).

3   Sydney Smith, letter to Miss G. Harcourt (1838).

4   Anthony Trollope, *Clergymen of the Church of England* (1866).

5   John Sandford, *Parochialia; or Church, School, and Parish* (1845).

6   Richard Jefferies, *Hodge and His Masters* (1880).

7   Jenny Woolf, *The Mystery of Lewis Carroll* (Haus, 2010).

8   Dawson, *A Short History of Embleton Church and the Fortified Vicarage.*

9   Erasmus, in his letter to Wolsey's physician (1524); see G. G. Coulter, Mediaeval Panorama (Cambridge University Press, 1949), p. 305.

10   <www.newworldencyclopedia.org/entry/Thomas_Babington_Macaulay>.

11   K. T. Street, *Poems of Two Lincolnshire Villages* (illustrated booklet with unnumbered pages).

12   Obituary, Register, *The Times*, 7 December 2010.

13   James Woodforde, *The Diary of a Country Parson 1758-1802*, entry dated 15 April 1778.

14   *Transactions of the Ancient Monuments Society*, Vol. 55 (2011), p. 19.

15   *The Ecclesiologist* 24 (1863), pp. 374–5.

16   James Bettley, *In the Footsteps of William of Wykeham: Anglican Priest-Architects of the Nineteenth Century* (Transactions of the Ancient Monuments Society, Volume 55, 2011).

17   S. R. Hole, *A Book about the Garden and the Gardener* (Edward Arnold, 1892).

18   Sabine Baring-Gould, *Devonshire Characters and Strange Events* (1908).

19   Tindal Hart, *The Country Priest in English History* (Phoenix House, 1959), p. 87.

20   Hart, *The Country Priest in English History*, p. 88.

21   Hart, *The Country Priest in English History*, p. 84.

22   Hart, *The Country Priest in English History*, p. 138.

23   Malcolm Johnson, "Wittier than the two halfwits", *Church Times*, 4 March 2016.

24   John Horder, *Camden New Journal*, 31 May 2007.

25   *Church Times*, 11 November 2016, News, p. 7.

26   *The Times Magazine*, 2 December 2006.

27   Paul Thompson, *William Butterfield* (Routledge & Kegan Paul, 1971), p. 452.

28   Jane Brown, *Lutyens and the Edwardians* (Viking, 1996).

29   Deborah Devonshire, *Wait For Me!* (John Murray, 2010), p. 331.

30   Selby Whittingham, in an email to the author, 5 February 2014.

Part Six: The Future

"An' in convarting public trusts to very privit uses"

James Russell Lowell

CHAPTER 15

The Working Parsonage

In Chapter 12, we concluded that the "great sell-off" has been in great measure a product of the centralisation of control over parish clergy. That explains the process which has enabled it to happen. We have also tried to examine the motivating factors. But has it all just been a reactive process, viewed as the inevitable consequence of decline, or does the Church see it as a thoroughly positive end in itself? After all, it could easily have taken the view that it had a duty to keep, conserve, and cherish its finest parsonages, but it has not. It might have taken the view that the Church is a frail institution without its valuable assets. Are those marvellous houses being sold off with any regret, or just with relief? The discussions I have had with Church officials suggest that it is mainly the latter.

So, is there any future now for the traditional parsonage except in the hands of the private buyer?

At the time of writing the first edition of this book, I took a figure of about 5 per cent remaining out of 14,000 good houses once owned by the Church, one for each parish, leaving about 700 pre-1939, mainly Georgian and Victorian, parsonages in Church ownership, equating to 16.27 parsonages per diocese. What research was available from the few diocesan surveyors who responded to enquiries suggests that is about right. For example, in 2007, I was told that Norwich diocese had only 18 remaining pre-1939 houses. Some dioceses, like Bath and Wells, had more, some fewer, but as an average the figure was as good as any. More will now have gone, if not at the same rate as before.

The rest of the clergy are now rehoused in small compact boxes with no distinguishing features, usually some way from the church, or at the edge of town. Is it worth trying to save those six or seven hundred? Even if it is, can they be saved? Here we should note that common sense can prevail. When the seventeenth-century vicarage at Fairfield, Derbyshire, was recently threatened with sale, the governors of the chapel and almshouses commissioned an architect to draw up plans for separating the parish office from the private areas of the house, and these were accepted by the diocese. The Diocesan Parsonages Committee then agreed to spend money on the house and grounds and the Parochial Church Council (PCC) agreed to be responsible for the internal redecoration.

That is a thoroughly sensible outcome, but it is rare. The Church has by far the greatest proportion of Grade I and Grade II* listed buildings in its care; more than any other organisation or institution, including the National Trust, but diocesan secretaries will happily tell you they never take the architectural quality of a building into consideration as a reason for not selling it. A Church committee recently concluded that buildings can be "a positive encumbrance". It is obvious to many of us that traditional rectories are fine buildings that must be cherished, but we noted in Chapter 12 that the Church sees them as a burden that must be cast off. The administrators nowadays see themselves primarily as business people, and that business is one of selling. Getting rid of another house is achieving a target. The idea that the Church will repurchase its former rectories when they come onto the market, sweeping away the swimming pools, decking and designer furnishings, triumphantly restoring the faded rugs and allowing the weeds to reclaim the gardens, is clearly a fantasy. It could not afford to buy them back even if the penny suddenly dropped.

Parishioners, churchwardens, PCC members, volunteers, even the stipendiary clergy, all have little power to change these attitudes. The latter, for career reasons, lack motivation; it is important that they have a reasonable working relationship with their archdeacon. In the business world, no company retail representative will ask the board of directors to halt the sale of its marketing operations in England. There are occasional mutterings that there should now be a swing away from centralisation and that parishes are becoming more active. But centralisation has probably gone too far to be reversed now. So there is neither the wish for change at the centre, nor the power to effect it in the parish.

In some countries, the parish priest must provide his or her own house. Should the Church just sell off all its parsonages? A lot of capital would be realised, but there would need to be a large increase in stipends, or housing allowances for clergy, loans for house purchase, and so on. And a recent poll strongly suggested the clergy prefer the present system. The money may be better invested even in the new inferior houses. Of course, money is important. Diocesan officers do sometimes say they would be more ready to listen to "outside" ideas if the parish, or anyone, has funding to offer. Simple ideas like replacing the traditional Easter offering with a donation to a parsonage fund may help—for a while. It is only money that will keep the last traditional parsonages afloat—or blackmail: in one case where the diocese was hoping to sell off the parsonage, the boilers for the church were in the parsonage cellar!

John Marshall was a white baker who lived in Southwark and died in 1631 in the reign of Charles I. He left the residue of his estate to a trust for parsonages in England and Wales occupied by a rector or vicar. Grants are made for the building, purchase, or improvement of a property. But parishioners, PCC members, or churchwardens cannot apply for grants, only the dioceses.

The "heritage" lobby consists of a number of bodies, government agencies, the amenity bodies which require to be consulted on planning applications, and pressure groups, differing in their specific functions and aims but united in their concern for our heritage. It has several times been suggested to me by their representatives that the Church should take a look at its key remaining good houses and draw up a list of "core parsonages" purely on grounds of architecture and heritage, and then put them in a separate category, not for disposal. There is some mystification that this comparatively simple step has not been taken. It would mollify many people, not least parishioners and conservationists. As part of that initiative, a list could be made of those parsonages deemed both architecturally important and suitable for ministry, or at least for alternative uses, for example as retreat houses or even holiday lettings. To the extent the two lists overlap, there is a solution. The Church has little enthusiasm for this, and has said it has no money or resources to devote to such peripheral ideas, but surely a retired conservation architect could be found to take on such a satisfying project. The fact is that the will is not there. So that is it, then. But we should still be positive. There is no policy of selling or destroying old churches in favour of new, smaller ones. On the contrary, new ways of using working churches are being found. Even the sale of church halls to pay for church repairs is regularly criticised as shortsighted. There is a convincing economic case. Those assets may be needed for future generations. Even bishops' palaces have so far fared better—they have been subdivided and alternative uses have been found. Why are parsonages any different?

As the middle classes migrate from the town to the country, there is the potential for a revival of the Church in our market towns and rural villages, provided that it is prepared to welcome the incomers. They may not mostly be churchgoers, but even so, community facilities are needed. There is a move to adapt churches, often by building unsightly annexes, to provide communal space. That would not have been necessary if the good parsonage had not gone, and it is not necessary if a wing of a good remaining one is used.

Parsonage trusts

I have spoken to people of many different disciplines, financiers, lawyers, surveyors, architectural historians, and conservationists, who go further and say that the Church should never sell any parsonage. Houses that are surplus to present needs should be kept in a property portfolio and treated as investments, for letting out, thus preserving capital and ensuring access to continuing income.

It does seem odd that at the same time it is telling a parish that the next parsonage is to be sold, the Church is talking about the urgent need for housing for retired clergy. This is always high on the agenda. The Church of England Pensions Board buys properties for retired clergy under its CHARM (Church's Housing Assistance for the Retired Ministry) scheme. It now has about 2,000 houses in rental or shared ownership schemes. While it is busily so engaged, the dioceses are selling off parsonages. It seems breathtakingly inefficient. They may say the parsonages are too big, but houses can be subdivided. If housing retired clergy does not initially bring in a market income (though the clergy are always being asked to contribute more themselves), it avoids the capital expenditure of buying houses, and the use of some houses for holiday lettings, which are very lucrative, would subsidise the others. The Landmark Trust has been party to such schemes. All the expense of buying and selling is avoided.

Setting up a new trust for "redundant" parsonages would represent a fundamental shift in policy, and the Church would have to "buy in" to the idea. The question then is whether the new body should be an independent one, like the Churches Conservation Trust, or part of the Church. It would seem much better for it to be part of the Church, but if not, a new vehicle, a parsonages trust, would have to be set up, find its own funding, and get these redundant parsonages transferred to it. As part of the Church, the diocesan parsonage boards could administer the scheme in each diocese, hiring agents to let the houses out and bring in valuable income without losing all that capital value. However, the dioceses at present want nothing to do with any such scheme, and the central Church institutions take the same view. It is difficult to know why. Perhaps it springs from the epidemic of short-termism that led an archdeacon to say, when selling off a Georgian rectory recently advertised as "one of the finest Georgian houses in the area", that he had no brief to look further than five years ahead.

Chrysalis Holidays provides educational holidays for the mentally disabled:

> Chrysalis teamed up with Lowton Methodist Church, which lent the deposit for the purchase of a residential centre on a deferred-payment basis.

This was not solely a philanthropic gesture. The church would share in the value of the property's net worth, and get free use of it for its conferences. Five years later, the centre is booming, Lowton Church has a significant return on its investment, and Chrysalis is planning further expansion.[1]

Social enterprises are essentially businesses, but with social objectives, surpluses being reinvested in the business on behalf of the community, not shareholders. "Redundant" parsonages could be saved in this way. There should be a real opportunity here for the Church to regain its lost credibility.

Notes

[1] *Church Times*, 9 March 2006.

CHAPTER 16

The Old Rectory

Predicting the future is usually fraught with difficulty. But there is one future that can quite confidently be predicted—that of the ex-parsonage. We noted in Chapter 2 that there have been more than 13,000 parishes in England, and if they have had an average of three parsonages during their history, and possibly more, that makes a working figure of at least 50,000 pre-1939 houses. Most of those are still there. If fewer than 1,000 are now in Church use, that amounts to a lot of ex-parsonages being used for purposes for which they were not intended. The prospect of any more than a fraction of these houses reverting to their original use is low. So the parsonage certainly has a future in private hands. Is it a satisfactory and fitting future? How are these fine houses faring in their new ownership?

The great majority of conservation and amenity bodies agree that it is most desirable, if it is possible, for a building to continue to be used for the purpose for which it was originally designed. The physical location of the parsonage in relation to the church was historically no accident—it was informal yet planned. Many, including Betjeman and Pevsner,[1] have seen this juxtaposition as one of the glories of the English countryside, and uniquely characteristic of it. The relationships between the buildings create a harmony intended to reflect the glory of God, not that of the retired fund manager. On the other hand, when we tried to analyse the form and function of the parsonage, we saw that many working parsonages were never built for that purpose in the first place. We have also seen that the design of the parsonage has had an important influence on the design of the private house. As such, it should be eminently adaptable. The evidence seems to confirm that. Former rectories and vicarages have proved to be as highly valued by private buyers as they once were for their true purpose. The larger ones have also proved useful for commercial and institutional purposes. So, are there any problems?

Private use

The grown-up children of a parsonage often cultivate unconsciously in their own homes a reminder of every vicarage and rectory, whereas the layman involuntarily destroys this atmosphere within a few weeks of buying a parsonage house.

Bax[2]

That comment by Bax seems harsh. But his use of the word "involuntarily" suggests that he considers this process inevitable, however well-meaning the layman. Some of the former character of any parsonage will, to whatever degree and however sensitive any restoration, inevitably be lost in private hands. Who else but a country parson can create the atmosphere of academicism, public service, unpretentiousness, unworldliness, chaos, and disdain for style and fashion of a country parsonage?

I said in Chapter 1 that architects of a certain persuasion love gutting buildings and reworking them. Conservationists see that as insensitive and destructive, but architects in turn see conservationists as merely anachronistic. It seems to me that any private buyer of a parsonage who instructs a practitioner of "steel and glass" to "modernise" is asking for trouble. There is an even more insidious danger. There is a view, which has gained mainstream respectability, that, while radical new work is certainly not justified if the existing building is intact and fully serviceable, nevertheless if alteration or addition is needed, the new work must not be "pastiche" but "of its time". This perceived need to distinguish between the old and the new is on the face of it understandable, and a principle even adopted by some conservationists, notably SPAB. But it is an approach that brings its own problems. In practice, the indiscriminate use of the term "pastiche" these days seems to have come to mean "anything that is not of the modernist school". In the same way, the phrase "of its time" nowadays means "in conformity with the modernist school". Without going into all this in greater detail, I can confidently say that if an old rectory is given a modernist interior, however much repair it needs, it has lost its character as an old rectory. That is called common sense. I do get worried when people talk enthusiastically about "renovation". The motive is often to stamp their own personality on the house. That should not be allowed to happen to any good house, let alone a good parsonage. Every house has its own character. Every parsonage has its own character. That character is not the same as the character of its temporal custodian, the current owner. The owner has a duty to the house, not the other way around. There is no more irreversible way of destroying the character of an old house than by "renovation".

> "We re-plastered, put in underfloor heating, knocked down a couple of walls and painted the lot white", says Chloe of her kitchen-diner. Now shining with stainless steel, it was once the parlour where the vicar gave counsel to his parishioners.[3]

The vulgarisation of key features or their destruction for what is deemed "state of the art" in that way is an insult to any good house. Even restoration can cause problems. Over-restoration may result in loss of character, even if features are carefully retained. I have visited many houses that look so good on the outside, but have been completely scrubbed inside. Character is lost for a perceived but wholly misconceived gain. All this is often done with the best of motives.

The press tries to promote this mania for "modernisation" in the property columns all the time. Typical is a newspaper advert for The Old Vicarage, St Issey, Cornwall, which says: "Downside. You may wish to modernise the property as the interiors look quite dark and outdated." That can be translated quite simply. It means, "Most buyers will want to destroy the character of this historic house in order to appear trendy and fashionable, through ignorance, insensitivity and disrespect for the past".

Even when those dangers are avoided, owners can be slaves to the fashion of the day; the favoured old rectory interior décor, judging by the estate agents' websites at the time of writing, seems to be of the smart Belgravia townhouse or country house hotel variety, all-purpose "Georgian" gilt looking glass firmly in place above every mantelpiece, regardless of whether the house is medieval, Queen Anne, or Victorian; on the walls and in the furnishings washed-out pale greys, creams, or beiges proliferate, as though everything has been bleached, again regardless of period. No doubt that will change with the whims of fashion, but again all will look the same.

Having got that off my chest, I am well aware that most private owners of parsonages are genuinely fond of their houses, want to treat them well, and do so. I have myself never encountered any private buyer who has not cherished the former parsonage, or not had the best of intentions for it. Some may be more commercial than others, buying in order to "renovate" and sell, and some are architecturally illiterate, but most just want to do the best for their home. I have seen many interiors of former parsonages that have been restored with great sensitivity. The scourge of plastic glazing bars has very largely been avoided. The perhaps inevitable swimming pool is sometimes rightly sited in a distant copse. These houses are cared for, and that is important.

Commercial uses

> Old Parsonage, 1 Banbury Road, Oxford. This ancient building is one of the city's culinary gems . . . As lunch ends, a diverse mix of students, academics and shoppers seamlessly fill the place for scones, finger sandwiches and home made cakes . . . Cooking combines old-school skill with a modern sensibility.[4]

Some ex-parsonages are in commercial or institutional use, as hotels and guest houses, solicitors' or accountants' offices, local authority offices, and old people's homes. They have generally proved well suited to these uses. Their architectural integrity will have been compromised by inappropriate additions and materials. The destruction of mouldings, detailing, and fireplaces, the insertion of suspended polystyrene ceilings, woodchip paper, and false partitioning, and the glaring and ugly notices of the dreaded "health and safety" culture, will have removed most of their character. A house that is now a solicitors' office in Peterborough has metal shelving brackets screwed into seventeenth-century beams. On the other hand, there may be well-preserved original features behind the hastily assembled partitioning in some of these ill-fated houses, and fireplaces that can eventually be restored, unlike those torn from an Arts and Crafts parsonage in private hands in favour of inappropriate Rococo marble.

Serving the parish

Waiting for my wife at a shop in the deepest Lincolnshire fens, I read a notice announcing a coffee morning for the benefit of St Mary's Church "to be held at the Old Vicarage by kind permission of the owners, Mr and Mrs X". The Church has to rely on such favours nowadays.

Some former parsonages continue to provide a useful service to the parish as cottage hospitals, care homes, or retreat houses, and to a lesser extent the same is true of those that are now hotels or serve local authorities. Do private owners see themselves as having responsibilities to the community, knowing that the house once chattered with the vicar's coffee mornings and the garden rang with shrieking children while their parents discussed the forthcoming fête? I recently asked someone who writes for an estate agent's magazine whether secular buyers of parsonages see themselves as having responsibilities to the community. Some have twinges of conscience, he said, but basically the answer is "no".

In my experience, many private buyers are sensitive about the past, understand the loss, and move in with all good intentions. They are keen to be seen as good citizens. They will allow the garden to be used for fêtes. They are ready to surrender the garden to tombola stalls and coconut shies as before. Others start off well, but good intentions can fade. And, of course, owners change. A new owner moves in. A chain or gate goes across the path that leads from the church. Next, a sign abuts it, apparently mocking the church: "Private Property". But that sign is no more than the truth. The house is no longer in the service of the Church. It is shocking that the Church has been so glad to rid itself of it, but the house is now private. The relevant question is this: why should the owner have any public responsibility at all?

Conclusion

The evidence suggests that the new owners of traditional parsonages are good custodians of these houses. Private buyers take delight in them for all the reasons we have discussed. They often express astonishment that the Church could have sold such wonderful houses at such bargain prices, and cannot believe their luck. Commercial and public buyers have found a new use for them. That can only be good for their survival which, barring totally unforeseen circumstances, seems assured. The fact is that many former parsonages have been saved and not destroyed.

Notes

1   Church and parsonage together make "a feature in the English villagescape to which the
     Continent has no parallel"—Pevsner's foreword to Savidge, *The Parsonage in England*.
2   Bax, *The English Parsonage*, p. 6.
3   *The Times Magazine*.
4   *The Times*, "The Big Eat", The Knowledge, 8–14 November 2008.

CHAPTER 17

Final Thoughts

"Where there is no vision the people also perish"

Proverbs

Most of us remember the rectory or vicarage in the town or village where we grew up. Its presence always had an impact, even if only subliminal. It was part of life, even if we were never churchgoers. That was not just because of what it symbolised, but what it was. It taught us about the Church, which was an integral part of community life, it taught us about architecture and history, it taught us about heritage and tradition.

Community relies on identity. The "theology of place" is what makes the parsonage important to the parishioner. Those who move to the country go there in order to find stability, not change. The Church seems to be going in the opposite direction. The perception that England is an increasingly rootless society has led it to contemplate the demise of the parish system. If the Church starts seeing the geographical parish as a thing of the past, it follows that there is no longer a need for a parish church. Presumably there is no need for a parsonage either.

The bishops and the bureaucrats, the Church Commissioners, and much of General Synod alike remain resolutely sceptical of the importance of architecture and history, heritage and tradition, and the part they play in our life. Some take positive pride in that. If that is what they think even about our wonderful churches, little thought is going to be wasted on a Georgian or Victorian vicarage. If the subject of the parsonage arises, it is in the context of yet another committee debating clergy needs, clergy status, and the possibility of legislation making it even easier to dispossess its occupants and sell the house. It is deeply unsettling to parishioners.

Financial and pastoral considerations, heating costs, maintenance costs are debated *ad infinitum*. The humanity, grace, and propriety of the traditional parsonage is what really matters, but that cannot even be discussed. If any parsonages are seen as an asset, it is those on the new estates that spread relentlessly out from the suburbs of our country towns, the ones least distinguishable as parsonages.

Even in 1964, at the height of the "great sell-off", B. Anthony Bax in *The English Parsonage* was minded to write: "The Church certainly has an aesthetic as well as a spiritual duty."[1] He cites St John's Rectory at Bedford, the Interpreter's House of *Pilgrim's Progress* where Bunyan received succour from John Gifford, and "the historic rectory at Trowbridge, Wiltshire, where the poet George Crabbe worked for 10 years". "Some people feel", he goes on, "that hallowed stones, properly used, could preach better sermons than many clergymen." Both parish and diocese were to blame. "In 1962 the Ministry of Housing tried to preserve the eighteenth-century vicarage of St John the Baptist at Hillingdon, Middlesex, but the parishioners supported a builder who wished to pull it down and develop the site . . . the old vicarage was doomed and the desert of ugliness that is suburban Middlesex moved forward, like the engulfing sands of the Sahara, to obliterate another building worthy of preservation." He adds: "The only interesting house in Long Ditton, Surrey, was said to be the rectory. It has been pulled down."

Alan Savidge, in *The Parsonage in England*, is less sentimental, but then he had been assistant secretary to the Church Commissioners. "In this increasingly materialistic, bewildered age . . . he would be a rash man who would take more than a short view." But his comment, "we appear to be within striking distance of the happy day when parsonages are generally suitable to their occupants", would not be accepted by today's diocesan parsonage boards, which are still dissatisfied, 40 years on.[2]

Yet Bax's dilapidated house with its "beetling gables, narrow windows and unmellowed polychromatic walls" is precisely what we used to love about the Church of England. It represented its Englishness. The Church goes about the business of dismantling tradition in the name of progress. But tradition is not against change. There will always be change. But we need change that encourages the best from the new and conserves what is good about the old. It is difficult to avoid the conclusion that the worst enemy of the Anglican Church these days is no longer Catholicism or even the atheists or the communists, not even the chattering classes, the intellectuals or the more blinkered scientists, and certainly not the people of England, but the Church itself. If society has become fragmented, the Church must seek to provide roots, not pander to that fragmentation.

Looking ahead, Savidge envisages fleets of mobile parsonages parked at diocesan headquarters, "available to be hooked up and trailed off to house the new man at Little Meander with Old Womansleigh". I know some Church officials who would like that idea. In fact, it occurs to me that if "New Age" supersedes the Church of England as our established religion, perhaps the gypsy caravan will be the new parsonage. The traditional one, with folk lettering and fancy paintwork, will be that of the leader of the community. The blank, unadorned plastic camper van will be that of the disestablished vicar, now seen as a Dissenter.

In Chapter 1, we said our love of history and tradition was one reason why old rectories are so popular. There is a growing sense these days that our heritage is a vital part of our identity, and a realisation that our buildings are the most powerful manifestation of that identity. The climate of the times, in which we have seen our fine buildings destroyed by developers, has greatly encouraged this sentiment. Only the Church is unmoved.

Another reason for their popularity is our love of rural England, and that is linked. We see ever more of our precious landscape disappearing. The greater the state of flux, the greater is our need for permanence. The need for tranquillity speaks of the pace of life and is deep within us. Chronic overpopulation has brought pressure, stress, no escape. Except to the Old Rectory. So even if our love for the Old Rectory is really just the idyllic dream of an England that simply no longer exists, an England that, as the hardcore and tarmac spreads, can only now exist in the mind, or within the bounds of the croquet lawns, it seems it will thrive. Embattled by forces beyond our control, we can retreat within its walls, like the besieged Saxon thegn or Norman baron. There, we have the illusion that we can still live properly. The flight to the Old Rectory becomes an escape from the reality of life, and a potent commentary on it.

There are even more worrying thoughts. Every day more of our countryside is being concreted over with no more vision for our landscape on the part of our leaders than that more and more people must be housed, and if that means ravaging our environment, so be it. Let us take more and more of what was once untouched; besides, it may stimulate our badly managed economy. There has long been no wilderness left in England, and already great swathes of the South-East are no more than suburbia. No politician can be expected to have the vision to see that England is being destroyed, and we have now ceased to expect or even hope for that vision. Those who do understand what is happening are not prepared to admit it, much less do anything about it. Even those we expect to be concerned provide little solace. The Council for the Protection of Rural England has told me it is not its policy to oppose this continual process of development.[3] So the cult of the Old Rectory may be more than just a middle-class, middle-England preoccupation. It may be a requiem for our country. The story of the Old Rectory is perhaps, in fact, the opposite of what it seems—not one of complacent well-being at all, but one of fear and distress. It may be the story of nothing less than the demise of England itself. If you think that view is too apocalyptic, we can surely at least all nowadays agree that the preservation of our finest buildings and the struggle to preserve our countryside are worthy aims. The Old Rectory may be a parsonage no longer, but it is by and large well cared for. That is probably good enough for most of us.

The last word should go to a diocesan secretary, attempting to justify the sale of yet another rectory. He wrote: "The main reason for the sale of the vicarage is its unsuitability for modern living."[4]

And that is where we came in.

Notes

[1]   Bax, *The English Parsonage*, p. 205.

[2]   Savidge, *The Parsonage in England*, pp. 201-202.

[3]   Press officer, CPRE.

[4]   Chichester Diocesan Secretary, of the Georgian Amberley Vicarage, 2005.

Appendix A: Definitions

Advowson: The right of presentation to a benefice.

Benefice or living: An estate traditionally held for life conditional on performing duties. In the physical sense the benefice was originally one parish, but is now usually several. Until the 2009 legislation, rectors and vicars owned what is called a freehold. New incumbents no longer have freehold of office, but still have the freehold of the parsonage.

Chantry: A foundation for the chanting of masses for an individual or family or specified persons and, by extension, the chapel erected for that purpose.

Chantry House: The dwelling house of the chantry priest.

Curate: Originally, someone having the care of souls in the parish. It has come to mean an assistant to the rector or vicar.

Freehold: A complex term which does not have its strict legal meaning. It is explained in Chapter 4.

Glebe: Land constituting capital endowment providing income for the incumbent. These days it is no longer owned by the incumbent, or even available for him or her, having been appropriated by the diocese.

Incumbent: The holder of the benefice or living, thus the rector or vicar appointed to the parish, but not a priest-in-charge.

Minister: Latin for servant, emphasising the priest's duties towards his or her parishioners.

Parish: A community served by a rector or vicar, priest-in-charge, team or group, defined by physical boundaries. It has its Parochial Church Council (PCC), while the secular parish has its parish council, the two often being co-extensive. From the early days of the Church, the obligation on parishioners to pay tithes made it important to establish precise boundaries. Due to the decline of congregations and of the stipendiary priesthood, the parish and its PCC nowadays often find themselves grouped with a number of others to form a combined benefice. In most cases the original parish survives as part of the combined benefice.

Parson: The rector or vicar was the *persona* of the Church, hence the parson.

Parsonage: A Church of England rectory, vicarage, priest's house or clergy house. Priests' houses are the early and medieval versions of parsonages. The parsonage is a private house, but on retirement goes to the vicar's successor rather than dependants or family. Wealthy vicars might therefore also have large private houses, particularly in the late Georgian and Victorian periods.

Patron: The person having the right of presentation of a priest to a benefice. Patronage has had the power of conferring a life income and the advowson has therefore been treated as property. Because it gave value, the right of presentation was in the past bought and sold.

Prebend: An endowment for a cathedral or conventual church in order to provide a living for a secular cleric. If in the form of an estate or manor, it was often originally given by the king to the bishop.

Prebendary: The cleric given the benefit of the prebend. The prebendary represents the collegiate church in the parish, as does the vicar his rector.

Rector: The person or body entitled to the tithe, glebe, and other income of the rectory, who may institute a vicar to perform his, her, or its duties.

Rectory: The endowment constituting the rights and duties of the rector. The term denotes the house itself only by extension.

Secular clergy: Clergy not in seclusion, hence non-monastic clergy.

Tithe: The "tenth", the share of income historically payable by parishioners to sustain the incumbent.

Vicar: Someone assigned to do the work of the rector in the parish, a *vicarius* or substitute for the rector, who still usually had his own security of tenure.

Vicarage: This denotes the rights and duties of the vicar, not just the house, though it is not often used in this precise sense.

Appendix B: *The Buildings Of England*—The 20 Best Counties

The table below is not definitive and is solely based on the numbers of parsonages mentioned in *The Buildings of England* as at 2009. The newer editions are more comprehensive (of the first 10 parsonages in the current Lincolnshire volume, for example, only two or three feature in the first edition). In many counties there are no doubt houses, for example former priest's houses, which remain unidentified.

1. Gloucestershire
2. Lincolnshire
3. Yorkshire
4. London
5. Norfolk
6. Oxfordshire
7. Devonshire
8. Buckinghamshire
9. Northamptonshire
10. Lancashire
11. Northumberland
12. Hampshire
13. Wiltshire
14. Hertfordshire
15. Kent
16. Suffolk
17. Dorset
18. Somerset
19. Cheshire and Nottinghamshire

Appendix C: The 84 "Best Parsonages"

Farnborough, Berkshire; Inkpen, Berkshire; Lambourn, Berkshire; Wantage, Berkshire; Amersham, Buckinghamshire; Beaconsfield, Buckinghamshire (2); Marlow, Buckinghamshire; Twyford, Buckinghamshire; Weston Turville, Buckinghamshire; Grantchester, Cambridgeshire; Landbeach, Cambridgeshire; Gawsworth, Cheshire; Morwenstow, Cornwall; Lanercost, Cumbria; Kentisbeare, Devon; Sampford Peverell, Devon; Puddletown, Dorset; Winterborne Came, Dorset; Ryton, Durham; Sedgefield, Durham; Bradwell, Essex; Great Baddow, Essex; Great Yeldham, Essex; Bourton-on-the-Hill, Gloucestershire; Coalpit Heath, Gloucestershire; Droxford, Hampshire; Marchwood, Hampshire; Ayot St Laurence, Hertfordshire; Borehamwood, Hertfordshire; Sacombe Green, Hertfordshire; All Saints Westbrook, Margate, Kent; Wingham, Kent; Penshurst, Kent; Southfleet, Kent; Barnack, Huntingdonshire; Croston, Lancashire; Warton, Lancashire; Church Langton, Leicestershire; Cossington, Leicestershire; Epworth, Lincolnshire; Market Deeping, Lincolnshire; Somersby, Lincolnshire; St Agnes, Liverpool; Tottenham, London; Old Deanery, London; Hampton Wick, London; Great Snoring, Norfolk; Easton-on-the-Hill, Northamptonshire; Lamport, Northamptonshire; Wappenham, Northamptonshire; Averham, Nottinghamshire; Alnham, Northumberland; Corbridge, Northumberland; Elsdon, Northumberland; Embleton, Northumberland; Ford, Northumberland; Ponteland, Northumberland; Shilbottle, Northumberland; Simonburn, Northumberland; Iffley, Oxfordshire; Claverley, Salop; Edgmond, Salop; Ludlow, Salop; Congresbury, Somerset; Winford, Somerset; Charlton Mackrell, Somerset; Martock, Somerset; Muchelney, Somerset; Barsham, Suffolk; Haverhill, Suffolk; Alfriston, Sussex; West Dean, Sussex; West Hoathly, Sussex; Shepperton, Surrey; Alveston, Warwickshire; Hampton Lucy, Warwickshire; Bemerton, Wiltshire; Bremhill, Wiltshire; Bredon, Worcestershire; Ripple, Worcestershire; Bolton Abbey, Yorkshire; Campsall, Yorkshire; Guiseley, Yorkshire.

In order of numbers per county, the counties rank as follows: 1. Northumberland; 2. Buckinghamshire; 3. Somerset; 4. Berkshire and Kent; 6. Essex, Hertfordshire, Lancashire, Lincolnshire, London, Shropshire, Sussex, Yorkshire; then the rest.

Appendix D: *The Buildings Of England*'s 73 "Best"

Kings Norton, Birmingham; Drayton Parslow, Buckinghamshire; Haddenham, Buckinghamshire; Marlow, Buckinghamshire; Twyford, Buckinghamshire; Colyton, Devon; Kingsteignton, Devon; Whitestone, Devon; Hamworthy, Dorset; Pulham, Dorset; Witchampton, Dorset; Seaton Holme, Durham; Houghton-le-Spring, Durham; Bradwell, Essex; Buckland St Michael, Gloucestershire; Wootton under Edge, Gloucestershire; Bishops Cleeve, Gloucestershire; Coalpit Heath, Gloucestershire; Standish, Gloucestershire; Netherton, Hampshire; Therfield, Hertfordshire; Bredgar, Kent; Ickham, Kent; Middleton, Lancashire; Church Langton, Leicestershire; Cossington, Leicestershire; Loughborough, Leicestershire; Great Ponton, Lincolnshire; Market Deeping, Lincolnshire; West Ashby, Lincolnshire; Tottenham, London; Didsbury, Manchester; Buckenham, Norfolk; Great Snoring, Norfolk; Great Yarmouth, Norfolk; Methwold, Norfolk; North Creake, Norfolk; Saxlingham Nethergate, Norfolk; Upwell, Norfolk; Kislingbury, Northamptonshire; Bywell, Northumberland; Corbridge, Northumberland; Elsdon, Northumberland; Embleton, Northumberland; Hartburn, Northumberland; Ovingham, Northumberland; Shilbottle, Northumberland; Stamfordham, Northumberland; Broughton, Oxfordshire; Burford, Oxfordshire; Deddington, Oxfordshire; Iffley, Oxfordshire; Kingham, Oxfordshire; Stanton Harcourt, Oxfordshire; Chew Stoke, Somerset; Congresbury, Somerset; Wookey, Somerset; Yatton, Somerset; Martock, Somerset; Walton, Somerset; Sheen, Staffordshire; Battle, Sussex; West Dean, Sussex; Bremhill, Wiltshire; Donhead, Wiltshire; Stratford-sub-Castle, Wiltshire; Martley, Worcestershire; Guiseley, West Yorkshire; Bewholme, East Yorkshire; Goodmanham, East Yorkshire; Seaton, Wassard Hall, East Yorkshire; Thorganby, Thicket Priory, East Yorkshire; Winestead, East Yorkshire.

Distribution of these by county is as follows: Northumberland 8; Norfolk 7; Oxfordshire, Somerset, Yorkshire 6 each; Gloucestershire 5; Buckinghamshire

4; Devon, Dorset, Leicestershire, Lincolnshire, Wiltshire 3 each; Durham, Kent, Sussex 2 each; the remaining 10 houses are all in separate counties. By this criterion, therefore, Northumberland is the best county, though largely for its pele houses; Norfolk is next with a very diverse selection.

Appendix E: Research Methodology

My architectural research, perhaps inevitably, began with *The Buildings of England*. Looking through every volume of the series, I found mention of a total of 2,267 houses that are or were either Church of England parsonages or private houses of the clergy (that number will now have increased as new editions have come out). I will call them all parsonages here. I then made notes on an additional 494 buildings (mainly good Catholic presbyteries, Nonconformist manses, deaneries, church houses, and church farms) bringing the total up to 2,761. From those 2,761 buildings, I selected a shortlist of 1,076. Having done that, I looked at my other sources, discussed below, to see how this list compared with the houses mentioned in them. As I said in the Introduction, the two main books on parsonages are *The English Parsonage* (Bax) and *The Parsonage in England* (Savidge). First, just out of curiosity, I took a random selection (42) of houses featured in both Bax and Savidge, then looked for them in *The Buildings of England*. Thirty-two were mentioned, ten were not, so it seemed that the latter corroborated them but did not cover the whole story.[1]

I then methodically noted all those in Bax and Savidge and those in Hammond and Jones[2] (Timothy Brittain-Catlin's book[3] had not yet come out, but in any case he limits himself to a specific short period in the history of parsonages, important though that period is), listing all houses that were mentioned broadly for their architecture. There are other books that refer to parsonages, but these are either on clergy history or about architects, and rarely discuss specific parsonages (see the Bibliography). There are also regional books, like Henry Thorold's engaging *Lincolnshire Houses*, which do discuss some good parsonages, but to include these without counterbalance would create area bias.

In 2008, *Country Life* held its "England's finest parsonage" competition, and the article announcing the shortlist featured six that were mentioned in the other sources. Together with Pevsner, Bax, Savidge, Hammond, and Jones, this was my final source.

On the system of two points for a mention in any two of the above, 23 per cent of the parsonages in my Pevsner list were in one or more of Bax, Savidge, Jones, Hammond, and *Country Life*, a shortlist of 252.[4]

I then narrowed the field further. Of these 252, 84 had three mentions in these sources. Those 84, together with their counties in order of numbers, are listed in Appendix C.

Notes

[1]   There are inevitable inconsistencies. In Alveston, Warwickshire, three parsonages are mentioned in Savidge; one is early, the second Gothic by Gibson of 1859, and the third, still large, in Arts and Crafts style by Temple Moore. Only the first is in *The Buildings of England*. Stone-in-Oxney, Kent, is described in *The Buildings of England* as a Wealden house but not a parsonage.

[2]   Peter C. Hammond, *The Parson and the Victorian Parish* (Ecclesia Books, 1977) and Jones, *1000 Years of the English Parish*.

[3]   Timothy Brittain-Catlin, *The English Parsonage in the Early Nineteenth Century* (Spire Books, 2008).

[4]   Bax mentions about 600 parsonages, Savidge about 400. Of my "Pevsner thousand", 158 are mentioned in Bax, or 16 per cent, and 147 are mentioned in Savidge, or 15 per cent. Bax has 83 not mentioned by Savidge. Savidge has 72 not mentioned in Bax.

Bibliography

See also sources quoted in footnotes

Church history and law

Godfrey, John, *The English Parish 600–1300* (SPCK, 1969).

Hartridge, R. A. R., *Vicarages in the Middle Ages* (Cambridge University Press, 1930).

Higgins, Michael, *The Vicar's House* (Churchman Publishing, 1988).

Jones, Anthea, *A Thousand Years of the English Parish* (Windrush Press, 2000).

Pounds, N. J. G., *A History of the English Parish* (Cambridge University Press, 2000).

Clergy and clergy history

Addison, William, *The English Country Parson* (J. M. Dent, 1947).

Brendon, Piers, *Hawker of Morwenstow* (Jonathan Cape, 1975).

Cutts, E. L., *Parish Priests and their People in the Middle Ages in England* (SPCK, 1898).

Ditchfield, Peter Hampson, *The Old-Time Parson* (1908).

Goodenough, Simon, *The Country Parson* (David & Charles, 1983).

Hammond, Peter C., *The Parson and the Victorian Parish* (Ecclesia Books, Hodder & Stoughton, 1977).

Plomer, William (ed.), *Kilvert's Diary, 1870–1879* (Pimlico, 1999).

Tindal Hart, A., *The Country Priest in English History* (Phoenix House, 1959).

Tindal Hart, A., *The Curate's Lot: The Story of the Unbeneficed English Clergy* (John Baker, 1970).

Tindal Hart, A., *Some Clerical Oddities in the Church of England from Medieval to Modern Times* (New Horizon, 1980).
Woodforde, James, *Diary of a Country Parson, 1758–1802*, 5 vols, ed. John Beresford (Oxford University Press, 1949).

Parsonages

Bax, B. Anthony, *The English Parsonage* (John Murray, 1964).
Brittain-Catlin, Timothy, *The English Parsonage in the Early Nineteenth Century* (Spire Books, 2008).
Savidge, Alan, *The Parsonage in England* (SPCK, 1964).

Architecture

Aldrich, Megan, *Gothic Revival* (Phaidon, 1994).
Arciszewska, Barbara, and McKellar, Elizabeth (eds), *Articulating British Classicism: New Approaches to Eighteenth Century Architecture* (Ashgate, 2004).
Betjeman, John, *A Pictorial History of English Architecture* (John Murray, c. 1970–72).
Braun, Hugh, *An Introduction to English Mediaeval Architecture* (Faber & Faber, 1951).
Brunskill, R. W., *Vernacular Architecture: An Illustrated Handbook* (Faber & Faber, 1971).
Brunskill, R. W., *Traditional Buildings of Britain* (Victor Gollancz in assn. with Peter Crawley, 1981).
Clark, Kenneth, *The Gothic Revival* (Constable, 1950).
Colquhoun, Alan, *Modern Architecture* (Oxford University Press, 2002).
Colvin, Howard, *A Biographical Dictionary of British Architects 1600–1840* (Yale University Press, 1995).
Cowley, Patrick, *The Church Houses* (SPCK, 1970).

Cunnington, Pamela, *Change of Use: The Conversion of Old Buildings* (Alphabooks, 1988).

Curl, James Stevens, *Victorian Architecture* (David & Charles, 1990).

Curl, James Stevens, *Georgian Architecture* (David & Charles, 1993).

Davey, Peter, *Arts and Crafts Architecture: The Search for Earthly Paradise* (The Architectural Press, 1980).

Dixon, Roger, and Muthesius, Stefan, *Victorian Architecture* (Thames & Hudson, 1978).

Eastlake, Charles L., *A History of the Gothic Revival* (Longmans, Green & Co, 1872).

Evers, Bernd (preface), *Architectural Theory from the Renaissance to the Present* (Taschen, 2006).

Garrigan, Kristine Ottesen, *Ruskin on Architecture: His Thought and Influence* (University of Wisconsin Press, 1973).

Gray, Stuart, *Edwardian Architecture: a Biographical Dictionary* (Duckworth, 1985).

Grenville, Jane, *Medieval Housing* (Leicester University Press, 1997).

Harvey, John, *English Mediaeval Architects: A Biographical Dictionary down to 1550* (Alan Sutton, 1984).

Hitchcock, Henry-Russell, *Early Victorian Architecture in Britain* (The Architectural Press and Yale University Press, 1954).

Howard, Maurice, *The Building of Elizabethan and Jacobean England* (Yale University Press, 2007).

James, Thomas Beaumont, *The Palaces of Medieval England* (Seaby, 1990).

Jenkins, Simon, *England's Thousand Best Houses* (Allen Lane, 2003).

Kuyper, W., *Dutch Classicist Architecture* (Delft University Press, 1980).

Lewis, Philippa, *Details: A Guide to House Design in Britain* (Prestel, 2003).

Muthesius, Stefan, *The High Victorian Movement in Architecture 1850–1870* (Routledge & Kegan Paul, 1972).

Norberg-Schulz, Christian, *Norwegian Architecture* (Norwegian University Press, 1986).

Parissien, Steven, *The Georgian Group Book of the Georgian House* (Aurum, 1995).

Paulsson, Thomas, *Scandinavian Architecture* (Leonard Hill Books, 1958).

Pevsner, Nikolaus, and others, *The Buildings of England,* 54 volumes (Yale University Press, 1951–).

Platt, Colin, *The Great Rebuildings of Tudor and Stuart England: Revolutions in Architectural Taste* (UCL Press, 1994).

Pugin, A.W. N., *Contrasts: or, a Parallel between the Noble Edifices of the Middle Ages and the Corresponding Buildings of the Present Day; Shewing the Present Decay of Taste* (Charles Dolman, 1841).

Pugin, A. W. N., *The True Principles of Pointed or Christian Architecture* (John Weale, 1841).

Quiney, Anthony, *Period Houses: A Guide to Authentic Architectural Features* (George Philip, 1989).

Reid, Richard, *The Georgian House and its Details* (Bishopsgate, 1989).

Service, Alastair, *Edwardian Architecture: Handbook to Building Design in Britain, 1890-1914* (Thames & Hudson, 1977).

Service, Alastair, *The Buildings of Britain: Anglo-Saxon and Norman* (Barrie & Jenkins, 1982).

Sitwell, Sacheverell, *British Architects and Craftsmen* (Batsford, 1945).

Summerson, John, *Architecture in Britain, 1530–1830* (Penguin, 1953).

Thorold, Henry, *Lincolnshire Houses* (Michael Russell, 1999).

Viney, Charles, *London Doors* (Oldcastle Books, 1989).

Ware, Dora, *A Short Dictionary of British Architects* (George Allen & Unwin, 1967).

Wilkinson, William, *English Country Houses* (James Parker & Co, 1875).

Wilson, William Carus, *Helps to the Building of Churches and Parsonage Houses* (Arthur Foster, 1835).

Wodehouse, L., *British Architects 1840–1976: A Guide to Information Sources* (Gale, 1978).

Young, David, *Bats In The Belfry* (David & Charles, 1987).

Specific architects

Allibone, Jill, *Anthony Salvin, Pioneer of Gothic Revival Architecture* (Lutterworth Press, 1988).

Archer, Lucy, *Raymond Erith, Architect* (The Cygnet Press, 1985).

Aslet, Clive, *Quinlan Terry: The Revival of Architecture* (Viking, 1986).

Atterbury, Paul, and Wainwright, Clive (eds), *Pugin: A Gothic Passion* (Yale University Press, 1994).

Bold, John, *John Webb* (Clarendon Press, 1989).

Briggs, Nancy, *John Johnson, Georgian Architect and County Surveyor of Essex* (Essex Record Office, 1991).

Brown, Jane, *Lutyens and the Edwardians* (Viking, 1966).

Brown, Roderick (ed.), *The Architectural Outsiders* (Waterstone, 1985).

Chadwick, George F., *The Works of Sir Joseph Paxton, 1803-1865* (The Architectural Press, 1961).

Cole, David, *The Work of Sir Gilbert Scott* (The Architectural Press, 1980).

Crook, J. Mordaunt, *William Burges and the High Victorian Dream* (John Murray, 1981).

Curl, James Stevens, *The Life and Work of Henry Roberts, 1803-1876* (Phillimore, 1983).

Darby, Michael, *John Pollard Seddon* (Victoria and Albert Museum, 1983).

Fellows, Richard A., *Sir Reginald Blomfield, An Edwardian Architect* (Zwemmer, 1985).

Gloag, John, *Mr Loudon's England* (Oriel Press, 1970).

Hart, Vaughan, *Nicholas Hawksmoor: Rebuilding Ancient Wonders* (Yale University Press, 2002).

Harvey, John H., *Henry Yevele, c. 1320 to 1400: The Life of an English Architect* (Batsford, 1944).

Hawkes, Dean (ed.), *Modern Country Houses in England: The Arts and Crafts Architecture of Barry Parker* (Cambridge University Press, 1986).

Hobhouse, Hermione, *Thomas Cubitt, Master Builder* (Macmillan, 1971).

Hubbard, Edward, *The Work of John Douglas* (The Victorian Society, 1991).

Hussey, Christopher, *The Life of Sir Edwin Lutyens* (Country Life, 1950).

King, David, *The Complete Works of Robert and James Adam* (Butterworth Architecture, 1991).

Kirk, Sheila, *Philip Webb: Pioneer of Arts & Crafts Architecture* (Wiley-Academy, 2005).

Kornwolf, James D., and Baillie, M. H., *Scott and the Arts and Crafts Movement* (Johns Hopkins Press, 1972).

Leach, Peter, *James Paine* (Zwemmer, 1988).

Linstrum, Derek, *Towers and Colonnades: the Architecture of Cuthbert Brodrick* (L. P. L. S., 1999).

Lukacher, Brian, *Joseph Gandy: An Architectural Visionary in Georgian England* (Thames & Hudson, 2006).

Mansbridge, Michael, *John Nash: A Complete Catalogue* (Phaidon, 1991).

Miller, Philip, *Decimus Burton, 1800-1881: A Guide to the Exhibition of his Work* (The Building Centre Trust, 1981).

Mordaunt Crook, J., *William Burges and the High Victorian Dream* (John Murray, 1981).

Mowl, Timothy, *William Kent: Architect, Designer, Opportunist* (Jonathan Cape, 2006).

Pace, Peter, *The Architecture of George Pace* (Batsford, 1990).

Quiney, Anthony, *John Loughborough Pearson* (Yale University Press, 1979).

Robinson, John Martin, *The Wyatts: An Architectural Dynasty* (Oxford University Press, 1979).

Saint, Andrew, *Richard Norman Shaw* (Yale University Press, 1976).

Saunders, Edward, *Joseph Pickford of Derby, A Georgian Architect* (Alan Sutton, 1993).

Scott-Moncrieff, W. W., *John Francis Bentley* (Ernest Benn Ltd, 1924).

Stanton, Phoebe, *Pugin* (Thames & Hudson, 1971).

Stroud, Dorothy, *George Dance, Architect, 1741–1825* (Faber & Faber, 1971).

Stroud, Dorothy, *Sir John Soane, Architect* (Faber & Faber, 1984).

Stutchbury, Howard E., *The Architecture of Colen Campbell* (Manchester University Press, 1967).

Thompson, Paul, *William Butterfield* (Routledge & Kegan Paul, 1971).

Watkin, David, *The Life and Work of C. R. Cockerell* (Zwemmer, 1974).

Wilkes, Lyall, *John Dobson, Architect and Landscape Gardener* (Oriel Press, 1980).

Williams, Guy, *Augustus Pugin versus Decimus Burton: A Victorian Architectural Duel* (Cassell, 1990).

General

The AA Book of British Villages (Drive Publications, 1980).

Aslet, Clive, "Parson Jack Russell", in *Landmarks of Britain* (Hodder & Stoughton, 2005).

Archer, Mary, *Rupert Brooke and the Old Vicarage, Grantchester* (Silent Books, 1989).

Bailey, Brian, *Stone Villages of England* (Robert Hale, 1982).

Betjeman, John, and Piper, John (eds), *The Shell Guides* (Faber & Faber, 1939-1984).

Bisgrove, Richard, *The National Trust Book of the English Garden* (Viking, 1990).

Brown, Jane, *The Art and Architecture of English Gardens* (Weidenfeld & Nicholson, 1989).

Clarke, B. F. L., *Parish Churches of London* (Batsford, 1966).

Coulton, G. G., *Medieval Panorama*, Vol. 1 (Cambridge University Press, 1938).

Cowley, Patrick, *The Church Houses* (SPCK, 1970).

Grigson, Geoffrey, and others, *The Shell Country Book* (Phoenix House, 1962).

Hadfield, Miles, *A History of British Gardening* (John Murray, 1960).

Hadfield, Miles, Harling, Robert, and Highton, Leonie, *British Gardeners: A Biographical Dictionary* (Zwemmer, 1980).

Hodgson, Tony, *Country People: An Endangered Species* (SMH Books, 2000).

Mee, Arthur (ed.), *The King's England* (41 volumes by county) (Hodder & Stoughton, 1936).

Needham, A., *How to Study an Old Church* (Batsford, 1944).

Powicke, Maurice, *The 13th Century, 1216–1307* (Oxford History of England, Clarendon Press, 1962).

Price, Harry, *The Most Haunted House in England* (Longmans, Green & Co, 1940).

Tames, Richard, *Bloomsbury Past* (Historical Publications Ltd, 1993).

Thacker, Christopher, *The History of Gardens* (Croom Helm, 1979).

Wright, Geoffrey, *The Stone Villages of Britain* (David & Charles, 1985).

Religion

Cohn-Sherbok, Lavinia, *Who's Who in Christianity* (Routledge, 1998).

Littell, Franklin H., *Illustrated History of Christianity* (Continuum, 1976/2001).

Periodicals, magazines, handbooks, and papers

Ancient Monuments Society (1954), *Gawsworth Old Rectory* (reprinted from the Transactions of the AMS, Vol. II, pp. 71–86, 1955).

Archaeological Journal and Review, Vol. 5 (Bemrose and Sons, 1891).

The Bronte Society, *Bronte Parsonage Museum* (1962).

Church Commissioners, Pastoral Division, *Parsonages: A Design Guide* (Church Commissioners, 1998).

Church Commissioners, *Annual Report* (2004).

Church Heritage Forum, *Building Faith in our Future* (Church House Publishing, 2004).

Congresbury History Group, *The Refectory, Congresbury* (2003).

***Country Life*:**

Hanson, M., "Making more parsonages redundant", 6 April 1978.

Hanson, M., "More parsonages to become redundant", 9 November 1978.

Hanson, M., "The rising cost of parsonage houses", 1 November 1979.

Hanson, M., "Of churches, parsonages and glebe", 7 July 1983.

Hanson, M., "More than the tithes", 5 July 1984.

Hanson, M., "No end of old parsonages", 4 July 1985.

Hanson, M., "Why the Church is selling", 9 July 1987.

Hanson, M., "Replanning the parson's plot", 14 July 1988.

Jackson-Stops, G. A., "Parsonage to be proud of", 31 August 1989.

Mallalieu, H., "And then the Heaven espy", 20 July 1989.

Worsley, G., "Reflecting a position", 11 April 1991.

Wright, G., "Priests in Residence", 22 June 1978.

Dawson, R. B., *A Short History of Embleton Church and the Fortified Vicarage* (The British Publishing Company Ltd, 1933).

Etchells, Frederick, "Le Corbusier, A Pioneer of Modern European Architecture", in *Studio* No. 96 (1928), pp. 156-163.

Faith in the City: A Call for Action by Church and Nation, Archbishop's Commission on Urban Priority Areas (Church of England, 1985).

Faith in the Countryside, Archbishops' Commission on Rural Areas (Churchman, 1990).

Francis, Leslie, Martineau, Jeremy, and Francis, Peter (eds), *Changing Rural Life: A Christian response to Life and Work in the Countryside* (Canterbury Press, 2004).

General Synod, *An Overview of Church of England Finances*, May 2006.

Goodhart-Rendel, H. S., "Rogue Architects of the Victorian Era", in *RIBA* Journal, Vol. 56 (April 1949).

Hodges, Charles Clement, *The Pele Towers of Northumberland* (Reliquary, January 1891).
Hummerstone, J., *Historic Parsonages in Devon* (Save Our Parsonages, 1995).
Review of Clergy Terms of Service: Part Two (Church House Publishing, 2005).
Save Our Parsonages Newsletters, 1995–2008.
The Landmark Trust Handbook (Landmark Trust).
The National Trust Handbook for Members and Visitors, 2004.

Academic thesis (unpublished)

Wellby, R., "Parsonage Houses, An Analysis of Change of Use" (1996).

Photograph and Illustration Acknowledgements

Plates

Anthea and Glyn Jones: 1, 9, 15, 18, 19, 20, 21, 23, 25, 26, 27, 28, 29, 30, 31, 43, 53
Cluttons: 2
Images of England: 3, 7, 14
Mary Hallett: 4
Anthony Jennings: 5, 6, 10, 24, 37, 41, 42, 45, 46, 47, 49, 50, 51, 52, 54, 57, 58, 59, 60, 61, 62, 64, 65
The Landmark Trust: 8, 36, 67, 68
Peter Condon: 11
Peter Neumann: 12
Graham Booth: 13
Alec Hamilton: 16
Jasper Jennings: 17
Felix Jennings: 22, 44, 55
Julian Litten: 32
Associated Newspapers: 33, 34
Tony Hodgson: 35
Rod Searle: 38
Savills: 39, 40
Marie Winckler: 48
Christopher Purvis: 56
Jeremy Hummerstone: 63
Geoffrey and Rosemary Pengelly: 66

Figures

Michael Thompson: 1A to 1D
Lois Fletcher: 2
Gloucester Archives, Gloucester Diocesan Records/Anthea Jones: 3
Richard Wellby: 4A and 4B
Graham Booth: 5
Chris and Penney Thompson: 6
Vicar and Lecturer of Dedham: 7
Hugh Bedford: 8
Dr C. Jolliffe: 9
Cathedral and Church Buildings Library: 10A and 10B

Index of Houses and Places

See also Appendices C and D

Index of Architects

General Index

Methodism 31, 33, 115, 255
Mies van der Rohe 72
Milne, A. A. 280
Milton, John 28, 253
Milton, William 280
Mitford, Deborah 280
Mitford, John 251
Mompesson, William 251
Montgomery, Field Marshal 275
More, Sir Thomas 25, 246
Moreton, W. 265
Morris, Marcus 252
Morris, William 133, 140, 169, 174, 177, 276
Moss, Fletcher 125
Mossman, T. W. 252
Mossop, J. 259
Moule, H. 262

National Churches Trust 205
National Trust xv, 98, 102, 280, 286
Neale, John Mason 252
Nelson, Lord 109, 167, 275, 276
Newby, R. 263
Newman, Cardinal 245, 249, 252, 273
Newton, Isaac 254, 275
Newton, John 252
Noel, Conrad 264

Oates, Titus 252
Odo 263
Olivier, Edith 232
Olivier, Laurence 276
Owen, Wilfred 280
Oxford or Tractarian Movement 33, 93, 116,
    224, 242, 249, 251, 252, 256, 264, 281

Paley, William 252
Palgrave 244
Palladianism 65, 158, 220, 226
Palladio 63, 65, 226
Parish clerk 22
Parish system 22
Parkyns, T. 281
Parsonage, meaning of, xi–xiii
Parsonages, A Design Guide 36, 38, 73, 202, 211
Patten, Father 252
Patteson, John Coleridge 253
Peck, Francis 253
Pemberton, J. H. 260

Perceval, Spencer 253
Pevsner, Nikolaus xv, 13, 97, 132, 148, 153,
    170, 223, 257, 291, 307, 308
Pickard-Cambridge, O. 259
Plath, Sylvia 279
Poore, Richard 257
Powys, J. C. and T. F. 276
Presbyterianism 4, 28, 112, 250
Presbyteries xi, xvii, 54, 69, 169
Prince, John 253
Pusey, E. B. 249, 252
Puseyites 256

Queen Anne's Bounty 11, 29, 31, 33, 35, 68,
    89, 143, 164, 199, 200, 241, 268

Raikes, Robert 228
Regency, definition of 67
Reynolds, Joshua 276
Rhodes, Cecil 276
Riley, Noël xiv, 83, 211
Robinson, William 229, 261
Rollo Meyer, H. 261
Rose, C. 269
Rose, H. J. 256
Royal Institution of British Architects 68
Ruskin, John 102, 171, 177
Russell, Jack 264

St Guthlac 101, 181
St Pega 181
Save Our Parsonages xv, 14, 83, 211, 212
Savidge, A. xv, 11, 57, 70, 71, 72, 105, 107,
    115, 135, 185, 223, 298
Sayers, Dorothy 276
Scott, Sir Walter 186, 249, 262
Scott, Thomas 258, 276
Scrope, R. 263
Sedgwick, Adam 262, 279
Sewell, Anna 280
Shaw, George Bernard 135, 153, 280
Sheppard, David 265
Sheppard, Dick 253
Simeon, Charles 251, 253
Skelton, John 253
Slingsby, Charles 253
Smith, G. E. 194
Smith, Sydney 31, 32, 46, 242, 251, 257, 268
Smythe, John 253